The Wilderness Itineraries

HISTORY, ARCHAEOLOGY, AND CULTURE OF THE LEVANT

Edited by

JEFFREY A. BLAKELY *University of Wisconsin, Madison*
K. LAWSON YOUNGER *Trinity Evangelical Divinity School*

The Wilderness Itineraries

*Genre, Geography, and
the Growth of Torah*

ANGELA R. ROSKOP

Winona Lake, Indiana
EISENBRAUNS
2011

Library of Congress Cataloging-in-Publication Data

Roskop, Angela R.
   The wilderness itineraries : genre, geography, and the growth of Torah / Angela
   R. Roskop.
        p.   cm. — (History, archaeology, and culture of the Levant ; vol. 3)
   Includes bibliographical references and indexes.
   ISBN 978-1-57506-212-9
   1. Bible. O.T. Pentateuch—Criticism, Narrative.   2. Bible. O.T. Numbers
XXXIII—Criticism, interpretation, etc.   3. Bible. O.T. Pentateuch—
Geography.   4. Travel in the Bible.   5. Bible. O.T. Pentateuch—Chronology.
6. Chronology, Historical.   I. Title.
   BS1225.52.R67   2011
   222′.1066—dc22

                                                              2011010052

In Memoriam

Milo Francis Hagan
1922–1991

אשר אדם מצא חכמא ואדם יפיק תבובה: כי טוב סחרה מסחר־כסף
ומחרוץ תבואתה: יקרה היא מפניים וכל־חפציך לא ישוו־בה:
ארך ימים בימינה בשמאולה עשר וכבוד:
דרכיה דרכי־נעם וכל־נתיבותיה שלום:
עץ־חיים היא למחזיקים בה ותמכיה מאשר:
משלי ג:יג–יח

We have to learn to think differently—in order, at last,
perhaps very late on, to attain even more: to feel differently.

Friedrich Nietzsche

Contents

List of Tables and Figures

List of Tables

List of Figures

Preface

This study emerged out of a deep love for the Bible. Like a partner in any good relationship, it brings joy and confounds, it pleases and sometimes aggravates. But it never fails to be life-giving. This study also emerged out of a deep frustration with the way that we often engage one another about the Bible. I entered graduate school as the terms *maximalist* and *minimalist* became fashionable and have only watched them—as labels often do—degrade into tired and even violent stereotypes that hinder more than help our ability to understand the text. I have always found this tragic. The book you are about to read is both my protest and the fruit of my own search for a better way. The wilderness narrative, the subject of this study, resists classification at every turn. This may be part of what makes it so irrepressibly fresh each time we encounter it anew. I have come to understand that, to honor it well, I as a reader must resist classification as well.

The pages that follow are a revised version of my doctoral dissertation, submitted to the faculty of Hebrew Union College–Jewish Institute of Religion (Cincinnati) in 2008. The transition from student to scholar has been a long journey through the wilderness, and the correlation between this professional rite of passage and the subject matter of this study has never been lost on me. Scholars who study ritual help us understand that such journeys involve hunger and thirst, complaining, mistakes, fear, false starts, confusion, loneliness, pain, uncertainty, even rebellion. The wilderness narrative offers a marvelous template for understanding these experiences. As we travel this sort of route, however, we also find inspiration, companionship, faithfulness, beauty, insight, and grace along the way. These things are what allow us to see the journey not as aimless wandering but as a triumphal march, whether with prescience as we walk or in hindsight once we have had the good fortune to arrive home.

I would never even have begun the journey were it not for Professors Leonard Thompson, Daniel Taylor, and Timothy Spurgin, who had faith in my potential when I could barely see it, encouraged me to pursue a budding interest, and helped me be accepted into graduate school in the first place, even when the numbers did not add up. I was fortunate to have *two* Professors Fox as mentors through my years in graduate school. Michael V. Fox is the kind of scholar I hope I can be someday. He taught me the meaning of intellectual discipline, and his work, a model of precision in detail coupled with breadth and depth of thought and always elegantly expressed, is a paradigm to which I continue to aspire. Nili S. Fox taught me the importance and value of taking risks to help students learn. I am always reminded by her personal example that scholars should be servants to others and that scholarship should be fun as well as hard work. I am grateful to Jeff Blakely and Lawson Younger for accepting my work for this series. The worth of a good editor is beyond rubies; my thanks to Jim Eisenbraun and Beverly McCoy for making it real.

Professors David H. Aaron and Samuel Greengus saw me through the wilderness portion of this journey. It is an enormous stretch to transition from course papers to a book, and one encounters unanticipated and often hostile terrain. To them I am grateful for helping me navigate, whether offering a ready solution, guiding me to possible answers, or leaving me to learn the process by traveling blind. They issued challenges that afforded me opportunities to show my mettle, both academic and personal. I learned new tools but also found and honed tools I already had. Their generosity with their time, energy, and insights has been a grace along the way, and it has been a privilege to engage in *talmud Torah* with them.

Others, especially my friends and family, have been a wonderful source of support, but I owe a debt of gratitude to a few specific individuals: Allen Gimbel, an unwitting matchmaker, introduced me to Hebrew through music, and I have been in love ever since. Very special thanks go to Gary Zola of The American Jewish Archives, who gave me access to resources without which I would have been unable to complete this project. I am grateful for the time and wisdom offered by Charles Halton, Kimberly Frankenhoff, Kari Hofmaister-Tuling, Noah Fabricant, and Shad Wenzlaff, who read drafts and offered invaluable suggestions for improving the manuscript. My colleagues at Xavier University have given me a temporary intellectual home that is supportive and nourishing. Kristine Henriksen Garroway has been an absolutely unending source of moral support throughout the entire project. Finally, profound gratitude goes to my husband, John Erisman, who is the most patient man I know other than my father. Thanks to him, German Riesling flowed from the rock and the quail came served with a fragrant rose petal sauce.

This book is dedicated to the memory of my grandfather. As was typical for boys who grew up on Minnesota farms in the 1930s, he completed only the eighth grade. But there never has been and probably never will be a more ardent supporter of my education and intellectual life. When I was nine or ten,

I announced at the dinner table at a family gathering that I was going to get a Ph.D. at Harvard—an outburst that provoked some skeptical but indulging smiles among the adults. Well, the Harvard part may not have worked out, but my grandfather was not laughing, and no one would have been prouder to share in this achievement.

ANGELA RAE ROSKOP
Cincinnati, Ohio
March 7, 2010

Abbreviations

General

A.	Louvre Museum siglum
ABL	texts in *Assyrian and Babylonian Letters Belonging to the Kouyunjik Collections of the British Museum*. Edited by R. F. Harper. 14 vols. Chicago: University of Chicago Press, 1892–1914
ADD	texts in *Assyrian Deeds and Documents Recording the Transfer of Property*. Edited by C. H. W. Johns. 3 vols. Cambridge: Deighton Bell, 1901
A.0.	texts in RIMA
B	Bulletin
c	common (grammatical Hebrew gender)
CH	Code of Hammurapi
DeZ	registration number of texts found at Deir ez-Zor
E	texts in RIME
IM	tablets in the collection of the Iraq Museum, Baghdad
K.	tablets in the Kouyunjik collection of the British Museum
m	masculine
M.	registration number of texts found at Mari
obv.	obverse
p	plural
P	Poem
pron.	pronoun/pronominal
rev.	reverse
s	singular
SH	texts from Shemshara
UIOM	tablets in the collections of the University of Illinois Oriental Museum
YBC	tablets in the Babylonian Collection, Yale University Library

Reference Works

AARAS	American Academy of Religion Academy Series
AASOR	*Annual of the American Schools of Oriental Research*
AB	The Anchor Bible
ABRL	The Anchor Bible Reference Library
AcOr	*Acta Orientalia*
AfO	*Archiv für Orientforschung*
AnOr	Analecta Orientalia

AOAT	Alter Orient und Altes Testament
AoF	*Altorientalische Forschungen*
AOS	American Oriental Series
ARM	Archives Royales de Mari
ARMT	Archives Royales de Mari, textes et traduites
ArOr	*Archív Orientální*
ASOR Books	American Schools of Oriental Research Books Series
BA	*Biblical Archaeologist*
BAR	*Biblical Archaeology Review*
BAR International Series	British Archaeological Reports International Series
BASOR	*Bulletin of the American Schools of Oriental Research*
BBET	Beiträge zur biblischen Exegese und Theologie
BEATAJ	Beiträge zur Erforschung des Alten Testaments und des Antiken Judentums
Bib	*Biblica*
BibInt	*Biblical Interpretation*
BJS	Brown Judaic Studies
BN	*Biblische Notizen*
BO	*Bibliotheca Orientalis*
BSOAS	*Bulletin of the School of Oriental and African Studies*
BZAW	Beiheft zur Zeitschrift für die alttestamentliche Wissenschaft
CAD	*Chicago Assyrian Dictionary*
CahRB	Cahiers de la Revue Biblique
CANE	*Civilizations of the Ancient Near East.* Edited by J. Sasson. 4 vols. New York: Scribner, 1995
CBC	Cambridge Bible Commentary
CBQ	*Catholic Biblical Quarterly*
CHANE	Culture and History of the Ancient Near East
ConBOT	Coniectanea Biblica, Old Testament Series
COS	*Context of Scripture.* Edited by W. W. Hallo. 3 vols. Leiden: Brill, 1997–2003
EncJud	*Encyclopaedia Judaica.* 16 vols. Jerusalem: Keter, 1972
FOTL	Forms of the Old Testament Literature
FRLANT	Forschungen zur Religion und Literatur des Alten und Neuten Testaments
GBS	Guides to Biblical Scholarship
GTA	Göttinger Theologische Arbeiten
HALOT	Koehler, L., and W. Baumgartner. *The Hebrew and Aramaic Lexicon of the Old Testament.* Study edition. 2 vols. Translated and edited by M. E. J. Richardson. Leiden: Brill, 2001
HAR	*Hebrew Annual Review*
HSM	Harvard Semitic Monographs
HSS	Harvard Semitic Studies
HUCA	*Hebrew Union College Annual*
IAA Reports	Israel Antiquities Authority Reports
IBC	Interpretation: A Bible Commentary for Teaching and Preaching
ICC	International Critical Commentary
IEJ	*Israel Exploration Journal*

Int	*Interpretation*
IOS	Israel Oriental Studies
JANER	*Journal of Ancient Near Eastern Religions*
JANESCU	*Journal of the Ancient Near Eastern Society of Columbia University*
JAOS	*Journal of the American Oriental Society*
JARCE	*Journal of the American Research Center in Egypt*
JBL	*Journal of Biblical Literature*
JCS	*Journal of Cuneiform Studies*
JEA	*Journal of Egyptian Archaeology*
JESHO	*Journal of the Economic and Social History of the Orient*
JNES	*Journal of Near Eastern Studies*
JNSL	*Journal of Northwest Semitic Languages*
JPS Torah Commentary	Jewish Publication Society Torah Commentary
JQR	*Jewish Quarterly Review*
JR	*Journal of Religion*
JSOT	*Journal for the Study of the Old Testament*
JSOTSup	Journal for the Study of the Old Testament Supplement Series
JSSEA	*Journal of the Society for the Study of Egyptian Antiquities*
LHBOTS	Library of Hebrew Bible/Old Testament Studies
MDOG	*Mitteilungen der Deutschen Orient-Gesellschaft*
MSL	Materialien zum sumerischen Lexicon
NABU	*Nouvelles assyriologiques breves et utilitaires*
NAC	New American Commentary
NCB	New Century Bible
NCBC	New Cambridge Bible Commentary
NEA	*Near Eastern Archaeology*
NICOT	New International Commentary on the Old Testament
OEAE	*Oxford Encyclopedia of Ancient Egypt*
OLA	Orientalia Lovaniensia Analecta
Or	*Orientalia*
OrAnt	*Oriens Antiquus*
OTL	Old Testament Library
OtSt	Oudtestamentische Studiën
PEQ	*Palestine Exploration Quarterly*
RA	*Revue d'Assyriologie*
RANE	Records of the Ancient Near East
RB	*Revue Biblique*
RelSRev	*Religious Studies Review*
RIMA	Royal Inscriptions of Mesopotamia, Assyrian Periods
RIME	Royal Inscriptions of Mesopotamia, Early Periods
SAA	State Archives of Assyria
SAAB	*State Archives of Assyria Bulletin*
SAAS	State Archives of Assyria Studies
SBLDS	Society of Biblical Literature Dissertation Series
SBLMS	Society of Biblical Literature Monograph Series
SBLSymS	Society of Biblical Literature Symposium Series

SBLWAW	Society of Biblical Literature Writings from the Ancient World
ScrHier	Scripta Hierosolymitana
SemeiaSt	Semeia Studies
SSEA	Society for the Study of Egyptian Antiquities Publications
ST	*Studia Theologica*
Sumer	*Sumer: A Journal of Archaeology and History in Iraq*
TA	*Tel Aviv*
TAPS	Transactions of the American Philological Society
TynBul	*Tyndale Bulletin*
Urk. IV	Sethe, K. *Urkunden der 18. Dynastie*, vol. 4: *Historisch-Biographische Urkunden*. Leipzig: Hinrichs, 1909
VT	*Vetus Testamentum*
VTSup	Vetus Testamentum Supplements
WBC	Word Biblical Commentary
YNER	Yale Near Eastern Researches
ZA	*Zeitschrift für Assyriologie*
ZÄS	*Zeitschrift für ägyptische Sprache und Altertumskunde*
ZDPV	*Zeitschrift des Deutsche Palästina-Vereins*

Chapter 1

The Torah as History:
Rethinking Genre

*A classic is not a classic because it conforms to
certain structural rules or fits certain definitions.
It is a classic because of a certain eternal
and irrepressible freshness.*
—Edith Wharton

In his classic work *Zakhor: Jewish History and Jewish Memory*, Yosef Hayim Yerushalmi explores a deeply felt tension between the drive to study and
record the past and the drive to remember the past in a way that sustains the life
of a community. Memory of the past has always been central to Jewish experience but has rarely taken on the intellectual or literary form of historiography.
History and memory were, in Yerushalmi's view, intertwined in the Bible but
pulled apart in postbiblical Judaism. The rabbis were concerned with the past
but sought to explore its meaning through other forms, forms that would creatively preserve Jewish identity and values: "As for the sages themselves—they
salvaged what they felt to be relevant to the ongoing religious and communal
(hence also the 'national') life of the Jewish people."[1] Pieces of the past took
on "legendary dimensions" and, as such, became an active part of communal
life through retelling in a literature is ahistorical yet has a deeply historical
character.[2] Yerushalmi notes that the "difficulty in grasping this apparent incongruity lies in a poverty of language that forces us, *faute de mieux*, to apply
the term 'history'" to both the object of study for historians and the content of
tradition.[3]

This poverty of language is a challenge for us as we encounter the Torah
itself. In fact, the problem may be more acute because the Torah, unlike rab-

1. Y. H. Yerushalmi, *Zakhor: Jewish History and Jewish Memory* (Seattle: University
of Washington Press, 1996) 25.
2. Ibid., 19.
3. Ibid., 26.

1

binic literature, *does* take on historiographical form. We encounter a number of history-like elements, particularly in the wilderness narrative, including the apparent use of sources; names, places, and dates that appear to be historical data; and an apparently unified linear chronological framework.[4] These elements are not altogether unlike things we might expect to find in a history even today. More specifically, features of the wilderness narrative such as itinerary notices, date formulas, and place-names bring to mind formal elements of chronicles and annals, historiographical genres commonly used in the ancient Near Eastern milieu in which the Bible took shape.

Although these history-like elements are similar in *form* to other historiographical genres used in the ancient Near East, the *content* raises some questions about whether the wilderness narrative really is a history. As Brian Peckham observes in his study of how various ancient texts depict time, history "supposes the continuity of past, present, and future" in a linear fashion.[5] The apparently linear chronological framework of the wilderness narrative is supplied by the itinerary notices and date formulas that structure it. Date formulas are also the backbone of chronicles and key formal elements in Neo-Assyrian annals. The biblical dates are formally quite similar to these, illustrated by the following comparison of an itinerary notice from the wilderness narrative to a date from the Neo-Assyrian annals:

וַיְהִי בַּשָּׁנָה הַשֵּׁנִית בַּחֹדֶשׁ הַשֵּׁנִי בְּעֶשְׂרִים בַּחֹדֶשׁ נַעֲלָה הֶעָנָן מֵעַל מִשְׁכַּן הָעֵדֻת׃

In the second year, in the second month, on the twentieth of the month, the cloud lifted off the Tabernacle of the *edut*. (Num 10:12)

ina līme [md]*Šamaš-nūrī ina qibit* [d]*Aššur bēli rabê bēliya ina* [iti]*Iyyar* UD.13. KAM *ištu* [uru]*Kalḫi attumuš*

In the eponymy of Shamash-nuri, by the command of Ashur, the great lord, my lord, on the thirteenth day of Iyyar, I departed from Calah. (A.0.101.1 iii 92–93)[6]

---

4. J. Barr, "Story and History in Biblical Theology," *JR* 56 (1976) 6–7. See also M. Sternberg, *The Poetics of Biblical Narrative: Ideological Literature and the Drama of Reading* (ed. R. M. Polzin; Indiana Literary Biblical Series; Bloomington: Indiana University Press, 1985) 41. For the term *history-like*, see H. Frei, *The Eclipse of Biblical Narrative: A Study in Eighteenth and Nineteenth Century Hermeneutics* (New Haven, CT: Yale University Press, 1974) 11.

5. B. Peckham, "History and Time," in *Ki Baruch Hu: Ancient Near Eastern, Biblical, and Judaic Studies in Honor of Baruch A. Levine* (ed. R. Chazan, W. W. Hallo, and L. H. Schiffman; Winona Lake, IN: Eisenbrauns, 1999) 295.

6. Throughout this volume, I refer to Neo-Assyrian royal inscriptions using the numbers assigned by A. Kirk Grayson in his RIMA series where possible, because these

But form and content do not always go together as we might expect. Mark S. Smith has pointed out that the date formulas in the wilderness narrative often contain liturgically significant dates. As such, the date formulas offer a chronology that is not linear, as would be characteristic of a chronicle or an annal, but cyclical, extending from the Pesah associated with the departure from Egypt to the first and second Pesah after the Tabernacle is constructed.[7] Following the completion of this liturgical year on the Israelites' departure from Sinai, date formulas rarely appear again in the wilderness narrative. Aside from a partial date in Num 20:1 marking the arrival of the people at Kadesh, the only other date formulas mark their entry into the land: They emerge from the Jordan on the 10th day of the 1st month, the day of preparation for Pesah (Josh 4:19; see Exod 12:3) and observe Pesah on the 14th day of the 1st month at Gilgal (Josh 5:10). While the date formulas are historiographic in form, the content relates to the ritual calendar.

Another history-like feature of the wilderness narrative is its putative use of a source document. Many redaction-critical studies of the wilderness narrative, including studies by Smith as well as Frank Moore Cross, Graham I. Davies, and William Johnstone, argue that the scribes who edited the wilderness narrative copied entries from the itinerary currently found in Num 33:1–49 into the narrative in order to shape it.[8] Although it is found within a narrative context, Num 33:1–49 is quite close in form to an administrative document. Davies compared its form with other itineraries throughout the ancient Near East and Mediterranean in a form-critical study that serves as a necessary foundation

---

are the text editions on which I have principally relied. All translations of Hebrew, Akkadian, and Egyptian texts in this volume are mine unless otherwise noted.

7. M. S. Smith, *The Memoirs of God: History, Memory, and the Experience of the Divine in Ancient Israel* (Minneapolis: Fortress, 2004) 81; idem, *The Pilgrimage Pattern in Exodus* (JSOTSup 239; Sheffield: Sheffield Academic Press, 1997) 290–98. Other scholars have also pointed out the liturgical nature of some of the dates, for example, J. Sturdy, *Numbers* (CBC; Cambridge: Cambridge University Press, 1976) 13, 76–77; and W. W. Lee, *Punishment and Forgiveness in Israel's Migratory Campaign* (Grand Rapids, MI: Eerdmans, 2003) 90.

8. F. M. Cross, *Canaanite Myth and Hebrew Epic: Essays in the History of the Religion of Israel* (Cambridge: Harvard University Press, 1973); G. I. Davies, "The Wilderness Itineraries and the Composition of the Pentateuch," *VT* 33 (1983) 1–13; M. S. Smith, "The Literary Arrangement of the Priestly Redaction of Exodus: A Preliminary Investigation," *CBQ* 58 (1996) 25–50; idem, *Pilgrimage Pattern*; idem, "Matters of Space and Time in Exodus and Numbers," in *Theological Exegesis: Essays in Honor of Brevard S. Childs* (ed. C. Seitz and K. E. Greene-McCreight; Grand Rapids, MI: Eerdmans, 1999) 182–207; W. Johnstone, *Chronicles and Exodus: An Analogy and Its Application* (JSOTSup 275; Sheffield: Sheffield Academic Press, 1998).

for any study of the wilderness itineraries. His survey of these texts showed that itineraries are typically administrative documents produced by scribal bureaucrats in an official context.[9] Davies recognized that itineraries must be adapted when they are used in the context of a narrative. He deemed Num 33:1–49 to be comparable to campaign narratives of early Neo-Assyrian kings along the Habur River, because both appear to have been minimally adapted by the use of narrative verb forms. The itinerary notices scattered throughout the wilderness narrative, on the other hand, were more substantively adapted to fit with the various episodes that are not included in Num 33:1–49.[10] Whatever the modifications, according to Davies, all of these instances have at their core an administrative document. He assumed that if a text looks like an administrative document, it must be or have been one, even if only in a former textual life. When we encounter an itinerary notice in any of these narratives, then, we often understand a historian to be at work with his sources.

As with the date formulas in the wilderness narrative, however, we encounter the potential for disconnect between form and content. Num 33:1–49 figures prominently in Benjamin Edidin Scolnic's 1995 study *Theme and Context in Biblical Lists*, which raised important questions about how we understand this text. Although Scolnic misidentified its genre (as Davies demonstrated, it is an itinerary rather than merely a list of place-names), his observations remain key to our consideration of itineraries. Scolnic explored the question of what an author might gain from imitating a list in a narrative context, simply *using the genre* rather than employing a source document. He argued that we cannot assume lists in narrative to have been distinct documents that had a separate existence outside of and were incorporated into biblical narrative, because they may also be literary creations themselves.[11] John Van Seters, who viewed Num 33:1–49 as a late version of the wilderness sojourn dependent on the wilderness narrative (a view previously articulated by Martin Noth), also captured this idea when he asserted that "the nature of this list does not correspond to any such official document *in substance*," even though it does in form.[12]

---

9. G. I. Davies, "The Wilderness Itineraries: A Comparative Study," *TynBul* 25 (1974) 47.

10. Ibid., 58.

11. B. E. Scolnic, *Theme and Context in Biblical Lists* (South Florida Studies in the History of Judaism 119; Atlanta: Scholars Press, 1995).

12. J. Van Seters, *The Life of Moses: The Yahwist as Historian in Exodus–Numbers* (Louisville: Westminster John Knox, 1994) 161; see pp. 153–64 for full argument; see also M. Noth, "Der Wallfahrtsweg zum Sinai (Nu 33)," in *Aufsätze zur biblischen Landes- und Altertumskunde* (ed. H. W. Wolff; 2 vols.; Neukirchen-Vluyn: Neukirchener Verlag, 1971) 1.55–74.

While Davies assumed that every specific instance of a genre has more or less the same form and function and was produced in the typical social context for the typical purpose, Scolnic pointed out that a "genre may be used as a literary device in order to make a point or to create an effect."[13] In his view, the author of Num 33:1–49 used the form of a list knowing it to be the kind of document that an ancient audience, based on experience with the genre, would have responded to as authentic. Verisimilitude is an implied characteristic of the list genre, a characteristic the author could draw on—even without using an actual source—in order to serve his literary goal of composing a text that a reader would receive as authoritative.

> The list may achieve meaning in a Biblical context by making the remote imminent. If we are told exactly how many men were involved in an event, if we read all the details of the stages of the journey, . . . we feel that we are close to the events. It is a closeness which springs from knowledge of details, from the sense that we are "there," that matters are tangible, concrete, so true-to-life that we seem to have a strong sense of exactly what happened.[14]

Num 33:1–49 has had a similar effect on modern scholars like Charles R. Krahmalkov who have attempted to reconstruct the route of this march on the assumption that the verisimilitude of the text is a function of its content as much as its form.

> The account sounds credible enough, even authoritative, as if based on real and reliable sources. It certainly creates in the mind of even the most critical reader the impression of historical fact. After all, the historian is absolute and specific. . . . On the face of it, this passage is an impressive and credible piece of ancient historical writing. Traditional Bible scholars always regarded it as such. For them, the account's extraordinary specificity and precision of detail strongly indicate that the ancient historian who wrote it had sources that accurately preserved the memory of a road used in very early times.[15]

When a genre is used as a literary device, however, this synergy between form and content may be loosened or broken. This is especially true when a scribe uses a genre creatively, blending it with other literary motifs and content

---

13. Scolnic, *Theme and Context*, 84.
14. Ibid., 165.
15. C. R. Krahmalkov, "Exodus Itinerary Confirmed by Egyptian Evidence," *BAR* 20 (1994) 56; see also J. D. Currid, *Ancient Egypt and the Old Testament* (Grand Rapids, MI: Baker, 1997) 121–22.

that may not typically be associated with it. Scolnic recognized that both the geographical content and the list (or itinerary) form *serve the author's literary goals*, whether or not they are historically accurate. As for the form, he made the important observation that verisimilitude is an *effect* created not strictly by the content but also by formal features of the genre and the expectations they create in an audience.[16] So, even if the formal features of the itinerary genre are blended with content that is not typical of itineraries, the genre still has the same effect on the reader.

Understanding how a text uses genre is a basic foundation for reading it. As Iain Provan, V. Phillips Long, and Tremper Longman III emphasized in *A Biblical History of Israel*, "Historians must read biblical texts, and indeed all texts, with as high a degree of literary competence as possible."[17] Assessing genre is sometimes quite simple. If you are holding in your hand a small cuneiform tablet whose first line reads *ina bēlī qibima* 'Say to my lord', you can be fairly certain you are reading a letter. In other cases, however, understanding the genre of a text can be a rather complicated matter. As we read the wilderness narrative, we are confronted with a wide variety of cues that shape our sense of what kind of narrative it is, often in conflicting ways. The wilderness narrative in some ways looks like history. But history-like features are combined in the wilderness narrative with a variety of other genres that are *not* historiographical. Interspersed with itineraries, date formulas, and putative source documents, we also encounter legends, sagas, myths, songs, and laws from the domains of folklore and didactic literature. How, in light of this complexity, do we assess the genre of the wilderness narrative?

George W. Coats and Rolf P. Knierim struggled nobly with this difficult question. In the initial discussion of genre in their commentary on Numbers, they suggested legend or saga, although they vacillated between the two throughout the commentary and even suggested that the genre changed from saga in pre-P material to legend in P.[18] They ultimately settled on *saga of a migrating sanctuary campaign*. *Saga* accounts for the folkloristic elements, *migrating* expresses the idea of an ethnic group moving from one place to another, and *sanctuary* reflects the focus on the Tabernacle, while *campaign* captures the aspects of the wilderness narrative that have a military flavor. The advantage of this genre label is that it is very descriptive. On one level, this is exactly what

---

16. Scolnic, *Theme and Context*, 101.

17. I. Provan, V. P. Long, and T. Longman III, *A Biblical History of Israel* (Louisville: Westminster John Knox, 2003) 99.

18. R. P. Knierim and G. W. Coats, *Numbers* (FOTL 4; Grand Rapids, MI: Eerdmans, 2005) 17–18, 34–35, 37.

we have in the wilderness narrative. The problem? The wilderness narrative is the *only* saga of a migrating sanctuary campaign there is. Perhaps we have simply not found another one yet, but Coats and Knierim acknowledge that, outside the wilderness narrative, sagas and annals are entirely unrelated to one another.[19] Although the saga of a migrating sanctuary campaign captures the complexity of the wilderness narrative, it seems reasonable to question whether ancient scribes had a genre of this sort in their repertoire that they would have used to frame more texts than just this one.

This unique genre label is the product of Knierim's conceptual approach to genre, developed out of frustration with Herrmann Gunkel's strong link between form, content, and mood that set the tone for a rather rigid approach to form criticism in biblical studies for much of the twentieth century.[20] Knierim strove to offer a better explanation for the flexibility we find in the structure, content, and social setting of genres in his 1973 article "Old Testament Form Criticism Reconsidered," since no one of these factors defines a genre in every instance of its use. He turned to structuralism in order to discover a reliable way to define a genre and argued that the genre of a text should be defined in terms of its basic underlying *concepts*.[21] The authors of the wilderness narrative depicted the ancestors of the Israelites marching through the desert with their portable shrine. So the genre is best understood as a saga of a migrating sanctuary campaign, since this is the concept that shapes the narrative.

The flexibility of genre is, however, not best explained by Knierim's conceptual approach because structuralism does not focus on how the *use* of a genre in a particular text might differ from what is typical. The limitations of the approach can be illustrated by Robert Alton Bascom's 1986 study of itineraries and journey narratives. Because he was concerned to define the genre based on a core concept that underlies all examples in the Bible, Bascom defined an itinerary as a broadly-construed concept of directional movement that can arise in a variety of social situations, including commercial activity and nomadism— too many to situate the genre in a specific type of context.[22] Although they use

19. G. W. Coats, *Exodus 1–18* (FOTL 2A; Grand Rapids, MI: Eerdmans, 1999) 105; see also Knierim and Coats, *Numbers*, 20.

20. For a concise review of Gunkel's views on genre, see T. Longman III, "Israelite Genres in their Ancient Near Eastern Context," in *The Changing Face of Form Criticism for the Twenty-First Century* (ed. M. A. Sweeney and E. Ben Zvi; Grand Rapids, MI: Eerdmans, 2003) 181–82.

21. R. P. Knierim, "Old Testament Form Criticism Reconsidered," *Int* 27 (1973) 435–68.

22. R. A. Bascom, *Prolegomena to the Study of the Itinerary Genre in the Old Testament and Beyond* (Ph.D. diss., Claremont Graduate School, 1986).

different methods, his understanding of the itineraries is, in the end, not much different from that of Noth, who used the term *itinerary* quite broadly to refer to the arrangement of traditions insofar as they reflect geographical concerns and suggest the concept of a route.[23] Noth recognized that the itinerary notices had unique stylistic criteria such as a stopping place, a date, and stereotypical verbs and syntax, but he wavered about whether these were characteristics of the P source document or of the itinerary as something unique.[24] The comparative form-critical study of extant itineraries undertaken by Davies solved this conundrum by demonstrating that the itinerary is not just any text that depicts directed movement but a specific type of administrative document with a well-defined form, produced in official contexts for a limited set of purposes—namely, to record and report on military or commercial maneuvers or plan out a future route.[25] The wide range of biblical narratives about journeys does not necessitate a broader definition of the itinerary genre. Rather, it suggests that the itinerary genre has been *used* in a variety of ways, some of which may differ substantially from the typical use of the genre Davies defined. Coats and Knierim quite beautifully captured the concepts, or *literary goals*, that shaped the wilderness narrative. But how ancient Israelite scribes used *genre* to achieve these goals is a question that still lacks an adequate answer.

The wilderness narrative is ostensibly a story about Israel's past, but history is not the only kind of narrative one can write about the past. We have already seen signs that the wilderness narrative is not historiographical in the typical sense. Although its chronology echoes the linear form of ancient Near Eastern chronicles and annals that relate the journeys of kings and armies, its content

---

23. M. Noth, *A History of Pentateuchal Traditions* (trans. B. W. Anderson; Englewood Cliffs, NJ: Prentice Hall, 1972) 220–21.

24. Idem, *Exodus: A Commentary* (OTL; Philadelphia: Westminster, 1962) 108, 127, 133.

25. We must be careful to distinguish *itinerary* as it refers to a kind of *text* that describes a route and *itinerary* as it refers more generally to the movement of people and things; contrast M. Porter, "Iter Itinerarii," *KASKAL* 3 (2006) 109; with F. M. Fales, "Treading the (Military, Comercial, and Cultural) Itineraries of the Ancient Near East (Udine, September 1–3, 2004): An Introduction," *KASKAL* 3 (2006) 105–8. For form-critical study of the itinerary notices in the wilderness narrative, see G. W. Coats, "The Wilderness Itinerary," *CBQ* 34 (1972) 135–52; and G. I. Davies, "Wilderness Itineraries: A Comparative Study," 47. The latter article along with *The Way of the Wilderness: A Geographical Study of the Wilderness Itineraries in the Old Testament* (Cambridge: Cambridge University Press, 1979) and "Wilderness Itineraries and the Composition of the Pentateuch" were developed on the basis of Davies's dissertation (*The Wilderness Itineraries in the Old Testament* [Ph.D. diss., University of Cambridge, 1975]).

is the cyclical ritual calendar that structures Israelite social and religious life. In fact, the overall content of the wilderness narrative, with its concern for Israel's laws and leadership roles as well as establishing its relationship to Yahweh is unquestionably formative for the community. As David H. Aaron put it in his 2006 volume *Etched in Stone: The Emergence of the Decalogue,*

> the Torah was written to serve as a *generative* document. That is, it was created for the sake of forming a community, a culture, a worldview at the very moment that the institutions normally responsible for such things had crumbled. The other historiographies are *derivative* rather than *generative*. They assume a set ideology and promote that ideology through their narration of past events. [26]

This epic narrative of Israel's origins is governed by a *valorized* rather than a historical concept of time. [27] As Peckham points out, the conception of time in history is linear, connecting past and present. History is still happening, and we are connected to it backward through time. [28] The epic past, on the other hand, is distant from the present and, more importantly, inaccessible to it. While an origin narrative offers the story of a group's past just as a history might, this past is not open to question or evaluation but can only be "accepted with reverence." As such, it becomes a repository for a group's formative traditions, lending them authority to define the community. [29]

We often think of origin narratives as *myth* but misuse this term by placing it in a dualistic relationship with history in such a way that it comes to have the overtones of something that is false. But a generative text is not exactly the stuff of fantasy. E. Theodore Mullen, in *Ethnic Myths and Pentateuchal Foundations,* understood the Torah as a type of narrative consisting of elements of shared culture that are "projected into the 'traditional' past and become part of the history and identity of the group from 'primordial' times." [30] Mullen emphasized that one reason Israelite scribes wrote this narrative was to establish

---

26. D. H. Aaron, *Etched in Stone: The Emergence of the Decalogue* (New York: T. & T. Clark, 2006) 44.

27. Ibid., 323; on myths of ethnic origin, see A. D. Smith, *The Ethnic Origins of Nations* (Hoboken, NJ: Wiley-Blackwell, 1991).

28. Peckham, "History and Time," 295.

29. M. Bakhtin, "Epic and Novel: Toward a Methodology for the Study of the Novel," in *The Dialogic Imagination: Four Essays* (ed. M. Holquist; trans. C. Emerson and M. Holquist; University of Texas Press Slavic Series 1; Austin: University of Texas Press, 1981) 13–17.

30. E. T. Mullen Jr., *Ethnic Myths and Pentateuchal Foundations: A New Approach to the Formation of the Pentateuch* (Atlanta: Scholars Press, 1997) 70.

continuity between life before the exile and the envisioned life after it, especially for the individuals who were born in exile.[31] Elements of shared culture
can come from a group's own traditions, be adopted from another culture as
its own, or be invented. Israel's legal traditions clearly play an important role
in shaping the wilderness narrative, and the ritual calendar, however it might
have been altered for use in a postexilic context, also would have provided this
sort of continuity in social practice.[32] The new is thus formed from pieces of
the old. Mullen's perspective not only holds promise for understanding how
the Israelites envisioned possibilities for social restoration. It may also account
for the literary shape of the Torah itself, as Israelite scribes drew on elements
of their own culture, borrowed from others, and innovated where necessary in
order to create this unique text.

The history-like character of the wilderness narrative is also created by
the presence of factual data. The toponyms and routes articulated in the wilderness narrative understandably prompt geographers and archaeologists such
as James K. Hoffmeier to search for physical evidence of them. Hoffmeier's
groundbreaking synthesis of the historical geography of the eastern Nile Delta
in his 2005 work *Ancient Israel in Sinai: The Evidence for the Authenticity of the
Wilderness Tradition* and other related publications is driven by the assumption
that archaeology, geography, and paleoenvironmental research "may uncover
evidence that corresponds to the textual materials."[33] The results of this sort
of work are undoubtedly valuable for understanding how a text relates to the
ancient world in which it was produced. For example, we now understand the
Mediterranean coastline prior to the Greco-Roman period to have been significantly farther south than it currently is and that the barrier island around Lake
Sirbonis did not connect to the mainland on its eastern end, rendering Otto
Eissfeldt's classic northern route for the exodus implausible.[34]

---

31. Ibid., 65.

32. Mullen assumes that, although the Temple cult was likely reorganized with
some foreign influence, particularly to fit within a Persian imperial context, there would
have been some continuity with the preexilic cult (*Ethnic Myths*, 204–5). This is also
suggested by studies that understand some Priestly literature to have been preexilic and
some postexilic, for example, I. Knohl, *The Sanctuary of Silence: The Priestly Torah and
the Holiness School* (Minneapolis: Fortress, 1995).

33. J. K. Hoffmeier, "The North Sinai Archaeological Project's Excavations at Tell
el-Borg (Sinai): An Example of the 'New' Biblical Archaeology," in *The Future of Biblical Archaeology: Reassessing Methodologies and Assumptions* (ed. J. K. Hoffmeier and
A. Millard; Grand Rapids, MI: Eerdmans, 2004) 60.

34. J. K. Hoffmeier, *Ancient Israel in Sinai: The Evidence for the Authenticity of the
Wilderness Tradition* (Oxford: Oxford University Press, 2005) 73, 88. For the northern

Many kinds of text contain references to real places that can be identified, whether they can still be seen, excavated, or learned about through other textual sources. Administrative documents such as itineraries certainly refer to places, as do military narratives, and the wilderness narrative is no exception. Hoffmeier thought geography might help us identify the genre of the exodus and wilderness narratives:

> A concocted story written centuries after the purported event would likely not bother with such trivial details as geography. No archaeologist to my knowledge has attempted to discover, for example, The Shire or Mordor from the *Lord of the Rings* trilogy, because they recognize that these great stories are novels, modern mythology that flowed from the creative imagination of J. R. R. Tolkien. They are not history.[35]

Because key sites such as Ramses are identifiable in a period to which an exodus event is plausibly dated, according to Hoffmeier, the exodus and wilderness narratives constitute an accurate historical report, whether written in the second millennium or based on an oral tradition extending back that far.[36]

But we cannot assess the genre of a text on the basis of the data in it alone. Geographical details in various kinds of literature are not at all trivial but are chosen for various reasons in order to serve the author's literary goals, and they do not always come from the imagination. The Shire may exist only in a fantasy world, but Thomas Hardy set his novels in Wessex, and Gustave Flaubert set *Madame Bovary* in the Norman countryside—real places that we can visit today.[37] Connecting a place mentioned in the Bible or any other text with a place known on the ground does not itself tell us much about the kind of narrative in which the place functions. Ramses is indeed a real place, but is its function in the Torah more like that of Aqaba in *Seven Pillars of Wisdom* or Dublin in *Ulysses*? Understanding how a text relates to the ancient world in which it was produced involves asking how and why ancient scribes represented pieces of that world in the text. We should ask: "Why did a scribe use the place-name Ramses at this point in the narrative?" and "How does Kadesh serve his goals in shaping the narrative?" The answers are not self-evident but involve detailed

---

route, see O. Eissfeldt, *Baal Zaphon, Zeus Kasios, und der Durchzug der Israeliten durchs Meer* (Halle: Max Niemeyer, 1932).

35. J. K. Hoffmeier, "Out of Egypt: The Archaeological Context of the Exodus," *BAR* 33/1 (2007) 35–36.

36. For identification of biblical narrative as a report, see idem, "Out of Egypt," 30, 33; for the conclusion of historical accuracy, see idem, "North Sinai," 60.

37. J. D. Johansen, *Literary Discourse: A Semiotic-Pragmatic Approach to Literature* (Toronto: University of Toronto Press, 2002) 113–73.

study of both the text and the ancient world in which it is deeply embedded by virtue of its many references not only to physical things but also ideas that were part of that world and would have been meaningful to the text's author and audience. This literary approach does not mean categorically dismissing the possibility that a text is history. If the authors of the wilderness narrative sought to write history in the same sense that other ancient Near Eastern scribes did, all signs, both literary and geographical, should indicate that this was so. If not, we might inquire about the *character* of its historicity as we consider how the ancient scribes used real pieces of their world, past or present, to shape this generative document.

Genre itself is an element of the ancient world, accessible to us through the texts it shaped just as ancient geography is accessible to us through archaeology. The wilderness narrative is situated within a whole network of different texts that use the itinerary genre, including reports and records as well as military narratives from Egypt and Assyria. Each text in this network is the product of a decision by a scribe in a particular historical and social context to use the itinerary genre as a means of communicating something to someone. But each text is also part of a process of how genre is altered through its use in different historical and social situations.[38] New contexts and shifting purposes, as we will see, generated innovation. David Damrosch has studied generic innovation in *The Narrative Covenant: Transformations of Genre in the Growth of Biblical Literature*, and his understanding of how genre works is important:

> The norms of genre are fundamental to the construction of meaning in texts, but at the same time, paradoxically, they are susceptible of constant alteration, deliberate or inadvertent, as new authors attempt to adapt old forms to changed circumstances and purposes.[39]

Using genre need not involve only borrowing a set of norms. It can also involve merging and transforming otherwise distinct genres to create texts that serve an author's particular set of goals in any given instance. In this book, I will show that the wilderness narrative, a story of the Israelites marching through the desert with their portable shrine, came about as scribes transformed standard ancient Near Eastern administrative and historiographical genres in order to serve purposes other than those for which they were typically used.

---

38. Ralph Cohen, "Afterword: The Problems of Generic Transformation," in *Romance: Generic Transformation from Chrétien de Troyes to Cervantes* (ed. K. Brownlee and M. S. Brownlee; Hanover, NH: University Press of New England, 1985) 269, 275; J. Frow, *Genre* (The New Critical Idiom; London: Routledge, 2006) 68–69.

39. D. Damrosch, *The Narrative Covenant: Transformations of Genre in the Growth of Biblical Literature* (San Francisco: Harper & Row, 1987) 37–38.

Innovation in the use of genre is not limited to the wilderness narrative. Each time the itinerary genre is used to compose a new text, it contributes something to a literary history. Hans Robert Jauss describes literary history as

> a process of founding and altering of horizons. The new text evokes for the reader (listener) the horizon of expectations and "rules of the game" familiar to him from earlier texts, which as such can then be varied, extended, corrected, but also transformed, crossed out, or simply reproduced. Variation, extension, and correction determine the latitude of a generic structure; a break with convention on the one hand and mere reproduction on the other determines its boundaries.[40]

We will find some uses of the itinerary genre to be quite typical, with no significant departures in form or context. These are simply reproductions, in Jauss's terms, and will be valuable to us insofar as they define a horizon of expectations for the itinerary genre. Other uses of the itinerary genre both in Egypt and Assyria transformed it, creating new genres, which in turn became normative and generated new sets of expectations. In fact, we will see that these experiments with genre set the stage for the transformations made by the authors of the wilderness narrative, transformations we can see only by situating it in the context of these "neighboring genres."[41] Although the wilderness narrative defies classification in a single genre category, it is nonetheless profoundly shaped by other genres in the network and, as a work of historiography without parallel, has its own place in literary history. My overall goal in this study is to shed some light on what this place is.

---

40. H. R. Jauss, *Toward an Aesthetic of Reception* (Theory and History of Literature 2; Minneapolis: University of Minnesota Press, 1982) 88.

41. C. Pelling, "Epilogue," in *The Limits of Historiography: Genre and Narrative in Ancient Historical Texts* (ed. C. S. Kraus; Leiden: Brill, 1999) 337–39.

Chapter 2

Emplotment and Repertoire: A Reading Strategy

> *Essentially, all models are wrong, but some are useful.*
> —George Box

Even the most enduring texts were written and are read in specific historical and social contexts. We open the Torah with a whole set of historically conditioned assumptions about it that influence our reading, even as we may often (and rightly) work hard to set at least some of these assumptions aside. The authors of the Torah likewise brought to their work a set of skills, resources, and knowledge about their world that were conditioned by their historical context. Perhaps because all we have left of these scribes is the literature they produced, it is easy to focus on the text and speak of its composition process as though it were unmanned. Rolf P. Knierim calls on historical critics to put the scribe back at the center of efforts to interpret biblical literature:

> Finally, historical exegesis should always be aware of the anthropological factor in the texts. This does not mean the human mind underneath the texts, nor does it mean that the focus of exegesis should move away from the texts to the humans behind them. The anthropological factor is the presence of the speakers and writers in their texts. These texts did not come into existence mechanically. They owe their existence to human beings, i.e., to their concerns, attentions, efforts, decisions, learnedness, and intentions. These humans speak in the texts and are part of their historicality.[1]

It is easy to forget about the scribes because we cannot, of course, directly access what was in their minds. The text itself is in front of us, and we can learn

---

1. R. P. Knierim, "Criticism of Literary Features, Form, Tradition, and Redaction," in *The Hebrew Bible and Its Modern Interpreters* (ed. D. A. Knight and G. M. Tucker; Minneapolis: Fortress, 1985) 157.

something about the historical and social contexts in which it might have been produced through historical research. Matching text to historical context is notoriously difficult, a difficulty that is often compounded by lack of adequate reflection on mimetics, or how a text represents the world. A common assumption is that a text *mirrors* the world, and when we have found the reality that best matches the image, we have succeeded in identifying the appropriate historical context. But rather than viewing the text as a mirror, we are better positioned to view it as *embedded* in a "multitudinous web of socio-cultural-historical forces" that influenced the scribes who wrote it.[2] The representations of genres, places, and social customs we find in a text got there because a scribe put them there. His craftsmanship is the link between the text and the world(s) represented in it. We cannot put the scribes themselves back at the center of our exegetical efforts, nor should this be our goal. But, through detailed study of both the text and the ancient world, we can focus on how they used their craft and their knowledge of the world around them to shape the texts that, in turn, shaped their ancient audiences and continue to shape us as we read them today.

What determines the meaning of a text? We can think about this question using the model offered by literary critic M. H. Abrams in his classic *Mirror and the Lamp*, which involves the four elements in the process of written communication: author, text, world outside the text, and reader. Abrams explains that different critical theories are oriented toward one or another of these four elements. Theories focused on the author articulate how literature expresses feeling and emotion, while reader-centered theories are concerned with the effects of literature. Theories focused on the world are concerned with how a text relates to the world, and text-centered theories focus on how language conveys meaning.[3] Within biblical studies, historical-critical methods tend to privilege the author and his historical context as the determinants of meaning, while efforts to correlate the text with the results of archaeology privilege the world. Literary studies have tended to situate meaning in the text itself, and reader-response approaches emphasize the role of the reader in producing meaning.[4]

---

2. F. Dobbs-Allsopp, "Rethinking Historical Criticism," *BibInt* 7 (1999) 242.

3. M. H. Abrams classifies them as expressive (author), mimetic (world), objective (text), and pragmatic (reader) (*The Mirror and the Lamp: Romantic Theory and the Critical Tradition* [New York: Norton, 1958] 3–29).

4. L. M. Poland, *Literary Criticism and Biblical Hermeneutics: A Critique of Formalist Approaches* (ed. C. A. Raschke; AARAS 48; Chico, CA: Scholars Press, 1985) 67–70; G. A. Yee, "The Author/Text/Reader and Power: Suggestions for a Critical Framework for Biblical Studies," in *Biblical Studies Alternatively: An Introductory Reader* (ed. S. Scholz; Upper Saddle River, NJ: Prentice Hall, 2003) 22–30; J. Barton, *The Nature of Biblical Criticism* (Louisville: Westminster John Knox, 2007) 75. For a slightly different

When we choose a particular tool with which to study the biblical text, then, we are also committing—however consciously—to a theory of meaning.

Any time we open the Torah, we are confronted with one whole text, whatever its history may have been and however difficult the residue of its development may sometimes make the reading process. Historical-critical methods have shed much light on this development, but they have not always helped us read the text with greater understanding of what it means. As Gerhard von Rad puts it, the source-critical method has often had a "profoundly disintegrating effect" on the text.[5] Frank Crüsemann names the implication: When historical criticism "breaks texts into rubble, it is time to switch methodology."[6] Scholars frustrated with the fragmented yield of historical criticism wanted a way to understand the biblical text as a unified whole whatever its origins and development, since it is read this way by individuals in both confessional and secular contexts.[7] So they set aside historical concerns, concerns about the author and the world, and focused on the text. Influenced by Anglo-American literary criticism of the mid-twentieth century, or New Criticism, they emphasized that a text is a "self-sufficient verbal artifact," internally coherent and autonomous. Historical and contextual concerns such as the author's intent or the composition history of the narrative, while they may have played a role in creating a text, do not determine its meaning. Meaning is instead a feature of the "text itself," produced by the relationships among words and the use of literary devices. The interpreter engages in "close reading" in order to discover what this meaning is.[8]

Wolfgang Iser offered an important critique of New Criticism in *The Act of Reading: A Theory of Aesthetic Response*. New Criticism's formalist approach to understanding the act of interpretation assumes meaning to be the *object* of a text—an old, stable, hidden message to which a text refers and which one excavates the text in order to discover. There are two problems with this approach,

---

map of critical methods in biblical studies, see J. Barton, "Classifying Biblical Criticism," *JSOT* 29 (1984) 19–35.

5. G. von Rad, "The Form-Critical Problem of the Hexateuch," *The Problem of the Hexateuch and Other Essays* (London: SCM, 1984) 1.

6. F. Crüsemann, *The Torah: Theology and Social History of Old Testament Law* (trans. A. W. Mahnke; Edinburgh: T. & T. Clark, 1989) 30.

7. E.g., J. Barr, *The Bible in the Modern World* (New York: Harper & Row, 1973) 59–65.

8. L. F. Searle, "New Criticism," in *Johns Hopkins Guide to Literary Theory and Criticism* (ed. M. Groden, M. Kreiswirth, and I. Szeman; Baltimore: Johns Hopkins University Press, 2005) 1; W. K. Wimsatt and M. C. Beardsley, *The Verbal Icon: Studies in the Meaning of Poetry* (Lexington: University of Kentucky Press, 1954) 4–18, 21–39.

according to Iser. First, it cannot explain why a given text can generate a variety of quite defensible interpretations even when read closely. Second, and perhaps more importantly, if we view meaning as something that we recover, all we are left with when we finish reading is admiration for the text, and all we can do is "congratulate" ourselves that we found the meaning.[9]

But this is not why we read, and it is not all we get out of reading. Iser was concerned to explain not just how texts mean but how they affect a reader's understanding of the world. He understood literature to have *significance* as well as meaning. Literature does not simply represent or explain but appeals to our imaginations and "enables us to view things differently from what they seem to be," showing us new possibilites for what we, our societies, and our world could be.[10] The Torah shapes the lives of many of its present-day readers and is generally held to have shaped its ancient readers as well. The wilderness narrative does not tell a story about the past simply for its own sake but in order to shape a nascent Israelite society, establishing a law, a social structure, and a relationship with Yahweh that will govern the Israelites' existence once they arrive in the land. New Criticism does a good job of articulating how texts work but falls short of telling us how they convey meaning and significance.[11]

Iser's critique of literary formalism can be extended to studies that appeal to archaeology and historical geography to interpret biblical texts, because they also view meaning as an object to be recovered. In studies such as *The Geographical and Topographical Texts of the Old Testament*, a "geographical commentary" by J. Simons, the task of interpretation is understood to involve quite literally excavating and identifying a historical and geographical reality to which the text is understood to correspond. Simons compiled information on every place-name found in the Bible, including a list of all the texts in which they occur and a discussion of their most likely identifications. When "all recognizable elements [could] be incorporated into a single itinerary without contradicting or neglecting any definitely acquired piece of evidence," Simons overlooked textually problematic passages in the wilderness narrative such as the sometimes strange sequences of events, be it the Israelites' turning

---

9. W. Iser, *The Act of Reading: A Theory of Aesthetic Response* (Baltimore: Johns Hopkins University Press, 1978) 4.

10. Idem, *Prospecting: From Reader Response to Literary Anthropology* (Baltimore: Johns Hopkins University Press, 1989) 273–78; idem, "What Is Literary Anthropology? The Difference between Explanatory and Exploratory Fictions," in *Revenge of the Aesthetic: The Place of Literature in Theory Today* (ed. M. P. Clark; Berkeley: University of California Press, 2000) 157–79.

11. Poland, *Literary Criticism*, 75–76, 85, 88, 159–60.

back from the wilderness toward the sea in Exod 14:2 or the ambiguity about whether they went around or through Edom and Moab in Numbers 20–21.[12] When it was difficult or impossible to reconstruct the route of the wilderness sojourn, he attributed the problem to lack of clarity about what physical reality is represented in the text or inadequate exploration of the Sinai Peninsula and Transjordan. On this view, meaning is understood to lie outside the text in the historical and topographical reality that the text mirrors, those external realities dictate how we read the text, and the solution to interpretive problems is more archaeological and topographical data. More data certainly give us more knowledge that we can use as we work out how a text relates to the world. But archaeological data cannot tell us how a text was composed or how it conveys meaning and significance.

Rather than as an *object* to be recovered, Iser advocates that we view meaning as an *effect* of a text: a coherent, albeit indeterminate understanding produced through interaction between a reader and a text. This interaction is guided by an author as he arranges words and information in various ways to guide the reading process.[13] The text, as Iser understands it, consists of a "network of response-inviting structures, which impel the reader to grasp" it.[14] Meaning takes shape as the reader navigates these instructions. She aligns herself with certain perspectives, puts questions to the narrative, evaluates based on her own expectations and those set up in the text, resolves tensions and, ultimately, synthesizes in a process Iser refers to as *consistency-building*.[15] At any given point in her reading process, the reader has a *Gestalt*, or overall sense of the narrative that she acquired by creating mental images based on her response to cues in the text. While the cues in the text constitute *potentials* for meaning, this *Gestalt* is the meaning.[16]

Meaning is thus not inherent in the formal structure of the text itself or in the world outside the text.[17] It takes place in the *brain*. Iser's theory of meaning has philosophical foundations, because it is deeply rooted in the work of Roman Ingarden, who was a student of the phenomenologist Edmund Husserl.[18]

---

12. J. Simons, *The Geographical and Topographical Texts of the Old Testament: A Concise Commentary in XXXII Chapters* (Leiden: Brill, 1959) 243.

13. Iser, *Act of Reading*, 5–10.

14. Ibid., 34.

15. Ibid., 18, 118–20.

16. Ibid., 95, 137–40.

17. Ibid., 120.

18. For an overview of Ingarden's work, see E. V. McKnight, *The Bible and the Reader: An Introduction to Literary Criticism* (Philadelphia: Fortress, 1985) 26–36.

Like philosophers and literary theorists, cognitive linguists explore how our brains process text, but they do so from the perspectives of linguistics, psychology, and neuroscience.[19] New Criticism and other formalist and structuralist literary approaches assume that language encodes meaning, but there is much about language that this approach does not explain well. Gilles Fauconnier observes:

> we are struck by the contrast between the extreme brevity of the linguistic form and the spectacular wealth of the corresponding meaning construction. . . . What is clear is that language is radically different from an information carrying and information preserving system, such as a code or telecommunications. Language forms carry very little information *per se*, but can latch on to rich preexistent networks in the subjects' brains.[20]

Studies in cognitive linguistics suggest that we connect the words we read with things we already know and build up a "mental representation of the discourse" as we, for example, envision the setting of a narrative or assess its genre.[21] As Fauconnier and Eve Sweetser describe the process, the "basic idea is that, as we think and talk [and read], mental spaces are set up, structured, and linked under pressure from grammar, context, and culture. The effect is to create a network of spaces through which we move as discourse unfolds."[22]

Fauconnier understands why it is attractive to think that meaning resides in the text or the world outside the text. We read a sentence, and meaning comes to us instantly. We see an object and assume that what "we perceive is indeed directly the very essence of the object perceived, out there in the world and independent of us."[23] In both cases, it appears to us as though meaning is

---

19. For the methods and assumptions of cognitive linguistics, see V. Evans, B. K. Bergen, and J. Zinken, "The Cognitive Linguistics Enterprise: An Overiew," in *The Cognitive Linguistics Reader* (ed. V. Evans, B. K. Bergen, and J. Zinken; Advances in Cognitive Linguistics; London: Equinox, 2007) 2–4.

20. G. Fauconnier, "Methods and Generalizations," in *Cognitive Linguistics: Foundations, Scope, and Methodology* (ed. T. Janssen and G. Redeker; Cognitive Linguistics Research 15; Berlin: de Gruyter, 1999) 98–99.

21. P. Werth, "How to Build a World (in a lot less than six days, and using only what's in your head)," in *New Essays in Deixis: Discourse, Narrative, Literature* (ed. K. Green; Costerus New Series 103; Amsterdam: Rodopi, 1995) 54, 60.

22. E. Sweetser and G. Fauconnier, "Cognitive Links and Domains: Basic Aspects of Mental Space Theory," in *Spaces, Worlds, and Grammar* (ed. G. Fauconnier and E. Sweetser; Chicago: University of Chicago Press, 1996) 11; see also Werth, "How to Build a World," 54.

23. Fauconnier, "Methods and Generalizations," 99; see also idem, "Mental Spaces, Language Modalities, and Conceptual Integration," in *The New Psychology of Language:*

in the thing we perceive. But this appearance is misleading. We are simply not conscious of the perception (how our eyes process visual stimuli, for example) and cognitive activity (how our brains turn these stimuli into concepts) that are involved in the way that we process information as we determine what it means.[24]

Although meaning is constructed in the mind of the reader, according to Iser, it is not determined by the author *or* the text *or* the world *or even* the reader. It is, rather, the result of a *process* involving all four, mediated by the text, which is fundamentally a set of instructions created by the author that guides the reading process.[25] It is important to emphasize that neither Iser nor cognitive linguists offer a relativist theory of meaning. George Lakoff emphasizes that meaning is "neither wholly objective nor wholly subjective."[26] Indeed, he points out a number of things that this approach has in common with objectivism:

> (*a*) a commitment to the existence of the real world, (*b*) a recognition that reality places constraints on concepts, (*c*) a conception of truth that goes beyond mere internal coherence, (*d*) a commitment to the existence of stable knowledge of the world.[27]

The claim is not that meaning is formed in the brain, *completely independent* of the world outside it. The claim is that meaning is formed in the brain, *in dialogue with* the world outside it that people who communicate with one another share.[28] So, although the text and the world represented in it do not determine meaning, they are still relevant for how we construct meaning. We should not abandon close reading or study of archaeology. We should simply think differently about their role in the process of interpretation.

Cognitive and Functional Approaches to Language Structure (ed. M. Tomasello; Mahwah, NJ: Lawrence Erlbaum, 1998) 251–52.

24. R. Jackendoff, *Foundations of Language: Brain, Meaning, Grammar, Evolution* (Oxford: Oxford University Press, 2002) 306–9.

25. Iser, *Act of Reading*, 64–65.

26. G. Lakoff, "Cognitive models and prototype theory," in *Concepts and Conceptual Development: Ecological and Intellectual Factors in Categorization* (ed. U. Neisser; Emory Symposia in Cognition; Cambridge: Cambridge University Press, 1987) 65.

27. G. Lakoff, *Women, Fire, and Dangerous Things: What Categories Reveal about the Mind* (Chicago: University of Chicago Press, 1987) xv.

28. C. Sinha, "Grounding, mapping, and acts of meaning," in *Cognitive Linguistics: Foundations, Scope, and Methodology* (ed. T. Janssen and G. Redeker; Cognitive Linguistics Research 15; Berlin: de Gruyter, 1999) 223–55. Basic-level categories and image schemas are among the ways in which our cognitive models are shaped by the world; see Lakoff, *Women, Fire, and Dangerous Things*, 282.

When we think about the world outside the biblical text, we often concentrate on tangible physical things that we know about through archaeology and historical geography, such as stone weights, city walls, road networks, or topography. But the world outside the biblical text contains much more: social conventions, other texts, political and social structures, ideologies, intellectual trends, current events, history. Indeed, the world outside a given text involves an entire culture in which it was produced, and we are arguably best positioned to understand a text by seeking to understand how it uses various elements of that culture—physical, literary, social, ideological—to help the reader construct meaning. Iser referred to these elements of culture as *repertoire*.[29] Genres are part of a culture's repertoire just as much as the places people live in or visit.

Iser argues that an author selects elements of repertoire such as genres and place-names from different cultural backgrounds, and he foregrounds, or projects them into the text.[30] Knowledge of these background contexts is important for the reader's process of consistency-building. Cognitive linguistics can help us understand selection and foregrounding, especially in complex texts such as the wilderness narrative that bring together material from different background contexts. Fauconnier, along with Mark Turner, has proposed a theory of *blending*, or conceptual integration, which may explain linguistic phenomena as well as nonlinguistic thought processes. The computer desktop is a nonlinguistic example of conceptual integration that involves blending knowledge from two different backgrounds—knowledge of how computers work and knowledge of the way that physical offices work—to create the new space in which we operate when we use a computer. When we use a computer, we rely on our background knowledge of how physical offices work to create "documents" that we move from one "folder" to another or to the "trash" when we no longer need them.[31] Likewise, in order to interpret the wilderness

---

29. Iser, *Act of Reading*, 68–79.

30. Ibid., 93.

31. M. Turner and G. Fauconnier, "Conceptual Integration and Formal Expression," *Metaphor and Symbol* 10 (1995) 183–204; M. Turner, *The Literary Mind* (New York: Oxford University Press, 1996); idem and G. Fauconnier, "Conceptual Integration Networks," *Cognitive Science* 22 (1998) 133–87 (I have used an updated version of this article posted online 10 February 2001 at http://markturner.org/cin.web/cin.html, accessed 6/28/2008); Fauconnier, "Mental Spaces, Language Modalities"; idem and M. Turner, *The Way We Think: Conceptual Blending and the Mind's Hidden Complexities* (New York: Basic Books, 2002). For application of conceptual integration theory to generically complex texts, see M. Sinding, "Genera Mixta: Conceptual Blending and Mixed Genres in Ulysses," *New Literary History* 36 (2005) 589–619. Although I use the model articulated by Turner and Fauconnier, it is important to acknowledge that other

narrative or a Neo-Assyrian annal well, we need knowledge of ancient literary and geographical repertoire, knowledge that archaeology can help us acquire by producing texts and other artifacts for us to study.

But when elements of repertoire are represented in a text, they do not only point to the cultural backgrounds from which they were selected. They also shape the text and create potentials for meaning. Although it is informed by features of a physical office, the computer desktop has its own internal logic; it is not a three-dimensional office but a new two-dimensional space on the computer screen. Our knowledge of how to use a computer is a blended mental space shaped not only by our knowledge of how physical offices work but also by our knowledge of computer operations. A literary text as Iser understood it can be viewed as a kind of blend, because it cues the reader to form a new, emergent mental space—a *Gestalt*—that has its own internal logic, shaped in part by the reader's knowledge of the elements of repertoire used in the text.

Representation should, in Iser's view, be understood as performance rather than as passive reflection of repertoire because the author actively *does something with* the repertoire in the text.[32] Elements of repertoire take on new connections in the text as they are combined with other elements, just as elements of a physical office are blended with computer code in order to make a computer desktop operate. These new connections are just as important to the process of communication as the background contexts because they are what helps us see the significance of the subject matter that the author aims to convey. We find the same idea in Benjamin Harshav's study of poetics: "even when relying heavily on the external world, imitating it or using its referents, the literary text selects elements and reshuffles their hierarchies while creating its own autonomous Field."[33] A text refers to elements of the world but creates its own distinct textual world in order to say something about the real one. A reader must understand the referents as well as what the author does with the repertoire in the text in order to understand the text. A parody, for example, requires some understanding of the object in its background context in order to work. But the author turns this object on its head in the text in order to make

---

linguists think blending is an important model for explaining language even as they question Turner and Fauconnier's specific way of understanding how it happens (mapping elements from a source to a target); e.g., R. Jackendoff and D. Aaron, "Review of More than Cool Reason: A Field Guide to Poetic Metaphor by George Lakoff and Mark Turner," *Language* 67 (1991) 334.

   32. Iser, *Act of Reading*, 237–38.

   33. B. Harshav, *Explorations in Poetics* (Stanford: Stanford University Press, 2007) 14.

light of or undercut it, prompting a reader to view it differently.[34] With the help of repertoire, the process of communication that Iser describes produces a *new perspective on*—a new way of seeing, relating to, thinking about—something, whether it be the king, a campaign, relationship with foreign peoples, one's role and responsibilities in a community, God, or the past. Close reading, with sensitive attention to details, remains important to the process of interpretation because it enables us to see what the author does with the repertoire, to make the connections that enable us to appreciate the significance of a text.

A complex text such as the wilderness narrative or a Neo-Assyrian an-nal can be understood as a blend of several elements of repertoire, building materials assembled with a particular goal or set of goals in mind. These texts do not function merely as passive reflections, or reports, of military campaigns or a journey through the desert but actively prompt readers to find a certain significance in the world around them, whether it relates to imperial power, as in the case of Egyptian and Assyrian military narratives, or ethnic cohesion and identity, as in the case of the wilderness narrative. The authors of these texts serve compositional, aesthetic, and ideological goals. Compositional goals re-late to the formal shape of the narrative. Given that the itinerary genre connects places together in a framework of linear movement through space and time, it has great potential for framing various parts of a narrative within a coherent and connected whole, and we will see authors capitalize on this potential.

Aesthetic goals relate to the reader's involvement in the narrative. We will consider how authors used elements of repertoire to create tension and drama in the narrative by, for example, guiding the reader to anticipate outcomes in the plot or form particular views of the characters' roles in the plot. We will also consider how repertoire was used to help the reader navigate contradic-tions in the setting, chronology, or ideology of a narrative that are typically read as indicators of diachronic development. The chain of itinerary notices in the wilderness narrative is an important example of this problem, because there are fractures in the chain where notices are in a different form, do not connect to previous notices, or present a conflated route. Historical criticism has typically identified these fractures and aimed to explain how they got there but has been notoriously deficient in explaining how we read the text now that they *are* there. Iser did not deal with the problem of composite texts, but his approach does give us a way of "reading the fractures" of this sort of text.[35] How authors used cultural repertoire to achieve the aesthetic goal of helping us read

---

34. Iser, *Act of Reading*, 35, 79–81.

35. The allusion is to D. M. Carr, *Reading the Fractures of Genesis: Historical and Literary Approaches* (Louisville: Westminster John Knox, 1996).

a composite as a whole will have significant implications for our understanding of the composition history of the wilderness narrative.

Ideological goals involve an effort to persuade a reader to buy into the interests and values of a particular social group, such as a royal administration or a priestly caste. The term *ideology* is slippery because it is used in a variety of ways ranging from the very generic and neutral *world view* to the very specific and derogatory *propaganda*.[36] I have in mind here Terry Eagleton's definition of ideology as "the *promotion* and *legitimation* of the interests of such social groups in the face of opposing interests."[37] I find this definition useful because it acknowledges that ideology involves both ideas and power without placing a positive or negative value on the concept; as such, it can be usefully applied to a wide variety of texts and other cultural products such as stelas and reliefs. The authors of the narratives we will consider here were interested in controlling geographical territory and the human and material resources within it. But they were also interested in controlling ideas: ideas about the king, about God, and about the shape of their society's past and future. In some cases, we must infer the opposing interests. In other cases, we will be able to see the advocates of different ideologies in dialogue with one another.

An author uses cultural repertoire selectively and sometimes quite creatively in order to achieve these goals. When repertoire is foregrounded in a text, only *some* of its attributes will function in the new context.[38] Iser noted that

> cultural norms and literary allusions . . . are incorporated into every new literary text in such a way that the structure and semantics of the systems concerned are decomposed. . . . [They are] broken up and rearranged when selected features appear in the text.[39]

Knowledge about how physical offices operate helps us work in the two-dimensional space of a computer, but not all elements of a physical office function in the blend: computer desktops do not have filing cabinets. And some are even a bit out of place: the trash can, which is on the floor in a real office but on the desktop in the computer, is an accommodation to the two-dimensional

---

36. T. Eagleton, *Ideology: An Introduction* (London: Verso, 1991) 1–31; D. J. A. Clines, *Interested Parties: The Ideology of Writers and Readers of the Hebrew Bible* (JSOTSup 205; Sheffield: Sheffield Academic Press, 1995) 9–16.

37. Ibid., 29.

38. For the selective use of elements from a background (or input space, in the terminology of conceptual blending), see Sinding, "Genera Mixta," 594; Turner and Fauconnier, "Conceptual Integration Networks," n.p.

39. W. Iser, *How to Do Theory* (Malden, MA: Blackwell, 2006) 60–61.

space of the computer. Benjamin Edidin Scolnic, as discussed in the previous chapter, essentially argued that the itinerary in Num 33:1–49 is not a source document copied wholesale into the text but a *selective* use of the itinerary genre for its attribute of verisimilitude in order to create the effects of realism and authoritativeness for the text. We should not necessarily assume that the place-names in Num 33:1–49 also constitute a single coherent route that can be identified geographically or historically.

How can the series of place-names and other formal features of the itinerary genre we read in texts carry such intangible qualities as verisimilitude? Michael Sinding, whose approach to genre theory draws heavily on cognitive linguistics (particularly the work of Lakoff), shows that genre can be viewed as a cognitive model.[40] Genre is typically understood as a pattern of formal features. According to the cognitive approach, however, a genre also involves the intangible attributes related to these features, the relationships among them, and knowledge about how the whole model works.[41] Although cognitive models exist only in the brain, they are not disconnected from the world outside the brain because, according to Lakoff, we form them through interaction with the world.[42] We have knowledge of how offices work because we have worked in offices or have at least seen or heard about people working in offices. Likewise, a genre is learned through exposure to texts, whether reading them, hearing them, or—for ancient scribes—learning to write them as part of scribal training, most likely by copying exemplars.[43] Our exposure to texts involves

---

40. M. Sinding, "After Definitions: Genre, Categories, and Cognitive Science," *Genre* 35 (2002) 196–97; idem, "Beyond essence (or, getting over 'there'): Cognitive and dialectical theories of genre," *Semiotica* 149 (2004) 377–95; Sinding, "Genera Mixta." For an evaluation of the potential of this work for biblical studies, see C. A. Newsom, "Spying Out the Land: A Report from Genology," in *Bakhtin and Genre Theory in Biblical Studies* (SemeiaSt 63; Atlanta: Society of Biblical Literature, 2007) 19–30.

41. D. E. Rumelhart, "Schemata: The Building Blocks of Cognition," in *Theoretical Issues in Reading Comprehension Perspectives from Cognitive Psychology, Linguistics, Artificial Intelligence, and Education* (ed. R. J. Spiro, B. C. Bruce, and W. F. Brewer; Hillsdale, NJ: Lawrence Erlbaum, 1980) 33–35; D. A. Cruse and W. Croft, *Cognitive Linguistics* (Cambridge: Cambridge University Press, 2004) 14–28.

42. Lakoff, "Cognitive Models," 65; Lakoff, *Women, Fire, and Dangerous Things*, 112, 280–83.

43. Sinding, "After Definitions," 182 n. 10, 193; see also E. D. Hirsch, *Validity in Interpretation* (New Haven, CT: Yale University Press, 1967) 73–74; J. Culler, *Structuralist Poetics: Structuralism, Linguistics and the Study of Literature* (Ithaca, NY: Cornell University Press, 1975). Newsom offered the caveat that genre competence need not be expressly inter*textual* because the pattern itself is cognitive; it could also be acquired in other ways ("Spying Out the Land," 23–24).

cultural and social experience as well as our faculties of perception and our conceptualizing capacity. [44] So we learn not just its formal features but also the contexts in which it is typically used, who typically uses it, what assumptions they make about it when they write and read it, and what they typically use it to communicate. All of these intangibles become just as much a part of the cognitive model as the formal features.

Cognitive models carry not just tangible elements like trash cans (for an office) or place-names (for an itinerary) but a whole network of associations, *any* of which might be useful for writing or reading a text. We are accustomed to thinking of genre in biblical studies as a particular thematic content and set of typical formal features (*Gattung*) that are used in a specific social context (*Sitz im Leben*). [45] Graham I. Davies defined the itinerary genre in just this way: a type of text containing departure and arrival notices written in administrative contexts by members of a bureaucracy. [46] But genre also involves situation of address, structure of implication, and rhetorical function. Rhetorical function involves a text's purpose—for example, to report or to convince. Situation of address involves the social positions of the author and audience. Structure of implication refers to assumptions involved in communication that are not directly expressed in the text but nonetheless generate meaning. These assumptions include, for example, the authority and credibility of the speaker and the message as well as the implied reality status. [47] While these assumptions are not

---

44. Lakoff, "Cognitive Models," 65; Lakoff, *Women, Fire, and Dangerous Things*, 112, 280–83. For the relationship between Fauconnier's mental spaces and cognitive models, see ibid., 68, 281–82.

45. I deliberately avoid the terms *Gattung* and *Sitz im Leben* in this study for two reasons. The first is the frequent imprecise use of the term *Sitz im Leben*. It is often extended beyond its specific reference to the social circumstances that called for the use of a particular *Gattung* (for example, use of the itinerary to make a report to one's boss in a bureaucratic context) to refer to specific historical circumstances (for example, the exilic period) or even to the literary context. For incisive comment on these sorts of ambiguities, see E. Blum, "*Formgeschichte*—A Misleading Category? Some Critical Remarks," in *The Changing Face of Form Criticism for the Twenty-First Century* (ed. M. A. Sweeney and E. Ben Zvi; Grand Rapids, MI: Eerdmans, 2003) 32–46. This confusion can be avoided and greater precision gained by referring specifically to the "social context," "historical context," or "literary context." Furthermore, I use terms such as "genre" and "social context" rather than *Gattung* and *Sitz im Leben* in order to make this book more easily accessible to a broader audience familiar with contemporary genre theory.

46. G. I. Davies, "The Wilderness Itineraries: A Comparative Study," *TynBul* 25 (1974) 47.

47. J. Frow, *Genre* (The New Critical Idiom; London: Routledge, 2006) 9–10, 73–80. See K. L. Sparks, *Ancient Texts for the Study of the Hebrew Bible: A Guide to the*

explicit in the formal features of a text, they are part of a cognitive model, developed out of experience with writing, reading, and using texts in that genre. Such experience would generate knowledge not only of its formal features but of its purposes and assumptions as well. Verisimilitude is just as much an attribute of the itinerary genre as a place-name is because, as we will see in the next chapter, itineraries typically function as reports and are therefore assumed to be accurate.

As Hans Robert Jauss intimated when he suggested that a genre might be "simply reproduced," an author might choose to use a genre in a way that conforms quite closely to the cognitive model, using all the necessary formal features in the typical social context for the typical purpose.[48] An author can also, however, capitalize on one or another of a genre's attributes in a creative way to achieve his literary goals. This is especially the case when an author uses a genre in a context with an *atypical* situation of address or for an *atypical* purpose. Scolnic, for example, argued that the author of Num 33:1–49 capitalized on the implication of versimilitude in order to create authority for his narrative, which in other ways is *not* just an itinerary.

We may have a difficult time identifying and understanding such creative uses of genre if we focus on classifying a text as one genre or another, especially since some texts resist or even defy classification. Some considerations of genre within biblical studies adopt the idea that a text has an intrinsic genre and, if we identify the genre based on necessary and sufficient features, we know how to read the text. Because not every text of a given genre has exactly the same set of features, we might understand texts to fall nominally in a particular genre and recognize that they may be classified differently when analyzed.[49] If our job as readers and critics is to identify the intrinsic genre of a text, how do we classify texts that are as generically complex as the wilderness narrative? This is just the dilemma Knierim and George W. Coats faced when trying to identify the genre of the wilderness narrative. They recognized that this narrative

---

Background Literature (Peabody, MA: Hendrickson, 2005) 18 for a similar list, which is, however, weak in its recognition of rhetorical features.

48. H. R. Jauss, *Toward an Aesthetic of Reception* (Theory and History of Literature 2; Minneapolis: University of Minnesota Press, 1982) 88.

49. Sparks refers to the genre that actually shapes a text as *intrinsic genre* and the critic's after-the-fact classifications as *analytical genre* (*Ancient Texts*, 10–11). While he recognizes that a text can be classified differently when analyzed by various critics, he does not deal with the problem of how we understand the genre of a text when it *defies* classification. For dogmatism, nominalism, and skepticism as principle-based approaches to genre contrasted to the pragmatic approach I adopt here, see T. Pavel, "Literary Genres as Norms and Good Habits," *New Literary History* 34 (2003) 201–10.

might mix genres, but the need to identify a single intrinsic genre generated a "genre"—saga of a migrating sanctuary campaign—that is otherwise unattested in ancient Near Eastern literature. It could be that the wilderness narrative is the only extant example of a saga of a migrating sanctuary campaign from the ancient Near East and that there are more of them to be excavated or located in a genizah. But the subgenres that make up this complex text are quite identifiable and, before appealing to absence of evidence, we ought to explore whether we owe the present shape of the wilderness narrative to a creative *blend* of various genres and other elements of cultural repertoire.

Instead of trying to classify, we may fare better if we consider how the genre or genres used by an author create potentials for meaning and influence how we read a text. John Frow described genre in this way:

> Genre, we might say, is a set of conventional and highly organised constraints on the production and interpretation of meaning. In using the word "constraint" I don't mean to say that genre is simply a restriction. Rather, its structuring effects are productive of meaning; they shape and guide, in the way that a builder's form gives shape to a pour of concrete, or a sculptor's mould shapes and gives structure to its materials. Generic structure both enables and restricts meaning, and is a basic condition for meaning to take place. [50]

We should therefore read "for an awareness of how the subtleties of text are generically formed and governed." [51] Although Num 33:1–49, according to Scolnic, is not an itinerary per se, the itinerary genre, with its attribute of verisimilitude, is one factor that helps us interpret this text as authoritative. Instead of asking, "What genre is this text?"—a question that locks us into one genre or another—we should ask, "How does genre *shape* this text?"—a question that allows for multiple influences.

I will focus in this book on one simple element of cultural repertoire: the itinerary genre. Since itineraries involve place-names, however, we must consider how geography, also an element of cultural repertoire, shapes the wilderness narrative as well. Cognitive models are invoked by linguists to explain our capacity for language, but they may also apply to other cognitive capacities such as vision, music, social cognition, or movement. [52] Humanistic geogra-

---

50. Frow, *Genre*, 10.

51. Ibid., 101.

52. R. Jackendoff, "Linguistics in Cognitive Science: The State of the Art," *The Linguistic Review* 24 (2007) 355–57. For the idea that mental spaces have strong potential to explain how we think generally, see also Fauconnier, "Mental Spaces, Language Modalities," 268–69; and idem and Turner, *Way We Think*. Caution is warranted since,

phers have suggested that we form *mental maps* of place. A mental map is "a spatial image of a place that is carried in the mind."[53] This map may involve the physical dimensions of a place out there in the world that can be perceived, measured, and described just as the formal features of a text can be. Historical geography typically gets at these attributes by studying archaeology, toponymy, climate, geology, settlement patterns, and trade routes.[54] But a mental map also involves knowledge about a place and its history—however accurate or flawed—as well as attitudes, preferences, and aesthetic and social values.[55] Our mental maps can also involve elements of landscape, even fictional elements, that have become part of our cultural tradition, as well as memories of a landscape no longer physically present.

Yi-Fu Tuan, the founder of humanistic geography, points out that mental maps are not pictures, as though reflected by the mind's mirror or taken with the mind's camera, but cognitive models of place that involve the spatial relationships among things, their typical uses, and the values assigned to them.[56] Just as we learn genres by exposure to texts, we develop mental maps based on experience of living and interacting in a place, reading and hearing about it, or seeing how it is represented in texts and visual imagery. Our cognitive models for place enable us to give directions, remember things by locating them spatially, draw maps, write about places, remember the landscapes of the past, and imagine what future landscapes might look like.[57] The same, of course, would have been true for ancient scribes. A cognitive approach to geography is important for us as we try to understand how place-names are used. An ancient scribe could have foregrounded a particular place-name in the text, not

according to Jackendoff, the overlap between different types of cognition is currently being studied.

53. G. R. Pitzl, *Encyclopedia of Human Geography* (Westport, CT: Greenwood, 2004) 137.

54. A. F. Rainey and R. S. Notley, *The Sacred Bridge: Carta's Atlas of the Biblical World* (Jerusalem: Carta, 2006) 10.

55. For example, P. C. Adams, S. Hoelscher, and K. E. Till, "Place in Context: Rethinking Humanist Geographies," in *Textures of Place: Exploring Humanist Geographies* (ed. P. C. Adams, S. Hoelscher, and K. E. Till; Minneapolis: University of Minnesota Press, 2001) xiii–xxxiii.

56. For a brief explanation of the "mental picture" model of representation and critique of this model, see P. Werth, *Text Worlds: Representing Conceptual Space in Discourse* (Textual Explorations; New York: Longman, 1999) 36–38.

57. Y. Tuan, "Images and Mental Maps," *Annals of the Association of American Geographers* 65 (1975) 205–13; C. Renfrew and P. Bahn, *Archaeology: Theories, Methods, and Practice* (2nd ed.; London: Thames and Hudson, 1991) 370; M. Porter, "Iter Itinerarii," *KASKAL* 3 (2006) 110.

merely because the place exists physically, but also for some of the knowledge or values associated with it in his mental map. As Jon Berquist has noted, our understanding of place within biblical narrative should consider "concepts of distance, height, width, breadth, orientation, and direction, and also human perceptions, constructions, and uses of these aspects."[58]

Geographical features in the biblical text are sometimes treated simply as neutral data while the meaning or significance of the text comes from the events related and thoughts expressed against this geographical background, which has been described as "often almost incidental to the message."[59] But place-names, as elements of repertoire, help to shape the meaning of a text just as genre does. Leonard Lutwack devoted his study *The Role of Place in Literature* to a consideration of how geography is foregrounded in literature. An author can

> manipulate the wide range of effects places may have. The physical quali-
> ties of place are expressive only as they are assimilated to the over-all liter-
> ary complexion of the work. Like sounds in poetry, they must be made to
> seem appropriate and symbolic within the range of meaning prepared for
> them by the arts of language.[60]

A place-name in a narrative can evoke any or all of the physical, conceptual, or social facets of a place in a mental map. An author might choose to foreground a place-name because an event took place there but also because of its size, its shape, its dimensions, its status (as a remote area nobody knows about or the center of a tribal territory, for example), the kind of place it is (urban area or desert way station), when it was occupied (or the fact that it is no longer oc-

---

58. J. L. Berquist, "Critical Spatiality and the Construction of the Ancient World," in *'Imagining' Biblical Worlds: Studies in Spatial and Historical Constructs in Honor of James W. Flanagan* (ed. D. M. Gunn and P. McNutt; JSOTSup 359; Sheffield: Sheffield Academic Press, 2002) 15; see also J. W. Flanagan, "Ancient Perceptions of Space/Perceptions of Ancient Space," in *The Social World of the Hebrew Bible: Twenty-Five Years of the Social Sciences in the Academy* (ed. R. L. Simkins and S. L. Cook; Semeia 87; Atlanta: Society of Biblical Literature, 1999) 15–44.

59. Rainey and Notley, *Sacred Bridge*, 9. This view of place is rooted in Aristotle's *Physics*; see E. Relph, "Place," in *Companion Encyclopedia of Geography: The Environment and Humankind* (ed. I. Douglas, R. Huggett, and M. Robinson; London: Routledge, 1996) 907.

60. L. Lutwack, *The Role of Place in Literature* (Syracuse, NY: Syracuse University Press, 1984) 34. For recognition of literary significance of place in the Bible specifically, see S. Bar-Efrat, *Narrative Art and the Bible* (JSOTSup 70; Sheffield: Sheffield Academic Press, 1997) 194; Y. Amit, *Reading Biblical Narratives: Literary Criticism and the Hebrew Bible* (Minneapolis: Fortress, 2001) 119–25.

cupied), the kind of activity that typically takes place in it, or ideas or memories associated with it. Its location—whether on a particular route, whether inside or outside political boundaries—is yet another potentially useful facet of a place. An author may have one or more of these facets in mind as a reason to select and foreground a particular place-name in the service of his literary goals.

By selecting, foregrounding, and establishing connections among elements of repertoire such as genre and geography, an author creates a discourse world. As we read, we construct a mental image, or *Gestalt*, of this discourse world based on cues in the text. As Paul Werth noted, "all situations must be represented in the minds of the participants, whether they refer to the real world, to memory, or to imagination."[61] Elements of repertoire such as the city of Ramses, the oasis at Kadesh, or an itinerary are not represented in the wilderness narrative in such a way that the text simply mirrors a single real-world situation involving all three. These elements of repertoire *may or may not* have anything to do with one another in the real world or in the cognitive models that a reader already has. Elements of repertoire from separate background contexts, from separate cognitive models, can take on new connections as they are combined in the text.[62] The discourse world may fit well with a single real-world historical and geographical situation, as it would be expected to do in a historical narrative. But it also may not.[63] As Iser notes, "We have to bear in mind that literary texts do not relate to contingent reality as such, but to systems through which the contingencies and complexities of reality are reduced to meaningful structures."[64]

Even historians shape their narratives in order to provide a new perspective on the past. Hayden White argues that historical narratives do not simply correspond to the events they depict but often share literary elements in common with fictional genres. Writing history certainly involves researching and accurately representing data about events, but it also involves metahistorical issues that are not related to the data at all. These include ideology and *mode of emplotment*, or the particular literary framework that we might use to tell the story in a given instance. White argued that a historian could take the same set

---

61. Werth, "How to Build a World," 64.

62. Iser, *Act of Reading*, 93.

63. G. Fauconnier, *Mental Spaces: Aspects of Meaning Construction in Natural Language* (Cambridge, MA: MIT Press, 1985) 152; Lakoff, *Women, Fire, and Dangerous Things*, 70; Sweetser and Fauconnier, "Cognitive Links," 11; idem, *Mappings in Thought and Language* (Cambridge: Cambridge University Press, 1997) 69. For more detail on creating discourse worlds, see also Werth, "How to Build a World."

64. Iser, *How to Do Theory*, 60–61.

of data and tell the story, for example, either as a tragedy or a satire, depending on how these data are cast in the narrative.[65] While collecting data is about answering the "who-what-when-where" questions, writing the narrative addresses the questions "why" and "so what." Writing history is thus not simply about researching and representing data but also about choosing frameworks within which to give the data *meaning*. Narrative, as opposed to other forms such as the chronicle, has a formal and conceptual coherence that enables the author not merely to record the data but to make sense of them by telling us something significant about them.[66] Iser acknowledged that reading historical narrative involves consistency-building, just as reading fiction does, so that we finish a history not simply with a knowledge of what happened but with some sense of what it means and why it matters as well.[67]

Although histories represent real-world data, the meaning of a historical narrative still has much to do with how an author manipulates words, just as the meaning of a portrait has much to do with the the way in which the artist manipulates shape, line, and color. Iain Provan, V. Phillips Long, and Tremper Longman III argue in *A Biblical History of Israel* that a historical narrative is a verbal picture of the past just as a portrait is a visual picture of its sitter.

> Indeed, the ability to place the features in right relationship to one another distinguishes a good portrait artist from a bad one. Similarly, the ability to place the individual historical "facts" in right relationship to one another distinguishes a good historian from a bad one. Individual brushstrokes must be "accurate"—which is to say, they must achieve their representational objective (a single stroke may suffice to represent, say, an eyebrow quite accurately). But even more importantly, the total effect of the brushstrokes in combination must "accurately" achieve its representational objective.[68]

---

65. H. V. White, *Metahistory: The Historical Imagination in Nineteenth-Century Europe* (Baltimore: Johns Hopkins University Press, 1973) 7–11.

66. H. V. White, "The Historical Text as Literary Artifact," *Tropics of Discourse: Essays in Cultural Criticism* (Baltimore: Johns Hopkins University Press, 1978) 81–100; idem, "The Value of Narrativity," *The Content of the Form: Narrative Discourse and Historical Representation* (Baltimore: Johns Hopkins University Press, 1987) 1–25. For more in-depth discussion of the philosophical and linguistic issues involved in the question of how a text represents its referent, see idem, "The Context in the Text," *The Content of the Form: Narrative Discourse and Historical Representation* (Baltimore: Johns Hopkins University Press, 1987) 185–213.

67. Iser, *Prospecting*, 56.

68. I. Provan, V. P. Long, and T. Longman III, *A Biblical History of Israel* (Louisville: Westminster John Knox, 2003) 87–88. See also V. P. Long, *The Art of Biblical His-*

By this view, a history is valuable only to the extent that it resembles the past, just as a portrait is only as good as it resembles the sitter, and the narrative artistry is cosmetic.

We can see the flaw in this view by pushing the art analogy a bit further. Pablo Picasso's *Portrait of Daniel-Henry Kahnweiler*, an important example of analytical cubism, does not resemble its sitter at all. An author or an artist can depict aspects of the world around him, but these are situated within a narrative or artistic framework when they are represented. The narrative or artwork need not be realistic to be representational. As Roland Barthes has pointed out, realism is a form of discourse that seeks to appear true to life. Although it is traditionally characteristic of historical narrative, it is also used by authors of fiction.[69] Moreover, historical discourse need not be realistic. Historians have recently experimented with other forms of discourse that can address specific problems that they face—such as how to convey multiple points of view in a single narrative—that traditional historical discourse cannot.[70] Picasso strove to push the boundaries of representation away from realism, as do other types of literary discourse. While a cubist painting represents Kahnweiler just as much as a realistic painting would, each would tell us something different about him, about the nature of human beings and things in the world around us more generally, and even something about how we viewers see and understand this world.

It may be helpful for our purposes here to frame the difference between fiction and history not primarily as a difference of nature (representational or not) but a difference of constraints. The author of a history works with more constraints on his use of geography (and other data) than an author of realistic fiction or fantasy literature. If an author's goals are historiographical, we should expect to see a stronger adherence to sources and accurate data, because histories report as well as emplot.[71] In the next chapter, we will study administrative

tory (Foundations of Contemporary Interpretation 5; Grand Rapids, MI: Zondervan, 1994) 17–26.

69. R. Barthes, "The Discourse of History," in *Comparative Criticism: A Yearbook* 3 (ed. E. S. Shaffer; Cambridge: Cambridge University Press, 1981) 3–20; and idem, "The Reality Effect," *The Rustle of Language* (New York: Hill and Wang, 1986) 141–48. See also the incisive comments on this issue by White, *Metahistory*, 2 n. 4.

70. For discussion of such efforts, see P. Burke, "History of Events and the Revival of Narrative," *New Perspectives on Historical Writing* (University Park: Pennsylvania State University Press, 2001) 283–300.

71. J. Marincola notes that scholars often hold two positions at odds—the idea that historians tried to get it right (report) and the idea that they tried to create artistically crafted narrative (emplot)—and rightly points out that this is a false dichtotomy (*Greek Historians* [New Surveys in the Classics 31; Oxford: Oxford University Press, 2001] 7).

texts that report or otherwise serve pragmatic goals. An author may make a
report of a journey, a text that has little meaning beyond being simply true
or false. He might also lay out the route of a journey for a future traveler or
convince someone to choose one route to a destination over another—in other
words, to act in a certain way in response to the text. The Egyptian and Neo-
Assyrian military narratives we will study in chap. 4 are standard examples
of ancient Near Eastern historiography. We will see that they also exhibit a
concern to report because at points they actually incorporate administrative
documents. When an author incorporates part or all of such a document into a
historical narrative, it retains its nature as a report *but is also put in the service
of new goals* that were not operative in its primary context, goals that relate
to emplotment. We will see these authors use their sources creatively as they
balance the goals of reporting and emplotting, even in one case straining their
accuracy—but only so far.

Authors of various types of fiction continue to use real-world information.
They just do so with fewer constraints. J. R. R. Tolkien not only *could* invent
places like Mordor and the Shire, but he *needed* to do so in order to displace his
social and philosophical commentary onto an imagined world. Even so, while
the Shire may exist only in the imagination, its character is deeply informed
by the realities of the English countryside. This and other elements of reality
represented in Tolkien's literature help us grasp the significance of his message
for us and the world we live in. Iser emphasizes that a "literary text is a mixture
of reality and fictions, and as such it brings about an interaction between the
given and the imagined."[72] Authors of realist fiction can mix actual geography
with fictional characters or even mix actual and invented places, as Gustave
Flaubert does in *Madame Bovary*, in order to serve their literary goals. We
would not comprehend or benefit from reading literature—literature would
have no significance for us—if there were no familiar elements of reality represented in it.[73]

While origin narratives are set in the past, even they are not subject to the
same constraints as historical narrative. As we discussed in chap. 1, history is
set in real-time and thus open to question, criticism, and revision, while an
origin narrative is set in valorized time, in the epic past. The epic past becomes
the repository for a group's formative traditions; here they acquire authority

---

72. W. Iser, *The Fictive and the Imaginary: Charting Literary Anthropology* (Baltimore: Johns Hopkins University Press, 1993) 1.

73. H. M. Barstad, "The History of Ancient Israel: What Directions Should We
Take?" in *Understanding the History of Israel* (ed. H. G. M. Williamson; Proceedings of
the British Academy 143; Oxford: Oxford University Press, 2007) 32–34.

because this past is closed off and must be "accepted with reverence."[74] Some of these traditions in the wilderness narrative are ritual, such as the calendar that governs the Israelites' collective life and, as Mark S. Smith argued, is written into the itinerary notices. Some are social, such as the roles of priests and levites. Israelite legal tradition certainly plays a prominent role. Some of these traditions may even be historical. The authors of the wilderness narrative had more room for flexibility and creativity in their use of diverse traditions, diverse elements of cultural repertoire, than did the authors of Egyptian and Neo-Assyrian military narratives. Reading the wilderness narrative is like looking at Israelite history and culture through a kaleidoscope.

However an author combines elements of repertoire from different backgrounds, he constructs a narrative that optimally achieves his literary goals, one that can ideally be read as a coherent whole. Iser argues that an author provides cues to guide our process of consistency-building by constructing various perspectives within the text, including the perspectives of the narrator, various characters, and plot structure. The reader is guided to identify with one of these perspectives at any given moment and to evaluate this perspective from the point of view of the other perspectives.[75] We establish a *theme* for a text as we determine its dominant characteristics, the ones with which we identify. For example, we do not need to read too far into the wilderness narrative before we have seen enough itinerary notices to characterize it as the story of a journey. But, as we read, we are constantly encountering new things or other perspectives that we must fit into the *Gestalt* we have already built up at any given point in the process. A *horizon*, or point of tension, occurs when we encounter something that prompts us to renegotiate the theme. The author thus guides the reader to read the text in a certain way: "[T]he structure of theme and horizon organizes the attitudes of the reader."[76]

Theme and horizon are important for *both* synchronic *and* diachronic analysis of the wilderness narrative. We build consistency when we read a text such as the Torah that was created out of disparate materials over time by multiple authors, just as much as we do when we read a novel created by a single author. Horizons need not be fractures in a text that tip us off to its diachronic

---

74. M. Bakhtin, "Epic and Novel: Toward a Methodology for the Study of the Novel," in *The Dialogic Imagination: Four Essays* (ed. M. Holquist; trans. C. Emerson and M. Holquist; University of Texas Press Slavic Series 1; Austin: University of Texas Press, 1981) 13–17.

75. Iser, *Act of Reading*, 96.

76. Ibid., 97. For a similar process described from the perspective of cognitive linguistics, see Sweetser and Fauconnier, "Cognitive Links," 12.

development. In fact, creating and resolving horizons is how an author develops a narrative. Horizons can, however, also be created when a text is revised, but not flawlessly so. How do we tell the difference? Horizons that are tensions within a well-constructed narrative are productive and eventually either resolved or left in such a way as to contribute to the meaning of a narrative. We encounter a number of horizons in the wilderness narrative that are not resolvable in this way because they grate against what we know to be true about geography or about the itinerary genre. It is reasonable to consider the presence of these horizons as a sign of compositional problems.

We might see the redactors of the Torah as striving to create an optimally functional blend out of disparate materials. The classic understanding of the redactor within the Documentary Hypothesis paradigm does not assign much creativity or skill to redactors, who just supply the editorial glue to hold the original sources (which are thought to yield the insight about Israel's literary and religious history) together in an artificial whole. But appreciation for the work of redactors has grown to the point of seeing them as authors rather than editors, responsible for the literary and ideological shape of the narrative we now have.[77] Rather than simply shift the emphasis from sources to redaction, more recent redaction-critical studies fundamentally challenge the Documentary Hypothesis and strive to rethink the nature of the Torah's composition history, offering suggestions for other models.[78]

One such model is offered by William Johnstone in his 1998 work, *Chronicles and Exodus: An Analogy and Its Application*. Building on Erhard Blum's model of a Deuteronomistic and a Priestly version of the Pentateuch, the latter a revision of the former, Johnstone proposed two editions that are to be distinguished from one another not on the basis of stylistic criteria or vocabulary (which are commonly used to distinguish the classical Documentary sources from one another) but on the basis of internal consistency and coherence of both ideology and compositional technique. Each author had his own particular view about the shape of Israel's society and wrote a narrative that served these interests. The wilderness narrative, then, according to Johnstone, resulted

---

77. L. G. Stone, "Redaction Criticism: Whence, Whither, and Why? Or, Going beyond Source and Form Criticism without Leaving Them Behind," in *A Biblical Itinerary: In Search of Method, Form and Content* (ed. E. E. Carpenter; JSOTSup 240; Sheffield: Sheffield Academic Press, 1997) 77–90.

78. See the review of a number of recent studies and state-of-the-art comments in D. M. Carr, "Controversy and Convergence in Recent Studies of the Formation of the Pentateuch," *RelSRev* 23 (1997) 22–31; and R. Rendtorff, "The Paradigm Is Changing: Hopes—and Fears," *BibInt* 1 (1993) 34–53.

not from the redaction of multiple source documents but from purposeful *composition* and *revision*, not altogether different in nature from the way we might go about writing and rewriting texts today.[79] Recognizing that penta-teuchal studies is currently in flux and, consequently, that any discussions of composition history are tentative, I here modify and extend Johnstone's model in the hope of making a small contribution to the effort to move toward a new paradigm.

The goal of creating a coherent, readable whole—or a whole that is as co-herent as possible—places constraints on the way an author uses repertoire. Turner and Fauconnier articulate a series of principles for creating an optimal blend. The blend has to function on its own as a unit, and elements in the blend should serve some meaningful function within it. Elements must also maintain "appropriate connections" to the cognitive models in which they originate. As I discussed above, a blend does not make use of every feature and attribute that a genre or place-name would have in its background context. But the use of an element of cultural repertoire in the blend should not violate its use in these models.[80] In other words, even a composite text should read as much as possible as a single whole and remain plausible. I suggest that this is not just an assumption that modern readers bring to a text but that the ancient Israel-ite scribes who produced this composite text made a similar assumption and wrote partly with this goal in mind, even if they did not always fully succeed. Examples I will discuss later in the book bear this out.

These optimality principles are ideal, and a perfect blend cannot always be fully achieved. Sometimes elements of repertoire from different backgrounds do not fit seamlessly together. In some cases, the ill-fitting combination has

---

79. W. Johnstone, *Chronicles and Exodus: An Analogy and Its Application* (JSOTSup 275; Sheffield: Sheffield Academic Press, 1998). While Johnstone offers a substantive cri-tique of Blum's work, his model of composition rests on the foundation established in E. Blum, *Studien zur Komposition des Pentateuch* (BZAW 189; Berlin: de Gruyter, 1990). Although both Blum and Johnstone use the sigla D and P in their works, I have delib-erately used the full terms *Deuteronomistic* and *Priestly* in order to avoid the impression that I am working within the Documentary Hypothesis paradigm. I also use *priestly* with a lowercase letter to refer to priestly materials in general when I do not mean to associate them with the Priestly version of the wilderness narrative. I will continue to use this terminology throughout the book except where I mean to refer to a classical Documentary source, since it recognizes the existence of literature that belongs to or is influenced by these ideological schools without referring to a specific (if hypothetical) text, such as the classically-defined P source document.

80. Fauconnier, *Mental Spaces*, 186; Turner and Fauconnier, "Conceptual Integra-tion Networks," n.p.

no significant bearing on the coherence of the blend. Returning to Turner and Fauconnier's computer example, the presence of the trash can *on* the desktop rather than on the floor *beneath* it, as it is in a real office, is easy to negotiate. We relax our expectations and ignore this conflict between the trash can's place in a real office and its place on a computer desktop because there is no third dimension in the computer for the trash can to sit on. The two-dimensional parameters of the blend force the conflict, but it does not get in the way of the trash can's function as the place where you put items to delete them, or throw them away, which is the same on the computer as it is in a physical office. Despite a conflict with the background context, the element of repertoire still plays a necessary and uncomplicated role in the way the blend functions as a whole. We will encounter similar conflicts in the wilderness narrative, particularly where there are fractures in the chain of itinerary notices. Each of these problems is a horizon, and we must decide how to integrate it with the overall itinerary theme that dominates the wilderness narrative. In many cases, despite the conflict, we will see that the itinerary notices are critical in our process of consistency-building and, perhaps ironically, *help* us read the narrative as a whole.

In other cases, however, conflicts have negative consequences for the coherence of the blend. Although you drag folders and documents to the trash can in order to discard them, you also drag disk icons to the trash in order to eject the disk from the computer. This is a significant problem for the coherence of the blend, according to Turner and Fauconnier, because the trash can has two roles *in the blend itself* that conflict with one another. You use the trash can to *delete* folders and documents, but you also use it to *save* items when you move a disk to the trash in order to eject it. Saving items by moving a disk to the trash further conflicts with the function of the trash can in the cognitive model for a physical office, since the wastebasket is not a place you put things you want to keep. This move is counterintuitive, and it is harder to relax our expectations and ignore the conflict, which is much more obvious than the simple presence of the trash can on the desktop rather than under it. Ultimately, however, we learn to do so in the interest of operating the computer, or making the blend work. [81]

We must negotiate similar conflicts as we read the wilderness narrative. The Israelites' route through Transjordan in Numbers 20–21 and 33 is a classic example. At some points, the Israelites appear to be going through Edom, while

---

81. Idem, "Conceptual Integration and Formal Expression," 183–204; idem, "Conceptual Integration Networks," n.p.

at others they appear to be going around it. The same is true for Moab at various points in the narrative. It is not clear on the whole which route the Israelites are taking. One way to approach these challenges is to assume that the narrative does describe a single, coherent journey that we would properly comprehend if only we had enough knowledge about the geography of Transjordan. But we might also view each challenge as a horizon at which we must determine how what we are currently reading fits with the theme, or the general picture that we have of the Israelites' route so far. These horizons are particularly challenging to navigate because there are conflicts within the narrative itself: a passage describes the Israelites going one way, and a few verses or chapters later they seem to be going a different way entirely. Moreover, there are conflicts with the way that repertoire works in its background contexts. The idea that the Israelites go both around and through Edom violates the linear character of the itinerary genre and the knowledge, gleaned from basic bodily experience, that people cannot be in or move through two places at once. Improving our knowledge of Transjordan's topography through archaeology and historical geography can undoubtedly contribute to a more thorough understanding of this narrative, but it will not make these particular violations of the way repertoire works in its background contexts go away. We must couple the study of archaeology with close reading—paying attention to textual details, navigating theme and horizon—in order to understand not only the repertoire itself but also the way it is used in the narrative.

Were authors in antiquity really so creative as to select and combine cultural repertoire to shape a text that would achieve a set of literary goals and read as a coherent whole? Johnstone, like Iser, assumes that authors had a purpose, a meaning they wanted to communicate, and that they were deliberate about shaping the text to serve this purpose. Such deliberateness is held by some to conflict with the view that authors in antiquity were caretakers and transmitters of literature rather than inventors of it. [82] At the heart of this discomfort is a concept of authorship that "involves the idea of an individual (singular) who is responsible for or who originates, who writes or composes, a (literary) text and who is thereby considered an inventor or founder" with godlike authority over the shape and interpretation of his text. [83] As Andrew Bennett points out in his study of authorship throughout literary history, this is a post-medieval and particularly Romantic concept of authorship that does not apply to antiquity. [84]

---

82. E.g., W. M. Schniedewind, *How the Bible Became a Book: The Textualization of Ancient Israel* (Cambridge: Cambridge University Press, 2004).

83. A. Bennett, *The Author* (The New Critical Idiom; London: Routledge, 2005) 7.

84. Ibid., 29–71.

Authors in the ancient Near East, with a few exceptions, remained anonymous, while works were attributed to prominent political or prophetic figures or to God in order to bolster their authority.

Although the rules of writing and reading were different in antiquity from what they are today, there is plenty of positive evidence for deliberate and creative shaping of the cultural tradition by ancient scribes. John Barton articulates a good approach to the authorship of ancient texts: "In trying to discover what a work means, we are not exploring the inside of its author's mind, but asking about how the assertions that compose the work cohere with each other to make a comprehensible whole." [85] The author as individual in fact drops out of the picture for Iser, because the reader can interact with the author only as he is implied in the structure of the text. Although an individual is responsible for constructing the text using repertoire from his cultural background, this person no longer has any bearing on the production of meaning once the text is written. [86] What is left to us of an author is implicit in the construction of the text. Whatever constraints the attitudes and practices of ancient scribal guilds placed on the production of literature, a text has a particular shape in part because of decisions that a scribe made about its shape.

Authors in antiquity were in any case not typically concerned to relate their private thoughts but instead spoke for the community of scribal and intellectual elite of which they were a part. In his recent work on scribal activity in the ancient Near East, Karel van der Toorn argues that a text

> expresses the common values, ideological and artistic, of the scribal community. The author is a craftsman. Individual talent, which would be as real a gift in antiquity as it is today, was not an instrument to express the private and the personal but was a way to attain the pinnacle of a collective art. [87]

---

85. Barton, *Nature of Biblical Criticism*, 106.

86. Iser, *How to Do Theory*, 68. This is Foucault's "author function" or Wayne Booth's "implied author" (M. Foucault, "What Is an Author?" in *Critical Theory since 1965* [ed. H. Adams and L. Searle; Tallahassee: Florida State University Press, 1986] 137–48; W. C. Booth, *The Rhetoric of Fiction* [Chicago: University of Chicago Press, 1961] 67–86); see also B. Lategan, "Reference: Reception, Redescription, and Reality," in *Text and Reality: Aspects of Reference in Biblical Texts* (ed. B. C. Lategan and W. S. Vorster; SemeiaSt; Atlanta: Scholars Press, 1985) 70–71; M. Sternberg, *The Poetics of Biblical Narrative: Ideological Literature and the Drama of Reading* (ed. R. M. Polzin; Indiana Literary Biblical Series; Bloomington: Indiana University Press, 1985) 9; Bennett, *Author*, 29–54.

87. K. van der Toorn, *Scribal Culture and the Making of the Hebrew Bible* (Cambridge: Harvard University Press, 2007) 46–47. See also Barton, *Nature of Biblical Criticism*, 78–79.

While ancient scribes were artisans whose responsibility, in part, was to preserve the cultural tradition, they shaped and reshaped this tradition, exhibiting
a high degree of individuality and creativity *even as* they transmitted it.[88]

Genre transformations are an important example of the creativity of ancient scribes. Longman suggests that ancient Near Eastern literature was less
rather than more innovative than modern literature, making the task of assessing the genre of a narrative easier because ancient authors were more
constrained by genre than modern authors.[89] Herman Vanstiphout, however,
discusses a number of genre innovations in Mesopotamian literature, including the *Tale of the Fox* and *Enki and the World Order*.[90] Hannes D. Galter has
pointed out some genre innovations that shaped Neo-Assyrian annals, and
I will consider others in chap. 4 of this book.[91] Moreover, as I will argue in
chaps. 5 and 6, we owe the present shape of wilderness narrative to profoundly
creative uses of genre. But the stability of genre to which Longman points is
an important part of the creative process. Creative use of a genre in an atypical and especially in a blended context involves transgressing norms but, as
Tsvetan Todorov put it in his own study of genre, transgression implies a norm

---

88. B. R. Foster, "On Authorship in Akkadian Literature," *Annali* 51 (1991) 19. Foster's article is devoted to the way these issues play out in Mesopotamian scribal culture;
for discussion of them in Israelite scribal culture, see Barton, "Classifying Biblical Criticism," 19; D. M. Carr, *Writing on the Tablet of the Heart: Origins of Scripture and Literature* (Oxford: Oxford University Press, 2005); J. Van Seters, *The Edited Bible: The Curious
History of the "Editor" in Biblical Criticism* (Winona Lake, IN: Eisenbrauns, 2006); idem,
"Author or Redactor?" *Journal of Hebrew Scriptures* 7, 5 October 2007, http://www.arts
.ualberta.ca/JHS/Articles/article_70.pdf; idem, "The Origins of the Hebrew Bible: Some
New Answers to Old Questions," *JANER* 7 (2007) 91; van der Toorn, *Scribal Culture*.

89. T. Longman III, "Israelite Genres in their Ancient Near Eastern Context," in
The Changing Face of Form Criticism for the Twenty-First Century (ed. M. A. Sweeney
and E. Ben Zvi; Grand Rapids, MI: Eerdmans, 2003) 180. Longman is perpetuating this
idea from R. P. Knierim, "Old Testament Form Criticism Reconsidered," *Int* 27 (1973)
435–36.

90. H. Vanstiphout, "'I Can Put Anything in Its Right Place': Generic and Typo-
logical Studies as Strategies for the Analysis and Evaluation of Mankind's Oldest Literature," in *Aspects of Genre and Type in Pre-Modern Literary Cultures* (ed. B. Roest and
H. Vanstiphout; COMERS Communications 1; Groningen: Styx, 1999) 79–99; H. Vanstiphout, "The Use(s) of Genre in Mesopotamian Literature: An Afterthought," *ArOr*
67 (1999) 703–17.

91. H. D. Galter, "Assyrische Königsinschriften des 2. Jahrtausends v. Chr.: Die
Entwicklung einer Textgattung," in *Assyrien im Wandel der Zeiten: XXXIXe Rencontre Assyriologique Internationale, Heidelberg, 6.–10. Juli 1992* (ed. H. Waetzoldt and
H. Hauptmann; Heidelberger Studien zum Alten Orient 6; Heidelberg: Heidelberg Orientverlag, 1997) 53–59.

that was transgressed.[92] Flexibility or creativity is incomprehensible without stability.[93] Moreover, what is creative can itself become a new norm; blended spaces can in turn be used to shape new blends.[94] Genres, through sometimes less and sometimes more creative use in different contexts over time generate new genres, and these shifts constitute literary history.[95]

Cognitive models matter not only because they are the background contexts out of which an *author* selects elements of repertoire but also because they are important for the *reader's* process of consistency-building. Iser indicated that, when an element of repertoire is foregrounded in a narrative, it retains some connection to the cultural background from which it was drawn, and this connection to context aids the reading process.[96] Cognitive linguists understand words, such as the formal features of the itinerary genre or place-names, to be "'points of access' to vast repositories of knowledge relating to a particular [cognitive model]"; they prompt a reader to draw on this knowledge in order to construct meaning.[97] As Harshav puts it in his study of poetics, a reader's "experience and interpretation of literary texts are not a matter of language alone" but are mediated through language.[98] When a reader encounters the formal features of the itinerary genre in the wilderness narrative, for example, she is cued to think of the whole model, including the formal elements as well as elements such as the structure of implication that are not directly represented in the text, and she uses this model to help her process the text.[99]

Just as Iser focuses on the author as implied by the creativity and skill evident in the construction of the text, he also focuses on an ideal reader who would follow all of the cues, cooperating with the implied author. This ideal reader, like the author, is fundamentally a textual strategy, implied in the composition of the text.[100] She would follow every single cue and fully share

---

92. T. Todorov, *Genres in Discourse* (trans. C. Porter; Cambridge: Cambridge University Press, 1990).

93. This point is made in many of the essays in R. Boer, ed., *Bakhtin and Genre Theory in Biblical Studies* (SemeiaSt 63; Atlanta: Society of Biblical Literature, 2007).

94. Turner and Fauconnier, "Conceptual Integration Networks," n.p.

95. Sinding, "After Definitions," 190–91; Jauss, *Toward an Aesthetic of Reception*.

96. Iser, *Act of Reading*, 69.

97. Evans, Bergen, and Zinken, "Cognitive Linguistics Enterprise," 8. For application of this idea to Biblical Hebrew lexicography, see the recent study by E. van Wolde, *Reframing Biblical Studies: When Language and Text Meet Culture, Cognition, and Context* (Winona Lake, IN: Eisenbrauns, 2009).

98. Harshav, *Explorations in Poetics*, 1.

99. On the relationship between formal features and cognitive models, see Turner and Fauconnier, "Conceptual Integration and Formal Expression."

100. Lategan, "Reference," 70–71.

the author's cultural context, enabling her to understand his use of repertoire because she would fully understand the background contexts from which it was drawn.[101] Dan Sperber and Dierdre Wilson talk about the importance of context for interpreting language. Context is not just the surrounding text or the particular physical and historical environment in which an utterance was produced or a text was written. It includes things like general cultural assumptions, knowledge, expectations, memories, and religious beliefs. These things are found in our cognitive models of the world.[102] Shared context can come about when people "share physical environments and have similar cognitive abilities."[103] An ideal reader of the wilderness narrative would have a cognitive model of the itinerary genre that perfectly matched the author's and would be able to relate all of the places mentioned to a mental map that would let her access the same set of associations the author had in his.

Fully shared context is an ideal. A shared physical environment and a shared culture provide the *potential* for an author and a reader to share the same cognitive models of genres, geography, and other things in this environment. But it is no guarantee that they will: "[T]o say that two people share a cognitive environment does not imply that they make the same assumptions: merely that they are capable of doing so."[104] Even when we share a physical environment and a culture, we form our models of the world as individuals, and they can differ due to a whole variety of factors. A number of factors unique to the ancient world limit the extent to which even readers in antiquity would have read—or, more broadly, received—texts such as a Neo-Assyrian annal or the wilderness narrative with a fully shared context.

Access is one limiting factor. While virtually anyone in the Western world can acquire a copy of a work of literature from a bookstore, Web site, or local library, access to the texts to be discussed here was quite restricted in antiquity. While commemorative inscriptions were in some cases publicly visible on the external walls of temples or on stelas, they were usually inscribed on the *inside* walls and floors of temples and palaces, to which only a limited segment of the population had access.[105] Furthermore, some copies of the Neo-Assyrian texts

---

101. Iser, *Act of Reading*, 69.

102. D. Sperber and D. Wilson, *Relevance: Communication and Cognition* (The Language and Thought Series; Cambridge: Harvard University Press, 1986) 15–16, 39–41. Paul Werth calls this shared context "frame knowledge" ("How to Build a World," 54–55).

103. Sperber and Wilson, *Relevance*, 41.

104. Ibid., 41.

105. A. L. Oppenheim, *Ancient Mesopotamia: Portrait of a Dead Civilization* (rev. ed.; Chicago: University of Chicago Press, 1977) 148–49; idem, "Neo-Assyrian and

to be considered were written on the backs of orthostats or on tablets or prisms placed in foundation deposits, where they would be seen only by the gods and kings who might undertake future building projects. For the Hebrew Bible, lack of extant manuscripts prior to the Dead Sea Scrolls leaves us to make educated guesses about what the context of reception might have been. It is clear, however, simply from the many instances of intertextuality across the Hebrew Bible that the texts were accessible at least to other scribes who were composing, copying, and storing them.

Literacy is a second factor that must be taken into account as we consider the ancient audience for these texts. While literacy is comparatively widespread in the modern Western world, it was likely quite limited in all ancient Near Eastern cultures. The ability to read and write at all was limited in Mesopotamia due to the amount of training needed to function with the cuneiform writing system. Moreover, evidence for scribal schools in both Mesopotamia and Egypt suggests that there were different levels of education for the administrative scribe and scholar, and it is reasonable to assume that the same would have been true in ancient Israel. The upper-level elite, who were responsible for maintaining and perpetuating the tradition, would have mastered it, while others may have learned it on different levels.[106] Some studies of epigraphic evidence for ancient Israel stress that literacy may have been less limited in Israel, especially beginning in the eighth century B.C.E., because evidence of writing is geographically widespread and not necessarily limited to certain classes.[107] But, even if more widespread, the extant evidence is limited to certain types of writing, generally to a repertoire of written genres used in political, military, and commercial contexts.[108] So we cannot assume that, just because some-

---

Neo-Babylonian Empires," in *Propaganda and Communication in World History*, vol. 1: *The Symbolic Instrument in Early Times* (ed. H. D. Lasswell, D. Lerner, and H. Speier; Honolulu: University Press of Hawaii, 1979) 111–44.

106. L. E. Pearce, "The Scribes and Scholars of Ancient Mesopotamia," *CANE* 4.2265; P. Piacentini, *Oxford Encyclopedia of Ancient Egypt*, 3.187–92; J. Baines, *Visual and Written Culture in Ancient Egypt* (Oxford: Oxford University Press, 2007) 50.

107. See, for example, M. D. Coogan, "Literacy and the Formation of Biblical Literature," in *Realia Dei: Essays in Archaeology and Biblical Interpretation in Honor of Edward F. Campbell, Jr.* (ed. P. H. Williams and T. Hiebert; Atlanta: Scholars Press, 1999) 47–61; R. S. Hess, "Literacy in Iron Age Israel," in *Windows into Old Testament History: Evidence, Argument, and the Crisis of "Biblical Israel"* (ed. V. P. Long, D. W. Baker, and G. J. Wenham; Grand Rapids, MI: Eerdmans, 2002) 82–102; and Schniedewind, *How the Bible*, 91–117.

108. S. Niditch, *Oral World and Written Word: Ancient Israelite Literature* (Library of Ancient Israel; Louisville: Westminster John Knox, 1996) 39–77.

one could write and read, his training extended to literature to such an extent that he would relate to one of the narratives to be discussed here on the same level—with a truly shared cultural repertoire—as the scribe who wrote it. We can relate to this issue even in the modern Western world as we consider the different levels and kinds of literacy possessed, for example, by a high school graduate, an English professor, and a lawyer. But our knowledge of schools in antiquity allows us to understand that differences may have been more pronounced in that context.

Finally, we must consider that the narrative texts to be considered here were not merely read. They were viewed and possibly heard as well. It has been suggested that texts such as Sargon II's letter to the god may have been read aloud publicly, and this is certainly a possibility for the Torah as well.[109] We can assume, at least on a basic level, that the creation of meaning through the listening process would have been much the same as through reading, since the language of the text is what conveys this meaning. But texts carved on monumental reliefs on the side of a temple, the threshold of a building, or the walls of a throne room also communicate meaning visually. While the writing is often accompanied by reliefs, the combination of the two—and even the writing itself insofar as it conveys command of knowledge and access to information—has an iconic function as well.[110] Those who could not read could still receive the message, and those who could had access to it in multiple dimensions. In some cases, the texts may even have been designed to be read in a variety of ways by different audiences. Texts can work on multiple levels, and they can be *intended* to work on multiple levels, as Barbara Neveling Porter has shown for Assyrian stelas and as is readily apparent to any adult who has seen an episode of the children's television show *Sesame Street*.[111]

---

109. W. W. Hallo suggests that monumental inscriptions in cuneiform would have been read aloud to an illiterate audience ("Introduction: The Bible and the Monuments," in *COS* 2.xxv). For the caveat that, while possible, there is no positive evidence that such readings actually took place, see See H. Tadmor, "Propaganda, Literature, Historiography: Cracking the Code of the Assyrian Royal Inscriptions," in *Assyria 1995: Proceedings of the 10th Anniversary Symposium of the Neo-Assyrian Text Corpus Project, Helsinki, September 7–11, 1995* (ed. S. Parpola and R. M. Whiting; Helsinki: Neo-Assyrian Text Corpus Project, 1997) 332. For oral performance of biblical literature, see Niditch, *Oral World*, 123–25.

110. On the iconic function of text, see ibid., 58.

111. B. N. Porter, "Language, Audience and Impact in Imperial Assyria," in *Language and Culture in the Near East* (IOS 15; ed. S. Izre'el and R. Drory; Leiden: Brill, 1995) 51–72.

As twenty-first-century readers of ancient texts, we are embedded in our own historical and social context.[112] Our modern assumptions about reading texts (and especially about reading the Bible) aside, we do not even share the physical, social, and cultural environment that would provide ready potential for shared context. This lack of context can have negative consequences for understanding texts. Ray Jackendoff offered a simple example in *Foundations of Language*. If someone says to you over the telephone, "Hey, will you look at THAT!" you can tell that he means to refer to something, but you cannot determine what, because you lack the shared visual context necessary to process a referent for "THAT."[113] The communication of meaning is not complete until the listener can somehow satisfy the referent for the word. Likewise, we can often tell that an ancient writer meant to refer to something, such as a place, but we cannot tell what he meant to refer to or why. Paul Werth discussed this problem in his article on discourse worlds, "How to Build a World (in a lot less than six days, and using only what's in your head)." Because the reader of a text is almost never in the same spatial, temporal, and cultural context as the one in which the text was written, there may be details of that context about which a reader is completely ignorant, be they details such as the location of a place that can be mapped in the physical world or the implications about reality status associated with the itinerary genre that exist only in a cognitive model.[114] This is as true when we read Shakespeare, Kafka, or even Barbara Kingsolver as it is when we read the Bible. An author might set a story in a place that he and his immediate audience knew well and for which they might have had a rich set of associations in their mental maps, yet this story may be the only one in the Bible that mentions it, leaving us to draw a blank about why the author chose this place and how it contributes to the meaning of the narrative.

What satisfies the referent of "THAT" in Jackendoff's example is not the thing in the world that is being referred to but the listener's *knowledge of it*.[115] You would not have to see the thing yourself. Your conversation partner could describe it over the telephone, effectively repairing his reference, and you would understand what he meant and the associations he made with it that prompted him to point it out. We lack the direct potential for shared context with the ancient scribes whose texts we read, and we certainly cannot ask them to explain what they meant. (If only we could. . . .) But we can bridge the gap by learning whatever we can about the world in which ancient texts were written,

---

112. Dobbs-Allsopp, "Rethinking Historical Criticism," 242.
113. Jackendoff, *Foundations of Language*, 324.
114. Werth, "How to Build a World," 54–55.
115. Jackendoff, *Foundations of Language*, 324.

by studying other ancient texts and archaeological remains. It is important to recognize that this knowledge creates only the *potential* for shared context. It gives us insight into the world *with which the scribes might have interacted* in order to form their cognitive models of the world, from which they drew the cultural repertoire with which they shaped the text.

We must be particularly mindful about what archaeology can and cannot do for us. It alone cannot satisfy referents in ancient texts to things in the world, because language does not refer *directly* to things in the world. When we use language, we express what we have already constructed in our brains based on our experience in the world.[116] In other words, when an element of the world is represented in a text, it is first filtered through the brain of the person who wrote the text. We may be able to identify a place in the archaeological record, but this alone does not give us access to the rich set of associations an ancient writer might have had about a place: what he knew about it, why it might have been important to him, what images or memories he might have associated with it. As Piotr Bienkowski put it, what archaeologists can see and measure is extremely valuable, but it "is obvious that such an approach has nothing to do with how landscape was experienced by those living in it: it tells us nothing about landscapes as relational webs of meaning."[117]

To share the author's cultural repertoire, we need to know not only where a place was and when it was occupied but also what the author of the text knew about it; where he thought it was; what assumptions he made about it; what values, ideas, or memories he assigned to it. We can get some sense of the author's mental map—instead of just the potential for shared context—when a place is mentioned in other biblical texts.[118] While it is important to recognize that cognitive models would have been formed by individuals, even if they were broadly shared throughout a culture, individual meaning is virtually impossible for us to perceive; Michael Shanks and Ian Hodder noted that "the

---

116. Fauconnier, *Mental Spaces*, 2. Ellen van Wolde's recent study of the word שַׁעַר 'city gate' is an example of how experience and cultural associations influence semantics (*Reframing Biblical Studies*, 72–103).

117. P. Bienkowski, "The Wadi Arabah: Meanings in a contested landscape," in *Crossing the Rift: Resources, routes, settlement patterns and interaction in the Wadi Arabah* (ed. P. Bienkowski and K. Galor; Levant Supplementary Series 3; Oxford: Oxbow, 2006) 16.

118. Colin Renfrew has emphasized the importance of texts and pictorial representations for understanding the cognitive maps of ancient peoples because they tell us what we can only infer from the archaeological record ("Towards a cognitive archaeology," in *The ancient mind: Elements of cognitive archaeology* [ed. C. Renfrew and E. B. Zubrow; Cambridge: Cambridge University Press, 1994] 11).

meanings that archaeologists reconstruct must on the whole be assumed to be general social and public meanings."[119] Texts can arguably reflect the views of an individual, but the character of ancient authorship suggests that what we find in many ancient texts, and particularly in the Torah (in contrast to, say, Qohelet), is more likely to speak on behalf of a community. So I will speak of genres and mental maps as though they are generally shared.

Our effort to interpret ancient texts should involve understanding the web of connections they have to the ancient world in which they are embedded: the events that had an impact on their authors; the ideas that shaped them; the genres, places, and other elements of cultural repertoire selected and foregrounded in them. The linguistic cues in the text and the information about the ancient world that we can glean through archaeology stand in a reciprocal relationship. As we will see in this book, sometimes information in a text is important for interpreting what we find in the archaeological record. In other cases, information from the archaeological record can help us interpret a text. As Baruch Halpern puts it, neither text nor archaeology is epistemically superior; "[w]hat occupies the high ground is intelligent analysis of both together."[120] If one cannot serve as the arbiter for interpreting the other, however, what becomes of objectivity and control? Shanks and Hodder point out that an objective intepretation is not an abstract ideal that we discover or achieve but a synthesis that is coherent, ties together and explains well as much data as possible, and remains open to verification or falsification.[121] No model can account for every last bit of data. In our study of antiquity, we are operating with a deficiency as a matter of course because we must work with the remains that are left to us.[122] Moreover, we are not completely external observers but are involved and implicated in our interpretations. The insights of various thinkers from literary theory, cognitive linguistics, geography, and archaeol-

---

119. M. Shanks and I. Hodder, "Processual, postprocessual and interpretive archaeologies," in *Interpreting Archaeology* (ed. I. Hodder et al.; London: Routledge, 1995) 17.

120. B. Halpern, "David Did It, Others Did Not: The creation of ancient Israel," in *The Bible and Radiocarbon Dating: Archaeology, Text and Science* (ed. T. E. Levy and T. Higham; London: Equinox, 2005) 436.

121. Shanks and Hodder, "Processual, postprocessual and interpretive archaeologies," 18–19; I. Hodder, *Theory and Practice in Archaeology* (Material Cultures; London: Routledge, 1992) 18–21. See also Renfrew, "Towards a cognitive archaeology," 5.

122. A. Millard, "Only Fragments from the Past: The Role of Accident in Our Knowledge of the Ancient Near East," in *Writing and Ancient Near Eastern Society: Papers in Honour of Alan R. Millard* (ed. P. Bienkowski, C. Mee, and E. Slater; New York: T. & T. Clark, 2005) 301–19.

ogy that I have laid out here in the form of a reading strategy have transformed my own understanding of both the Torah and the ancient world in which it is embedded. But they are merely interpretive tools. The texts themselves and the material remains of the ancient world in which their authors lived provide a shared context to which we must be all be kept honest. The usefulness of these tools lies in their ability to help us, however imperfectly, honor the texts and the scribes who wrote them.

Chapter 3

Itineraries:
Their Forms and Contexts

*He who chooses the beginning of the
road chooses the place it leads to.*
—Harry Emerson Fosdick

Our ability to comprehend successfully the meaning of an ancient text, no less than a modern text, depends in part on how well we understand the cultural repertoire used by its author. Wolfgang Iser emphasized that elements of repertoire are ideally shared by both author and reader.[1] If the speaker in a conversation refers to something with which the listener is not familiar, the listener must learn it by guessing or asking for clarification.[2] Moreover, if the listener is not simply ignorant of it but understands it to be something other than what the speaker is referring to, *mis*communication may occur. Interpreting written texts is subject to the same pitfalls. Correctly assessing the genre of a text—or, better, how one or more genres shape a text—is an interpretive task that involves, as we will see throughout the course of this book, identifying both the genres at work and how the author uses them.

In order to assess the genre of a text, we should not try to classify it. A prototype is a specific text that is judged to be a good or maybe even ideal example of the genre.[3] Looking at other examples, we would then see gradations of texts that we judge to be more or less like the prototype. These judgments are re-

---

1. W. Iser, *The Act of Reading: A Theory of Aesthetic Response* (Baltimore: Johns Hopkins University Press, 1978) 69.

2. D. Sperber and D. Wilson, *Relevance: Communication and Cognition* (Language and Thought Series; Cambridge: Harvard University Press, 1986) 16. On reference repair, see R. Jackendoff, *Foundations of Language: Brain, Meaning, Grammar, Evolution* (Oxford: Oxford University Press, 2002) 324–25.

3. G. Lakoff, *Women, Fire, and Dangerous Things: What Categories Reveal about the Mind* (Chicago: University of Chicago Press, 1987) 7.

ferred to by psychologists and cognitive linguists as *prototype effects*. Prototype effects are relevant to any type of category, not just genres: many people might judge a robin to be a more prototypical example of a bird than an ostrich is. The problem with viewing categories—including genres—in this way is that protoype effects do not "directly mirror category structure" or "constitute representations of categories" themselves.[4] We use our knowledge about categories when we make judgments of this sort, but psychological experiments have shown that the judgments do not tell us how this knowledge is stored in the human brain.[5] In fact, what constitutes a prototypical bird (or any other object) can differ according to culture; for some it is a robin, but for others a parrot or a sparrow serves as the prototype.[6] We make these judgments about prototypicality based on knowledge that is stored and structured in a cognitive model.

Assessing genre and how it is used in a particular text instead involves using a cognitive model that one has learned through exposure to "a set of prototypical examples" of texts that use the genre.[7] A cognitive model is not coterminous with any one text but, according to George Lakoff, is "defined relative to idealized circumstances rather than circumstances as they are known to exist."[8] A cognitive model for the itinerary genre does not necessarily fit with one particular itinerary but is *abstracted* from a variety of itineraries that might vary. We then use the idealized cognitive model we have developed based on our experience with reading and/or writing texts to understand new texts we encounter. When we judge an ostrich to be a marginal example of a bird, we invoke the same cognitive model we use to determine that a robin is a protoypical example. Not every bird we meet will fit the model exactly. Likewise, not every itinerary we encounter will look exactly the same.[9] My goal in this chapter is to develop an idealized cognitive model for the itinerary genre that approximates the cognitive model held by ancient Near Eastern scribes. I will be concerned in this chapter with the "robins" of the itinerary genre—texts that were likely judged to be prototypical. The model I develop will serve as a foundation as we study the more creative uses of the itinerary genre in the following chapters.

---

4. Ibid., 43.

5. Ibid., 40–46.

6. E. van Wolde, *Reframing Biblical Studies: When Language and Text Meet Culture, Cognition, and Context* (Winona Lake, IN: Eisenbrauns, 2009) 26–27.

7. M. Sinding, "Genera Mixta: Conceptual Blending and Mixed Genres in Ulysses," *New Literary History* 36 (2005) 594.

8. G. Lakoff, "Cognitive models and prototype theory," in *Concepts and Conceptual Development: Ecological and Intellectual Factors in Categorization* (ed. U. Neisser; Emory Symposia in Cognition; Cambridge: Cambridge University Press, 1987) 65–66.

9. Idem, *Women, Fire, and Dangerous Things*, 130.

In antiquity, exposure to the itinerary genre might have been acquired informally by those who actually used itineraries and/or formally through education, because ancient scribes probably learned the itinerary genre in a scribal school. The Rhind Mathematical Papyrus is primarily a scribal exercise consisting of a collection of mathematical problems related to fractions. Its reverse contains three nonmathematical sections, including a cryptogram; an account list; and a daybook (*hrwyt*), or a record of activities organized by date, like a journal or diary entry. Daybooks contain a wide variety of information, including lists of provisions, correspondence, directives from senior officials, the departures and arrivals of significant people to and from the crew of a ship, payment of crew rations, and notations on the time of day and weather conditions. In some cases, they also record the movement of a ship or an army from one place to the next and do so using the itinerary genre. The daybook and the other two exercises on the reverse of the papyrus are probably also scribal exercises, jotted in the blank portions on the obverse of the math exercise.[10] It appears that Egyptian scribes, at least, learned the itinerary genre in school.

While ancient scribes and officials probably learned the itinerary genre through formal training and direct use, we must learn it as best we can by studying cultural remains. Inscriptions provide a great opportunity for us to establish shared repertoire. In the Torah and other narrative contexts such as Neo-Assyrian annals, we find the itinerary genre used in complex literary environments. But inscriptions give us the most direct access to the way that genres were used in their primary contexts in antiquity.[11] Our sample is, of course, limited in quantity. Reports and records that use the itinerary genre include three records of a trip along more or less the same route to Emar from the Old Babylonian period (UIOM 2370, UIOM 2134, YBC 4499), a Middle Assyrian itinerary (DeZ 2521), and a Neo-Assyrian itinerary (K. 4675+). From Egypt, three daybooks in addition to the Rhind Mathematical Papyrus contain itineraries: Papyrus Turin 2008, Papyrus Leiden I 350, and Papyrus Boulaq 18. Letters also make use of the itinerary genre. Most of the extant examples are from the Old Babylonian period: one comes from Shemshara (SH 809) and three from Mari. The relevant Mari letters include one from Shamshi-Adad to Yasmah-

---

10. T. E. Peet, *The Rhind Mathematical Papyrus: British Museum 10057 and 10058* (London: The University Press of Liverpool, 1923) 5; G. Robins and C. Shute, *The Rhind Mathematical Papyrus: An Ancient Egyptian Text* (New York: Dover, 1990) 10–11. The daybook is contained in §87.

11. M. Rösel, "Inscriptional Evidence and the Question of Genre," in *The Changing Face of Form Criticism for the Twenty-First Century* (ed. M. A. Sweeney and E. Ben Zvi; Grand Rapids, MI: Eerdmans, 2003) 109.

Addu regarding the former's pending visit to Mari (ARM 1 26), another from Shamshi-Adad regarding a shipment of wood from Qatnum (ARM 1 7), and a third about a rendezvous between a group of Benjaminite messengers and their Eshnunean escorts (M. 5431).

Preservation quality is also a challenge in some cases, be it of the text itself or the context in which the text was used and deposited. A Neo-Assyrian letter containing an itinerary on the reverse (K. 1516) has such a poorly preserved obverse that we cannot discern who wrote it, to whom it was intended to be sent, or any clear information about the context.[12] Furthermore, not all of these documents are provenanced, and the lack of provenance, similar to poor preservation, can limit our ability to understand the social context. Despite the limitations of the sample, enough texts are preserved well enough and provenanced to such an extent that we are able to acquire a certain degree of competence in the ancient genre. We can thus overcome the problem of alterity, or the fact that the genres with which an ancient culture operated may not have been quite like the genres in our own culture.[13] Should we at some point in the future discover more itineraries, we will simply confirm or adjust our cognitive model for the genre through study of those new texts.

Although a prototype does not give us direct and full access to the cognitive model, prototype effects do give us some general and partial information about it.[14] Attributes that are repeated across different examples are likely to be part of the model. The texts to be discussed in this chapter all have the same basic thematic content—all relate a journey—and a fairly limited set of formal features, including place-names situated in linear spatial and temporal sequence. They all have an administrative situation of address and a pragmatic

---

12. For copy, see R. F. Harper, *Assyrian and Babylonian Letters Belonging to the Kouyunjik Collections of the British Museum* (14 vols.; Chicago: University of Chicago Press, 1892–1914) 4.687 (ABL 635). Transliteration of lines 1–9 of the reverse of the tablet, which contains the itinerary and is the only readable part of the tablet, can be found in A. Fadhil, *Studien zur Topographie und Prosopographie der Provinzstädte des Königsreichs Arraphe* (Baghdader Forschungen 6; Mainz am Rhein: von Zabern, 1983) 75.

13. A. Fowler, *Kinds of Literature: An Introduction to the Theory of Genres and Modes* (Cambridge: Harvard University Press, 1982). For discussion of alterity as it pertains to Egyptian literature, see R. B. Parkinson, *Poetry and Culture in Middle Kingdom Egypt: A Dark Side to Perfection* (London: Continuum, 2002) 33. Alterity as it pertains to ancient Mesopotamia is perhaps best understood in terms of Benno Landsberger's *Eigenbegrifflichkeit* approach; see discussion in H. Vanstiphout, "Some Thoughts on Genre in Mesopotamian Literature," in *Keilschriftliche Literaturen: Ausgewählte Vorträge der XXXII. Rencontre Assyriologique Internationale, Münster, 8.–12.7.1985* (Berliner Beiträge zum Vorderen Orient 6; Berlin: Reimer, 1986) 1–11.

14. Lakoff, *Women, Fire, and Dangerous Things*, 43.

rhetorical function, or purpose. There is some variation among these texts, but it is constrained within the parameters I have just described. Thus all of the texts to be discussed in this chapter can be considered prototypical.[15]

The situation of address and rhetorical function in the texts to be discussed in this chapter are relatively constrained. The situation of address can vary somewhat but is always administrative in nature, as Graham I. Davies discussed, since the authors and intended readers, insofar as we can determine them, wrote and read in administrative roles. The author of the Middle Assyrian itinerary is mentioned in the colophon as Ashur-iddin, who was the *sukkallu*, or governor, at Dur-Katlimmu (Sheikh Hamid).[16] Dur-Katlimmu was a provincial site on the Habur River that was connected to Ashur by a road and controlled access to points farther west via the river. It played a key role in the expansion of Assyria after the collapse of the Mittanian Empire, evident in letters from Tuttul, Washukanni, and Carchemish in Ashur-iddin's archive, where this itinerary was found. Ashur-iddin was thus in charge of newly acquired Assyrian territory in the west and the administrative duties that went with this job.[17] The Shemshara letter was written by Shamshi-Adad to Kuwari, his official

---

15. To be clear: *prototype effects* (judgments a person makes about what is prototypical based on an idealized cognitive model) are not the same thing as a *prototype* (a particular text that serves as a model against which all other examples are judged). The texts we are about to discuss are prototypical in the first sense.

16. W. Röllig, "Ein Itinerar aus Dur-Katlimmu," *Damaszener Mitteilungen* 1 (1983) 281. For more in-depth discussion of his role, see E. C. Cancik-Kirschbaum, *Die Mittelassyrischen Briefe aus Tall Seh Hamad* (Berichte der Ausgrabung Tall Seh Hamad/Dur-Katlimmu 4; Berlin: Reimer, 1996) 19.

17. On the nature of Middle Assyrian control of this area, see W. Röllig, "Dur-Katlimmu," *Or* 47 (1978) 428; and P. Machinist, *Provincial Governance in Middle Assyria and Some New Texts from Yale* (Assur 3/2; Malibu, CA: Undena, 1982). Mario Liverani argued, based in part on the evidence of Dur-Katlimmu, that Assyria was a territorial empire in the Middle Assyrian period and that the later Neo-Assyrian Empire was founded on a political organization that was never entirely dissolved, despite the interruption suggested by the lack of historical inscriptions. Although control of various sites such as Dur-Katlimmu became localized, the local dynasties appear to have remained dependent on Assyria ("The Growth of the Assyrian Empire in the Habur / Middle Euphrates Area: A New Paradigm," *SAAB* 2 [1988] 86–91). This perspective is picked up by H. Kühne, "The Assyrians on the Middle Euphrates and the Habur," in *Neo-Assyrian Geography* (ed. M. Liverani; Quaderni di Geografia Storica 5; Padua: Sargon srl, 1995) 72, 75; idem, "La Djézireh à l'époque médio-assyrienne et au primier millénaire av. J.-C.," in *En Syrie: Aux Origines de l'Écriture* (ed. E. Gubel; Turnhout: Brepols, 1998) 140; idem, "Tall Šēḫ Ḥamad—The Assyrian City of Dur-Katlimmu: A Historic-Geographical Approach," in *Essays on Ancient Anatolia in the Second Millennium B.C.* (ed. T. Mikasa; Bulletin of the Middle Eastern Culture Center in Japan 10; Wiesbaden: Harrassowitz,

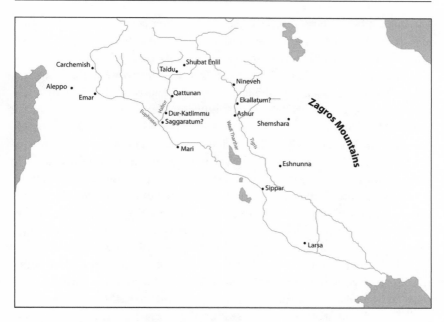

Fig. 1. Key Sites on Administrative Itineraries.

stationed at Shemshara, a provincial outpost that controlled a route into the Zagros Mountains and may have played an important role in the tin trade.[18] Although Shemshara was later incorporated into the Kingdom of Ashur, the relationship seems to have been a diplomatic one at the time this letter was written.[19] Kuwari was likely stationed at Shemshara to oversee shipments of

1998) 283–84; and idem, "Dur-Katlimmu and the Middle-Assyrian Empire," in *La Djéziré el l'Euphrate Syriens de la Protohistoire à la Fin du IIe Millénaire av. J.-C.* (ed. O. Rouault and M. Wäfler; Turnhout: Brepols, 2000) 271–80.

18. For the commonly held view that Shemshara imported tin from the east for export to the west, see J. Laessøe, "Akkadian *annakum*: 'Tin' or 'Lead'?" *AcOr* 24 (1959) 83–94; D. Oates, *Studies in the Ancient History of Northern Iraq* (London: Oxford University Press, 1968) 32–34; and J. Eidem, *The Shemshara Archives 2: The Administrative Texts* (Historisk-filosofiske Skrifter 15; Copenhagen: Muksgaard, 1992) 9, 41–42. But the most recent publication of Shemshara materials notes that tin moved in the opposite direction, from west to east; see J. Eidem and J. Laessøe, *The Shemshara Archives 1: The Letters* (Historisk-filosofiske Skrifter 23; Copenhagen: The Royal Danish Academy of Sciences and Letters, 2001) 29.

19. The archive in which this letter was found consists of two groups, the earlier group associated with a period during which Shemshara was independent but in diplomatic relationship with Ashur and the later after Shemshara was incorporated into the

grain and other materials to the capital.[20] The letter comes from his personal archive, which contains letters dealing with personal as well as administrative affairs.[21] The authors of the daybooks in Papyrus Leiden I 350 and Papyrus Turin 2008 were also administrators, in this case shipboard scribes. Papyrus Leiden I 350 provides a clue about the potential audience of these daybooks, because the scribe notes that he wrote numerous letters to the high priest of Ptah at Memphis, possibly the royal prince Khaemwese, who probably owned the ship or at least administered its activities on behalf of the divine estate.[22]

Although the situation of address involves administrative roles, each scribe wrote on a different type of occasion, and his purpose in that situation, as we will see later in the chapter, influenced his use of the itinerary genre. The itineraries we will study, then, have different rhetorical functions, but all seek to report or prompt some action and are pragmatic in nature. The occasions include troop requisitions, daily business activities, and military or commercial trips. The Middle Assyrian itinerary records one of Ashur-iddin's administrative acts as governor, the requisitioning of *ḫurādu*-troops. The requisition contains an itinerary for the transfer of the troops to Dur-Katlimmu from Taidu (Tall Hamidi), another governor's seat on the upper Habur. A *ḫurādu* is an individual or a group of men who perform *ilku*, or corvée labor, in exchange for payment, usually in land. This work can involve building roads, irrigation ditches, and public buildings as well as various types of military service. If soldiers, these would likely be reservists.[23] While it is clear that their purpose was

---

kingdom as a vassal. This text comes from the earlier period, evident by its place at the bottom of the jar and by the fact that Shamshi-Adad does not use titles associated with kingship as he does in letters from later in the collection, after Kuwari had become a vassal. SH 809 comes from the earlier group (Eidem and Laessøe, *Shemshara Archives 1*, 15, 43–44; and J. Eidem, "News from the Eastern Front: The Evidence from Tell Shemshara," *Iraq* 47 [1985] 95–96).

20. M. T. Larsen, "The Shemshara Archives," *Sumer* 42 (1986) 37; and Eidem, "News from the Eastern Front," 92. This explanation seems on the surface inconsistent with Eidem and Laessøe, *Shemshara Archives 1*, 14, which states that he was first a viceroy but then became a vassal, which suggests a different kind of role.

21. J. Laessøe, *The Shemshara Tablets: A Preliminary Report* (Copenhagen: Munksgaard, 1959) 60–65; W. F. Leemans, "Old Babylonian Letters and Economic History," *JESHO* 11 (1968) 173; Eidem, *Shemshara Archives 2*, 34.

22. J. J. Janssen, *Two Ancient Egyptian Ship's Logs: Papyrus Leiden I 350 verso and Papyrus Turin 2008+2016* (Leiden: Brill, 1961) 5–6.

23. On the nature of *ḫurādu*, see I. M. Diakonoff, who does not use this term but seems to be talking about the same thing ("Agrarian Conditions in Middle Assyria," in *Ancient Mesopotamia: Socio-Economic History* [Moscow: Nauka, 1969] 231); see also

to serve the state in some capacity, it is unclear in this instance why they were requistioned.[24] The purpose of this journey could relate to a military maneuver or a civil building or agricultural project.

The itinerary genre was also used to record the daily activities of a ship or an army. Egyptian daybooks were used by a variety of institutions including the temple, the king's house, the necropolis, and the treasury.[25] When they record movements using the itinerary genre, these journeys tend to be commercial or royal in nature. Papyrus Turin 2008 records the daily activities of a ship involved in garment trade, while Papyrus Leiden I 350 records a journey to Pi-Ramesses, the capital of the Egyptian Delta, concerned with redistribution of foodstuffs.[26] The daybook entry in Papyrus Boulaq 18 is very fragmentary, because this section is right where the papyrus is cut off, but it appears to be a journey undertaken by boat involving an overnight stay.[27] Although daybooks involving the king record his movements in general and are not necessarily military, the use of expressions characteristic of military inscriptions such as *ḥȝyt jm* 'great slaughter' suggest that it may be a campaign itinerary.[28]

Finally, itineraries may have been used to document business trips. The situation in which the Old Babylonian itineraries were written and read is a matter of dispute, complicated by the fact that they are unprovenanced. They probably come from Larsa (Tell Senkereh) and most likely date to the early-mid-

---

J. N. Postgate, "Land Tenure in the Middle Assyrian Period: A Reconstruction," *BSOAS* 34 (1971) 498–501; H. Freydank, "Untersuchungen zur sozialen Struktur in mittelassyrischer Zeit," *AoF* 4 (1976) 111–15; M. Heltzer, "Some Problems of the Military Organization of Ugarit (Ugaritic *ḫrd* and Middle-Assyrian *ḫurādu*)," *OrAnt* 18 (1979) 247, 250–51; and Machinist, *Provincial Governance*, 26–27. *ḫurādu* may originally have been a Hurrian military term borrowed into Akkadian and Ugaritic, so its application to groups who do various types of *ilku* service may be secondary; see R. R. Stieglitz, "Ugaritic *ḫrd* 'Warrior': A Hurrian Loanword," *JAOS* 101 (1981) 371–72.

24. Röllig, "Ein Itinerar," 281, 283.

25. D. B. Redford, *Pharaonic King-Lists, Annals, and Day-Books: A Contribution to the Study of the Egyptian Sense of History* (SSEA Publication 4; Mississauga, ON: Benben, 1986) 101–3, 121.

26. See J. J. Janssen, *Two Ancient Egyptian Ship's Logs: Papyrus Leiden I 350 Verso and Papyrus Turin 2008+2016* (Leiden: Brill, 1961) 1–5, 105.

27. A. Scharff, "Ein Rechnungsbuch des königlichen Hofes aus der 13. Dynastie (Papyrus Boulaq Nr. 18)," *ZÄS* 57 (1922) 61.

28. S. G. Quirke, *The Administration of Egypt in the Late Middle Kingdom: The Hieratic Documents* (Surrey: SIA, 1990) 31 n. 30; A. J. Spalinger, *Aspects of the Military Documents of the Ancient Egyptians* (YNER 9; New Haven, CT: Yale University Press, 1982) 77.

eighteenth century B.C.E.[29] Albrecht Goetze and William Hallo, who initially published them, understood them as first-person records of a royal military campaign. Goetze based this assessment on the mention of troops in two of the notes included with the place-name entries of UIOM 2134 (ERIN$_2$.ḪA$_2$ in I 18 and *ummanātum* in II 8).[30] But the presence of troops does not necessarily point to a royal military expedition. Commercial as well as military expeditions would likely have used the same routes, and troops may have accompanied commercial expeditions due to the threat of losing goods to an attack, a possibility reflected in §103 of the Code of Hammurapi.[31] Hallo recognized the possibility that the journey may have been commercial but offered no discussion of this option.[32]

Merchants and their agents often employed scribes to document their business activity. This was the norm, at least as reflected in texts related to

29. For primary publication of these texts, see A. Goetze, "An Old Babylonian Itinerary," *JCS* 7 (1953) 51–72; and W. W. Hallo, "The Road to Emar," *JCS* 18 (1964) 57–88. A collation of UIOM 2134 iv 2'–4' can be found in N. Ziegler, "À propos de l'itinéraire paléo-babylonien UIOM 2134 iv 2'–4'," *NABU* (2000) 48. Larsa was systematically plundered, and tablets and artifacts allegedly from this site flooded the antiquities market after World War II. These tablets were most likely acquired under these sorts of circumstances and probably come from Larsa (Dr. Benjamin R. Foster, personal communication; my thanks to Dr. Foster and his staff at the Yale Babylonian Collection for taking the time to check their records). Because the place-name Dur-Apil-Sin appears in the itinerary, these texts must be later than the reign of Apil-Sin (1830–1813 B.C.E.), after whom the site was probably named. For more in-depth discussion of date, which is tied up with one's understanding of the nature of the journey, see Goetze, "Old Babylonian Itinerary," 70–71; Hallo, "Road to Emar," 86; Leemans, "Old Babylonian Letters," 212; J. D. Muhly, *Copper and Tin: The Distribution of Mineral Resources and the Nature of the Metals Trade in the Bronze Age* (Transactions of the Connecticut Academy of Arts and Sciences 43; Hamden, CT: Archon, 1973) 299; and M. Stol, *Studies in Old Babylonian History* (Istanbul: Nederlands Historisch-Archaeologisch Institut, 1976) 32.

30. Goetze, "Old Babylonian Itinerary," 55, 71. For comment on how difficult it is to understand the background and use of these sorts of documents when their context is unknown, see K. R. Veenhof, "Cuneiform Archives: An Introduction," in *Cuneiform Archives and Libraries: Papers Read at the 30e Rencontre Assyriologique Internationale, Leiden, 4–8 July 1983* (ed. K. R. Veenhof; Leiden: Nederlands Historisch-Archaeologisch Institut te Istanbul, 1986) 32.

31. P. Garelli, "La notion de route dans les textes," *RA* 52 (1958) 123; L. Le Breton, "De l'état de notre connaissance des itinéraires antiques," *RA* 52 (1958) 115; G. I. Davies, "The Wilderness Itineraries: A Comparative Study," *TynBul* 25 (1974) 54–55; Liverani, "Growth of the Assyrian Empire," 87–88. For citation and discussion of CH §103, see W. F. Leemans, *The Old Babylonian Merchant: His Business and His Social Position* (Studia et Documenta ad Iura Orientis Antiqui Pertinentia 3; Leiden: Brill, 1950) 26.

32. Hallo, "Road to Emar," 85.

Old Assyrian commercial activity at Kanesh. But there is evidence that some merchants and agents were literate enough to keep their own records, making the first-person Old Babylonian itineraries at least as likely to be commercial as military.[33] Sections 100 and 104–5 of the Code of Hammurapi, for example, refer to an agent's entering items into his account. In favor of interpreting the itineraries as business records is the fact that some of the sites mentioned in the itinerary played an important role during the height of Old Babylonian commercial activity. W. F. Leemans argued that these documents are best understood to depict commercial missions, perhaps on behalf of the king of Larsa, since the journeys depicted in YBC 4499 and UIOM 2134 begin and end there.[34] Larsa and Sippar were major centers for both private and government trade in the Old Babylonian period, particularly for the export of wool from Sippar and reexport of tin procured in the east (see UIOM 2134 I 10–12; YBC 4499 does not mention Sippar because its itinerary begins after the departure from Dur-Apil-Sin, which is north of Sippar and Babylon). Trade went north along the Euphrates through Babylon to Mari, Emar, Carchemish, and Aleppo using boats on the river and donkeys overland.[35] Emar, the final destination of these itineraries, was a key point on the usual trade route up the Euphrates River where goods were transferred to donkeys for overland transport.[36] The Old Babylonian itineraries do include an overland detour from this usual route that avoids Mari (YBC 4499 lines 15–32; UIOM 2134 I 27–II 8), probably due to political tensions between Larsa and Mari.[37] This detour leads James Muhly to

---

33. Leemans, *Old Babylonian Merchant*, 23–24, 26; L. E. Pearce, "The Scribes and Scholars of Ancient Mesopotamia," *CANE* 4.2265.

34. Leemans, "Old Babylonian Letters," 211–12. While the beginning of UIOM 2134 is broken, the return trip ends in Larsa (UD.UNUG^{ki}, IV 12), and Goetze ("Old Babylonian Itinerary," 64) supposes it began there as well. YBC 4499, in turn, departs simply from URU 'city' (line 4), but the kings of the Larsa Dynasty often used this designation to refer to their city (Hallo, "Road to Emar," 66).

35. Leemans, *Old Babylonian Merchant*; W. F. Leemans, *Foreign Trade in the Old Babylonian Period as Revealed by Texts from Southern Mesopotamia* (Studia et Documenta and Iura Orientis Antiqui Pertinentia 6; Leiden: Brill, 1960) 99. While the tin trade was managed by Ashur in the Old Assyrian period and possibly to some degree during Shamshi-Adad's reign, it is possible that the Babylonians became involved after Hammurapi's reign; see Leemans, "Old Babylonian Letters," 171–226; and W. Heimpel, *Letters to the King of Mari: A New Translation, with Historical Introduction, Notes, and Commentary* (Mesopotamian Civilizations 12; Winona Lake, IN: Eisenbrauns, 2003) 38.

36. A. Goetze, "Remarks on the Old Babylonian Itinerary," *JCS* 18 (1964) 115.

37. Muhly, *Copper and Tin*, 299; B. J. Beitzel, "From Ḫarran to Imar along the Old Babylonian Itinerary: The Evidence from the Archives Royales de Mari," in *Biblical and*

question Leemans's conclusion that the journey was commercial, but political hostilities could cause a detour no matter what the character of a journey.[38]

Even with the constrained situation of address and rhetorical function, there is a good deal of variety in the formal features used to express an itinerary. Some elements, such as a series of place-names, are common to all extant itineraries. These place-names are specific sites at which someone traveling the route could stop, rest, and perhaps engage in some sort of activity. The names of roads and rivers traveled are not typically used. Instead, the route is defined by the series of sites along it. But a series of place-names *alone* does not constitute a use of the itinerary genre, because it contains no formal features to tell us how to read it. Lists of place-names can be arranged on any principle. They can be alphabetical, as are the place-names in the lexical series ḪAR.RA = *ḫubullu*.[39] Towns can be listed by administrative district.[40] Other lists of toponyms appear to be arranged based on "political or religious considerations, assonance of names, and the like."[41] Where the organizing principle is not entirely transparent to us, we have difficulty interpreting the list or must guess. The Egyptian topographical lists, for example, have been understood as simple lists of places conquered along a route, administrative districts, itineraries, or extracts from a daybook.[42] The Assyrian Dreambook records dreams associated with particu-

---

Near Eastern Studies: Essays in Honor of William Sanford LaSor (ed. G. A. Tuttle; Grand Rapids, MI: Eerdmans, 1978) 217 n. 8.

38. Muhly, *Copper and Tin*, 299–300. A more recent discussion of the Old Babylonian itineraries mentions both commercial and military as possibilities; see S. W. Cole and H. Gasche, "Second- and First-Millennium BC Rivers in Northern Babylonia," in *Changing Watercourses in Babylonia: Towards a Reconstruction of the Ancient Environment in Lower Mesopotamia* (ed. H. Gasche and M. Tanret; Mesopotamian History and Environment 2/5; Chicago: Oriental Institute of the University of Chicago, 1998) 20.

39. The entire series ḪAR.RA = *ḫubullu* occupies seven volumes of Materialien zum sumerischen Lexicon; the tablets containing toponyms occupy one of these volumes: E. Reiner and M. Civil, eds., The Series ḪAR-RA = *ḫubullu* Tablets *XX–XXIV* (MSL 11; Rome: Pontifical Biblical Institute, 1974). For its alphabetical arrangement, see Hallo, "Road to Emar," 61.

40. F. M. Fales and J. N. Postgate, *Imperial Administrative Records, Part II: Provincial and Military Administration* (SAA 11; Helsinki: Neo-Assyrian Text Corpus Project, 1995) 4.

41. D. R. Frayne, *The Early Dynastic List of Geographical Names* (AOS 74; New Haven, CT: American Oriental Society, 1992) 3. On the distinction between these lists and geographical texts, see D. O. Edzard, "The Ideas of Babylonian Geography," *Sumer* 41 (1985) 113–14.

42. D. B. Redford, "A Bronze Age Itinerary in Transjordan (Nos. 89–101 of Thutmose III's List of Asiatic Toponyms)," *JSSEA* 12 (1982) 55–74; and idem, "Contact between Egypt and Jordan in the New Kingdom: Some Comments on Sources," in *Studies*

lar geographical locations, which appear to be organized geographically and possibly along a route. [43] Some lists, such as the Early Dynastic ḪA.GIDIM list or the list of Canaanite place-names in Papyrus Anastasi I do identify places on a route, but we know this only because we can identify the places and routes to which the lists refer. [44] The character of the text as an itinerary in such cases is a matter of *content*, not of genre.

Because a list of place-names can be read in a variety of ways, the itinerary genre involves one or more formal features that cue us to read a list of place-names in *linear* spatial and temporal sequence, specifically as sites along a route. Robert Wilson makes the same observation about genealogies in his seminal study on this genre: if a text consists of nothing but a series of personal names, without the relationships made explicit, "the names simply constitute a list and are not a genealogy." [45] The expressions "son of" or "sons of" are required to invoke the cognitive model for a genealogy. Likewise, itineraries typically involve one or more of the following elements: repetition of the place-name, prepositions that convey spatial relationships, temporal expressions, and verbs that express movement. While the author of an itinerary can use any combination of these features, the list of place-names is combined with at least one of them. Otherwise the text is merely a list of names, and we must infer its organizing principle. Rolf P. Knierim and George W. Coats defined an itinerary as a simple list of place-names, which led them to understand the verbs for movement that occur in some texts as turning an itinerary into a travelogue or campaign narrative. [46] Verbs for movement are instead part of the itinerary genre. They do not occur in every prototypical example of an itinerary because other features can also do the job of expressing linear movement through time and space. The fact that one scribe used temporal expressions and another scribe used verbs does not make one text more prototypical than the other.

---

in the History and Archaeology of Jordan I (ed. A. Hadidi; Amman: Department of Antiquities, 1982) 117–18.

43. A. Leo Oppenheim understood the Assyrian Dreambook to generally reflect the geography of its time (*The Interpretation of Dreams in the Ancient Near East. With a Translation of an Assyrian Dream Book* [TAPS 46; Philadelphia: American Philosophical Society, 1956]), while Albrecht Goetze more specifically posited that it is an itinerary ("The Syrian Town of Emar," *BASOR* 147 [1957] 22–27).

44. For the ḪA.GIDIM list, see Frayne, *Early Dynastic List*, 53. For discussion of pl. 20 of Papyrus Anastasi I, see Redford, *Pharaonic King-Lists*, 126 n. 87.

45. R. R. Wilson, *Genealogy and History in the Biblical World* (YNER 7; New Haven, CT: Yale University Press, 1977) 10.

46. R. P. Knierim and G. W. Coats, *Numbers* (FOTL 4; Grand Rapids, MI: Eerdmans, 2005) 14–15.

When confronted with an itinerary, we do not need to know where any of the places are in order to read them as sites along a route because elements of the *genre* cue us to do so.

The four Egyptian daybooks illustrate the basic formal features of an itinerary. Davies recognized the potential value of daybooks for study of the itinerary genre, but he excluded them from consideration because they do not focus exclusively on movement but contain notes about other activities such as business transactions and visiting officials.[47] This was an issue for him because he sought to define a single prototype for the itinerary genre based on a fairly rigid core set of formal features. But, not only do daybooks fit the situation of address and rhetorical function of the itinerary genre, they also sometimes make significant use of its formal features, as is evident in this excerpt from Papyrus Turin 2008 (recto II 22–23, III 7–9):

> *ḥsbt 7 ꜣbd 1 prt sw 28 mḥ sw ꜣbd 2 sw 12 n wḏꜣ nwt wḏꜣ mryt mn-nfr mjnj ḥr mryt n3 bḫnw n pr-wsjr . . . ḥsbt 7 ꜣbd 2 prt sw 1 mḥ sw ꜣbd 2 sw 15 n wḏꜣ nwt mḥ sw 4 ḥr mryt n3 bḫnw n pr-wsjr wḏꜣ st tn mjnj ḥr mryt t3 m3wt n3 bḫnw n pr-wsjr*

> Year 7, first month of Growing, day 28: second month, twelfth day since the departure from Thebes. Departing from the river bank at Memphis. Mooring at the river bank of "The Pylons of the House of Osiris." . . . Year 7, second month of Growing, day 1: second month, fifteenth day since the departure from Thebes; fourth day at the river bank of "The Pylons of the House of Osiris." Departing from this place. Mooring at the river bank of "The New Land of the Pylons of the House of Osiris."[48]

The list of place-names includes Memphis, The Pylons of the House of Osiris, and The New Land of the Pylons of the House of Osiris. The author of this daybook uses three features to connect these names in a linear continuum. He repeats the place-names, in one case using *st tn* 'this place' instead of writing out the place-name a second time. He also uses a formulaic set of verbs to express movement, including *wḏꜣ* ('proceeding') and *mjnj* or *ꜥq* ('mooring' or 'entering'). The forms are usually infinitives and thus constitute simple notes.[49]

---

47. G. I. Davies, "Wilderness Itineraries: A Comparative Study," 60–62, esp. p. 61 n. 46.

48. See Janssen, *Two Ancient Egyptian Ship's Logs*, 60–61 for copy; 75ff., 78ff. for translation and notes. Transliteration and translation are mine, following Janssen's notes.

49. It can be difficult to distinguish an infinitive form from one of the six *sḏm.f* forms, because the infinitive, like the *sḏm.f* form, is often simply the base; see J. P. Allen, *Middle Egyptian: An Introduction to the Language and Culture of Hieroglyphs* (Cambridge: Cambridge University Press, 2000) §14.3 and §21.15. Redford noted that §87 of

These two features explicitly depict movement through space and only imply movement through time. But the use of a date formula at each entry makes the movement through time explicit as well. While these features do not dominate daybooks the way they do itineraries from Mesopotamia, they do constitute a prototypical use of the itinerary genre.

When verbs for movement are used, the particular verbs chosen can relate to the specific rhetorical function of the text. The colophon of the Middle Assyrian itinerary (DeZ 2521 lines 16–19) identifies it as 'the stages [*mardiātu*] of the *ḫurādu*-troops which Ashur-iddin arranged in Dur-Katlimmu'; the stages are depicted as follows (lines 1–15):[50]

ḫurādu ištu Taidi	The *ḫurādu*-troops will set out
inassaḫa	from Taidi.
ina Marirte	At the river Marirte
ibīat ištu [id]KI.MIN	they will stay the night. From 'ditto',
ina Makrisi	at Makrisi
ibīat ištu [uru]KI.MIN	they will stay the night. From 'ditto',
ina Napraṣi	at Napraṣi
ibīat	they will stay the night.
ištu [uru]KI.MIN	From 'ditto',
ina [L]a[t]iḫi	at [L]a[t]ihi
[i]bī[a]t	[th]ey will stay [the] night.
ištu [uru]KI.MIN *ina Qatun*	From 'ditto', at Qatun
ibīat ištu Qatun	they will stay the night. From Qatun
ana Dūr-katlimu	to Dur-katlimmu
ittallaka	they will come.

This document repeats the place-names and employs a formulaic set of verbs, as does Papyrus Turin 2008. The Middle Assyrian itinerary also expresses the repetition in shorthand, here through the use of KI.MIN, or the 'ditto' sign,

---

the Rhind Papyrus includes one clear *sḏm.f* form and only one clear infinitive form, making the syntax somewhat difficult to sort out (*Pharaonic King-Lists*, 110). Given that daybooks are generally characterized by the use of infinitive forms, it seems to me appropriate to assume that the ambiguous cases should be read as infinitives and the presence of a passive *sḏm.f* (II 3) attributed to variability, the need to use a passive, or the possibility that this is a scribal exercise and the student made a mistake.

50. The primary publication of this text is in Röllig, "Ein Itinerar." For basic historical background on this period, see A. Kuhrt, *The Ancient Near East c. 3000–330 B.C.* (2 vols.; Routledge History of the Ancient World; London: Routledge, 1995) 1.348–65; and M. Roaf, *Cultural Atlas of Mesopotamia and the Ancient Near East* (New York: Facts on File, 1990) 140 (map), 148–49.

rather than a noun phrase such as *st tn*. While the typical verbs in Papyrus Turin 2008, cited above—especially *mjnj* 'mooring'—are keyed to the movement of ships, the verbs here suit the quartering of travelers. Departure from the starting point is expressed with *nasāḫu* 'to set out' while the overnight stops are indicated consistently with *biātu* 'to stay overnight'.

In some cases, the meaning of a formal feature is ambiguous. This is the case with the prepositions *ištu* and *ina* or *ana*, used in the Middle Assyrian itinerary to convey movement between one site and the next. The word *ina* marks the overnight stops, while *ana* is used with the final destination, Dur-Katlimmu. The words *ištu* and *ina* or *ana* need not, however, convey linear movement when used with place-names; they can also express spatial relationships. Some scholars have referred to *The Sargon Geography* as an itinerary because it contains repeated place-names and the prepositions *ištu* and *adu*.[51] The prepositions are used in this case, however, to outline the extent of the empire said to have been controlled by Sargon of Akkad by noting two points that define the borders of each area conquered and, as such, the extent of a particular territory from (*ištu*) one point to (*adu*) another. The repeated names likely indicate neighboring territories rather than points on a route.[52] Use of repeated place-names with *ištu* and *adu* to define territorial boundaries is not uncommon in Neo-Assyrian royal inscriptions (e.g., A.0.87.10 lines 36–37 and A.0.102.6 iv 3–7), and Josh 12:1–5 defines the Israelite tribal territories in a similar manner, using the equivalent prepositions מִן and עַד. In these texts, repetition of place-names and prepositions are used in a strictly spatial manner. In order to constitute an itinerary, they must be combined with another feature—such as the formulaic verbs in the Middle Assyrian itinerary—that indicate linear movement through time as well as space.

While date formulas were used in the daybooks alongside repeated place-names and verbs for movement, the three Old Babylonian itineraries (YBC 4499, UIOM 2134, and UIOM 2370) rely solely on expressions for time to cue

---

51. Garelli, "La notion de route," 120, 126; Beitzel, "From Ḥarran to Imar," 217 n. 8. Beitzel cites W. F. Albright as evidence that *The Sargon Geography* is an itinerary, but Albright refers to this text *not* as an itinerary but as a "geographical commentary" on an epic about Sargon I that gives the "extreme boundaries" of the regions he conquered (W. F. Albright, "A Babylonian Geographical Treatise on Sargon of Akkad's Empire," *JAOS* 45 [1925] 193–245); see also A. K. Grayson, "The Empire of Sargon of Akkad," *AfO* 25 (1974–77) 57. Graham I. Davies understood *The Sargon Geography* to have an unspecified "connection with" itineraries ("Wilderness Itineraries: A Comparative Study," 70–71).

52. W. Horowitz, *Mesopotamian Cosmic Geography* (Mesopotamian Civilizations 8; Winona Lake, IN: Eisenbrauns, 1998) 75.

the reader to read the list of place-names as an itinerary. Here we find no repeated place-names, no prepositions, and no verbs. This excerpt from YBC
4499 (lines 20–30) shows the use of temporal expressions to mark the overnight stays:

[UD.1.KAM] ap-qum	[1 day,] Apqum
[UD.1.KAM UD.]20.KAM ki-iš-ki-iš	[1 day, (total)] 20 days, Kishkish
[UD.1.KAM] ia-ap-tu-rum	[1 day,] Iapturum
[UD.1.KAM] ta-ar-ḫu-uš	[1 day,] Tarhush
[UD.]3.KAM šu-ba-at-^dEN.LÍL.LÁ	**3 [days,] Shubat-Enlil**
UD.1.KAM šu-na-a	**1 day, Shuna**
UD.3.KAM aš-na-ak-ki	3 days, Ashnakku
UD.1.KAM 10 a-la-an	1 day, (total) 10 (days), Alan
UD.1.KAM pa-na-aḫ-zu-ú	1 day, Panahzu
UD.1.KAM ma-am-a-qi-ri	1 day, Mamaqiru

The left edge of YBC 4499 gives a total time for the entire trip: ŠU.NÍGIN ITI.2
UD.27.KAM 'Total: 2 months and 27 days'. This total includes the 38 days it took
to travel to Dur-Apil-Sin according to line 3 and the total sum of the overnight
stays, which is 49. Interim totals are given at various points throughout the
itinerary, such as the 20 days in line 21 and the 10 days in line 27 cited above.
Within this temporal framework, UD.X.KAM can in theory refer either to the
travel time between sites or the length of stay at each site. It more likely refers
to the number of days spent at each site mentioned in the itinerary, however,
since the number with a particular site sometimes varies between one of the
Old Babylonian itineraries and another. If we read UD.X.KAM as the travel time
between sites, the time between Shubat-Enlil and Shuna on the outbound trip
in UIOM 2134, for example, is 1 day (obv. II 5–6), just as it is in the excerpt from
YBC 4499 cited above. But on the return trip in UIOM 2134, it is 9 days with an
extra stop in between (rev. III 21–25):

UD.10.KAM aš-na-ak-ki	10 days, Ashnakku
UD.1.KAM ur-ge-eš	1 day, Urgesh
UD.26.KAM šu-na-a	**26 days, Shuna**
UD.1.KAM ḫa-ar-sí	**1 day, Harsi**
UD.8.KAM šu-pa-at-^dZUEN	**8 days, Shubat-Enlil**
UD.1.KAM ta-ar-ḫu-uš	1 day, Tarhush

If the time between Shubat-Enlil and Shuna took 8 days longer than usual, we
might expect to see a full list of the extra stops that would have been made and
not just the one additional stop at Harsi, given that these itineraries appear to

be thorough in their lists of stops. The Old Babylonian itineraries also include short notes about what took place at some of the stops. These do not occur in any other extant itinerary from Mesopotamia, although they are akin to the more extensive descriptions of events at each stop in Egyptian daybooks such as Papyrus Turin 2008.

Temporal expressions do not always function as part of the itinerary genre even when they occur in itineraries. Like the Egyptian daybooks, the Middle Assyrian itinerary contains a date formula, but its function has nothing to do with the itinerary genre. It occurs in the colophon and dates the text to the 22nd day of the month of Shakinate, a scribal practice for archival documents. The date formulas in Egyptian daybooks also reflect conventions for archival texts, because they are sometimes differentiated from the content of the entry in a visual way by using red rather than black ink, a common feature of Egyptian administrative documents that may make them easier to locate and refer to in an archive.[53] Nonetheless, while they date each entry according to standard practice, they also mark temporal progression along the route. This is not the case in the Middle Assyrian itinerary.

Although it may seem logical that distance measures indicating how far each stage of a journey was from the previous would be a standard feature of itineraries, the only extant text in which they occur is the Neo-Assyrian itinerary (K. 4675+). This text dates to the reign of Sargon II (721–705 B.C.E.) on the basis of its paleography and depicts a route through the province of Zamua.[54] It was among the texts brought to the British Museum from Tell Kuyunjik by Austen Henry Layard in the late ninth century and is presumably from the palace archives at Nineveh, which contained a variety of documents pertaining to internal palace affairs and temple offerings.[55] Lines 28–36 on the reverse of the tablet offer a sample of the itinerary's form:

---

53. For the various uses of red ink in Egyptian papyri, see G. Posener, "Sur l'emploi de l'encre rouge dans les manuscrits égyptiens," *JEA* 37 (1951) 75–80.

54. The primary publication of this document can be found in L. D. Levine, "The Zamua Itinerary," *SAAB* 3 (1989) 75–91; see also Fales and Postgate, *Imperial Administrative Records II*, #14. It was previously published as ADD 1096 in C. H. W. Johns, *Assyrian Deeds and Documents Recording the Transfer of Property* (3 vols.; Cambridge: Deighton Bell, 1901) 2.306–8; see also F. E. Peiser, "Ein assyrisches Itinerar," *Mitteilungen der Vorderasiatischen Gesellschaft* 6 (1901) 134–40. For the date of the inscription, see Fales and Postgate, *Imperial Administrative Records II*, xv.

55. F. M. Fales and J. N. Postgate, *Imperial Administrative Records, Part I: Palace and Temple Administration* (SAA 7; Helsinki: Helsinki University Press, 1992) xii–xiv. Louis Levine suggested that it may have been from the royal chancellery ("Zamua Itinerary," 89–90). Its location is ultimately unknown due to the way in which texts from

[*ištu Dūr-Aššur ad*]*u Sizini*	[From Dur-Ashur t]o Sizini,
[*ištu Sizini*] *adu Ban*[*b*]*ala*	[from Sizini] to Ban[b]ala,
[x DANNA x UŠ x NINDA *iš*]*tu Dūr-Aššur adu Banbala*	[x DANNA x UŠ x NINDA fr]om Dur-Ashur to Banbala
[UD.15.KAM *samuntu*] *mardītu*	[15th day, 8th] stage

[*ištu Banbala*] *a*[*du Ḫalṣ*]*u ša Quraya*	[From Banbala] t[o Halṣ]u of Quraya,
[*ištu Ḫalṣ*]*u ša Qu*[*raya*]	[from Halṣu of Qu[raya]
[*adu Gupni š*]*a Bēl-Ḫar*[*rān* x] *bēru* 5 UŠ 50 NINDA	[to Gupni o]f Bel-Har[ran x] double hours, 5 UŠ, 50 NINDA[55]
[*ištu Banbala a*]*du Gupni ša Bēl-Ḫarrān*	[from Banbala t]o Gupni of Bel-Harran
[UD.16].KAM *tesūtu mardētu*	[16th day,] 9th stage

Here we find repeated place-names combined with prepositions, different from the Middle Assyrian itinerary only in the variant *adu*, typical of Neo-Assyrian, instead of *ana*. While the Middle Assyrian itinerary has a series of verbs situating the place-names along a linear spatial-temporal continuum, the Neo-Assyrian itinerary uses temporal expressions, not unlike the Old Babylonian itineraries, and numbers the stages of the journey.

As we have now seen, formal features of the itinerary genre as we can learn it from extant examples across the ancient Near East vary from one text to another. Davies explained this variation by suggesting that there are formal subcategories of the itinerary genre: "backward-looking" and "forward-looking" itineraries. He proposed these subcategories mainly based on the purpose of a given text, be it to describe a journey that has already taken place or to plan one that is yet to take place. But each subcategory tends to have certain formal features. Features such as dates, numbered overnight stays, totals for travel time, and narrative incidents are associated with backward-looking itineraries.

the Kuyunjik Collection were numbered. For further detail on the reconstruction of the Nineveh archives, see J. Reade, "Archaeology and the Kuyunjik Archives," in *Cuneiform Archives and Libraries: Papers Read at the 30ᵉ Rencontre Assyriologique Internationale, Leiden, 4–8 July 1983* (ed. K. R. Veenhof; Leiden: Nederlands Historisch-Archaeologisch Institut te Istanbul, 1986) 213–22; and S. Parpola, "The Royal Archives of Nineveh," in *Cuneiform Archives and Libraries: Papers Read at the 30ᵉ Rencontre Assyriologique Internationale, Leiden, 4–8 July 1983* (ed. K. R. Veenhof; Leiden: Nederlands Historisch-Archaeologisch Institut te Istanbul, 1986) 223–36.

56. UŠ and NINDA seem to be units of distance smaller than a *bēru*; their pronunciations are unknown. For discussion, see L. D Levine, "Zamua Itinerary," 82.

Forward-looking itineraries tend to have distances, repetition of place-names, prepositions, and no verbs.[57]

Davies recognized that certain itineraries present a problem for these subcategories of the itinerary genre because, while they generally fit in one category, they use a formal feature "that would be equally appropriate" to the other.[58] The Egyptian daybooks blur the distinction, since they have verbs (characteristic of backward-looking itineraries) but also repeat the place-names (characteristic of forward-looking itineraries). These subcategories actually illustrate the problem with classifying texts based on categories that are equated with a prototype rather than understanding that our judgments about what is prototypical are based on an idealized cognitive model. No matter how one constructs a formal category, some text will come along that does not fit it. Then either the validity of the category becomes questionable, or a new subcategory is generated. Benedetto Croce rejected the notion of genre altogether because efforts to account for individuality within a system by using formal generic categories, extended to their logical conclusion, end up simply describing individual texts rather than generating a tool that can be used to interpret other texts—which is what genre should be.[59] Croce has a point. Rather than discarding the whole idea of genre as a potentially useful interpretive tool, however, we are better off to rethink our approach to genre. Instead of attempting to classify a text, we should consider how its author *used* a particular genre, or drew on elements of an idealized cognitive model, when he wrote a text. We can then see that he would have chosen whichever features of the genre best suited his purpose in any given instance. This is true not only for prototypical examples of the genre but also, as we will see in subsequent chapters, for examples in which the itinerary genre is used in ways that stretch or break its norms.

Variation in the formal features of the itinerary genre from one text to another may, to some degree, reflect scribal conventions that constrained how an itinerary happened to have been written in a particular period or geographical area. It is possible that a scribe in the Old Babylonian period might only have thought to write an itinerary using a list of place-names with temporal expressions, while an Assyrian scribe would have used repeated place-names and prepositions as a matter of course, as both the Middle and Neo-Assyrian itiner-

---

57. G. I. Davies, "Wilderness Itineraries: A Comparative Study," 76–77; see pp. 53–70 for fuller discussion of the features of backward-looking itineraries and pp. 70–76 for forward-looking itineraries.

58. Ibid., 77.

59. B. Croce, "Criticism of the Theory of Artistic and Literary Kinds," in *Modern Genre Theory* (ed. D. Duff; London: Longman, 2000) 25–28.

aries do. Although we have enough examples to understand the basic model for the itinerary genre as it was used in the ancient Near East quite broadly, they are scattered throughout different geographical areas and time periods, and we often have only one exemplar from a given region and period. It is therefore very difficult, if not impossible in most cases, to assess the extent to which scribal convention influences the differences we see among itineraries across the ancient Near East. It appears, however, that the pair *nasāḫu* 'to set out' and *biātu* 'to stay overnight' is a convention for the itinerary genre in Assyrian, because they are used not only in the Middle Assyrian itinerary but also in the military narratives from the tenth–ninth centuries B.C.E. that I will discuss in the next chapter. They also correspond closely to the verbs נסע and חנה used in the itineraries of both Num 33:1–49 and the wilderness narrative—the former as a cognate and the latter as a semantic equivalent.

It is easier to say something meaningful about the way in which variation among itineraries is influenced by the rhetorical function of a given text, particularly the specific purpose an author might have for writing an itinerary on a particular occasion. We have already seen this in the use of specific verb forms such as *mjnj* 'mooring' to convey the movement of ships in Papyrus Turin 2008, compared with *nasāḫu* 'to set out' and *biātu* 'to stay overnight' to depict the quartering of travelers in the Middle Assyrian itinerary. We can see this sort of variation even more clearly by considering the letters that make use of the itinerary genre. All of the reports, instructions, and records that we have so far considered are comprehensive in their coverage of whatever journey they convey. They typically have a starting and an ending point and relate every stop the travelers made or were intended to make. Letters, on the other hand, use the itinerary genre more selectively. Unlike reports, records, and instructions, which need to be thorough to serve their goals, letters assume a high degree of shared context. In some cases, assumed knowledge is simply left out. When details are given, what information is provided and how it is presented are quite closely controlled by the author's goals, as we will see in the following examples.

There is no need to define a well-known route by providing a thorough list of stops in a letter, because it is assumed knowledge on the part of the sender and the recipient. In ARM 1 26, Shamshi-Adad wrote to let his son, Yasmah-Adad, know that he was about to pay a visit to Mari. [60] The purpose of the visit is not stated or even implied in the letter. Yasmah-Adad's shaky ability to rule and his relationship with his father, who did not seem to trust him, may shed

---

60. For primary publication of this text, see G. Dossin, *Correspondance de Samsi-Addu et de ses fils* (ARMT 1; Paris: Imprimerie Nationale, 1950) 67–68; and idem, *Lettres* (ARM 1; Paris: Geuthner, 1946) 66–69.

light on the situation.[61] If so, we might understand Shamshi-Adad's visit as a checkup and the advance warning of it as a signal to Yasmah-Adad to make sure that affairs are in order as they should be. It is not clear why Shamshi-Adad outlines his pending movement from Shubat-Enlil only as far as Saggaratum (lines 14–23), which seems to be located at the confluence of the Habur and the Euphrates, and not all the way to Mari. It is probably assumed that the king would follow the river the short remaining distance to Mari, obviating the need to articulate this leg of the route.[62] Contrast the route outlined in stop-by-stop detail in the Old Babylonian itineraries. The route is clearly well known, which is evident from the fact that we have multiple extant itineraries that articulate it. But the purpose of these texts as reports necessitates mentioning every stop so there is a record of exactly where the goods (assuming they do record commercial trips) went and how long the caravan spent at each stop.

An itinerary, especially in a letter, does not always articulate every stop even when the whole route is given. Rather, a scribe can choose to mention only the stops that are important in some way to the message of the letter. Shamshi-Adad took up two matters with his son in ARM 1 7, a census and instructions for what to do with a shipment of aromatic lumber from Qatnum.[63] The shipment was to be divided in three, and one-third sent to each of Ekallatum, Nineveh, and Shubat-Enlil. He gave specific instructions for how to get the shipment to Shubat-Enlil (lines 22–31). Here the basic form of prepositions and the repetition of place-names are combined with verbs that specify the actions that need to be taken at each stage of this journey:

ša ana Šubat-Enlil	What you send
tušabbalam	to Shubat-Enlil,
ina eleppēti ana Saggaratim	let them receive in Saggaratum
limaḫḫirū ištu Saggarati[m]	in boats. From Saggaratu[m]
ana Qattunan	to Qattunan.
ištu Qattunan	From Qattunan
ina ereqqī	in wagons

---

61. For basic historical overviews of Shamshi-Adad's reign, see J. Laessøe, *People of Ancient Assyria: Their Inscriptions and Correspondence* (trans. F. S. Leigh-Browne; London: Routledge & Kegan Paul, 1963) 40; Oates, *Studies in the Ancient History*, 37ff.; Roaf, *Cultural Atlas*, 114–16; and P. Villard, "Shamshi-Adad and Sons: The Rise and Fall of an Upper Mesopotamian Empire," *CANE* 2.873–83.

62. G. I. Davies, "Wilderness Itineraries: A Comparative Study," 71.

63. For primary publication of this text, see Dossin, *Correspondance de Samsi-Addu*, 34–37.

Qattunanayya	let the Qattunaneans
lil[qū]nimma	ta[ke] it.
ana Šubat-Enlil liblūnim	Let them carry it to Shubat-Enlil.

This letter is concerned not only with *where* to send the shipment but also *how*, and the instructions about how to manage the shipment govern the selection of places mentioned in the itinerary. The goods were to be taken by boat to Saggaratum and then Qattunan, where they were to be transferred to wagons and taken overland to Shubat-Enlil by the men of Qattunan. Saggaratum was the point at which the contingent needed to leave the Euphrates and take the Habur, while Qattunan was the point at which the goods were transferred to wagons. These are surely not the only places the contingent passed en route to Shubat-Enlil, but they are the places at which the crew needed to take important actions.

M. 5431 is another text in which sites are selected and verbs are used to note turning points and key actions in the course of a journey. This letter relates that a group of Benjaminite messengers met Eshnunean troops who accompanied them on the rest of their journey south to Eshnunna as well as the geographical details of their return trip north. The author and recipient of this letter are unclear, because the name of the author (obv. 3) is broken, and the recipient is simply referred to as *bēliya* 'my lord' (obv. 1), although this probably refers to Zimri-Lim, given that the letter probably came from his archive.[64] Given this plausible context, we might understand this letter as providing Zimri-Lim with intelligence about Benjaminite troop movements; Francis Joannès suggested that it be understood against the background of a conflict between Zimri-Lim and the Benjaminites early in the former's reign at Mari, during which the Benjaminites sought alliance with Eshnunna.[65] The first section of the letter, which employs the itinerary genre to articulate the trip south (lines 9–13), highlights Karana, the place where the Benjaminites met up with their Eshnunean escort.

---

64. F. Joannès, "Une mission secrète à Esnunna," in *La circulation des biens, des personnes et des idées dans le Proche-Orient ancien: Actes de la XXXVIIIe Rencontre Assyriologique Internationale (Paris, 8–10 juillet 1991)* (ed. D. Charpin and F. Johannès; Paris: Éditions Recherche sur les Civilisations, 1992) 185.

65. Ibid., 188–89. For a broader look at the relationship between the Benjaminites and Mari during the reign of Zimri-Lim, see J. Kupper, *Les nomades en Mésopotamie au temps des rois de Mari* (Paris: Les Belles Lettres, 1957) 47; and G. Dossin, "Benjaminites dans les Textes de Mari," in *Recueil Georges Dossin: Mélanges d'Assyriologie (1934–1959)* (Akkadica Supplement 1; Leuven: Peeters, 1983) 150–65.

. . . mārī šipri ša [Mārī]-iamina ištu [x]-da ana Karana ištu Karana itti ṣābi Eš[nun]na iṣṣabtunimma ana Ešnunna illikunim

. . . The messengers of the [Benja]minites went from [GN] to Karana, [then] joined up with Esh[nun]ean troops [and] went from Karana to Eshnunna.

It is not clear why the place-names between Karana and Eshnunna are omitted. If we understand the purpose of the letter to be military intelligence, we might suppose that the author received no information on the whereabouts of Benjaminites once they had met up with their Eshnunean escort.

Select stops rather than a comprehensive list are also found when an author seeks to outline an atypical route.[66] The Shemshara itinerary (SH 809) mainly concerns the shifting alliances of Yashub-Adad, another provincial ruler.[67] Near the end of the letter (lines 49–63), however, Shamshi-Adad inquires about why his representative, Kushiya, was still at Shemshara and provides an itinerary for his return, presumably to Shamshi-Adad's capital at Shubat-Enlil. The route is defined here because it is not the most obvious or easiest route (rev. 54–59):

. . . ištu Zasli	. . . from Zasli
ana Šegibbu ištu Šegibbu	to Shegibbu, from Shegibbu
ana Zikum ištu Zikum	to Zikum, from Zikum
ana U[ra]u ištu U[ra]u	to U[ra]u, from U[ra]u
ana Lutpiš ištu Lutpiš	to Lutpish, from Lutpish
ana m[āt] Ḫaburatim	to the la[nd] of Haburatum

Not every stop is given here, which is evident from the fact that the land of Haburatum is the last mentioned, and it is assumed that the route from there to Shubat-Enlil would be known.[68] The places in the itinerary seem to have been chosen to provide enough information to clarify the uncertain part of the route. In order to achieve his purpose, Shamshi-Adad needed only a few

---

66. F. Joannès, "Routes et voies de communication dans les Archives de Mari," in *Mari, Ébla et les Hourrites: Dix ans de Travaux, Première Partie* (ed. J.-M. Durand; Amurru 1; Paris: Éditions Recherche sur les Civilisations, 1996) 329.

67. For primary publication of this text (= IM 62089), see Eidem and Laessøe, *Shemshara Archives 1*, 70–72.

68. Eidem, *Shemshara Archives 2*, 12; and M. C. Astour, "Semites and Hurrians in Northern Transtigris," in *General Studies and Excavations at Nuzi 9/1* (ed. D. I. Owen and M. A. Morrison; Studies on the Civilization and Culture of Nuzi and the Hurrians 2; Winona Lake, IN: Eisenbrauns, 1987) 9, 45–46. This is noted by G. I. Davies, "Wilderness Itineraries: A Comparative Study," 71–72.

strategic place-names and the basic form of repetition and prepositions. These places probably did not convey where Kushiya was supposed to stop and rest overnight, because the overarching concern was not to secure his provision, as in the Middle Assyrian itinerary, but to define the route that would get him back to Shubat-Enlil as quickly as possible.

The letter explicitly states that this route goes through the mountains and involves the risk of road blockages due to inclement winter weather (lines 60ff.) but does not explicitly state why this sort of route would have been necessary. The concerns in the first part of the letter suggest that the alternate route may have been designed to avoid Yashub-Adad's potentially hostile territory by going through the foothills of the Zagros and around to the north. SH 894, another letter that shortly followed or perhaps even accompanied SH 809, states that Kushiya should now return on the route via Kumme (lines 43ff.). No itinerary is specified here.[69] The usual route via Kumme did not need to be spelled out. Shamshi-Adad could leave this information out with no concern that his instruction would be misunderstood because the route was well known, a shared element of repertoire.

We find another instance of defining an alternate route to avoid danger on the typical route in the second section of M. 5431 (lines 18–31), which relates the Benjaminites' return from Eshnunna to Karana. The usual route north was likely the one articulated in the Old Babylonian itineraries, which runs along the west side of the Tigris, between the Tigris and Wadi Tharthar, through the area of Ashur and Ekallatum. Benjaminites avoided this route on their return, taking a route east of the Tigris through the foothills of the Zagros, just as Kushiya was advised to do in SH 809.

[*harrāna mārī šipr*]*i*	[The route of the messenger]s
[*ša Mārī-ia*]*mina*	[of the Benjamin]ites
[*birīt Ešnunna*] *u Karana*	[between Eshnunna] and Karana
[*ulammidan*]*ni*	[he will inform] me
[*kiam ana Dū*]*r-Sin-ma*	[thus: to Du]r-Sin,
[*ištu Dūr-Si*]*n ana Arra*[*apḫi*]	[from Dur-Si]n to Arr[apha],

---

69. For the text of this letter, see Eidem and Laessøe, *Shemshara Archives 1*, 72. Although Eidem initially suggested that SH 894 was written later in the winter after the roads had cleared, this is unlikely, since the route for which weather is a concern is the alternate mountain route rather than the usual route through the plains. It is more likely, as Eidem and Laessøe later suggest, that the political situation changed enough that the usual route was safe (Eidem, "News from the Eastern Front," 96; Eidem and Laessøe, *Shemshara Archives 1*, 45).

[*ištu Ar*]*raphi*[*i*]*m*	[from Ar]raph[a]
[*ana Kaw*]*al*[*hi*]*m*	[to Kaw]al[hu]m,
[*išt*]*u* [*K*]*awa*[*lhi*]*im*	[fro]m [K]awa[lhu]m
[*a*]*na Razama ša Iamut-baal*	[t]o Razama of Iamut-baal,
ištu Razama ša Iamut-b[*a*]*al*	from Razama of Iamut-b[a]al
ana Karana ištu Kar[*an*]*a*	to Karana, from Kar[an]a
ana Allahad [*an*]*a* GÚ <ID>-[*da*^KI]	to Allahad, [to]?
harrānašunu kia[*m*]	Their route was thu[s].

The alternate route suggests that the Benjaminites had no Eshnunean escort on the return and took a route that avoided territory friendly to Mari, as Ashur and Ekallatum were, where they might encounter resistance.[70] Although this itinerary is quite detailed and includes a fair number of place-names, these sites were not likely overnight stays, because the distance between some of the places must have been more than a day's journey. The stretch from Eshnunna to Kawalhum, for example, includes only two places, Dur-Sin and Arrapha.[71] Why these particular sites might have been important to mention is simply not transparent.

The formal features of the itinerary genre used in a text can sometimes offer a clue to its purpose where this is otherwise unclear. We have no clear information either in the Neo-Assyrian itinerary or outside it to help us understand who wrote this itinerary, for whom, or for what purpose. It has been interpreted as a report of a cultic procession, a journey of an official, or a record related to Ashurnasirpal II's eastern campaigns.[72] Louis D. Levine has understood this text as an addendum to ABL 408, a letter in which the author makes an ardent claim that he provided mules for a royal messenger and arranged posting for the company in Dur-Talite and Lagalagi, two sites mentioned in the itinerary as well, suggesting that he has been accused in a previous letter of failing to do so. The itinerary would have been attached to support his claim, just as the Middle Assyrian itinerary from Dur-Katlimmu may have accompanied a letter or have been an archival copy of such a supporting document, as I

---

70. Joannès, "Une mission secrète," 189–92.

71. Ibid., 189. On Arrapha, see Fadhil, *Studien zur Topographie*.

72. For the view that it may be a cultic procession or a journey of an official, see Peiser, "Ein assyrisches Itinerar," 139. For association with Ashurnasirpal's campaigns, see A. T. Olmstead, "The Calculated Frightfulness of Ashur Nasir Apal," *JAOS* 38 (1918) 230 n. 48; E. Speiser ("Southern Kurdistan in the Annals of Ashurnasirpal and Today," *AASOR* 8 [1928] 7), who actually only states that K. 4675+ deals with the same route as Ashurnasirpal's campaigns; and Liverani, "Growth of the Assyrian Empire," 87 n. 16.

will discuss below. The temporal rhythm of the journey indicated by the dates in each section is broken only in the seventh stage (lines 21–27), which took three days rather than the customary one. This deviation may be the reason for the report, perhaps to justify a journey that took place in a manner other than expected but did, nonetheless, take place.[73]

None of these explanations, however, addresses the unique features of this itinerary—namely, the use of distance measures and the enumerated *mardiātu*. Ernst Weidner suggested, based on the importance of distance measures in this text, that it may have been a record made en route during a campaign by an accompanying surveyor who measured the distances.[74] The *mardiātu* are stops for rest and provisions established by the administration along royal roads between the Assyrian centers and the seats of provincial governors.[75] These stops even functioned as a postal service. In K. 4785, a letter to Esarhaddon, the author mentions that his letters are delivered via these *bīt mardiāte*.[76] One might assume that the distances between *mardiātu* on an *established* route would have been known and therefore did not need to be mentioned. A possibility not heretofore considered is that the Neo-Assyrian itinerary may be a record of a journey to map out and survey the distances for *mardiātu* along a *new* royal road, which might also have served as a blueprint for the construction of the stations.

The purpose of a text can be multifaceted; it is not necessary to assume that a particular text only ever had *one* purpose. The Middle Assyrian itinerary

---

73. L. D. Levine, "Zamua Itinerary," 88, 90. For ABL 408, see R. F. Harper, "The Letters of the Rm. 2 Collection of the British Museum," *ZA* 8 (1893) 343–45; G. R. Berry, "The Letters of the Rm 2 Collection (ZA VIII, pp. 341–359)," *Hebraica* 11 (1894–95) 178–79; C. Bezold, *Catalogue of the Cuneiform Tablets in the Kouyunjik Collection of the British Museum* (5 vols.; London: British Museum, 1896) 4.1636; Harper, *Assyrian and Babylonian Letters*, 4.428–29; Fadhil, *Studien zur Topographie*, 74–75.

74. E. Weidner, "Assyrische Itinerare," *AfO* 21 (1966) 43, 45.

75. L. D. Levine, "Zamua Itinerary," 90. For discussion of royal roads and *mardiātu*, see S. Favaro, *Voyages et voyageurs à l'époque Néo-Assyrienne* (SAAS 18; Helsinki: The Neo-Assyrian Text Corpus Project, 2007) 57–60, 67–72; on royal roads, see also Weidner, "Assyrische Itinerare," 43; and K. Kessler, "'Royal Roads' and other Questions of the Neo-Assyrian Communication System," in *Assyria 1995: Proceedings of the 10th Anniversary Symposium of the Neo-Assyrian Text Corpus Project, Helsinki, September 7–11, 1995* (ed. S. Parpola and R. M. Whiting; Helsinki: The Neo-Assyrian Text Corpus Project, 1997) 129–36.

76. K. 4785 rev. 4. An edition of this text (= ABL 1021) is published in S. Parpola, *Letters from Assyrian Scholars to the Kings Esarhaddon and Assurbanipal* (2 vols.; AOAT 5/2; Kevelaer: Butzon & Bercker, 1970–83) #294, 1.250–51, 2.301–2. The copy can be found in Harper, *Assyrian and Babylonian Letters*, #1021.

discussed above served as a set of instructions but also, after the fact, as a record. This itinerary may have accompanied a letter to Taidu, to whoever would have been responsible for seeing that the *ḫurādu*-troops came to Dur-Katlimmu according to the stated schedule.[77] The route that connects these sites may be similar to the road that connects Dur-Katlimmu to Ashur, a road that is evident today from the presence of wells and water holes at regular intervals of about 40 km (about one day's journey), each of which is probably a *mardītu*.[78] Mention of the *mardiātu* in the Middle Assyrian itinerary likely relates to the quartering and provisioning of the *ḫurādu*-troops on their journey. Given the likelihood that these stops, as *mardiātu*, would have been well known, the thorough list of sites along this journey may have been included to make sure that the journey was undertaken according to plan and/or to secure provisions from officials at each individual site. But this set of instructions later functioned as a record. The colophon (lines 20–21) contains a date of composition, suggesting that this document was an archival copy of the original set of instructions.[79]

Davies recognized that a text could serve multiple functions; in particular, he noted that a record of travel can serve as a guide in planning future trips.[80] He made this comment about the Neo-Assyrian itinerary, the distance mea-

---

77. Two of the letters in the Dur-Katlimmu archive also mention *ḫurādu*-troops, although neither seems to shed light on this itinerary. DeZ 3836+ simply mentions them in passing with no clear context (line 44). DeZ 3293 mentions them in the context of what appears to be an issue with a city's water supply related to a military conflict, and the sender notes the impending arrival of the *ḫurādu*-troops. According to Eva Christiane Cancik-Kirschbaum, this letter is probably addressed *to* Ashur-idin; in that case, the *ḫurādu*-troops would be coming not to Dur-Katlimmu, as in the itinerary, but to whatever city the sender is from; as such, this episode probably does not provide the context for the itinerary. For these texts, see Cancik-Kirschbaum, *Mittelassyrischen Briefe*.

78. The word *mardītu* can also refer to a road and is sometimes used to refer to the course of a river (*CAD* M/1 278). See also L. D. Levine, "Zamua Itinerary," 81–82; and the comment in J. N. Postgate, *Taxation and Conscription in the Assyrian Empire* (Studia Pohl: Series Maior 3; Rome: Pontifical Biblical Institute, 1974) 383. For discussion of the Ashur-Dur-Katlimmu road, see Kühne, "Dur-Katlimmu and the Middle-Assyrian Empire," 273–75; and Weidner, "Assyrische Itinerare," 42–46 for the Assyrian road system more generally. See also maps in Kühne, "The Assyrians on the Middle Euphrates," 70–71. It may be that the *mardītu* is specifically a feature of the Assyrian road system, because it is attested primarily in Neo-Assyrian texts (*CAD* M/1 278), which may explain why the term does not appear in any of the Babylonian itineraries. This suggestion of course remains tentative, since there are so few itineraries.

79. Röllig, "Ein Itinerar," 283.

80. G. I. Davies, "Wilderness Itineraries: A Comparative Study," 70, 76.

sures of which could be useful in this way, but it may apply to the Old Babylonian itineraries as well. All three of the texts—UIOM 2134, YBC 4499, and
UIOM 2370, a small tablet containing a portion of the itinerary—have many
of the same stops and even the same number of days spent at particular stops.
For example:

> 4 days at Mankisum (UIOM 2134 I.17 // YBC 4499 line 9)
> 3 days at Shubat-Enlil (UIOM 2134 II.5 // YBC 4499 line 24)
> 3 days at Ashnakku (UIOM 2134 II.7 // YBC 4499 line 26)

Hallo thought that these three texts were copies of one another, YBC 4499 being a "virtual duplicate" of the outbound portion of UIOM 2134.[81] He chalked
up the differences among all three texts to "minor scribal variants," noting also
the absence of narrative statements in YBC 4499 that are present in UIOM 2134
and the addition of travel-time subtotals in YBC 4499 lines 21 and 27, which
are not present in UIOM 2134.[82] These differences are minor enough, in Hallo's
view, to warrant seeing YBC 4499 as a variant text.

Hallo explained these three copies as administrative texts on their way to
becoming canonical literature: the small tablet was probably made en route,
one of the longer tablets was an archival copy, and the other is a stage in the
evolution of the archival document into a royal campaign narrative, not unlike
the "King of Battle Epic" (*šar tamḫāri*). His basis for this argument is two-
fold: he reads YBC 4499 line 5 in such a way as to suggest a military context—
the troops 'girded themselves [for battle] in Dur-Apil-Sin' (*ina Dūr Apil-Sin
nizzuḫū*)—and he assumes that the presence of a copy means that a text cannot
be a "simple administrative record."[83]

Hallo's interpretation is problematic for a number of reasons. First, the
"King of Battle Epic" is about Sargon's journey to Purushkhanda on a military
campaign, but it does not make use of the itinerary genre as it is defined by
Davies and in this book. It can be considered an itinerary and thus an "epic
parallel" to the Old Babylonian itineraries only in the broadest sense. Second,
the Old Babylonian itineraries may not be military at all. Marten Stol calls into
question the military character of the text with his new reading of YBC 4499
line 5 as 'after we had departed from Dur-Apilsin' (*ištu Dūr Apil-Sin nissuḫu*).
While Hallo reads *ni-iz-zu-ḫu-u₂*, an N 3mp stative from *ezēḫu*, Stol reads *ni-is-*

---

81. Hallo, "Road to Emar," 63; see also p. 84, where he refers to it as a version of
the same text.

82. Ibid., 66 n. 2.

83. Ibid., 63, 65 (for reading of line 5) and pp. 84–85. It is not altogether clear in §75
on p. 84 which text Hallo thinks is the archival copy and which he thinks is the text on
its way to becoming literature.

su₂-ḫu-u₂, a G 1cs preterite subjunctive from *nasāḫu*.[84] Stol's reading no longer leaves us with evidence of battle activity, but it is a better reading, in part because it corresponds to the use of *nasāḫu* to indicate departure in line 2 of the Middle Assyrian itinerary and is quite at home in the itinerary genre. The use of this verb to denote departure from a place is also frequently attested in Old Assyrian and Old Babylonian/Mari texts, so we should not be surprised to see it used as the formulaic verb for departure in itineraries.[85] Finally, Davies noted that Hallo is too ready to assume that only literary texts exist in more than one copy. All three texts could be administrative in character.[86]

Davies interpreted YBC 4499 and UIOM 2134 as two administrative texts with different purposes. Both texts contain administrative features such as totals for travel time. Hallo accounted for this by suggesting that the text is only partially canonized as literature, at which point he would expect to see the administrative features removed.[87] Davies rightly suggested that the many administrative features are best explained if *both* texts are understood as administrative documents. He argued that the purpose of UIOM 2134, which contains notes about activity that took place at some of the stages, was to justify delays, while YBC 4499, which does not have these notes, was meant to serve as a permanent record.[88] His suggestion that the notes justify delays is attractive, albeit difficult to substantiate because the lines cannot all be read with certainty. Lines I 18–19 of UIOM 2134 note that the four-day stop at Mankisum is *inūma ṣābū ipp[aḫrū] u eleppētum illikānim* 'when the troops assembled and the boats came', while lines II 8–9 may be relating the receipt of supplies during the three-day stop at Ashnakku: *ašar ummānātum ša [. . .] imḫurū* 'where the troops which [. . .] received'.[89] Another note appears in line I 25, although its reading is unclear.[90] But Davies's argument that these two texts have different

84. Stol, *Studies in Old Babylonian History*, 40 n. 20.

85. *CAD* Ṣ 10, no. 7.

86. G. I. Davies, "Wilderness Itineraries: A Comparative Study," 56–57.

87. Hallo, "Road to Emar," 85.

88. G. I. Davies, "Wilderness Itineraries: A Comparative Study," 56–57.

89. In UIOM 2134 I 18–19, Hallo reads *i-nu-ma* ERIM.ḪI.A *ip-pa-aṭ-rŭ u* ᴳᴵˢMÀ.ḪI.A *i-tu-ru-ú* 'when the troops left and the ship went back', following a reading suggested by Landsberger, given without citation ("Road to Emar," 69). Goetze strenuously objects to this reading ("Remarks on the Old Babylonian Itinerary," 115 n. 15). Cole and Gasche note that Landsberger's reading may actually have been *i-tu-ra* or *i-tu-ra-nim*, and that Goetze's copy reads TU, not LI, despite the fact that he reads *illikānim* ("Second- and First-Millennium BC Rivers," 20 n. 84).

90. For a hypothetical restoration of "where the troops rested for two days," see Hallo, "Road to Emar," 70.

purposes does not hold because *both* texts contain notes. The note in YBC 4499 line 42 is just as difficult to read as those in UIOM 2134, but its presence is undeniable.[91] Thus YBC 4499 and UIOM 2134 are probably both reports. Indeed, Stol's reading of YBC 4499 line 5 as *nissuḫū* reveals it to be a first-person report just as UIOM 2134 is, by virtue of its colophon.

I agree with Davies that YBC 4499 and UIOM 2134 are both administrative, but I suggest that they are distinct reports of *two different trips* along the same route—two different iterations of a regularly undertaken journey to Emar. The author of one of these texts probably copied an itinerary from a previous trip but not in order to make a duplicate. Rather, he used it as a template for his own record. The argument that these tablets are duplicates of one another rests on the view that the differences between them are scribal variants. This is true of the differences between the small tablet (UIOM 2370) and the larger tablet (UIOM 2134 III 23–32), which are in fact limited to orthographic variations. They involve different spellings (compare *za-ni-ba-a* in UIOM 2370 line 9 and *za-ni-pa-a* in UIOM 2134 III 31), omission of signs (compare UIOM 2370 line 2 with UIOM 2134 III 24, which omits a RU), and the use of sign variants (compare UIOM 2370 line 2, which uses SI, with UIOM 2134 III 24, which uses SI_2). Goetze suggests that UIOM 2134 may have been copied from a number of smaller texts such as UIOM 2370.[92] Since military records were kept while on campaign, Davies suggests that small texts such as UIOM 2370 were records made en route as notes made for use in composing a "final report" such as an annal.[93] The purely orthographic differences may also suggest, however,

---

91. Hallo notes two options for reading here. The first follows previously suggested readings and involves understanding BA.AḪ.RA as referring to the *bît qanê* 'reed chassis' of a chariot, as it appears and is read in ARM 1 50:14 and understanding the verb as *i-ṣi₂-ʾu* (from *naṣû* 'to repair, tear down'); with this reading, Hallo translated the clause 'where the chariot had to be repaired'. The second reading, Hallo's own, involves reading the verb as *i-zi-ḫu* (from *ezēḫu* 'to gird oneself') and BA.AḪ.RA as a reference to military troops "*via* an otherwise unattested Sumerian intermediary"; here he translates 'where the elite troops girded themselves (for battle)' ("Road to Emar," 80). Hallo maintains this second reading in "Choice in Sumerian," *JANESCU* 5 (1973) 165–72. An entirely different but tentative reading is offered by Stol (*Studies in Old Babylonian History*, 40 n. 20) in light of evidence for *ba-aḫ-ra* as a place-name and a reading of the verb as *i-ṣi₂-ḫu*: 'where Bahra revolts'.

92. Goetze, "Old Babylonian Itinerary," 51.

93. G. I. Davies, "Wilderness Itineraries: A Comparative Study," 56, 59–60. Davies points to the depiction in reliefs of scribes who appear to be recording the booty taken from a captured city as evidence that records in general were kept while on campaign; see also J. Glassner, *Mesopotamian Chronicles* (ed. B. R. Foster; SBLWAW 19; Atlanta: Society of Biblical Literature, 2004) 14.

that UIOM 2370 was a school text, a partial copy of a fuller itinerary made by someone learning to be a scribe. If so, we can understand UIOM 2370, like the Rhind Mathematical Papyrus, as evidence for formal training in the itinerary genre.

The differences between the two large tablets, however, are not merely orthographic and cannot be sufficiently explained as scribal variants resulting from the copying process. First, the lengths of stay at the same spot are different in some cases; for example, the travelers stay five days at Suqaqu in UIOM 2134 (I 24) and only two days in YBC 4499 (line 14). Second, the stops themselves are sometimes different:

UIOM 2134 III 7–4[94]	**YBC 4499 Lines 33–36**
[UD.X.KAM *A*]*pqum ša Balīḫâ*	UD.1.KAM *Apqū ša Balīḫâ*
	UD.1.KAM *Ṣaḫlala*
[..........]UD.1.KAM *Zalpa*[*ḫ*]	UD.1.KAM *Zalpaḫ*
[UD.X.KAM *A*]*ḫuna*	
	UD.1.KAM *Ṣerdi*[95]
[UD.X.KAM *T*]*ultul*	UD.2.KAM *Tultul*

Here UIOM 2134 has a stop at Ahuna, which YBC 4499 does not have, while YBC 4499 has stops at Sahlala and Serdi that are not found in UIOM 2134. Third, both texts have notes indicating activity at various stops, but they are in different places. The note in YBC 4499 line 42 discussed above occurs in a different place from the notes in UIOM 2134, while YBC 4499 has no notes in the places where notes appear in UIOM 2134. These minor differences that are not orthographic may be explained as deviations from the previous itinerary, be it a couple of extra (or fewer) days at a stop or a slightly different set of stops. The differences in the notes may be explained in terms of the noteworthy events' being different on each trip. A list of place-names organized into an itinerary by combining it with temporal expressions is a form with a great deal of flexibility. The absence of verb forms would make it easy to expand the basic

---

94. Since this section of the text is outbound in YBC 4499 but on the inbound part of the trip in UIOM 2134, the lines from UIOM 2134 are given here in reverse order for easier comparison.

95. Beitzel ("From Ḥarran to Imar," 212) reads YBC 4499 line 36 as *ṣe-er-di* rather than *ṣe-er-ki* (per Hallo), following the collation in G. Dossin, "Le Site de Tuttul-Sur-Balîḫ," *RA* 68 (1974) 25–34. This reading fits well with additional evidence from Mari that refers to a Serda near Tuttul as in the itinerary.

structure with a note where an event occurred.[96] Moreover, this rather skeletal form could be used to report a past trip *or* as a map for a future trip. The need to make records of multiple iterations of the same trip makes a good deal of sense if they are to be explained as trips along a regularly traveled commercial route. Copying the record of the last trip and making changes wherever necessary to reflect the particularities of the new trip may have been simply an efficient record-keeping process.

We have now acquired a certain degree of competence in the itinerary genre as it was used throughout the ancient Near East by studying the extant inscriptions that use it. Given the limits of our sample, our model may be skewed, but it does provide a solid base that can be adjusted in the future if more inscriptions of this sort are found. Itineraries articulate linear movement through space and time, from one site to another along a route. However, a list of place-names alone does not constitute an example of the itinerary genre. The formal features of the itinerary genre include a list of names combined with one or more other features such as prepositions, the repetition of place-names, temporal expressions, or verbs for movement. Features such as distance measures and notes about what took place at a given stop are sometimes included as well. The itinerary genre is used in a range of administrative situations—military, commercial, civic—to serve pragmatic goals, whether to make a report to a superior official, provide instructions, or create a record for deposit in an archive.

While there is some variation from one text to another in terms of the situation of address, rhetorical function, or formal features used, all of the texts studied here can be judged prototypical. In Jauss's terms, the itinerary genre is simply *reproduced* in these texts, and the texts establish a horizon of expectations for the itinerary genre. In other words, when we encounter a text that uses the itinerary genre, we have certain expectations about it that are generated by the idealized cognitive model that we have now developed based on our direct familiarity with these extant administrative documents and letters.

First, we expect itineraries to be accurate. The pragmatic goals that itineraries typically serve place constraints on the use of geography. Places have to be locatable and must be on a traversable route in order for instructions to be followed or for a report to be accurate. A report can of course be "fudged," but the need to fake a report instead of writing an accurate report itself reveals the

---

96. For use of the term *expansion* to refer to narrative clauses (in UIOM 2134, for example) that do not disturb the fundamental list-like structure of the itinerary, see G. I. Davies, "Wilderness Itineraries: A Comparative Study," 57. The term itself implies that the narrative statements are added to a basic text.

expectation that reports are accurate. When scholars understand Num 33:1–49 to be an accurate report, as Charles Krahmalkov does, or understand that its author capitalized on the verisimilitude of itineraries, as Benjamin Edidin Scolnic does, their judgments are based on knowledge of the itinerary genre that is a function of how it is typically *used*.

Second, we expect itineraries to be goal oriented and linear. All of the texts discussed here involve the travelers' getting to a designated endpoint for a reason, be it arriving at Emar with a shipment, arriving at Dur-Katlimmu ready for service, or returning safely back to Shubat-Enlil ready for the next diplomatic assignment. Moreover, the itinerary notices do not emphasize twists and turns in the route or travel through difficult terrain. This is not because there are no turns or ups and downs in the route. It is because *description* of the route in this kind of detail is not the purpose of an itinerary. Instead, in line with the typical pragmatic goals, such as reporting on overnight stops or outlining a route, an itinerary takes the traveler straight to the goal in a *linear* fashion through space and time.

We have seen variation in the way the itinerary genre was used to serve varying goals even within prototypical uses of the itinerary genre. Every stop is articulated in the Middle Assyrian itinerary in order to lay out the places where the troops should be quartered on each night of their journey. In the Shemshara letter, on the other hand, only enough sites are articulated to sketch out an alternate and unfamiliar route. When an author uses the itinerary genre in an *atypical* situation for an *atypical* purpose, as will be the case with texts that we will consider in the remainder of this book, his use of the genre stretches or breaks the norms of the genre. Even so, he engages some features of the genre to serve his literary goals. Formal features, situation of address, rhetorical function, and implications are facets of the itinerary genre in its background context as an element of cultural repertoire. The author of a campaign or other journey narrative might foreground the itinerary genre in order to make use of one or more of these features. Our ability as readers to understand these creative uses of genre hinges on our cognitive model as well as our ability to identify how the author is stretching or breaking its norms. It is to the creative uses that we now turn.

Chapter 4

Experimenting with Genre: Using Sources and Shaping Narratives

The secret to creativity is knowing how to hide your sources.
—Albert Einstein

We take it for granted that historians use sources. A trip to the archives to draw on whatever material might be available and useful in writing a narrative about a particular subject is a necessary part of the modern historian's work. Historians in antiquity also had access to and drew upon source material. We know this because they explicitly referred to sources within their narratives, because they sometimes did a less-than-careful job of integrating their sources, and because they left traces of the genre characteristics of their source documents. Louis D. Levine suggested that we might further explore the sources used for composing the Neo-Assyrian annals through form-critical study. He advocated learning about particular forms and the social contexts in which they were produced (which we have now done for itineraries) and then identifying them in the broader literary context of the annals.[1] We can recognize the use of itineraries in both Assyrian and Egyptian military narratives because features of these narratives invoke our cognitive model for that genre.

Although a historian's job is to write about the past, a historical narrative does not merely report past events in the same way that an itinerary reports the route of a journey, the length of time it took, and notable events that took place on it. A historian writes a narrative in order to explain what the past *means*,

---

1. L. D. Levine, "Manuscripts, Texts, and the Study of the Neo-Assyrian Royal Inscriptions," in *Assyrian Royal Inscriptions: New Horizons in Literary, Ideological, and Historical Analysis* (ed. F. M. Fales; Orientis Antiqui Collectio 17; Rome: Istituto per l'Oriente, 1981) 62.

how it is significant. He emplots as well as reports. Hayden White is not the only thinker to speak of the formal and conceptual coherence of historical narrative; in his essay "Interpretation in History," he points to the view of Claude Lévi-Strauss that "historical facts, originally constituted as data by the historian, must be constituted a second time as elements of a verbal structure which is always written for a specific (manifest or latent) purpose."[2] The historian may report, but he reports for a different purpose than a scribe who writes an itinerary. The historian's goals are not strictly pragmatic but also literary and ideological. One might choose to relate a particular battle in order to tell a story about the tragic loss of life, perhaps voicing a critique of war. One could also tell a story about human ingenuity in technological innovation; this story might bear a message about the ethics of using knowledge. The same battle could also be related as a story of heroism, creating a figure or figures whose values set an example to which members of a culture can aspire. The same sources and data would be available to authors of all three types of story, but each would choose data and cast it appropriately for the particular meaning he or she wished to convey.

Assyrian and Egyptian scribes had an important message to convey about the king: his fitness to rule. The king's ability to rule is expressed in religious terms as the ability to maintain order over chaos, which typically involved building and maintaining the cult. Royal activities such as restoring a temple would thus be duly noted in commemorative inscriptions. Assyrian commemorative inscriptions include statues and obelisks as well as foundation and wall deposits in temples and palaces. The latter were directed not only at the gods but also at future kings who would find the inscriptions during repair or renovation of a building.[3] They appealed to future kings to maintain the evidence of a previous king's piety by maintaining his construction projects, because building activity demonstrated his care of Ashur's city and cult.[4] Commemorative or dedicatory inscriptions in Egypt were usually carved on stelas, set up in temples, and directed at the deity in an effort to demonstrate that the king

---

2. H. V. White, "Interpretation in History," *Tropics of Discourse: Essays in Cultural Criticism* (Baltimore: Johns Hopkins University Press, 1978) 55–56. For discussion of White and emplotment, see pp. 31–33 above.

3. On foundation deposits, see R. S. Ellis, *Foundation Deposits in Ancient Mesopotamia* (New Haven, CT: Yale University Press, 1968).

4. J. Laessøe, *People of Ancient Assyria: Their Inscriptions and Correspondence* (trans. F. S. Leigh-Browne; London: Routledge & Kegan Paul, 1963) 160. There are records of finding such texts during the rebuilidng process; see A. Kuhrt, *The Ancient Near East c. 3000–330* B.C. (2 vols.; Routledge History of the Ancient World; London: Routledge, 1995) 2.475 for discussion of an example from the Persian period.

had executed his pious duty as high priest, which came with the responsibility to maintain the cult.[5]

But royal ideology developed in tandem with the emergence of the state. Scribes began to write narratives commemorating the king's *military* deeds during the Late Bronze Age, as Egypt and Assyria began to exercise imperial control over neighboring territories.[6] Assyria emerged as a territorial state during the Middle Assyrian period (thirteenth to mid-eleventh centuries B.C.E.), as Kassite Babylon to the south and the Kingdom of Mitanni (Hanigalbat) to the west grew weaker. Adad-nirari I (1305–1274 B.C.E.) succeeded in pushing the border with Babylon back to the Diyala River and eliminating Mitanni entirely, making Assyria a neighbor of the Hittites, and these conquests were consolidated by the kings who followed him.[7] Egypt, on the other hand, had extended its control north into Palestine throughout Dynasty XVIII (1552–1295 B.C.E.), bringing the Egyptians into relationship with the Hittites as well, and the battle between Ramesses II (1279–1212 B.C.E.) and Muwatallis at Qadesh in the pharaoh's fifth year established the boundary between the two.[8] Although the Egyptian empire waned in the mid-eleventh century B.C.E., there was merely a hiatus in expansion efforts in Assyria during the next century. The new millennium saw efforts to reestablish control over the territorial extent of Assyria established during the Middle Assyrian period and to extend the empire beyond this, continuing until the fall of Nineveh in 610.[9] The changing political and

---

5. J. Van Seters, *In Search of History: Historiography in the Ancient World and the Origins of Biblical History* (repr.: Winona Lake, IN: Eisenbrauns, 1997) 141–45; R. J. Leprohon, "Royal Ideology and State Administration in Pharaonic Egypt," *CANE* 1.273–74.

6. The itinerary genre seems to be used in two inscriptions from a much earlier period of imperial expansion: E2.1.4.2 from the reign of Naram-Sin (2254–2218 B.C.E.), commemorating his defeat of a coalition of Sumerian cities, and E.2.13.6.4 from the reign of Utu-hegal (2019–2013 B.C.E.), commemorating his defeat of Tirigan, king of the Guteans. For text, see D. R. Frayne, *Sargonic and Gutian Periods* (RIME 2; Toronto: University of Toronto Press, 1993). These will not be considered here.

7. For historical background of this period, see Kuhrt, *Ancient Near East*, 1.348–62. Dates of reign for Assyrian kings follow the dates given in M. Roaf, *Cultural Atlas of Mesopotamia and the Ancient Near East* (New York: Facts on File, 1990).

8. N. Grimal, *A History of Ancient Egypt* (trans. I. Shaw; Oxford: Blackwell, 1992) 250–58. For a recent, thorough study of Egyptian imperialism, see S. T. Smith, "State and Empire in the Middle and New Kingdoms," in *Anthropology and Egyptology: A Developing Dialogue* (ed. J. Lustig; Monographs in Mediterranean Archaeology 8; Sheffield: Sheffield Academic Press, 1997) 66–89; D. Warburton, *Egypt and the Near East: Politics in the Bronze Age* (Civilisations du Proche-Orient 4; Paris: Recherches et publications, 2001).

9. Kuhrt, *Ancient Near East*, 2.473–546. For the ninth-century focus on reestablishing traditional borders, see M. Liverani, "Assyria in the Ninth Century: Continuity

economic circumstances that accompanied imperialism motivated scribes in both cultures to give expression to a new image of the king as one who maintains order over chaos in the role of *conqueror* as well as the role of builder and maintainer of the cult. [10]

The image of the king as conqueror was not merely a religious ideal. It was also used to serve imperial interests. These texts no longer simply commemorated royal activities but conveyed a message designed to prompt cooperation with imperial interests, particularly the movement of material wealth into the Assyrian heartland. [11] Mario Liverani notes how Assyrian military inscriptions depict the territorial center as stable and the periphery as chaotic but potentially stable, "a failed cosmos, or one not yet realized but which could eventually be realized." [12] The realization of such an ordered cosmos (that is, empire) is depicted as the sole achievement of the king who alone, by his virtue, skill, and prowess is able to overcome binaries of space, time, people, and resources. The king carves out roads where none exist and goes places where no previous

---

or Change?" in *From the Upper Sea to the Lower Sea: Studies on the History of Assyria and Babylon in Honour of A. K. Grayson* (ed. G. Frame and L. Wilding; Leiden: Nederlands Instituut voor he Nabije Oosten, 2004) 213–26; K. L. Younger, "Neo-Assyrian and Israelite History in the Ninth Century: The Role of Shalmaneser III," in *Understanding the History of Israel* (ed. H. G. M. Williamson; Proceedings of the British Academy 143; Oxford: Oxford University Press, 2007) 243–46. For recent discussion of Assyrian imperialism in general, see B. J. Parker, *The Mechanics of Empire: The Northern Frontier of Assyria as a Case Study in Imperial Dynamics* (Helsinki: Neo-Assyrian Text Corpus Project, 2001) 249–71.

10. M. Liverani, "The Ideology of the Assyrian Empire," in *Power and Propaganda: A Symposium on Ancient Empires* (ed. M. T. Larsen; Mesopotamia 7; Copenhagen: Akademisk, 1979) 303–4. See also A. J. Spalinger, who points out that stelas relating military victories do not appear in Egypt prior to the New Kingdom (*Aspects of the Military Documents of the Ancient Egyptians* [YNER 9; New Haven, CT: Yale University Press, 1982] 121). J. Assmann makes this change in role explicit for Egyptian royal ideology, as he discusses the change in imagery from the king's "smiting the enemy" as expressing a cyclical view to the king in his chariot heading for battle as expressing a linear view of historical events as unique (*The Mind of Egypt: History and Meaning in the Time of the Pharaohs* [trans. A. Jenkins; New York: Metropolitan, 2002] 247–50). On the duty of the Assyrian king to expand the borders of Assyrian territory, see H. Tadmor, "World Dominion: The Expanding Horizon of the Assyrian Empire," in *Landscapes: Territories, Frontiers, and Horizons in the Ancient Near East. Papers Presented at the XLIV Rencontre Assyriologique Internationale, Venezia, 7–11 July 1997* (3 vols.; History of the Ancient Near East Monograph 3; Padua: Sargon srl, 1999–2000) 1.55–62.

11. See discussion of these practical ends in Liverani, "Ideology of the Assyrian Empire," 298; K. L. Younger, *Ancient Conquest Accounts: A Study in Ancient Near Eastern and Biblical History Writing* (JSOTSup 98; Sheffield: JSOT Press, 1990) 64.

12. Liverani, "Ideology of the Assyrian Empire," 306.

king has gone. He either assimilates or destroys enemy peoples and brings raw materials from the periphery to the center, where they are transformed into purposeful and useful objects.[13] The king is depicted as one who mercilessly acquires land and resources, particularly wealth, whether from voluntarily paid tribute or spoils collected at a violent price. The degree to which he is depicted as violent served both to reassure those at home—and perhaps himself—of his power and to illustrate to foreigners the price of resistance.[14]

As the purpose and message of commemorative inscriptions changed, so did the audience and the mode of delivery. Inscriptions that convey the role of the Assyrian king as conqueror were no longer aimed only at the gods and posterity but were inscribed all over the inside walls and floors of temples and palaces, conveying the king's role to others.[15] The impact of these texts is unavoidable. Ashurnasirpal II's (883–859 B.C.E.) annals, for example, were carved into stone slabs not only lining the walls of the palace and the Ninurta Temple but also on the thresholds where a visitor would walk directly over them.[16] Because they were on the inside of temples, only a limited segment of the population had access to these texts, but visitors would have included royal officials and courtiers as well as visiting dignitaries.[17] Even if members of this audience could not read the inscriptions, text carved on monumental reliefs on the side

---

13. Ibid., 306–13.

14. B. N. Porter, *Images, Power, and Politics: Figurative Aspects of Esarhaddon's Babylonian Policy* (Philadelphia: American Philosophical Society, 1993) 1. The king's concern for the security of his reign because of both outside enemies and the potential for internal disloyalty is implied in some prophetic texts, such as those from Esarhaddon's reign; see S. Parpola, *Assyrian Prophecies* (SAA 9; Helsinki: Helsinki University Press, 1997) 4–19.

15. For a concise summary of these functions and recognition of their role in serving state interests, see H. Tadmor, "Propaganda, Literature, Historiography: Cracking the Code of the Assyrian Royal Inscriptions," in *Assyria 1995: Proceedings of the 10th Anniversary Symposium of the Neo-Assyrian Text Corpus Project, Helsinki, September 7–11, 1995* (ed. S. Parpola and R. M. Whiting; Helsinki: Neo-Assyrian Text Corpus Project, 1997) 330–34.

16. See discussion in J. M. Russell, *The Writing on the Wall: Studies in the Architectural Context of Late Assyrian Palace Reliefs* (Mesopotamian Civilizations 9; Winona Lake, IN: Eisenbrauns, 1999) 50.

17. A. L. Oppenheim, *Ancient Mesopotamia: Portrait of a Dead Civilization* (rev. ed.; Chicago: University of Chicago Press, 1977) 148–49; idem, "Neo-Assyrian and Neo-Babylonian Empires," in *Propaganda and Communication in World History*, vol. 1: *The Symbolic Instrument in Early Times* (ed. H. D. Lasswell, D. Lerner, and H. Speier; Honolulu: University Press of Hawaii, 1979) 111–44. Self-indoctrination on the part of the scribes who composed them is also a possibility; see Liverani, "Ideology of the Assyrian Empire," 302.

of a temple, the threshold of a building, or the walls of a throne room also communicated meaning visually: writing meant mastery of technology, and mastery of technology meant power. Moreover, the texts were often combined with reliefs depicting the campaigns narrated in the texts. The combination of writing and reliefs had an iconic function as well as a communicative one. Both text and image became "visual icons of kingship."[18]

Egyptian military narratives probably also served as imperial propaganda. The Egyptian king's responsibilities as son of Amun were likewise to maintain order by protecting Egypt. Foreign peoples, especially those not aligned with Egypt's interests or in outright confrontation, were construed as inferior, "vile," and chaotic, and their rebellious actions were understood to disrupt cosmic order. The king carried out his responsibility to bring order in this context through military campaigns, success in which was construed as a gift from Amun or even as being carried out by Amun himself.[19] It has been argued that Egyptian inscriptions are more theological than political in nature, concerned more to establish the legitimacy of the king than to motivate actions that support Egypt's territorial and economic imperial ambitions or to create fear-driven obedience on the part of Egyptians or foreigners.[20] Military narratives were displayed as votive offerings to the god in celebration and thanks.[21]

---

18. Russell, *Writing on the Wall*, 230. On the iconic function of text, see S. Niditch, *Oral World and Written Word: Ancient Israelite Literature* (Library of Ancient Israel; Louisville: Westminster John Knox, 1996) 58. On the reliefs and how they communicate ideology, see I. J. Winter, "The Program of the Throneroom of Assurnasirpal II," in *Essays on Near Eastern Art and Archaeology in Honor of Charles Kyrle Wilkinson* (ed. P. O. Harper and H. Pittman; New York: Metropolitan Museum of Art, 1983) 15–32. Russell suggests that the reliefs and texts do not so much correspond as complement one another, although he concurs that the reliefs serve to increase the accessibility of the ideology communicated by the texts (*Writing on the Wall*, 41). See also Younger, *Ancient Conquest Accounts*, 67.

19. B. J. Kemp, "Imperialism and Empire in New Kingdom Egypt," in *Imperialism in the Ancient World* (Cambridge Classical Studies 33; ed. P. D. A. Garnsey and C. R. Whittaker; Cambridge: Cambridge University Press, 1978) 8–11; Younger, *Ancient Conquest Accounts*, 176–79, 183–84; Spalinger, *Aspects of the Military Documents*, 240; and Leprohon, "Royal Ideology," 273–74.

20. C. J. Eyre, "Is Egyptian historical literature 'historical' or 'literary'?" in *Ancient Egyptian Literature: History and Forms* (ed. A. Loprieno; Probleme der Ägyptologie 10; Leiden: Brill, 1996) 419; S. G. Quirke, "Narrative literature," in *Ancient Egyptian Literature: History and Forms* (ed. A. Loprieno; Probleme der Ägyptologie 10; Leiden: Brill, 1996) 265; and A. R. Schulman, "The Great Historical Inscription of Merneptah at Karnak: A Partial Reappraisal," *JARCE* 24 (1987) 22.

21. Kemp, "Imperialism and Empire," 8–9, 18–19; Spalinger, *Aspects of the Military Documents*, 238. For a detailed argument that the Kadesh reliefs of Ramesses II are

Sety I (1294–1279 B.C.E.), however, commemorated his military activities not in narrative, as did the Dynasty XVIII kings, but in pictorial relief on the *external* walls of temples at Thebes. Ramesses II continued this trend but combined the reliefs with narrative.[22] This shift to a public context and a combination of text with iconography, the message of which could be read even by the illiterate may have constituted an "attempt to influence the general public to support the governing institution and its programs."[23]

Creating this image of the king as conqueror required some ingenuity on the part of ancient scribes because neither the Egyptians nor the Assyrians had a genre in their repertoire that typically involved extended military narrative. In order to give voice to this royal image, scribes in both cultures adapted traditional commemorative forms that were already part of their repertoire by drawing on other forms of repertoire for the content, among them daybooks and itineraries written as administrative reports of the military campaigns. Scribes used these sorts of record both as sources of data and as the formal basis for their narratives. In some cases, the source document was simply copied into the text.

When a scribe used a source in this way, he had to combine two genres: that of the source document and that of the broader narrative. This required technical skill because, in terms of genre, a narrative and an itinerary are like oil and vinegar. An itinerary is close to being a list of place-names. As we saw in the previous chapter, if it has verbs at all, they are repetitive, they hardly constitute a fleshed-out story, and they are written in third person, which contrasts with the first-person character of many ancient Near Eastern royal inscriptions. A scribe may just throw the two together, in which case they sit one on top of another, clearly discernible, but make for a rather jarring narrative. But a scribe can also emulsify them, changing the properties of each in order to write a stable and palatable narrative. In this chapter, we will learn something of the techniques used by these scribes to accommodate an itinerary to a narrative context. We will be able to discern clearly that a source document was used only when we find characteristics of it that *do not* fit the narrative context that were either deliberately or mistakenly left in the text.

---

also votive in nature, see B. G. Ockinga, "On the Interpretation of the Kadesh Record," *Chronique d'Égypte* 62 (1987) 38–48.

22. Van Seters, *In Search of History*, 153.

23. Ibid., 172. On public display, see also D. B. Redford, *Egypt, Canaan, and Israel in Ancient Times* (Princeton: Princeton University Press, 1992) 142; idem, "Historical Sources: Textual Evidence," *OEAE* 2.104–8.

Using sources in this way requires creativity as well as technical skill. Even an administrative document copied wholesale into a new narrative context no longer functions as—or *merely* as—a report. It is ideally made to serve literary and ideological goals as well. Scribes did not just adapt sources in technical ways; they also made choices about which details to include and which to omit as well as choices about how to cast these details in the narrative by combining them with other elements. They even experimented with how features of the itinerary genre might be used to shape the military narrative. For example, a scribe might choose to capitalize on the implication of verisimilitude in order to make his account appear authoritative, whether or not it might be accurate. He might also use the linear and goal-oriented characteristic of itineraries to help him depict a king who moved swiftly to the site of battle. The author need not even use a *source document* at all in order to achieve these effects; all he needs are enough formal features of the itinerary *genre* to invoke the reader's cognitive model.

The innovations that resulted from experiments of this sort played a role in the creation of new genres. As we discuss how the Assyrian and Egyptian scribes used itineraries and other source documents, we will see Hans Robert Jauss's "process of founding and altering of horizons" at work.[24] As they experimented with ways that the itinerary genre might be used to shape a new type of narrative, they not only stretched and sometimes broke the conventions of the itinerary genre as it was used in administrative contexts, but they also established conventions for new genres. Egyptian scribes produced one of the standard forms for military narrative in the New Kingdom: the *nḫtw* genre, or narrative of the king's military victories based on a daybook.[25] Such experimentation also played an important role in shaping the annals genre in Assyria, particularly in examples from the reigns of Adad-nirari II (911–891 B.C.E.) to Shalmaneser III (858–824 B.C.E.), and it is with the annals that we will begin.

Neo-Assyrian Annals

The annals, so characteristic of Neo-Assyrian royal literature, are without precedent in the classical Babylonian corpus upon which most Assyrian literature depends. The annals genre was thought to have developed quickly under the influence of Hittite literature, but this idea has generally been rejected for

---

24. H. R. Jauss, *Toward an Aesthetic of Reception* (Theory and History of Literature 2; Minneapolis: University of Minnesota Press, 1982) 88.

25. Spalinger, *Aspects of the Military Documents*, 34–47; see also p. ix on experimentation.

lack of clear positive evidence for influence.[26] Although he does not rule out the possibility of some Hittite influence, Hannes D. Galter has instead argued that the annals genre is a native Assyrian development, the culmination of a slow series of innovations in royal inscriptions from the Middle Assyrian period onward.[27] In order to understand how the use of itineraries in the tenth and ninth centuries fits into this series of innovations, we must first understand how the annals genre itself developed out of a typical Middle Assyrian genre, the commemorative building inscription.

Commemorative building inscriptions are prevalent in both Babylonia and Assyria in various periods. These texts typically include royal epithets, a building account, a statement that the king deposited his clay cone or monumental inscription, and a concluding formula with blessings and curses, including a warning to a future king.[28] Figure 2 (p. 92) offers an example of a commemorative building inscription from the reign of Ashur-uballit (1363–1328 B.C.E.) and illustrates the genre in its Assyrian form. The epithets consist of the king's political/religious titles and genealogy. Use of the ENSI title (*iššak* ᵈ*Aššur* 'vice-regent') and genealogy is unique to Assyrian versions.[29] The main content of the inscription is a narrative of a building project in which the king is depicted as caretaker of the city. Here Ashur-uballit commemorates his reconstruction of a building that had become run down. The building was probably built by Puzur-Ashur, the ancestor to whom Ashur-uballit is traced in the

---

26. For acceptance of this idea, see H. Güterbock, "Die historische Tradition und ihre literarische Gestaltung bei Babyloniern und Hethitern bis 1200, Zweiter Teil: Hethiter," *ZA* 44 (1938) 98. For its rejection, see H. Tadmor, "Observations on Assyrian Historiography," in *Essays on the Ancient Near East in Memory of Jacob Joel Finkelstein* (ed. M. Ellis; Memoirs of the Connecticut Academy of Arts and Sciences 19; Hamden, CT: Archon, 1977) 209 n. 2; A. K. Grayson, "Assyria and Babylonia," *Or* 49 (1980) 163; idem, "Assyrian Royal Inscriptions: Literary Characteristics," in *Assyrian Royal Inscriptions: New Horizons in Literary, Ideological, and Historical Analysis* (Orientis Antiqui Collectio 17; ed. F. M. Fales; Rome: Istituto per l'Oriente, 1981) 41.

27. H. D. Galter, "Assyrische Königsinschriften des 2. Jahrtausends v. Chr.: Die Entwicklung einer Textgattung," in *Assyrien im Wandel der Zeiten: XXXIXᵉ Rencontre Assyriologique Internationale, Heidelberg, 6.–10. Juli 1992* (ed. H. Waetzoldt and H. Hauptmann; Heidelberger Studien zum Alten Orient 6; Heidelberg: Heidelberg Orientverlag, 1997) 53–59. For the view that the annals genre developed out of commemorative building inscriptions, see also A. Kuhrt, "Israelite and Near Eastern Historiography," in *Congress Volume, Oslo 1998* (ed. A. Lemaire and M. Saebø; VTSup 80; Leiden: Brill, 2000) 262.

28. Grayson, "Assyria and Babylonia," 153.

29. See comments in A. K. Grayson, *Assyrian Royal Inscriptions*, vol. 1: *From the Beginning to Ashur-resha-ishi I* (RANE; Wiesbaden: Harrassowitz, 1972) 80.

[epithets] Ashur-uballit, vice-regent of the god Ashur, son of Eriba-Adad; Eriba-Adad, vice-regent of the god Ashur, son of Ashur-bel-nisheshu; Ashur-bel-nisheshu, vice-regent of the god Ashur, son of Ashur-nirari; Ashur-nirari, vice-regent of the god Ashur, son of Ashur-rabi; Ashur-rabi, vice-regent of the god Ashur, son of Enlil-nasir; Enlil-nasir, vice-regent of the god Ashur, son of Puzur-Ashur, vice-regent of the god Ashur:

[building account] Ashur-uballit, appointee of Enlil, vice-regent of Ashur, [for his life] and the well-being of his city [...] of New City [which previously] had been built outside but now was situated within the city that Puzur-Ashur, my forefather, the prince, had previously built—(that building) had become dilapidated. I rebuilt (it) from foundation to parapet.

[statement of deposit] And I deposited my clay cone.

[concluding formula] As for a later prince, when that building becomes dilapidated and he rebuilds (it), Ashur, Adad, and Bel-sharri will listen to his prayer. May he restore my clay cone to its place. Month of Muhur-ilani, eponymy of Enlil-mudammiq.

Fig. 2. Building Inscription from the Reign of Ashur-uballit (A.0.73.1).

epithet section. While other royal activities relating to law and the economy are commemorated on occasion, most of these inscriptions focus on building projects. (For acts of justice and legal activities, see A.0.33.1; for economic activities, see A.0.33.2 and A.0.39.1.)

Beginning with the reign of Adad-nirari I (1305–1274 B.C.E.), scribes experimented with various ways to depict the king as conqueror in the context of the commemorative building inscription genre, which did not provide a precedent for doing so.[30] Reference to the king's military achievements is nothing

---

30. Idem, "Assyria and Babylonia," 154–55. Simple statements of the king's military achievements appear in Mesopotamian royal inscriptions as early as the reign of Sargon of Akkad in the third millennium B.C.E. See inscriptions from the reigns of Sargon (E2.1.1.1–3, 7, 11), Rimush (E2.1.2.1–8), Manishtushu (E2.1.3.1), Naram-Sin (E2.1.4.2, 6, 9–10, 13, 23–24, 29–31), Rim-Sin I (E4.2.14.9–10), (E4.3.6.4), Samsu-iluna (E4.3.7.3, 7), and Iahdun-Lim (E4.6.8.1–2). These texts can be found in Frayne, *Sargonic and Gutian Periods*; and idem, *Old Babylonian Period (2003–1595 BC)* (RIME 4; Toronto: University of Toronto Press, 1990). More extensive military narrative, characteristic of the Assyrian annals, is first included in Assyrian royal inscriptions during the reign of Shamshi-Adad I, although the few texts that contain this sort of narrative are broken, and their genre is

new in commemorative building inscriptions. But scribes during the Middle Assyrian period strove to commemorate *this role in particular* either by modifying the typical epithet section or by incorporating episodic military narrative. In some cases, such as the following text from the reign of Adad-nirari I, they retained the traditional Assyrian epithet section with its focus on genealogy but also created epithets such as *murappiš miṣrī u kudurrī* 'extender of borders and boundaries' that express his military role.

> *mār Arik-dīn-ili šakni ᵈEnlil iššiak ᵈAššur kāšid* ᵏᵘʳ*Turukki u* ᵏᵘʳ*Nigimḫi adi pāṭ gimrišu gimir malkī šadî u ḫuršāni pāṭ Quti rapalti kāšid* ᵏᵘʳ*Kutmuḫi u nagab rēṣišu gunnu Aḫlamî Sutî Iūrî u mātātišunu murappiš miṣrī u kudurrī*

> Son of Arik-din-ili, appointee of Enlil, vice-regent of Ashur, conqueror of Turukku and Nigimhu to its entire extent (and) all the rulers of the mountains and hills of the broad district of Qutu, conqueror of Katmuhu and all its help (as well as) the hoardes of Ahlamu, Sutu, (and) Iuru along with their lands, extender of borders and boundaries. (A.0.76.1 lines 18–24)

The epithet *murappiš miṣrī u kudurrī* 'extender of borders and boundaries' appears four times in this inscription, each time at or near the end of a section like the one cited here (A.0.76.1 lines 15, 24, 27, and 32). In each case, as here, the epithet is fleshed out with a litany of place-names that articulate the extent of territory that the king brought within Assyrian purview. The king is thus celebrated for his territorial achievements in addition to his construction activities.

In other cases, the scribes eliminated political/religious titles altogether in the epithet section in favor of military titles. Another of Adad-nirari I's building inscriptions, shown in fig. 3 (p. 94), commemorates the construction of a palace in the city of Taidu. The epithet section includes the title *šar kiššati* 'king of the universe'. This is not a new epithet, because it was adopted by Sargon of Akkad, probably when he defeated the city of Kish (E2.1.1.1) and was also used by Shamshi-Adad I (A.0.39.1–2, 8, 12). Here it is fleshed out not with place-names but with a full narrative about Adad-nirari I's victory over Mitanni, highlighting his valor and divine support rather than the extent of territory that he conquered. This narrative was used in a number of this king's building inscriptions, so this battle must have been regarded as a singular achievement, worthy of commemorating in a number of contexts.[31] Both the narrative and the title *šar kiššati* 'king of the universe', which is not used before the Middle

---

unclear; see A.0.39.1001 and A.0.75.8. See Galter, "Assyrische Königsinschriften," 57–58 for further discussion.

31. See Grayson, RIMA 1.135.

[epithet] Adad-nirari, king of the universe, strong king, mighty king, king of Assyria; son of Arik-din-ili, king of Assyria; son of Enlil-nerari, king of Assyria:

[military narrative] When Shattuara, king of the land Hanigalbat, rebelled against me and committed hostilities, by the command of Ashur, my lord and ally, and of the great gods who rule in my favor, I seized him and brought him to my city, Ashur. I made him take an oath and sent him back to his land. On an annual basis as long as he lived, I regularly received his audience-gift in my city, Ashur. After him, his son Uasashtatta revolted and rebelled against me. He committed hostilities. He went to the land of Hatti for aid. The Hittites took his bribes but did not render him assistance. With the strong weapons of the god Ashur, my lord, with the support of Anu, Enlil, and Ea, Sin, Shamash, Adad, Ishtar, and Nergal, most powerful among the gods, the terrifying gods, my lords, I captured and conquered Taidu, his great royal city, Amasaku, Kahat, Shuru, Nabula, Hurra, Shuduhu, and Wasshukanu. I took the possessions of those cities, the accumulated (wealth) of his fathers, the treasure of his palace, and brought (it) to my city, Ashur. I conquered, burned, (and) destroyed Irridu and sowed salt over it. The great gods allowed me to rule from Taidu to Irridu, Eluhat and Mt. Kashiiari in its entirety, the fortress of Sudu, the fortress of Harranu, to the bank of the Euphrates. As for the remainder of his people, I imposed upon (them) hoe, spade, and basket. But as for him, I took out from the city Irridu his "wife of the palace," his sons, his daughters, and his people. I brought them bound along with his possessions to my city, Ashur. I conquered, burned, (and) destroyed the city Irridu and the cities within the district of Irridu and sowed salt over them.

[building account] At that time the [...] of Taidu was old, and I improved it[s] dilapidation. I restored it to its place. I built (it) from its foundation to its parapet, and I deposited my steles.

[concluding formula] At a later time, when [that building has become ol]d and worn out, may a future prince [repair its] dilapidation. May he restore my inscri[bed] name to its place. (Then) [Ashur] will hear his prayers. (As for) the one [who alters] my inscription or [my] name, may [As]hur, my lord, overthrow his reign. May [Ish]tar, my mistress, bring [about] the defeat of [his land]. May he not stand befo[re his enemy]. [May] Adad [strike] h[is] land [with] terrible [lightning. May he inflict] his land with fa[mine.]

Fig. 3. Building Inscription from the Reign of Adad-nirari I (A.0.76.3–4).

Assyrian and Middle Babylonian periods, constitute a new type of content for commemorative inscriptions.[32]

Creating military epithets involved simply making a change to an already-existing feature of the commemorative building inscription genre. Since commemorative inscriptions prior to the reign of Adad-nirari I do not typically contain extensive military narrative, however, there was probably no precedent for fitting it into the typical presentation of epithets, building account, statement of deposit, and concluding formula illustrated in fig. 2. Scribes were thus confronted with the problem of where and how to integrate it. In every instance where the Mitanni narrative was used in Adad-nirari I's building inscriptions, the scribes simply placed it between the epithet section and the building account, as it appears in fig. 3. Shalmaneser I's (1273–1244 B.C.E.) scribes experimented with inserting the military narrative into the epithets using the word *enūma* 'when' or the clause *ina ūmešuma* 'at that time'. This technique made for a rather awkward text because the inclusion of an entire narrative episode within a list of epithets complicated the syntax.[33] Tukulti-Ninurta I's (1243–1207 B.C.E.) scribes tried both methods.[34] The fact that we no longer find military narrative included among the epithets in inscriptions after the reign of Tukulti-Ninurta I suggests that the practice of including it *after* the epithets was judged more effective and became the norm. Here we see the Assyrian scribes altering the horizons of the commemorative inscription genre by including new content and experimenting with how it should be included formally. The fact that evidence for experimentation ceases suggests that a new norm was established, a new horizon founded, and commemorative building inscriptions simply continued to be written in this new way.

While the inclusion of a single military narrative was a development within the commemorative building inscription genre, further developments pushed the limits of this genre, giving rise to a new genre: annals. Initially, scribes commemorated only one military event in a single episode, just as one building project was the focus of the building inscription. During the reigns of Shalmaneser I and Tukulti-Ninurta I, however, they begin to juxtapose *multiple* episodes. Just as the inclusion of military narrative was a response to new

---

32. Galter, "Assyrische Königsinschriften," 57. For use of the title, see M. Seux, *Épithètes Royales Akkadiennes et Sumériennes* (Paris: Letouzey et Ané, 1967) 308–12.

33. Grayson, RIMA 1.180. See discussion in Galter, "Assyrische Königsinschriften," 58.

34. Grayson, RIMA 1.231. See A.0.78.2 for an example of narrative included in the epithets, where the awkwardness of this method is readily apparent. A.0.78.23–24 are good examples of reversion to the method of including the narrative after the epithets.

importance placed on the role of the king as conqueror, the inclusion of multiple episodes may have been encouraged by the emergence of a new medium
for writing. Galter suggests that the eight-sided prism, used for the first time
during the reign of Tiglath-pileser I (1114–1076 B.C.E.), enabled scribes to include even lengthier narrative of even more campaigns.[35] These prism inscriptions are the first full-fledged examples of the annals genre. Annals are still
essentially commemorative inscriptions; they retain a connection to the commemorative building inscription genre from which they developed, because
they begin with royal epithets and often end with a building inscription. But
they no longer simply celebrate an exemplary deed. Annals offer a rudimentary narrative of the king's military exploits, characterized by episodes relating
battles and royal hunts, written in the first-person voice of the king, and arranged chronologically.[36]

When multiple episodes were first included, they had no connection to
one another or any explicit mode of organization. This lack may have confronted scribes with the problem of framing these episodes so that their spatial
and temporal organization would be explicit. How could they make the yearly
chronological structure clear? How might they create a spatial and temporal
connection between the episodes? Scribes experimented with potential solutions to both challenges by turning to resources offered by other genres in the
Assyrian repertoire—namely, the chronicle and the itinerary. Thus the shape
of the annals genre as it emerged in the early first millennium was the result of
blending formal elements from different genres.

Scribes ultimately addressed the first challenge—that of explicit chronological structure—by dating each campaign. For example, the campaign of
Tukulti-Ninurta II (890–884 B.C.E.) to Babylon and then north along the Habur
River, which I will discuss in detail below, is dated *ina* ^ITI*Nisânu ina* UD.26.KAM
ina līme ^m*Na'idi-ili* 'In the month of Nisan, on the 26th day, in the eponymy of
Na'idi-ili' (A.0.100.5 line 41). The Assyrians used a system of eponym dates in
which each year was named after the individual occupying the office of *limmu*
for that year. Before settling on eponym date formulas to mark each campaign,

_____

35. Galter, "Assyrische Königsinschriften," 58. These texts are edited together as
A.0.87.1. See Grayson, RIMA 2.77 for discussion of the various exemplars.

36. This definition of Neo-Assyrian annals, as distinct from other types of commemorative text, was articulated in essence by A. T. Olmstead (*Assyrian Historiography: A Source Study* [University of Missouri Social Science Series 3; Columbia, MO:
Univesity of Missouri, 1916] 3–6) and has been reiterated consistently in subsequent
studies on the royal inscriptions: Tadmor, "Observations on Assyrian Historiography,"
209; Grayson, "Assyria and Babylonia," 150–53; idem, "Assyrian Royal Inscriptions: Literary Characteristics," 37; idem, RIMA 2.7; M. Van de Mieroop, *Cuneiform Texts and
the Writing of History* (Approaching the Ancient World; London: Routledge, 1999) 41.

however, scribes experimented with various solutions for marking the chronological structure of the narrative. They first tried to use resources available to them within the commemorative building inscription genre itself. The five episodes included in Tiglath-pileser I's annals are simply juxtaposed with one another, with little or no logical connection drawn between them.[37] But the scribes did distinguish between one yearly episode and the next in two ways. First, they separated one from another visually by a ruled line on the prism. Second, they began each new episode with a very short epithet section so that the account of each new year's events would be introduced as though it were a new commemorative inscription (A.0.87.1 ii 85–88; iii 32–34; iv 40–42; and v 42–43).[38] But, while these features marked the structure, they still did not make its chronological nature explicit. We know that each episode relates activity from one regnal year only from the summary statement of Tiglath-pileser I's conquests at the end of the inscription, which indicates that the events took place *ištu rīš šarrūtiya adi 5 palîya* 'from my accession year to my fifth regnal year', each year corresponding to one of the five episodes (A.0.87.1 vi 44–45).

Date formulas offer the obvious solution for creating explicit chronological structure. From what background context did scribes draw these date formulas? Graham I. Davies suggests that they came from itineraries. He notes that each of the campaigns along the Habur River in the annals of Adad-nirari II, Tukulti-Ninurta II, and Ashurnasirpal II begins with a date header and compares it with the date header in administrative documents such as the Old Babylonian itineraries (YBC 4499).[39] But date formulas such as those that came to be used in the annals are found in a variety of contexts. They occur at the end of commemorative building inscriptions and are used to date archival documents, as in the itinerary from Dur-Katlimmu. In none of these contexts, however, are the date formulas used to mark a linear chronological progression. Although date formulas are used to summarize the length of the journey in the Old Babylonian itineraries, they are not typically used in itineraries to indicate progression along the journey, which is marked by use of the verb *biātu* 'to camp', as in the Dur-Katlimmu itinerary, or cardinal numerals such as UD.4.KAM, as in the Old Babylonian itineraries. We find date formulas used

---

37. The absence of causal links in Neo-Assyrian annals in general has been noted by Van de Mieroop, *Cuneiform Texts*, 82.

38. Further brief epithet sections (A.0.87.1 vi 55–57 and vii 36–59) set the hunting episode that follows the campaign narrative apart from the building inscription. These epithet sections, as well as multiple sections within each campaign episode, are also set off from one another with ruled lines on the prism.

39. G. I. Davies, "The Wilderness Itineraries: A Comparative Study," *TynBul* 25 (1974) 57.

to indicate linear chronology in *chronicles*, or compositions that relate a fairly lengthy sequence of reigns, noting a memorable event in each reign.[40]

The Broken Obelisk, from the reign of Ashur-bel-kala (1073–1056 B.C.E.), indicates that the chronicle genre is where at least one scribe turned for explicit chronological structure. This annal is the first in which date formulas including month, day, and eponym year mark each episode. Each new year is indicated with a full date formula, such as *ina* [iti]*Iyyar līme* [md]*Aššur-rêm-nišēšu* 'in the month Iyyar, eponymy of Ashur-rem-nisheshu', and each campaign episode within a given year is further marked off with *ina šattimma šiāti* 'in that same year' and the particular month (A.0.89.7 iii 3; see iii 2 for an example of *ina šattimma šiāti*). Although this inscription's building account is in the first person (A.0.89.7 v 1–37), the military narrative is in the *third* person, not the first-person voice of the king that is characteristic of the annals genre. The third-person narrative and date-by-date structure are features of the chronicle genre, and Haim Tadmor and A. Kirk Grayson have suggested that the author of this inscription either incorporated extracts from actual chronicles or used the chronicle genre.[41] Either way, the scribe who wrote the Broken Obelisk employed a chronicle-like style for the military narrative section while retaining the other elements of a typical commemorative building inscription, creating a blend of formal elements from two different genres.

The combination of first-person narrative, which had its origin in the commemorative building inscription genre, and third person narrative from the chronicle genre did not succeed in the long run. The Broken Obelisk stands out in this regard, and later scribes reverted to the first-person narrative typical of annals (e.g., A.0.101.1 i 43–44). Nonetheless, this experiment with genre impacted the typical shape of Neo-Assyrian annals. Although they abandoned third-person narrative, the authors of later annals continued to use date formulas to mark the chronological structure of their texts, and this practice became the norm.[42] The annals of Adad-nirari II, Tukulti-Ninurta II, and Ashurnasirpal II in the late tenth and ninth centuries B.C.E. all regularly use date formulas at the beginning of each campaign. While itinerary notices do not appear until

---

40. J. Glassner, *Mesopotamian Chronicles* (ed. B. R. Foster; SBLWAW 19; Atlanta: Society of Biblical Literature, 2004) 37.

41. H. Tadmor, "History and Ideology in the Assyrian Royal Inscriptions," in *Assyrian Royal Inscriptions: New Horizons in Literary, Ideological, and Historical Analysis* (Orientis Antiqui Collectio 17; ed. F. M. Fales; Rome: Istituto per l'Oriente, 1981) 17–18; Grayson, RIMA 2.99. For definition of the chronicle genre, see idem, "Assyria and Babylonia," 173.

42. Tadmor, "History and Ideology," 19.

the Habur campaigns in the annals of these three kings, date formulas had already become a norm by this time, indicating that the use of date formulas in the annals is a separate development from the use of itineraries.

Just as scribes were concerned with integrating the military narrative as well as possible into the commemorative building inscription genre during the Middle Assyrian period, so also did scribes in the Neo-Assyrian period integrate the date formulas by weaving their elements together with various features of the annals genre. In some cases, tropes otherwise characteristic of annals, such as the divine command to go on campaign, are mixed with elements of the date formula:

> *ina līme* [md]*Šamaš-nūrī ina qibit* [d]*Aššur bêli rabê bēliya ina* [iti]*Iyyar* UD.13. KAM *ištu* [uru]*Kalḫi attumuš*
>
> In the eponymy of Shamash-nuri, by the command of Ashur, the great lord, my lord, on the 13th day of Iyyar, I departed from Calah. (A.0.101.1 iii 92–93)

In other cases (e.g., A.0.101.1 iii 27–28), the date formula occurs not at the beginning but after a narrative relating the provocation for the campaign, usually the king's receiving a letter informing him of a rebellion in the provinces. In still another case (A.0.101.1 ii 49, 51), elements of the date formula are split up, with the eponym at the beginning of the episode, followed by the provocation report, and only then the month and day. While the author of the Broken Obelisk either copied entries from a chronicle or used the genre quite strictly according to its typical use, these scribes used date formulas—now a feature of the annals genre—in quite creative ways. [43]

Galter argued that the inclusion of date formulas by the author of the Broken Obelisk was the last step in the development of Assyrian royal inscriptions containing military narrative. [44] However, we do see a further development. While the chronicle genre offered resources for addressing the problem of explicit chronological structure in the annals, the scribes turned to a different

---

43. The use of date formulas to mark each year seems to have been an ideal, not consistently executed for a variety of reasons. For a sense of the problems, see, J. A. Brinkman, *A Political History of Post-Kassite Babylonia, 1158–722 B.C.* (AnOr 43; Rome: Pontifical Biblical Institute, 1968) 385–86; A. K. Grayson, "Studies in Neo-Assyrian History: The Ninth Century B.C.," *BO* 33 (1976) 138; J. Reade, "Neo-Assyrian Monuments in Their Historical Context," in *Assyrian Royal Inscriptions: New Horizons in Literary, Ideological, and Historical Analysis* (ed. F. M. Fales; Orientis Antiqui Collectio 17; Rome: Istituto per l'Oriente, 1981) 154–55; and E. Badalì et al., "Studies on the Annals of Assurnasirpal II: I. Morphological Analysis," *Vicino Oriente* 5 (1982) 21.

44. Galter, "Assyrische Königsinschriften," 58.

element of cultural repertoire—the itinerary genre—for help in creating spatial and temporal connections between the episodes by indicating movement between them. Just as the author of the Broken Obelisk tried to base an annal on a chronicle, Assyrian scribes in the ninth century tried to base a campaign narrative on an itinerary. Although this approach to writing campaign narrative ultimately fared no better in the long run than the use of chronicles, the scribes experimented in various ways with using the itinerary genre to connect one campaign episode to another, adapting features of the itinerary genre to the literary context of the annals, just as they did with the date formulas, in order to make a more coherent, unified narrative. [45]

Three episodes in annals from the reigns of Adad-nirari II (A.0.99.2 lines 105–19), Tukulti-Ninurta II (A.0.100.5 lines 41–127), and Ashurnasirpal II (A.0.101.1 iii 1–26), all of which relate campaigns along the Habur River, stand out quite radically from the typical battle episode in the annals as it is defined by K. Lawson Younger in his analysis of Neo-Assyrian royal inscriptions, *Ancient Conquest Accounts.* Younger showed that the episodes relating battles in annals, summary inscriptions, and letters to the god are consistently composed using standard content, characteristic vocabulary, and stock stereotypical expressions arranged in a pattern that is repeated with minimal variation in every episode. He demonstrated that these episodes relate not what actually took place on each individual campaign but, rather, the *idea* of what constitutes a campaign. [46] The king is provoked by a rebellion, to which he responds by appealing to the gods for help, gathering his troops, and heading to the site of battle. He overwhelms the enemy and proceeds to attack the city. He pursues the fleeing soldiers, engages them in battle, massacres them, and destroys their land. The enemy always submits in the end, and the king always imposes tribute. In some cases, he installs a governor or erects a statue in the city, but he returns home with the goods in the end, in some cases engaging in a hunt en route. [47] Each battle has the same series of events and always the same outcome: the king gains control over territory and succeeds in bringing material wealth

---

45. In his effort to illustrate his argument that the itinerary notices bring unity to the otherwise diverse collection of materials in the wilderness narrative, Coats appeals to the use of itineraries in Neo-Assyrian annals, which he suggests have the same function (G. W. Coats, "The Wilderness Itinerary," *CBQ* 34 [1972] 147–48). In one sense, the following argument puts flesh on this basic insight, showing how the scribes accomplished it.

46. Younger, *Ancient Conquest Accounts*, 123, an idea adopted from Badalì et al., "Studies on the Annals," 69–70.

47. Younger, *Ancient Conquest Accounts*, 72–79; see Badalì et al., "Studies on the Annals," 18–41.

back to the Assyrian capital. The specific details unique to a given campaign are not relevant to this message and simply get in the way.[48] An example of this stereotypical pattern can be found in Adad-nirari I's battle against Mitanni in fig. 3. The Habur campaigns are heavily laden with itinerary notices and only minimally employ this stereotypical plot and set of expressions.

E. Badalì and a team of Italian scholars tried to account for movement between one site and another in the campaign narratives using Vladimir Propp's formalist method for studying Russian folk tales as their model. According to Badalì's pattern, movement occurs at four points in a campaign: at the very beginning with the date formula, going to the site of battle after divine aid has been sought and the troops gathered, returning to camp after the battle, and returning home at the end of the campaign. Badalì and his team recognized the presence of itinerary notices, noting that they are limited to accompanying the date formula and the return to camp.[49] This may be true in some campaign narratives, but it certainly does not explain the Habur campaigns, which are dominated by movement almost to the exclusion of other plot elements. The Italians expressed discomfort with the way their scheme applies to Ashurnasirpal II's Habur campaign, but even in other campaign narratives that are not so dominated by movement, itinerary notices occur at a variety of points in the campaign, not only at the very beginning or at the return to camp.[50] The formalist model is inadequate to explain the varying use of itinerary notices in the annals because its explanatory power is limited to minor variations from the pattern such as differences in detail, different expressions, or the omission of certain functions. It breaks down in the face of significant differences, such as plot elements occurring out of order or one particular plot element dominating a campaign.

---

48. This is evident from the way the inscriptions deal with failure to achieve territorial control. Regarding Shalmaneser III's campaigns against the Damascus coalition in the 11th and 14th *palûs*, which I have cited in fig. 6 (p. 132), J. K. Kuan, states: "There is no evidence that the Assyrian army did any better against the coalition than on previous occasions" (*Neo-Assyrian Historical Inscriptions and Syria–Palestine: Israelite/Judean-Tyrian-Damascene Political and Commerical Relations in the Ninth–Eighth Centuries B.C.E.* [Jian Dao Dissertation Series 1; Hong Kong: Alliance Bible Seminary, 1995] 9). In fact, there is little evidence about any of the specifics of what the Assyrian army did; what matters is that, in the end, the rebellious army fled. Note that the use of battle elements stops at the flight of the enemy and the scribe does not record a defeat in the typical way. Rather than admit defeat, the scribes may have truncated the pattern to eliminate the elements that would consitute an outright falsehood.

49. Younger, *Ancient Conquest Accounts*, 72–79; see Badalì et al., "Studies on the Annals," 18–41.

50. Ibid., 26.

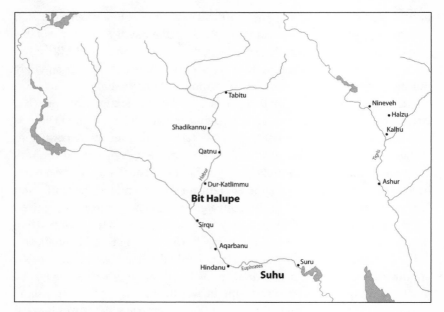

Fig. 4. The Habur Campaigns.

If analysis of typical structural patterns in the annals cannot explain the use of itinerary notices, what can? It is usually assumed that the purpose of these campaigns was different, that they did not involve battle but were "show-of-strength" campaigns, the primary aim of which was tribute collection.[51] This may indeed be the case. Sabrina Favaro suggests that itineraries carry an ideological message of dominance over territory because they convey detailed knowledge, and knowledge is control. Unlike landscape detail, which tends to be used in peripheral regions that are being conquered, itineraries convey mastery over known territory.[52] The early Neo-Assyrian kings would have had an interest in conveying control of the Habur area, since they were focused on regaining and consolidating control over sites such as Tabitu, Shadikannu, Qatnu, and Dur-Katlimmu that had been under direct Assyrian control during the Middle Assyrian period.[53] These sites and others relevant to the Habur

51. Grayson, RIMA 2.145.

52. S. Favaro, *Voyages et voyageurs à l'époque Néo-Assyrienne* (SAAS 18; Helsinki: The Neo Assyrian Text Corpus Project, 2007) 36–38, 101. See also S. Ponchia, "Mountain Routes in Assyrian Royal Inscriptions," *KASKAL* 1 (2004) 162.

53. H. Kühne, "The Assyrians on the Middle Euphrates and the Habur," in *Neo-Assyrian Geography* (ed. M. Liverani; Quaderni di Geografia Storica 5; Padua: Sargon srl, 1995) 72–77; Kuhrt, *Ancient Near East*, 478–81.

itineraries are shown in fig. 4. Consolidation involved regaining control over these very sites, which form the bulk of the Habur itineraries as well as establish a southern frontier against Aramean incursions and Babylonia.

Adad-nirari II's Habur campaign demonstrates his consolidated territory. He begins by bringing Mitanni under control. He then proceeds through the Habur on his way home, hitting Tabitu, Shadikannu, Qatnu, and Dur-Katlimmu, the key sites that had been part of Assyrian territory in the second millennium and are now again, and then skirting the Babylonian frontier with stops at Sirqu and Hindanu on the way home to Ashur.[54] Assurnasirpal II's Habur campaign is prompted by a rebellion at Suru, the main city of Suhu on the Euphrates, and is also an effort to demonstrate control over this region. The Suru rebellion represented a threat from the Babylonians, because it took place on the southern Assyrian frontier and was supported by Kassite troops. Ashurnasirpal II is successful and, at the end of the campaign, erects a statue intent on reminding the Babylonians of their defeat and deterring them from further incursions (A.0.101.1 iii 16–25). The itinerary leading up to the campaign may convey the idea of control that is impervious to the kind of outside threat that loosened Assyrian control in the second millennium.

But, irrespective of the nature of the events themselves, we must still contend with the question why their *literary form* is different, since a scribe could just as well have related even a tribute-collection mission using the stereotypical pattern that Younger defined, depicting it as a pseudo-battle. This sort of accommodation is not unknown.[55] The building account for the provincial city of Tushha in Ashurnasirpal II's Ninurta Temple reliefs (A.0.101.1 ii 2–12), for example, is included not at the end of an inscription, which is typical for the commemorative building inscription genre, but in the middle of a campaign narrative and ends, however awkwardly for a narrative of a *construction project*, with typical battle tropes such as the flight and submission of the enemy and collection of tribute. *Use of a source document* would explain the atypical literary form, and we find evidence for this in Tukulti-Ninurta II's Habur campaign. Like Adad-nirari II's Habur campaign, this inscription also demonstrates consolidation of the empire, because the itinerary through Babylon probably traces the Assyrian frontier.[56] But it is unusual compared with

---

54. Ibid., 482.

55. *Accommodation* is a technical linguistic term that refers to the "presentation of new information in a backgrounded way" so that, even though it is new, its "presence in the text world is presented as an unremarkable fact," and we read the new information as though it naturally belongs there (P. Werth, *Text Worlds: Representing Conceptual Space in Discourse* [Textual Explorations; New York: Longman, 1999] 280, 56).

56. Kuhrt, *Ancient Near East*, 482–83.

the campaigns of Adad-nirari II and Ashurnasirpal II because it goes south to Babylon first and only then north through the Habur region on the way to a campaign against Piru that is only briefly related. The focus of the campaign narrative is not a lengthy battle episode that precedes or follows the itinerary but the itinerary itself. This unusual route and unusual campaign may have prompted the scribe simply to use the administrative records—an itinerary and tribute list—to compose the narrative.

We can tell that a source document was used in a narrative when we find characteristics of the genre of the source document that do not fit the narrative context. Tukulti-Ninurta II's Habur campaign is characterized by fluctuation between first- and third-person verb forms. The third-person forms are out of place in the characteristically first-person voice of the annals genre, which led Tadmor to understand this fluctuation, in this campaign and elsewhere, to indicate that a third-person source document was used.[57] Grayson is more cautious. In his view, it *may* point to the use of a source, but conflation of sources cannot explain every instance, and in some cases it may be due simply to scribal carelessness.[58] A primary reason for Grayson's caution is the fact that this sort of fluctuation occurs in Assyrian building inscriptions as early as the Old Assyrian period, and these are clearly *not* employing sources like itineraries or tribute lists.[59] Grayson's openness to a variety of possible explanations for this phenomenon is thus well warranted. However, when we are able to find characteristics of an administrative genre that we know from extant documents and when the fluctuation is isolated and patterned rather than random, we can make a case that the scribe is dealing with some type of compositional challenge, such as how to accommodate a source document like an itinerary to the narrative context of the annals.

In order to make a good case that a source was used, then, we need to know the genre well. In some instances of fluctuation between first and third person, it can be difficult to discern whether or not a source was used because we lack knowledge of the genre of the alleged source document. The campaigns

---

57. H. Tadmor, "The Historical Inscriptions of Adad-nirari III," *Iraq* 35 (1973) 141–42; idem, "History and Ideology," 17–18; and idem, "Propaganda, Literature, Historiography," 329.

58. Grayson, "Assyria and Babylonia," 167; and idem, "Assyrian Royal Inscriptions: Literary Characteristics," 42; idem, RIMA 2.170.

59. Idem, "Assyria and Babylonia," 165 n. 126. The examples that he cites begin in third person and shift to first person, as in A.0.32.2, from the reign of Ilu-shumma (early twentieth century B.C.E.). Third person occurs in a statement that Ilu-shumma built the Temple for Ishtar, while first-person forms begin to occur early in the following narrative of its construction.

in Shalmaneser III's 27th–31st *palûs* are led not by the king himself, as is typical for the annals genre, but by the field marshal. Tadmor understands the shift between third and first person to reflect use of a "diary style" report.[60] The episode begins in first person (underline) until the king has commissioned the field marshal, then lapses into third person (**bold**) when the field marshal leads the effort. At the end of the episode, where we get the stereotypical language characteristic of battle episodes, the narrative returns to the first-person voice of the king.

> *ina 27 palêya narkabāti ṣābiya adki* ᵐ*Dayyān-Aššur* ˡᵘ*turtānu rab ṣābī rapši ina pānāt ṣābiya ana* ᵏᵘʳ*Urarṭi uma"er ašpur ana Bīt-*ᵏᵘʳ*Zamāni it-tarad ina nērebi ša* ᵘʳᵘ*Ammaš ērub* ⁱᵈ*Arṣania ēbir* ᵐ*Seduri* ᵏᵘʳ*Urarṭayya išmema ana gipiš ummānišu ma'di ittakilma ana epēš qabli tāḫāzi ana irtiya itbâ ittišu amdaḫḫiṣ dabdîšu aškun pagar qurādīšu ṣēru rapšu umalli*

In my 27th *palu*, I mustered my chariots and troops. I issued orders and sent Dayyan-Ashur, the field marshal, chief of my extensive army, to lead my army to Urartu. **He** went down to Bit-Zamani, **entered** the pass of the city Ammash, and **crossed** the river Arsania. When Seduru, the Urartian, heard, he relied on the might of his numerous army and attacked to wage war and battle. I fought with him. I defeated him. I filled the wide plain with the corpses of his warriors. (A.0.102.14 lines 141–46)[61]

The field marshal's route, according to Tadmor, would have come from a war diary. It is not impossible that war diaries existed, especially since we do have daybooks from Egypt (discussed in chap. 3), which were sometimes used to document military activity. But we have no extant example of a war diary from Mesopotamia that would give us a sense of a genre for war diaries in this culture.[62] So, while we cannot rule out the use of a source here, we cannot confirm it either.

---

60. Tadmor, "Historical Inscriptions," 141–42.

61. Note that the forms *ērub* (written ᴋᴜ₄-*ub*) and *ēbir* in A.0.102.14 line 143 can be 3ms as well as 1cs in Neo-Assyrian (J. Huehnergard, *A Grammar of Akkadian* [HSS 45; Atlanta: Scholars Press, 1997; 2nd ed. Winona Lake, IN: Eisenbrauns, 2005] 603). It is thus possible that these are to be read as 1cs verbs, with the king, not Dayyan-Ashur, as their subject. But then the clearly 3ms form *ittarad* must be seen as an anomaly, perhaps generated by the mention of Dayyan-Ashur. I prefer the explanation offered above because it explains the compositional process well, does so on the basis of extant material, and does not involve appealing to an incompetent scribe. Although there is evidence of scribal incompetence in some places, I prefer to avoid this explanation when others are plausible.

62. The Habur itineraries are often taken as evidence that campaign diaries were kept. This view has been expressed not only by Tadmor ("Historical Inscriptions,"

While we lack extant war diaries that we can use to acquire a cognitive model for this genre in the Assyrian cultural repertoire, we do not lack chronicles or tribute lists. It is thus relatively easy to identify these genres within a broader narrative context. We must keep in mind, however, that a bit of a narrative needs to fit only the cognitive model in order for us to identify the genre; it does not need to match an extant document. No extant chronicle looks exactly like the apparent excerpts in the Broken Obelisk, yet it is clear that the chronicle genre is being used because enough key features are present to invoke our knowledge of the genre. The same applies to the narrative of Adad-nirari III's (810–783 B.C.E.) campaign to Hatti and Amurru narrated on the Rimah Stela. While the campaign narrative is, as customary, related in the first person, the statements of tribute contain third-person verbs.

> ᵏᵘʳ*Amurri* ᵏᵘʳ*Hatte ana sihirtiša ina šēpiya lū ušakniš biltu madattu ana arkiāt ūmē muhhišunu lū ukīn . . . madattu ša* ᵐ*Marî' ša immerišu **imhur** madattu ša* ᵐ*Iu'asu* ᵏᵘʳ*Samerinayya* ᵏᵘʳ*Ṣurayya* ᵏᵘʳ*Ṣidunayya* **imhur**

> I subdued Amurru and Hatti in its entirety. I imposed upon them tax and tribute forever. **He received** . . . (list of goods) the tribute of Mari, the Damascene. **He received** the tribute of Joash, the Samarian, and of the people of Tyre and Sidon. (A.0.104.7 lines 5–9)[63]

Most if not all of our extant tribute lists are simple lists and do not contain verbs.[64] As we saw in the previous chapter, however, some itineraries, such as

---

141–42) but also G. I. Davies, "Wilderness Itineraries: A Comparative Study," 59–60; M. Cogan, "A Plaidoyer on Behalf of the Royal Scribes," in *Ah, Assyria . . . : Studies in Assyrian History and Ancient Near Eastern Historiography Presented to Hayim Tadmor* (ed. M. Cogan and I. Eph'al; ScrHier 33; Jerusalem: Magnes, 1991) 126–27. It is also reflected in J. Reade's view that the Habur campaigns reflect the use of an "undiluted diary" ("Neo-Assyrian Monuments," 154–55). Although Davies does not cite Tadmor, he points to the depiction in reliefs of scribes who appear to be recording the booty taken from a captured city as evidence that records in general were kept while on campaign. On this relief as evidence that records were kept en route and probably used by the authors of the annals, see also Glassner, *Mesopotamian Chronicles*, 14. I am inclined, however, to agree with Grayson that the evidence for such diaries in Mesopotamia is "ambiguous" ("Assyria and Babylonia," 167) and to rely on *extant* text types such as tribute lists and itineraries in my discussion of the use of sources.

63. For specific mention of this text as evidence for use of sources, see Tadmor, "Historical Inscriptions," 141–42; and Kuan, *Neo-Assyrian Historical Inscriptions*, 80.

64. For tribute lists, see W. J. Martin, *Tribut und Tributleistungen bei den Assyrern* (Helsinki: Der Finnischen Literaturgesellschaft, 1936); J. N. Postgate, *Taxation and Conscription in the Assyrian Empire* (Studia Pohl: Series Maior 3; Rome: Pontifical Biblical Institute, 1974) 4–6; M. De Odorico, *The Use of Numbers and Quantifications in the*

the Dur-Katlimmu itinerary, contain verbs, while others, such as the Old Baby-lonian itineraries, do not. The same may apply to tribute lists. So the lack of an extant tribute list that contains verbs should not undercut the possibility that a source with third-person verbs was used here. The scribe seems simply to have copied the entries without thinking to change the subject of the verb in order to accommodate it to the narrative context.

The Habur campaigns, with their long series of repeated place-names, overnight stops at many sites, and formulaic verbs for departure and arrival quite closely fit the model for the itinerary genre we developed in the previous chapter. Grayson questioned whether the Habur campaigns were really itiner-aries because the phraseology is quite different from that of an itinerary *as he knew the genre*. His model was based primarily on the Neo-Assyrian itinerary (K. 4675+) which, as we saw in the previous chapter, places a heavy focus on distance measures and contains no verb forms.[65] But the Middle Assyrian itin-erary from Dur-Katlimmu (DeZ 2521), which had not yet been published when Grayson made these observations, has helped flesh out our understanding of the genre. In fact, the Habur itineraries are very much like the Dur-Katlimmu itinerary in form: the place-names are repeated, using the prepositions *ištu* (sometimes written TA) and *ana* or *ina*. The arrival formula uses a form of *biātu* 'to spend the night', just as the Dur-Katlimmu itinerary does, although it is sometimes here accompanied by a form of *šakānu*, usually written GAR-an. The unique feature of these Habur itineraries, compared with the itineraries discussed in the previous chapter, is use of a form of *namāšu* 'to set out' in the departure formula. Grayson argued that this is not a technical term from the itinerary genre, since no extant itineraries that he knew typically employ a verb form in the departure notice.[66] But the Dur-Katlimmu itinerary does employ a verb (*nasāḫu*), at least in the initial departure notice. When we compare the Habur campaigns with the Dur-Katlimmu itinerary, the consistent and even formulaic use of *namāšu* and *biātu* in the Habur itineraries clearly reflects the itinerary genre.[67]

Assyrian Royal Inscriptions (SAAS 3; Helsinki: The Neo-Assyrian Text Corpus Project, 1995) 77.

65. Grayson, "Assyria and Babylonia," 165.

66. Ibid., 165 n. 124.

67. For discussion of the issue of sources, see Tadmor, "Historical Inscriptions," 141–42; Grayson, "Studies in Neo-Assyrian History," 136; idem, "Assyria and Babylonia," 164–67; idem, "Assyrian Royal Inscriptions, Literary Characteristics," 41–42; Reade, "Neo-Assyrian Monuments," 154–55; Tadmor, "History and Ideology," 17–18; and idem, "Propaganda, Literature, Historiography," 329.

In addition to being able to identify the genre clearly, we must also be able to show that the fluctuation between first- and third-person verbs is isolated and patterned rather than random. The pattern of fluctuation in Tukulti-Ninurta II's Habur campaign is different from the pattern in the examples we have just examined. In Adad-nirari III's tribute list and the campaigns led by Shalmaneser III's field marshal, we saw a chunk of third-person text framed by first-person text. But in Tukulti-Ninurta II's Habur campaign, as Grayson notes, "the person changes even within the account of one stage of the journey." [68] The apparently arbitrary fluctuation is, in his view, best attributed to forgetfulness on the part of the scribe that he was writing annals, which should be in first person. Had a scribe simply switched to copying an itinerary, we might expect to see *all* the verbs in third person. But the fluctuation is not general. If the scribe were generally forgetful or careless, we might expect to see evidence of it all over the inscription. However, the fluctuation is limited exclusively to the Habur campaign (A.0.100.5 lines 41–127) and is entirely absent elsewhere in the inscription, which is consistently in first person. Whatever the cause of the fluctuation, it is not general forgetfulness.

The fluctuation within the Habur campaign also has a consistent pattern, which we can see if if we note which verbs are in first person and which in third. I have arranged the text here by clause rather than by line so that the similarity to the itineraries discussed in chap. 3 is visually clear.

ištu ᵘʳᵘ*Dūr-*ᵐ*Kurigalzu* **ittumuš**	He departed from Dur-Kurigalzu.
ⁱᵈ*Patti-*ᵈ*Enlil ētebir* **issakan bēde**	I crossed the Patti-Enlil canal. **He pitched camp and spent the night**.
ištu ⁱᵈ*Patti-*ᵈ*Enlil attumuš*	I departed from the Patti-Enlil canal.
ina ᵘʳᵘ*Sippuru-ša-*ᵈˣ*Šamaš* **issakan bēde**	**He pitched camp and spent the night** in Sippar-of-Shamash.
ištu ᵘʳᵘ*Sippuru-ša-*ᵈˣ*Šamaš attumša*	I departed from Sippar-of-Shamash.
ana pūt ⁱᵈ*Puratte aṣṣabat*	I set out toward the Tigris.
ina ᵘʳᵘ*Salati* **issakan bēde**	**He pitched camp and spent the night** in Salatu.
ištu ᵘʳᵘ*Salate* **ittumuš**	**He departed** from Salatu.
ina pūt ᵘʳᵘ*Dūr-balāṭi* **issakan bēde**	**He pitched camp and spent the night** opposite Dur-balati.
ᵘʳᵘ*Dūr-balāṭi šēpi ammāte ša* ⁱᵈ*Puratte ṣāli*	(Dur-balati lies on the other bank of the Tigris.)
ištu ᵘʳᵘ*Dūr-balāṭi* **ittumša**	**He departed** from Dur-balati.

---

68. Grayson, "Assyria and Babylonia," 166.

ina ^{uru}*Raḫimme ša pūt* ^{uru}*Rapiqu*   **He pitched camp and spent the night**
issakan bēde   in Rahimmu, which is opposite
    Rapiqu. (A.0.100.5 lines 52–57)

The camping verb *issakan bēde* 'he pitched camp and spent the night' is characteristic of itineraries and is here always in third person, just as we would expect
it to appear in an administrative document. The fluctuation occurs with the
verb *namāšu*, characteristic of the departure formula in itineraries. Although
the king is the subject throughout the inscription, sometimes the verb is in first
person ('*I* departed from the Patti-Enlil canal') and sometimes in third ('*He*
departed from Salatu'). This isolated fluctuation is best explained as an error
made while a scribe simultaneously copied a third-person source document
and accommodated it to the annals context by changing the verbs to first person. Sometimes he remembered to change this verb to first person, and other
times he forgot.

Why do we not see the fluctuation between first and third person with
issakan bēde 'he pitched camp and spent the night', the other verb form from
the itinerary? The verb *issakan* is usually written as a logogram in this text—as
GAR with the phonetic complement *-an*. Because a logogram depicts a word as
a single symbol rather than spelling it out, the logogram for a verb can be read
in any person/number/gender that fits the context, rendering a change in signs
unnecessary. The scribe's eye probably kept going, and he proceeded to copy
bēde, also without stopping to change it to first person.

The fluctuation between first- and third-person verb forms in Tukulti-
Ninurta II's Habur campaign, then, is the result of dealing with a compositional
challenge. The scribe not only had to copy the itinerary but also to accommodate it to the annals genre. His job may have been even more challenging
because of the likelihood that he was juggling *two* types of source documents:
a tribute list as well as an itinerary.[69] The scribe indicated arrival at a site where
tribute was collected not with the typical itinerary arrival form *issakan bēde* 'he
pitched camp and spent the night' but with *aqṭirib* 'I approached'.

ana ^{uru}*Sirqi aqṭirib* . . . *nāmurtu ša* ^m*Ḫarāni* ^{kur}*Laqayya* . . . **ittaḫar** *ina*
^{uru}*Sirqu* **issakan bēde** ^{uru}*Sirqu šēpi ammāte ša* ^{id}*Puratte ṣālli ištu* ^{uru}*Sirqi*
ittumša

---

69. Grayson entertains this possibility even as he is quite skeptical about the use of
an itinerary source in the Habur campaigns ("Assyria and Babylonia," 165).

> I approached Sirqu. . . . **He received** the tribute of Harani of the Laqu. **He pitched camp and spent the night** in Sirqu. Sirqu lies on the other bank of the Tigris. **He departed** from Sirqu. (A.0.100.5 lines 90–95)[70]

He then copied the tribute statement into the text from the tribute record without changing the person of its verb form, which appears as *ittaḫar* 'he received' rather than *attaḫar* 'I received'. He then went back to copying the itinerary, also without changing the verb form. Most of the verbs in these statements of tribute are in the first person (*attaḫar* or *amḫuršu*), suggesting that the scribe usually succeeded in accommodating the tribute list to the first-person character of the annals genre. But this one slip allows us to see that the scribe strove to accommodate the excerpts from tribute lists to the annals genre just as he did the itinerary notices.

The effort to accommodate the itinerary to its new context in the annals narrative is not limited to changing the verb forms to first person. It also involves blending the itinerary with content typical of the annals genre. Other verbs that occur in the excerpt from Tukulti-Ninurta II's Habur itinerary cited above, such as *ētebir* and *aṣṣabat*, are not found in administrative documents but are found throughout the annals and are always in the first person, just as they are here. These have been included to help the itinerary appear more at home in its new narrative context. The scribe may also have capitalized on features of the source document such as notes about various things that took place along the way, not unlike the notes we find in the Old Babylonian itineraries, in order to include stereotypical annalistic content such as hunt and battle scenes. Davies notes that these events are "just what might be expected in the course of a royal expedition" and are probably a feature of the administrative document.[71] While some of these notes may in fact have been copied from the source, the scribes also used this feature of the itinerary genre creatively to make the Habur campaigns look more like a typical battle episode.

Notes relating the acquisition of water were most likely copied from the source document. These typically contain passive verbs such as *mû iḫtubū* 'water was drawn' (A.0.100.5 lines 42, 46, 48, and 63) and *battubatte būrātu uḫtappiū* 'all around the wells were exhausted' (A.0.100.5 line 48) or simple statements of circumstance such as *mû marrū karāšī lā ušabbu* 'the water was too bitter to satisfy the troops' (A.0.100.5 line 44) and *mû madūtu* 'water was

---

70. See also lines 49–50. This failure to update the form from a tribute list happens only this one time in the inscription; lines 73, 79, 85, 87, 89, 92, 103, and 107 all have the updated first-person form.

71. G. I. Davies, "The Wilderness Itineraries: A Comparative Study," 58.

abundant' (A.0.100.5 line 48).[72] Statements such as these are not at all at home among the characteristics of the annals genre. They are not first person, they are not explicitly about the achievements of the king, and nowhere else in the annals is the procurement of water an issue. In one case, the drawing of water is immediately followed by the king's leading the army into a desolate area, a *qaqqar ṣumāmēte* 'land of thirst' (A.0.100.5 lines 62–64). This juxtaposition suggests the idea that the king provides for the needs of his troops. But, were these expressions suited to the purpose of the annals genre, we should expect them to be phrased with the king as their subject, such as "I drew water" or "I exhausted all of the wells." The fact that these are in the passive, with the water as the subject, suggests that they came from the source document. Given that this route may have been traveled on a regular basis to collect tribute, since the same Habur route with slight variation appears in the reigns of all three kings, it may be that citing where water could be procured was an issue for the individuals involved in making and receiving the report. The failure to accommodate these expressions to the annals genre by making the king the subject and thus the provider for the troops could be viewed as an unexploited opportunity for glorifying the king.

Two notes about the royal hunt in Tukulti-Ninurta II's Habur itinerary may also have been taken from the administrative document. The hunt episodes that occur elsewhere in the annals have their own stereotypical language, because stock expressions are employed to relate how the king conquered his prey: *ina narkabātiya pattūte* 'from my open chariot'; *ina qitrub meṭlūtiya* 'with my macho assault'; *ina šēpiya lasmāte* 'on my swift feet'; and *ina pašḫi* 'with the spear' (A.0.99.2 lines 123–24; see A.0.100.5 line 35).[73] Their use as tropes is suggested by the fact that they recur in such episodes, are piled up together, and are sometimes contradictory: the king cannot hunt simultaneously from his chariot and on his swift feet. The function of these hunt episodes in the annals is to highlight the king's machismo and ability to control the chaos of the empire's periphery, which is symbolized by the wild animals.[74] The two notes in Tukulti-

---

72. The word *uḫ-tap-pi* occurs in line 43 and is translated as first person, 'I destroyed', by Grayson, RIMA 2.173. But the verb is in the Dt stem, which has a passive meaning. I am inclined to think that the scribe omitted the *-u*, that *uḫ-tap-pi* should read *uḫtappiū* in the passive, as is the case for the very same expression in line 48.

73. Grayson does not translate *pattūte* (see RIMA 2.154), but the more recent *CAD* volume does have an entry for this word and cites this passage ("*pattūtu*," *CAD* P 286).

74. On the function of the royal hunt, often simply a matter of sport, to indicate the king's ability to control chaos at the periphery of the empire, see E. Weissert, "Royal Hunt and Royal Triumph in a Prism Fragment of Ashurbanipal (82-5-22,2)," in *Assyria 1995: Proceedings of the 10th Anniversary Symposium of the Neo-Assyrian Text Corpus*

Ninurta II's Habur itinerary, on the other hand, are little more than simple statements and lack these expressions. Moreover, they may be in third person. The verb *dâku* 'to kill' is written logographically (e.g., A.0.100.5 line 80), so it could be either first or third person. The temporal expressions that introduce the scenes, however, refer to the king with a 3ms suffix: *ina gerrišu ša šiddī* [id-]*Tartara* 'on his expedition along the banks of Wadi Tharthar', *ina dayyalātešu ša ḫuribte* 'on his hunting forays in the desert', and *ina dayyalātešu ina šiddī* [id]*Puratte* 'on his hunting forays on the banks of the Euphrates' (A.0.100.5 lines 45, 80–81).

Other elements of the itinerary, however, cannot be explained as notes copied from the administrative document and should instead be viewed as efforts to accommodate them to the annals context. One example is the use of stereotypical expressions for movement, such as a river crossing (with *ebēru*) or movement in a general direction or along a particular route (with *ṣabātu* or *redû*). Statements of this sort are *not* found in itineraries, which stick to a very limited range of verbs to express forward movement and stopping at various sites, but they *are* a feature of the annals, commonly found in movement described at the beginning of an episode. The scribe combines the itinerary notices with these statements in order to make the itinerary appear more like an annal. Expressions relating the difficulty of the terrain, such as *ina libbi ḫamāte eqli namrāṣi artedi* 'I continued through the *ḫamātu*, difficult terrain' are frequently added to the itinerary between arrival and departure notices (A.0.100.5 lines 47–48). In other cases, they function in lieu of an arrival notice, and the place-name used in them is picked up in a following departure notice drawn from the source: [id]*Patti*-[d]*Enlil ētebir issakan bēde ištu* [id]*Patti*-[d]*Enlil attumus*, 'I crossed the Patti-Enlil canal. He pitched camp and spent the night. I departed from the Patti-Enlil canal' (A.0.100.5 lines 52–53).

The battle episodes are likewise efforts to accommodate the itinerary to its annals context. Tukulti-Ninurta II's scribe not only concluded the itinerary with the conquest of Piru but also incorporated a very brief battle episode into the main body of the itinerary in the form of a note. Unlike the notes about the royal hunt, this one employs stereotypical expressions characteristic of the battle episodes throughout the annals.

Project, Helsinki, September 7–11, 1995 (ed. S. Parpola and R. M. Whiting; Helsinki: Neo-Assyrian Text Corpus Project, 1997) 342–49. On its association with the ideology of kingship, the king's religious obligations, and possible association with the Ninurta myth, see C. E. Watanabe, *Animal Symbolism in Mesopotamia: A Contextual Approach* (Wiener Offene Orientalistik 1; Vienna: Institut für Orientalistik der Universität Wien, 2002) 69–88.

ana muḫḫi ^(id)*Idiglat aqṭiribma maškanāte ša* ^(kur)*Utuʾ adi* ^(uru)*kaprānišunu*
ša šitkunū [*muḫḫi*] ^(id)*Idiglat aktašad dabdâšunu adūk šallassunu maʾatta*
asala ina ^(uru)*Aṣuṣi* **issakan bēde**

I approached the Tigris and captured the settlements of Utu along with
their villages that are situated on the Tigris. I massacred them (and) carried off (?) numerous spoils from them. **He set up camp and spent the
night** at Asusi. (A.0.100.5 lines 49–50)[75]

This miniature battle episode is incorporated into the itinerary by using the
first-person *aqṭirib* (the same verb used to incorporate the tribute notice cited
above) and putting the third-person itinerary arrival formula at the end of the
episode. The battle episodes added to the end of the itinerary are either simply
appended after the last itinerary notice, as in the case of Ashurnasirpal II's
Habur campaign, or incorporated by noting a march to the area using the verb
alāku, as is common in annals.[76] The scribe seems to have capitalized on the
form of the notes that were included in the administrative document, imitating
them in order to include a miniature battle episode alongside the notes about
water and hunting.

Characteristics of the itinerary genre certainly dominate the Habur campaigns of Adad-nirari II and Assurnasirpal II, the kings preceding and following Tukulti-Ninurta II, although we do not find the same signs of a source
document's having been copied and accommodated to the narrative. There is
no evidence of fluctuation in person. Did they also use source documents? It is
harder to say. The goal of these itinerary-laden, show-of-strength campaigns,
as Favaro indicated, is to communicate dominance over known territory. The
selection of place-names in Adad-nirari II's Habur campaign narrative corresponds to the key sites on the Habur during the Middle Assyrian period (see
fig. 1, p. 55, and discussion of the Dur-Katlimmu itinerary in chap. 3) and
could easily have served his ideological goal of demonstrating renewed Assyrian control of those centers. Adad-nirari II's scribe certainly employed the
itinerary *genre*, since he uses *bēdāk* and *assakan bēdāk* 'I pitched camp and
spent the night', words that we know are characteristic of the itinerary genre
and do not appear in annals prior to this point. But he need not have drawn on

---

75. I am uncertain to what root a-sa-la in line 50 is related. Grayson translates 'to
carry off' but does not normalize the word or provide a note (Grayson, RIMA 2.173).

76. For incorporation of the battle episode in Ashurnasirpal II's Habur campaign,
see A.0.101.1 iii 16–24. For Tukulti-Ninurta II's with *alāku*, see A.0.100.5 lines 121–26
and compare, for example, A.0.99.2 lines 91 and 94 (Adad-nirari II) and A.0.87.1 iii 8
(Tiglath-pileser I).

a *source document* to accomplish this goal. In fact, itineraries in their typical administrative contexts do not carry the ideological weight that Favaro suggests. They serve pragmatic goals. A report of such a campaign would have been made to the palace for record-keeping purposes, not to show strength. The itineraries in the Habur campaigns do convey mastery of territory, but this is an ideological overtone that they *acquired* by being placed in the context of an annalistic narrative, where issues such as the king's control over territory are live. If the scribe did use a report, his use of it in this literary context gave it an added layer of meaning.

Assurnasirpal II's scribe either managed to do a flawless job of accommodating an itinerary to its new literary context in the annals or modeled his campaign narrative on Tukulti-Ninurta II's. Virtually all of the places mentioned in Assurnasirpal II's Habur campaign are also mentioned in Tukulti-Ninurta II's. This could mean that the former copied the names from the latter, omitting a number of names from Tukulti-Ninurta II's fuller list. On the other hand, many of these sites are main stops and logical places to quarter soldiers, so it should not be surprising to see the same list of sites. The arrival formula is extremely consistent throughout the text; *assakan bēdāk* 'I pitched camp and spent the night' is used exclusively all the way through, even at tribute collection sites such as Sirqu, Aqarbanu, and Hindanu, which are prefaced by *aqṭirib* 'I approached', along with the itinerary arrival formula *issakan bēde* 'he pitched camp and spent the night' in Tukulti-Ninurta II's campaign narrative. This could be an effort to be consistent where Tukulti-Ninurta II's scribe is not, creating a stereotypical form. On the other hand, it could simply mean that Assurnasirpal II's scribe did not use a tribute list. While the tribute lists in Tukulti-Ninurta II's narrative are very specific, they are reduced to trope in Assurnasirpal II's. Virtually every instance of tribute collection consists of silver, gold, tin, bronze casseroles, oxen, and sheep. Whether he is reliant on a source document or Tukulti-Ninurta II's narrative, what is clear is that Assurnasirpal II's scribe produced a form that became normative, since itinerary notices elsewhere in his own annals and in Shalmaneser III's use it.

Like the author of the Broken Obelisk, who turned to the chronicle genre, these scribes created a blend, or a genre hybrid, even if only for the space of the Habur campaigns. They created an episode that is atypical for the annals genre through use of a source document, not unlike the atypical—because chronistic—Broken Obelisk. Rather than simply drawing on the data it had to offer, Tukulti-Ninurta II's scribe (if not the others as well) copied it into the text and used it as the main framework for the episode. He supplemented the itinerary with entries from a tribute list, as is done elsewhere in the annals, and imitated the notes in order to accommodate the itinerary to the annals context, including battle episodes in the itinerary just like notes in an administrative document. If the source included notes about battles, they were changed to fit the stereotypical form of the battle episode in the annals. We can see, then, that the Habur campaign narratives are dominated by movement because they are not typical annalistic campaign narratives at all but had their roots in a recontextualized administrative document made to look like an annal.

However much it may also have functioned as royal propaganda, we can see from this foray into the use of source documents that historiography in ancient Assyria shares with modern historiography a propensity to report events. Itineraries in their primary contexts function as reports and records, and there is a residue of this function in these new literary contexts. But they are no longer *merely* reports. Wolfgang Iser points out that foregrounded repertoire is "decomposed" into its new context.[77] Although Tukulti-Ninurta II's scribe accommodated his source document to the narrative context by changing verb forms and including battle episodes, one could say that the "emulsification" is quite weak since his campaign still sits apart from other campaign episodes, retaining much of its character as a report rather than fully taking on the formulaic plot typical of battle episodes. The other Habur campaigns use the itinerary genre more strongly in service of their ideological goals, as scribes used substantive stretches of itinerary to convey the idea of control over Assyrian territory.

Egyptian Military Narratives

The ancient Egyptians shared with the Assyrians a propensity to report events even as they composed inscriptions with the goal of commemorating the king's deeds as conqueror and displaying imperial propaganda on their temple walls. Egyptian scribes during the New Kingdom established a whole new genre with the daybook as a framework. There has long been a consensus that key examples of New Kingdom military narrative, such as the account of Thutmose III's (1479–1425 B.C.E.) battle at Megiddo, are based on entries from a daybook or war diary.[78] Although the daybook is a well-known genre in a

---

77. W. Iser, *The Fictive and the Imaginary: Charting Literary Anthropology* (Baltimore: Johns Hopkins University Press, 1993) 4–6.

78. E.g., M. Noth, "Die Annalen Thutmoses III. als Geschichtsquelle," *ZDPV* 66 (1943) 156–74; H. Grapow, *Studien zu den Annalen Thutmosis des Dritten und zu ihnen Verwandten Historischen Berichten des Neuen Reiches* (Berlin: Akademie, 1949) 50; J. K.

variety of periods, and there are extant examples of daybooks kept when the
king was on campaign, none survives from the New Kingdom except as employed in royal inscriptions.[79] These inscriptions are narratives rather than the
simple notes about events that characterize the daybook, but they often contain infinitives where finite narrative verb forms might be expected. In *Aspects
of the Military Documents of the Ancient Egyptians*, Anthony Spalinger argues
that scribes actually built one type of military narrative, the *nḫtw*, or victory
narrative, around a daybook source and that these infinitives are not stylistic
peculiarities but evidence of the sources and techniques used to compose these
narratives.[80] According to Spalinger, the scribes probably used daybooks because they were available and contained plenty of information about the campaigns that could be used in a detailed narrative.[81]

But the daybook was not merely a source of information. It also provided
the framework for the narrative. Spalinger shows how the scribes copied entire entries directly out of the daybook with minimal alteration, as we can see
from a comparison of the following example from the account of Thutmose
III's battle of Megiddo with actual daybook entries.

*ḥsbt 23 tpj šmw sw 4 hrw n ḥb ḥ ʿw nsw r dmj n mḥ.n pꜣ ḥqꜣ Gḏt [rn.f n
Ḥr ḥsbt 23] tpj šmw sw 5 wḏt m st ṯn m qnt m [nḫtw] m wsrw m mꜣʿt r
sḥrt hrw pf ḥsy r swsḫ tꜣšw Kmt mj wḏ.n jtj.f [Jmn-r ʿ kn]j nḫt jṯt.f ḥsbt 23
tpj šmw sw 16 r dmj n Yhm*

**Year 23, first (month) of Harvest, day 4: day of the king's coronation
festival. At the city of that which the ruler had taken, Gaza [(being) its
Syrian name. Year 23,] first (month) of harvest, day 5: departing from
this place** in bravery, [in victory], in strength, in justice; in order to overthrow that feeble enemy; in order to expand the borders of Egypt as his
[brave] and victorious father [Amun-Re] decreed that he conquer. **Year
23, first (month) of Harvest, day 16: at the city of Yehem.**[82]

Hoffmeier, "The Structure of Joshua 1–11 and the Annals of Thutmose III," in *Faith, Tradition, and History: Old Testament Historiography in its Near Eastern Context* (ed. A. R.
Millard, J. K. Hoffmeier, and D. W. Baker; Winona Lake, IN: Eisenbrauns, 1994) 169–71.

79. See Redford, *Egypt, Canaan, and Israel*, 141; and fuller discussion in idem,
*Pharaonic King-Lists, Annals, and Day-Books: A Contribution to the Study of the Egyp-
tian Sense of History* (SSEA Publication 4; Mississauga, ON: Benben, 1986) 123–24.

80. Spalinger, *Aspects of the Literary Documents*. For the view that it is a stylistic
peculiarity, see, for example, A. H. Gardiner, *The Kadesh Inscriptions of Ramesses II* (Oxford: Griffith Institute, 1960) 31.

81. Spalinger, *Aspects of the Literary Documents*, 120–21.

82. *Urk. IV* 648.9–649.4. Identification of the daybook entries is dependent on
Spalinger, *Aspects of the Literary Documents*, 135. Transliteration and translation are

Spalinger reconstructs the daybook entries (**bold**) without reference to actual daybooks, since no military daybooks are extant from the New Kingdom. But comparison with the daybook genre, using two successive entries from Papyrus Turin 2008 + 2016 helps to make the genre features clear.

> ḥsbt 7 ʒbd 1 prt sw 28 mḥ sw ʒbd 2 sw 12 n wḏʒ nwt wḏʒ mryt mn-nfr mjnj ḥr mryt nʒ bḫnw n pr-wsjr

> ḥsbt 7 ʒbd 2 prt sw 1 mḥ sw ʒbd 2 sw 15 n wḏʒ nwt mḥ sw 4 ḥr mryt nʒ bḫnw n pr-wsjr wḏʒ st ṯn mjnj ḥr mryt tʒ mʒwt nʒ bḫnw n pr-wsjr

Year 7, first month of Growing, day 28: second month, twelfth day since the departure from Thebes. Departing from the river bank at Memphis. Mooring at the river bank of "The Pylons of the House of Osiris."

Year 7, second month of Growing, day 1: second month, fifteenth day since the departure from Thebes; fourth day at the river bank of "The Pylons of the House of Osiris." Departing from this place. Mooring at the river bank of "The New Land of the Pylons of the House of Osiris." (Pap. Turin 2008 + 2016 recto II 22–23, III 7–9) [83]

As in the Turin papyrus, the Megiddo campaign is characterized by a series of date formulas, and the events are related as simple notes. Moreover, both documents use *st tn* 'this place' to avoid repeating a place-name when movement from one site to the next is expressed. Spalinger suggests that the first two entries in the Megiddo campaign were consecutive entries in the daybook. [84] Comparison with the Turin papyrus helps us see in a very concrete way that his suggestion is grounded in the features of the daybook genre.

Creating a narrative out of daybook entries involved accommodating verb forms, just as incorporating the Habur itineraries into annals did for the Assyrian scribes. It also involved adding particles that express temporal and logical consecution. Thutmose III's arrival at Megiddo is a good example of the techniques used, as Spalinger demonstrates.

---

mine. For discussion of the use of ḥʒt-sp to mark the regnal year, see A. H. Gardiner, *Egyptian Grammar* (Oxford: Clarendon, 1927) 204; Spalinger follows this reading. J. P. Allen reads ḥsbt instead, noting that ḥʒt-sp is an erroneous reading (*Middle Egyptian: An Introduction to the Language and Culture of Hieroglyphs* [Cambridge: Cambridge University Press, 2000] 104). Since I am following Allen's transliteration system and conventions on the whole, and since his work is the most recent, I follow his reading here as well.

83. J. J. Janssen, *Two Ancient Egyptian Ship's Logs: Papyrus Leiden I 350 Verso and Papyrus Turin 2008+2016.* Leiden: Brill, 1961) 60–61. Transliteration and translation mine, with reference to Janssen's notes.

84. Spalinger, *Aspects of the Literary Documents*, 135.

spr.n ḥm.f r rsw Mkt ḥr spt ḥnw n Qn jw wnwt 7 jm wḏb m sw ꜥḥꜥ.n wꜣḥ
jhw jm n ḥm.f rdj.n.tw m ḥr n mšꜥ r ḏr.f r [ḏd] grg ṯn sspd ḫꜥw.tn r ntt jw.tw
*r ṯhn r ꜥḥꜣ ḥnꜥ ḥrw pf ḥzj m dwꜣw ḥr ntt tw.tw [   ] **ḥtp** m ꜥꜥny n ꜥnḫ wḏꜣ*
*snb **jrt** mḥrw srjw **wꜣḥ** n šmsw **sš** rsw n mšꜥ ḏd n sn mn jb mn jb rs tp rs*
tp rs m ꜥnḫ m jmꜣw n ꜥnḫ wḏꜣ snb jw.tw r ḏd n ḥm.f mrw snb mnfꜣt rswt
mḥtt r mjtt

His Majesty arrived south of Megiddo, on the banks of the Qina Brook,
when the seventh hour was turning in the day. Then the tent was set up
there for His Majesty. One made the following command to the whole
army, [saying], "Make your preparations, get your weapons ready, because one will engage in fighting with that vile enemy in the morning,
because one will. . . ." **Resting** in the enclosure of Life, Prosperity, and
Health. **Making** provisions for the officers. **Distributing rations** to the
attendants. **Posting** a guard for the army, **saying** to them, "Be courageous,
be courageous! Keep awake, keep awake!" **Awakening** in life in the tent of
Life, Prosperity, and Health. One came to say to His Majesty, "The coast is
clear, and the troops south and north are also." [85]

The presence of infinitives (**bold**) points to the use of multiple entries from
a daybook. Some of the daybook entries that underlie this passage, however,
have been accommodated to the narrative context. [86] In some cases, such as the
arrival at Megiddo, the infinitive has been given a subject ("His Majesty") and
changed to the narrative *sḏm.n.f* form (double underline). The next original
daybook entry is *wꜣḥ jhw jm* 'pitching a tent there'. It has been accommodated
by adding *ꜥḥꜥ.n* (dotted underline) without a change in the verb form. The word
ꜥḥꜥ.n adds the idea of consecution without requiring a change in the verb form

---

85. *Urk. IV* 655.12–656.16. I have generally followed J. K. Hoffmeier's translation
("The Annals of Thutmose III" [trans. J. K. Hoffmeier; *COS* 2.2A]), with a few very
minor exceptions that simply allow us to see the Egyptian features more clearly. One is
the time of arrival at Megiddo (*Urk. IV* 655.14), which Hoffmeier translates 'at seven in
the evening', while Spalinger (*Aspects of the Literary Documents*, 138) translates 'when
the seventh hour was turning in the day (= midday)'. I have followed Spalinger here
simply because his translation is more literal. Second, I have used 'One made the following command . . .' rather than Hoffmeier's 'Then he made the following command . . .'
in light of the use of 'One' for the impersonal suffix pronoun *.tw* when it refers to the
king (Allen, *Middle Egyptian*, 177) and the lack of *ꜥḥꜥ.n*, which expresses consecution,
with the verb form. Third, Hoffmeier translates *sš* (*Urk. IV* 656.9) as a passive, while I
have translated it as an infinitive. Either is possible, but I prefer the infinitive, given the
context of infinitives more broadly; see also the note to this effect in *Urk. IV* 656.9. For
the unusual meaning of the infinitive *wḥꜥ* 'to distribute rations' (*Urk. IV* 656.8), see R. O.
Faulkner, "The Battle of Megiddo," *JEA* 28 (1942) 10–11.

86. For the reconstructed daybook entries, see Spalinger, *Aspects of the Literary
Documents*, 139. On the infinitives, see p. 138. Contrast Faulkner, who reads them as
passives ("Battle of Megiddo," 4).

itself, which would simply be read as a passive rather than an infinitive in this context.[87]

The scribe could have changed all the infinitive forms from the daybook into narrative forms had he so wished. Spalinger suggests that the scribe deliberately chose to leave the infinitives, which report activity in the camp, "because they provided a kind of pre-battle tension—they are certainly striking and dramatic."[88] The concern here is not merely to report events. The scribe used the daybook entries in order to emplot the narrative and to achieve a set of literary goals. In addition to leaving the infinitives where they would create drama, the scribe also combined these entries with other elements of repertoire that contributed to the aesthetic effect. Direct speech depicts the action going on in the camp. The command to the army creates a picture of Egyptian soldiers anxiously gathering and readying their weapons, while the command to the guards evokes bored sentries being roused to attention. The *jw.tw* ('One came to say . . .') report (wavy underline) forms the basis for another genre of military narrative in the New Kingdom in which a report is brought to the king prompting him to undertake a campaign.[89] The scribe used this device here to create a sense of general readiness for the upcoming battle. The scribe has selected and combined various elements of repertoire—daybook entries, speeches, and *jw.tw* report—in order not just to report the event but to evoke a particular aesthetic response to it on the part of the reader, as she, along with the characters in the narrative, is waiting tensely for the battle to begin.

Spalinger emphasizes that the scribes had a degree of flexibility in their use of literary elements, to the point of artistic license.[90] I suggest that his author-as-artist model is also applicable to the daybook entries themselves. The scribes did not slavishly copy every entry in the daybooks. They selected, omitted, and even to some degree manipulated the daybook entries to serve their literary and ideological goals. We can see this in the Bulletin and Poem accounts of the battle of Qadesh, which allow us to compare two different narrative accounts of the same event.[91] Spalinger argued that both versions are based on the *same* daybook, which he reconstructs.[92]

---

87. For background on these grammatical phenomena, see Allen, *Middle Egyptian*, 178, 223–39.

88. Spalinger, *Aspects of the Literary Documents*, 138.

89. Ibid., 1–33.

90. Ibid., 43–76.

91. For overview and basic discussion of these inscriptions, see Gardiner, *Kadesh Inscriptions*, 3–4. For a detailed summary of their locations, see G. A. Gaballa, *Narrative in Egyptian Art* (Mainz am Rhein: von Zabern, 1976) 114.

92. For reconstruction of the basic daybook, see Spalinger, *Aspects of the Literary Documents*, 157–59.

The author of the Bulletin selected daybook entries and combined them with other elements of literary repertoire in order to create in the audience tension and excitement building up to the battle, in which the Egyptians are ambushed by the Hittites. In other words, his goal is primarily aesthetic. First, he focused his narrative on the battle scene by selecting only the daybook entries immediately preceding the battle. We know that the daybook for this campaign contained entries that articulate the departure from Egypt and the journey to Qadesh because some of them are used in the Poem. But the author of the Bulletin left these out in order to focus only on the battle and the circumstances leading up to it.[93] The focus on the battle alone in the Bulletin is reinforced by its close association with the pictorial reliefs, for which it is sometimes understood as an extended caption.[94]

Second, the scribe used these daybook entries and the events related in them to create tension in the narrative. By combining the daybook entries just prior to the battle with dialogue and narrative, the author leaves the Egyptians in the dark about the Hittite battle strategy until the last minute, while letting the reader in on it sooner in order to build tension in the reader about when the king will realize what he marched into. The arrival at Shabtuna (Spalinger's reconstructed daybook entry in **bold**) is used to set up the Hittite ambush, just as Thutmose III's scribe created tension before the battle at Megiddo by highlighting the preparations in the camp at Yehem. Shabtuna becomes the setting for dialogue with the Shasu, who come to persuade the king that the Hittites have fled.

> **The Lord [= the King] proceeded North, and (His Majesty) reached the area South of the town of Shabtuna.** There came 2 Shasu, from the Shasu tribesfolk, to say to His Majesty: "It is our brothers, who are tribal chiefs with the Fallen One of Hatti, who have sent us to His Majesty saying: 'We shall become servants of Pharaoh, LPH, and we shall separate ourselves from the Ruler of Hatti.'" Then said His Majesty to them: "Where are they, your brothers who [se]nt you to speak of this matter to His Majesty?" Then they said to His Majesty, "They are where the despicable Chief of Hatti is, for the Fallen One of Hatti is in the land of Aleppo, to the North

93. Van Seters, *In Search of History*, 155.

94. For detailed discussion of the reliefs, which I will not consider here, see A. J. Spalinger, "Notes on the Reliefs of the Battle of Kadesh," in *Perspectives on the Battle of Kadesh* (ed. H. Goedicke; Baltimore: Halgo, 1985) 1–42. For the bipartite analysis into "Literary Record" (= Poem) and "Pictorial Record" (= Bulletin and reliefs), see Gardiner, *Kadesh Inscriptions*, 2–3.

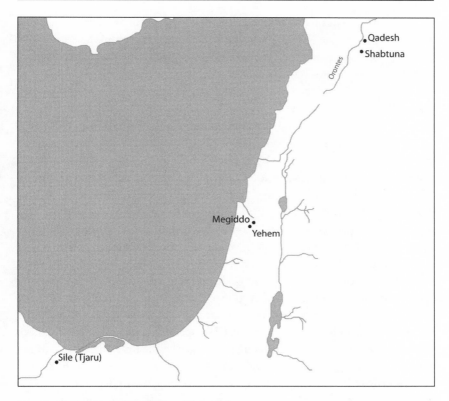

Fig. 5. The Battles of Qadesh and Megiddo.

of Tunip. He feared Pharaoh, LPH, too much to come southward, when he heard that Pharaoh, LPH, was coming northward."[95]

The narrator then tells the reader that the report was false, that the Shasu had been sent to collect military intelligence by the Hittite king who, unbeknown to Pharaoh, is actually waiting on the other side of Qadesh. The scribe thus combines dialogue with narration to build tension in the narrative as we, the audience, watch the king move straight into what we know to be an ambush. The scribe uses dialogue again to flesh out the daybook notice of arrival at Qadesh. Here the king is in dialogue with Hittite prisoners brought in by an

95. All translations of the Poem and Bulletin are taken from K. A. Kitchen, *Ramesside Inscriptions, Translated and Annotated: Translations* (2 vols.; Oxford: Blackwell, 1996).

Egyptian scout, who tell the king the truth, albeit a little too late, because he has already arrived at the site of the battle. This speech prompts a council with the king's officials, akin to the council at Yehem prior to the battle of Megiddo, and the king sends the vizier to hurry the army. The characters catch up to the reader in their knowledge of the situation only when it is too late to take an alternative course of action.

The author of the Poem has a different set of literary goals from the author of the Bulletin. He selected, foregrounded, and combined repertoire to create a narrative in which the army fails miserably while the king is left alone to handle the battle, highlighting his heroic and pious character. The ideology of kingship is a main concern in this account. While the author of the Bulletin began his narrative just before Qadesh in order to focus on setting up the ambush, the Poem begins in Egypt because the journey to Qadesh allowed him to show the army and the king preparing and traveling successfully together, creating a foil for the failure of the army later in the narrative (P25–30). The account begins with the supply of the troops in Egypt and a plan for the campaign. The king and his army leave Egypt together, prepared and with common purpose. The next daybook entry, however, is the arrival at Ramesses II, the town in the Valley of the Conifers. The author has telescoped the time and space that have passed since they left Egypt by using the phrase "some time after this" just before recording the arrival at Ramesses II, the town (P34–36). Even the stop at Shabtuna used so creatively by the author of the Bulletin is left out. Instead, the author of the Poem provides a statement about the ease with which Ramesses II and his army together navigated potential rebels as well as natural challenges, such as passes.

The Orontes crossing is a critical turning point in the Poem, because it allows the army to be attacked and fail while the king fights alone and claims divinely aided victory. The author of the Poem had the king cross the Orontes with one elite division, leaving the rest of the army behind (P37–40). Once the king has crossed, the geographical location of the rest of the army at Shabtuna and Arnam is given in detail, because they are now lagging behind the king, who "was all alone, with his followers," with the Orontes separating them (P56–63). Thus the information provided by the daybook about the army's location is not left out; it is just delayed until it serves this particular author's literary goals. Instead of serving as the setting for a dramatic scene, Shabtuna is used to locate the army at some distance from the king when the battle actually takes place. The Poem then goes on to narrate the ambush of the Egyptian army south of Qadesh, leaving the king truly alone for the climax of the narrative, his solo battle against the Hittites (P72–73).

The Bulletin also has an Orontes crossing, but it occurs near the *end* of the account, and it is the *Hittite army* that crossed the Orontes just south of Qadesh to ambush the rear guard of the Egyptian army as it headed north, not the Egyptian king who crossed the Orontes to separate himself from most of his army, as in the Poem (B75–83). Spalinger reconstructed the Orontes crossing as a daybook entry in the Poem but not in the Bulletin.[96] I suggest that both were based on the daybook. The author of the Bulletin simply moved the Orontes crossing to the end and made the Hittites the subject, slightly manipulating the daybook to serve the focus he wanted his narrative to have. The Hittite ambush is the climax of the Bulletin narrative, in which only the rear guard of the Egyptian army is attacked, and the king intervenes to save the day. In the Poem, however, the Orontes crossing functions to separate the king from the army, and the ambush is only the disappointing denouement of one scene, in which the Egyptian army fails. This failure sets up the climactic battle between the king and the Hittites still to come.

The physical separation of king and army created by the author's use of the Orontes crossing in the Poem allowed him to emphasize Ramesses II's role as son of Amun. After the Hittite ambush, the army and the king are distinguished from one another not only geographically but also in terms of courage. The contrast between the army and the king is made particularly evident as the king calls out to his troops—now watching from the other side of the river— during the battle: "Stand firm, be bold-hearted, my troops, see my triumph, on my own, with only Amun to be my protector, his hand with me" (P168–171). Moreover, the army is explicitly shamed by the notion that only the king's two horses and his shield bearer accompanied him into battle (P266–275). That the king fought alone is simply mentioned in the Bulletin in two places (B103 and 106). In the Poem, however, it is used to heighten his military prowess, as he lunges into battle "entirely on his own, no-one else with him," only then looking around to size up the enemy and find himself surrounded (P76–91).

Only the king and Amun with him are left to fight the Hittites. The final scene consists of a first-person poetic account of the battle in the voice of the king. He emphasizes his father/son relationship with Amun and lists his activities on behalf of the cult, both as an indication that he has loyally fulfilled his duty and as a rationale for his appeal to Amun to come to his aid now that he has been abandoned by his incompetent army and surrounded by the

---

96. Spalinger, *Aspects of the Literary Documents*, 157 (#10). Its presence in the Poem but not the Bulletin was also noted by Gardiner, *Kadesh Inscriptions*, 16.

Hittites.[97] Amun plays the key role as his aid in battle, and the king, as son of Amun, maintains the cosmos—in this case, on the battlefield. The first-person account in the Poem constitutes praise to Amun, employing the form typically used on stelas to express personal piety.[98] When, at the end of the Poem, the army comes to praise the king after the battle, they extol him as the "son of Amun" and the "Protector of Egypt" (P241–250).

While the Assyrian scribes who wrote the Habur campaigns incorporated more or less whole source documents into their annals narrative, the Egyptian scribes were quite selective about which daybook entries they used and which they left out. They were also creative in their use of daybooks, building a whole narrative around the selected entries. Spalinger argues that military narratives involved very little manipulation of the source document, and to a fundamental extent this is true.[99] The differences between the battle of Qadesh as recounted in the Poem and the Bulletin are minor. But the authors did take some license even with the daybook, which is evident in their manipulation of the Orontes crossing, and their use of the source was deeply influenced by the literary goals of their respective authors, both aesthetic and ideological.

Shaping Narratives

While scribes in Egypt continued to make use of daybooks as they wrote military inscriptions even into the Late Period (747–525 B.C.E.), the Assyrian scribes, inspired by the possibilities offered by their sources, further experimented with the itinerary genre in ways that suggest they may no longer have been dependent on administrative documents.[100] Simonetta Ponchia pointed out that Ashurnasirpal II's scribe used the itinerary structure to create a picture of a geographically contiguous empire and applied it beyond well-known Assyrian territories "to a mountainous environment, with a non-linear topographical development, and possibly more complex military tactics in which

---

97. S. Morschauser, "Observations on the Speeches of Ramesses II in the Literary Record of the Battle of Kadesh," in *Perspectives on the Battle of Kadesh* (ed. H. Goedicke; Baltimore: Halgo, 1985) 123–206; A. Ophel, "Lines 98–107 in the Kadesh Poem of Ramesses II," in *Pharaonic Egypt: The Bible and Christianity* (ed. S. Israelit-Groll; Jerusalem: Magnes, 1985) 146–56.

98. Assmann, *Mind of Egypt*, 263.

99. Spalinger, *Aspects of the Literary Documents*, 148. See also p. 163, where he again articulates the notion that the historical details come from the daybook extracts and not the narrative.

100. Grayson, *Assyrian Royal Inscriptions*, 80. For use of the daybook in military narrative from the Late Period, see Spalinger, *Aspects of the Literary Documents*, 185–90.

the action of peripheral strongholds is crucial."[101] While the Habur campaigns do not fit Badalì's formalist pattern because they are overdetermined by movement, other campaigns also present a problem because movement occurs in a wide variety of contexts and often varies from the proposed pattern. This variation is the result of scribes' *experimenting* with using the itinerary genre to create a more clearly structured and coherent narrative, connecting one episode to another in space and time. This goal is not only compositional but also has the ideological advantages to which Ponchia and Favaro refer. Grayson noted that "the sources used by the writer inevitably influence, whether consciously or unconsciously, his manner of literary expression."[102] In just this way, itinerary notices, like date formulas, became a normative part of the annals genre.

One such use of the itinerary genre involved movement to the site of battle. Movement out from the home site to the site of battle and back created a picture of a geographically coherent empire with the king going out from the center and wealth coming back to it. Movement to the site of battle was articulated in the annals even before the itinerary genre was first used in the Habur campaigns but only with a generic expression. The king moves to the site of battle in a typical introduction to military narrative containing a provocation, an appeal for divine aid, and mustering of the troops, as in the following example from Ashurnasirpal II's first campaign to Zamua:

> *ina līme* ᵐ*Aššur-iddin ṭēmu uttēruni mā* ᵐ*Nūr-Adad* ˡᵘ*nasīku ša* ᵏᵘʳ*Dagara ittabalkat* ᵏᵘʳ*Zamua ana siḫirtišu aḫaiš iṣbutū nērubu ša* ᵘʳᵘ*Babite dūra irṣipū ana epēš qabli u tāḫāzi ana libbiya itbûni ina tukulti Aššur bēli rabê bēliya u* ᵈ*urigallu ālik pāniya ina kakkī ezzūte ša Aššur bēli išruka ana iâši kakkī ṣābiya adki ana nērebe ša* ᵘʳᵘ*Babite* **allik**

> In the eponymy of Ashur-iddin, a report was brought back to me that Nur-Adad, the sheikh of Dagara, had rebelled. The entire land of Zamua had banded together. They had built a wall in the Babitu pass and had risen against me to wage war and battle. With the support of Ashur, the great lord, my lord, and the divine standard which goes before me, with the fierce weapons which Ashur, the lord, gave to me, I mustered my weapons and troops and **marched** to the pass of the city Babitu. (A.0.101.1 ii 23–27)

The only expression for movement used here is *ana* GN (*lū*) *allik*, which is characteristic of Tiglath-pileser I's prism inscriptions and used frequently in subsequent annals to indicate movement to the battle site.

---

101. Ponchia, "Mountain Routes," 167, 174.
102. Grayson, *Assyrian Royal Inscriptions*, 42.

Using an itinerary notice at the beginning of a campaign in addition to more-general expressions for movement out toward the periphery afforded the scribes an opportunity to include the name of a specific site in the Assyrian heartland as the departure point, because itinerary notices typically contain a place-name for departure as well as arrival. We find an example of this in Ashurnasirpal II's third campaign to Zamua:

> *ina līme* ᵐ*Miqti-adur ina* ᵘʳᵘ*Ninua usbākuni ṭēmu uttēruni mā* ᵐ*Ameka* ᵐ*Araštua madattu u kadurru ša Aššur bēliya lū iklu ina qibit Aššur bēli rabê bēliya u* ᵈ*urigalli ālik pāniya ina* ⁱᵗⁱ*Simāni* UD.1.KAM *šaluštešu ana* ᵏᵘʳ*Zamua aškuna dikûtu pān narkabāti u ummāniya lā adgul* **ištu** ᵘʳᵘ**Kalzi attumuš** ⁱᵈ*Zaba šaplî ētebir ina* ᵏᵘʳ*nērebī ša* ᵏᵘʳ*Babite ērub* ⁱᵈ*Radānu ētebir ina šēp šadê* ᵏᵘʳ*Simaki kal ūmeya aktuaš alpī immerī karāni madattu ša* ᵏᵘʳ*Dagara attaḫar* **ištu šēp** ᵏᵘʳ**Simaki** *narkabātu eṭlūtu pitḫallu ašarissu issiya asseqe mūšu adi namāri artedi* ⁱᵈ*Turnat ētebir ina mitḫār sānte* **ana** ᵘʳᵘ**Ammali āl dannūtišu ša** ᵐ**Araštua aqṭirib**

In the eponymy of Miqti-adur, I was in Nineveh. A report was brought back to me that Ameka (and) Arashtua withheld the tribute and corvee of Ashur, my lord. By the command of Ashur, the great lord, my lord and the divine standard which goes before me, I mustered (my army) for the third time against Zamua on the first of Simanu. I did not wait for the levy of my chariots and troops. **I departed from Kalzi.** I crossed the lower Zab. I entered the passes of Mt. Babitu. I crossed the river Radanu. I delayed all day at the foot of Mt. Simaki. I received the tribute of Dagara, oxen, sheep, (and) wine. **From the foot of Mt. Simaki** I took with me strong chariots, cavalry, (and) crack troops. I pressed on from night until dawn. I crossed the river Turnat. At dawn **I approached Ammali, the fortified city of Arashtua.** (A.0.101.1 ii 49–54) [103]

Names of Assyrian capitals, whether Ashur, Nineveh, Kalhu, or Halzu, do not appear in annals prior to Tukulti-Ninurta II's reign, even though movement to the site of battle does (see A.0.100.5 lines 13, 30, and 41). These names add a defined starting point to the king's movement, and the itinerary notices (**bold**) connect these capital cities to provincial sites of conquest in a direct linear spatial and temporal relationship. The multiple campaigns in an inscription, then, present a picture of the king traveling out in various radii from the Assyrian heartland over the extent of the empire, with the king departing from the Assyrian capital, to which he will also bring back tribute and spoils.

---

103. See also A.0.100.5 lines 11–29 and 30–40, where this phenomenon occurs in the annals of Tukulti-Ninurta II as well.

The way in which itinerary notices are combined with general expressions for movement in this example suggests that use of the itinerary genre in the annals generally was inspired by the Habur campaigns. Here we find a variety of expressions for movement (or lack of movement) including verbs such as *ebēru* 'to cross', *erēbu* 'to enter', and *kâšu* 'to delay'. Verbs such as these are characteristic of commemorative building inscriptions containing military narrative even in the Middle Assyrian period and continue to be used as a characteristic part of the annals genre. They are distinct from the typical itinerary verbs *namāšu* 'to depart' and *biātu* 'to stop overnight', which are *not* used in annals prior to the inclusion of the Habur itineraries. While the departure from Kalzu in this example is indicated with an itinerary notice using the typical verb *namāšu*, the arrival at Ammali is not indicated with the arrival formula *assakan bēdāk*. Instead, the scribe uses the verb *qerēbu* 'to approach'. This is the same verb used by the scribe who accommodated the Habur itinerary to Tukulti-Ninurta II's annals prior to incorporating a statement of tribute collection, as we saw in the arrival at Sirqu cited above (see also A.0.100.5 lines 69, 85, 90, 98, 102, 104, and 113) and in the Utu battle episode (A.0.100.5 lines 49–50). Like the itinerary notices, the verb *aqṭirib* is used for the *first time* in Assyrian military narrative in Tukulti-Ninurta II's annals. Its use here at the beginning of campaigns to mark arrival at the site of battle is likely related to the way the Habur itinerary was accommodated to the annals genre.

Itinerary notices are also used to create connections between the various episodes that make up a campaign. While the episodes in Tiglath-pileser I's annals are not connected at all, only two of Ashurnasirpal II's campaigns, as related in the Ninurta Temple reliefs, contain multiple episodes connected by generic terms such as *ina ūmešuma* (A.0.101.1 iii 26–50, including various episodes relating to the Laqu, and iii 51–56, relating to Bit-Adini). The remainder are explicitly joined to each other with itinerary notices to create a linear sequence of actions and movement between them. In some cases, this is done with a simple application of the itinerary genre. In his campaign to reconquer his royal city Damdammusa, Ashurnasirpal II fights in three different places, and the campaign ends with the reconstruction of the city of Tushha (A.0.101.1 i 101–ii 12). The three battle episodes are connected to one another by simple pairs of departure and arrival notices: *ana* ᵘʳᵘ*Kinabu āl dannūtišu ša* ᵐ*Ḫulayya aqṭirib* 'I approached Kinabu, the fortified city of Hulayya'; *ištu* ᵘʳᵘ*Kinabu attumuš ana* ᵘʳᵘ*Tēla aqṭirib* 'I departed from Kinabu. I approached Tela'; and *ištu* ᵘʳᵘ*Nirbi attumša ana* ᵘʳᵘ*Tušha aqṭirib* 'I departed from Nirbi. I approached Tushha' (A.0.101.1 i 106–7, 113, and ii 2–3).

When itinerary notices are used to connect one episode with another, they are not always just bare, as in the Tushha episode, but are sometimes combined with stereotypical expressions for heading out on a campaign. Even a second or third episode within a campaign is begun in the same way as an episode at the beginning: the king receives a report of rebellion, musters his troops with the support of the god Ashur, and heads out to handle the problem. This is not unlike the effort made by Tiglath-pileser I's scribe to mark the chronological structure of the episodes by effectively restarting the inscription with a new set of epithets. Here, however, the scribe creates a connection to the previous episode with the temporal expression *kī ina* GN *usbākuni* 'While I was in GN'. We saw this expression used at the beginning of Ashurnasirpal II's third campaign to Zamua, cited above, where he received a report of rebellion while he was in Nineveh. When this expression is used to connect two episodes in the middle of a campaign, the place-name is the site of the previous episode rather than an Assyrian capital (see, for example, A.0.101.1 i 74–75). Ashurnasirpal II's campaign to Katmuhu and the Nairi lands provides an example:

> *ina tukulti Aššur bēliya* **ištu ᵘʳᵘTušḫan attumuš** *narkabāti eṭlātu pitḫallu ašarissu issiya asseqe ina raksūte* ⁱᵈ*Idiglat ētebir kal mušīti artedi* **ana** **ᵘʳᵘPitura āl dannūtišunu ša ᵏᵘʳDirrayya aqṭirib**

> With the support of Ashur, my lord, **I departed from Tushha**. I took with me strong chariots, cavalry, (and) crack troops. I crossed the Tigris by means of a bridge of rafts. I travelled all night. **I approached Pitura, the fortified city of the Dirru**. (A.0.101.1 ii 103–4)

Here we see itinerary notices integrated with the appeal to Ashur and the mustering of troops characteristic of the beginning of a campaign, although in this case they are used to connect the eighth and ninth episodes in this extensive campaign.

It is possible and even in some cases likely that the authors are no longer using a source document in instances such as these. The itinerary notices that move Ashurnasirpal II from Kinabu to Tela and from Nirbu to Tushha on his campaign to Damdammusa are not all explicitly connected to one another by repetition of the place-name, as one expects from the itinerary genre, based on its typical use in administrative documents. The land of Nirbu, which is used in the third itinerary notice rather than repeating the city name Tela from the preceding itinerary notice, comes instead from the preceding *episode*, which suggests that the battle episodes and the itinerary notices were composed together, because their settings are intertwined. That the whole campaign was composed together is further suggested by the fact that episodes are not independent but have a causal connection to one another. The campaign to Kinabu generated a second battle episode at Tela, the fortified city of the Nirbu, because the people of Nirbu were unwise enough to have assisted Hulayya in his rebellion against the Assyrians at Kinabu (A.0.101.1 i 101–ii 12).[104] Moreover, the name Kinabu is given only in the itinerary notices. If the itinerary notices are not an integral part of the composition, the first battle site is left unidentified. If a source document was used to compose this narrative, it has been decomposed, as the Egyptian daybooks were, in order to create a coherent narrative.

While the use—or not—of a source document may be ambiguous in these sorts of examples, cases where itinerary notices are used in ways that depart quite radically from their typical appearance in administrative documents point to creative use of the itinerary *genre*. The camping notice *assakan bēdāk* is used in two ways that depart from its typical use in administrative documents. First, it is used to create denouement in the narrative. Ashurnasirpal II's campaign that is dated the 15th of Tishri contains three main episodes. The first two contain accounts of the conquest of Bunasi and Larbusa, two cities in the area of Mt. Nisir, while the third relates the conquest of a variety of unnamed cities in the Mt. Nisir plain (A.0.101.1 ii 33–49).[105] These episodes are connected with basic arrival and departure notices, but each ends with a camping notice similar to the following:

> *ana usmanniyama atūra bēdāk ištu usmanniyama atūra attumuš ana ālāni ša ṣēr* ^kur^*Nisir ša ašaršunu mamma lā ēmuru allik*

> I returned to my camp and spent the night. I departed from this camp. I marched to the cities in the plain of Mt. Nisir which no one had ever seen. (A.0.101.1 ii 38–39)

When Ashurnasirpal finishes the massacre, plunder, and destruction of Bunasi and its surrounding cities, he does not simply depart from Bunasi and move on to the next site but instead returns to his camp. Furthermore, his departure is not from Bunasi, as one might expect, but simply from the camp. Camping notices in administrative documents create temporal pauses that serve the pragmatic purposes of the documents, such as to indicate where the troops were to quarter along their journey in the Dur-Katlimmu itinerary. In the context of annals other than the Habur campaigns, however, they are used to create

---

104. This campaign continues with a tribute episode connected with the temporal clause *kī ina* ^uru^*Tušḫa usbākuni* 'While I was in Tushha . . .' (ii 12–15). The addition of such episodes at the end of campaigns in the Ninurta Temple reliefs is not uncommon.

105. This campaign also has a tribute episode appended to it with *ina ūmešuma*.

a pause in the action that allows the reader to breathe before the next violent episode, serving aesthetic rather than pragmatic goals.

Second, camping notices are used to depict radial movement out from a base camp. After Assurnasirpal II's conquest of Ammali, the fortified city of Arashtua, and its surrounding cities on his third campaign against Zamua (A.0.101.1 ii 49–86), he leaves that area and approaches the city of Zamru. After a brief tribute episode, he departs from Zamru and goes to Mt. Etinu, again to collect tribute. The scribe includes a denouement after this episode: *ana usmanniyama atūra bēdāk* 'I returned to my camp and spent the night'. The following departure notice is not from Mt. Etinu but from the camp: *ina rēšūte ša Aššur u* ^d*Šamaš ilāni tikliya ištu ušmanni annītema attumuš* 'With the help of Ashur and Shamash, the gods who support me, I departed this camp' (A.0.101.1 ii 65). The next episode is introduced by another departure from Zamru, this time to Arzizu and its surrounding cities; this episode ends in a return to the camp as well (A.0.101.1 ii 72–75). The next departure notice is, yet again, from the city of Zamru, this time for good. In this campaign, the author has used the camping notices not simply to create a pause in an otherwise linear episode but to convey the idea that the Assyrian king set up a base camp in Zamru from which he engaged in both the pursuit of Ameka and the battle against Arzizu. Only when these episodes are finished does he move on from Zamru. This type of radial movement out from a single site is never found in administrative documents and is a creative use of the itinerary genre.

Hans Robert Jauss understood the process of genre change within a culture to involve canonization, automatization, and reshuffling. A genre attains normative status and then is used or replicated until it undergoes substantive change internally or is replaced by another type of text.[106] By the ninth century, the annals genre had a stable form consisting of yearly campaign episodes, dated by eponym year and connected to one another with itinerary notices. We can now see that this form resulted from experimentation over a long time, from blending annals with chronicles and itineraries. But scribes did not retain blends like the Broken Obelisk or the Habur campaigns. Instead, date formulas and itineraries became a standard feature of the annals genre and were simply replicated in successive inscriptions as a typical part of writing an annal. Such uses of itinerary notices continued to be the norm in annals during the reign of Ashurnasirpal II and early in the reign of Shalmaneser III, in inscriptions such as a stone slab from the Nabu Temple at Calah (A.0.102.3), the Kurkh

---

106. Jauss, *Toward an Aesthetic of Reception*, 106.

Monolith (A.0.102.2), the Calah bulls (A.0.102.8), and a broken statue from Calah (A.0.102.16).[107]

Changes to the annals genre took place during Shalmaneser III's reign. Beginning in his ninth year, the practice of dating events to the eponym year was replaced by use of *palû* to count not only the first year, as had been the norm since the inscriptions of Tukulti-Ninurta I, but the successive years of reign.[108] Itinerary notices also eventually ceased to be part of the annals genre. Two inscriptions, both from Sargon II's reign, engage this itinerary-based structure for their campaign narratives in the same ways we have seen here: the letter to the god and the Iran stele, which relate his eighth and sixth campaigns, respectively.[109] But the accounts of these campaigns in Sargon II's annals do not employ this structure. Aside from these two texts, Shalmaneser III's annals are the last Assyrian royal inscriptions to use itinerary notices.

We can see that the role of the itinerary notices within the annals genre became less important by looking at how they fared when a campaign was revised in a later edition of Shalmaneser III's annals.[110] Comparing accounts of the campaign in Shalmaneser III's sixth regnal year in the two versions of the annals from Ashur on clay (842 B.C.E.; A.0.102.6) and a marble slab (839 B.C.E.; A.0.102.10), respectively, and on the Black Obelisk (828–827 B.C.E.; A.0.102.14), shown in fig. 6, allows us to see that itinerary notices were frequently omitted

---

107. Yamada, *Construction of the Assyrian Empire*, 76–85.

108. On use of the *palû* system, see H. Tadmor, "The Campaigns of Sargon II of Assur: A Chronological-Historical Study," *JCS* 12 (1958) 28–30; A. Fuchs, *Die Annalen des Jahres 711 v. Chr. nach Prismenfragmenten aus Ninive und Assur* (SAAS 8; Helsinki: Neo-Assyrian Text Corpus Project, 1998) 81–96; S. Yamada, *The Construction of the Assyrian Empire: A Historical Study of the Inscriptions of Shalmanesar III (859–824 B.C.) Relating to His Campaigns to the West* (CHANE 3; Leiden: Brill, 2000) 17 n. 24, 335–41.

109. For the letter to the god, see F. Thureau-Dangin, *Une relation de la huitième campagne de Sargon (714 av. J.-C.)* (Paris: Geuthner, 1912); and, for a more recent edition of the text, W. Mayer, "Sargons Feldzug gegen Urartu—714 v. Chr.: Text und Übersetzung," *MDOG* 115 (1983) 65–132. For the Iran stele, see L. D. Levine, *Two Neo-Assyrian Stelae from Iran* (Royal Ontario Museum Art and Archaeology Occasional Paper 23; Ontario: Royal Ontario Museum, 1972).

110. For the principle that later editions of the annals tend to abbreviate earlier campaigns to make room for fuller narration of more recent events, see Olmstead, *Assyrian Historiography*, 8. L. D. Levine has questioned this principle, which has often been axiomatically applied in studies on the annals in such a way that the compositional process has been oversimplified ("The Second Campaign of Sennacherib." *JNES* 32 [1973] 312). Whatever the reason, the earlier campaigns do tend to be shorter, at least in the case of the three texts I discuss here.

Ashur Annals (842 B.C.E.) A.0.102.6 ii 19–33	Ashur Annals (839 B.C.E.) A.0.102.10 ii 13–25	Black Obelisk (828–27 B.C.E.) A.0.102.14 lines 54–59
In my sixth regnal year, **I moved out from Nineveh.**	In my sixth regnal year,	In my sixth regnal year,
I approached the cities on the banks of the river Balih.	I approached the cities on the banks of the river Balih.	I approached the cities on the banks of the river Balih.
They became frightened in the face of my mighty weapons and killed Giammu, their city ruler. I entered Til-Turahi.	They killed Giammu, their city ruler. I entered Til-Turahi.	They killed Giammu, their city ruler. I entered Til-Turahi.
I claimed the city as my own. **I departed from the banks of the river Balih.**		
I crossed the Euphrates in flood and received tribute from the kings of Hatti.	I crossed the Euphrates in flood and received tribute from all the kings of the land Hatti.	I crossed the Euphrates in flood and received tribute from all the kings of the land Hatti.
I departed from Hatti. I approached Aleppo. I made sacrifices to Adad of Aleppo. **I departed from Aleppo.** I approached Qarqar.		

Fig. 6. Shalmaneser III's Campaign to Qarqar.

in later editions of the annals.[111] In the 842 annals, we can clearly see the continued use of arrival and departure notices to connect episodes, here including

111. I have included the campaigns up to the conflict with the Damascus coalition, which does not contain itinerary language and which contains little variation from one inscription to another. For the Ashur annals, the dates of composition are based on those explicitly given in the colophon; since the Black Obelisk has no colophon, the

tribute collection along the Balih River, collection of tribute from Hatti, sacrifices to Adad in Aleppo, and the conflict with the Damascus coalition at Qarqar in 843 B.C.E. The 839 annals are an abridgment of the 842 annals, and the Black Obelisk is one of the latest versions.[112] The initial departure notice is omitted and the arrival notice retained, while later itinerary notices are often left out altogether. The changes are probably part of an effort to shorten many of the campaigns to a single episode by omitting episodes entirely.[113] In other cases, such as the accounts of Shalmaneser III's fourth regnal year in the 842 annals (A.0.102.6 i 61–ii 2), the 839 annals (A.0.102.10 i 45–48), and the Black Obelisk (A.0.102.14 lines 41–44), we find a series of itinerary notices condensed, if not omitted altogether.

Use of the itinerary genre in Assyrian annals appears to be related to the focus during the ninth century on reestablishing control over territory that had already been incorporated into Assyria during the second millennium. Unlike the expansion beyond the traditional frontier achieved by Shalmaneser III, the territory around the Habur would have been familiar and the roads well known.[114] Indeed, the Middle Assyrian itinerary from Dur-Katlimmu, which articulates the route to be taken by a group of *ḫurādu*-troops, covers territory in the Habur region. Liverani speculated that the itinerary genre ceased to be used in royal inscriptions after the early years of Shalmaneser III, "since at that time the Assyrian army had to venture outside the administered territory, in regions less well known and out of control."[115] This view rests on the assumption that itineraries are records of regularly traversed territory and accurately reflects the fact that itinerary notices first came to be used in annals as they were copied into and accommodated to the narrative. And itinerary notices did indeed come to characterize the annals genre during the tenth–early eighth centuries B.C.E., which does coincide with the period in which Assyrian kings strove to regain control of traditionally held territory and began, during the reigns of Ashurnasirpal II and Shalmaneser III, to expand outside it.[116] But,

---

date of composition is based on the last campaign narrated. See Grayson, RIMA 3.32, 50, and 63.

112. Yamada, *Construction of the Assyrian Empire*, 20, 26.

113. See, in particular, the accounts of the second campaign (A.0.102.6 i 49–56; A.0.102.10 i 30–36; and A.0.102.14 lines 32–35), which is only one episode to begin with, but later editions omit the initial departure notice. Note that itinerary notices are not *always* omitted.

114. Liverani, "Assyria in the Ninth Century," 214.

115. Ibid., 214–15.

116. See the discussion of periodization in Younger, "Neo-Assyrian and Israelite History," 243–46.

as I have shown here, itinerary notices simply became a feature of the annals genre, and there is no reason that campaigns outside the Assyrian heartland could not have been rendered in this form. Whether subsequent changes in the annals genre, including the dissolution of itinerary notices, are also connected to changes in imperial goals or policy must be explored in another context.

Our study of how the itinerary genre is used in the literary context of military narratives from Egypt and Assyria has shown us that even creative uses of the genre in these contexts can be an outgrowth of the use of administrative documents. Egyptian scribes creatively selected entries from their daybook sources and combined them with dialogue, poetry, and other elements of literary repertoire in order to achieve aesthetic and ideological goals. Assyrian scribes, having tried to write a few campaigns based on administrative documents, instead experimented with using the features of the itinerary genre to help them write better annals narrative. Some of the techniques used by scribes in both cultures to accommodate the itinerary genre to its new literary context are quite mechanical, such as changing a verb form, while other accommodation techniques are quite creative, such as imitating the short notes characteristic of the source document in order to create miniature battle episodes. These narratives do not constitute just another set of prototypical examples of the itinerary genre from the ancient Near East. Rather, we can see the accommodation that Davies finds to be characteristic of the wilderness itineraries in the Torah operating already in Egyptian and Assyrian literature.

The horizon of expectations for an itinerary in its new literary context as part of an Egyptian *nḫtw* narrative or an Assyrian annal shifts somewhat. Apart from the example of radial movement discussed above, itinerary notices in this literary context still convey goal-directed, linear movement. We expect the king and army to arrive at the battle site just as we expect the merchants to deliver the goods to their destination. But the attribute of verisimilitude may be less important in these contexts. While it is essential for the pragmatic function of administrative documents, these military narratives can successfully achieve their core aesthetic and ideological goals even if the data are not accurate. That said, the fact that these scribes are using sources indicates a concern to base their narratives on what actually took place, however much they may be selective about what data are used in the narrative and how they are used.

Mario Fales has suggested that the Assyrian royal inscriptions are a "genre in the making."[117] By discussing how the scribes experimented with both the

---

117. F. M. Fales, "Assyrian Royal Inscriptions: Newer Horizons," *SAAB* 13 (1999–2001) 122.

chronicle and itinerary genres to shape the annals genre, I have shown in some detail one aspect of the evolution of the annals genre. The itinerary genre, once simply used to report the route of a journey in texts that would ultimately be filed in an archive, is now also used to emplot a highly ideological narrative displayed on a palace wall that communicates the king's mastery over territory and the geographical contiguity of his empire. The genre was transformed by its use in a new historical, social, and literary context and gave shape to a new genre. Thanks to experimentation with chronicles, date formulas now stand alongside itinerary notices in annals to mark explicitly the linear character of time. The army has been sidelined in favor of the king, who is now the focus of the narrative and the subject of the itinerary notices, leading the army to victory.

Chapter 5

An Israelite "Annal"

> *Originality is nothing but judicious imitation.*
> *The most original writers borrowed one from another.*
> —Voltaire

Innovative uses of the itinerary genre in Egyptian and Neo-Assyrian military narratives, as we have seen above, were driven at core by a shift in royal ideology. Kings were no longer simply builders and maintainers of the cult, their traditional roles in commemorative building inscriptions, but were also conquerors. Their scribes found a way not only to commemorate but also to promote this role by creating new literary forms. Despite the innovations involved in creating them, these new literary forms stretch the norms of itineraries and commemorative inscriptions only so far. Egyptian scribes continued to use source documents as a matter of practice when writing military narratives. Itinerary notices became a normative feature of the annals genre because Assyrian scribes were inspired by the potential of the source documents they were using. Yet, however much the annals genre differs in form and function from the commemorative building inscription genre out of which it grew, annals do continue to commemorate the king's deeds.

The itinerary in Num 33:1–49 is often understood to be a source document, and Frank Moore Cross argued that a redactor used it to structure the episodes in the wilderness narrative, abridging it with summary statements or regional designations where the combined JE source had no corresponding episode.[1] This view, or a variation on it, has long been commonly accepted.[2] I have now

---

1. F. M. Cross, *Canaanite Myth and Hebrew Epic: Essays in the History of the Religion of Israel* (Cambridge: Harvard University Press, 1973) 308–9.

2. E.g., H. Schmid, *Mose: Überlieferung und Geschichte* (BZAW 110; Berlin: Alfred Töpelmann, 1968) 22; G. I. Davies, *The Wilderness Itineraries in the Old Testament* (Ph.D. diss., University of Cambridge, 1975); idem, "The Wilderness Itineraries and the Composition of the Pentateuch," *VT* 33 (1983) 1–13; M. S. Smith, "The Literary Arrangement of the Priestly Redaction of Exodus: A Preliminary Investigation," *CBQ* 58 (1996) 25–50; idem, *The Pilgrimage Pattern in Exodus* (JSOTSup 239; Sheffield: Sheffield Academic

discussed in detail the techniques used by the Egyptian and Assyrian scribes to accommodate source documents to a narrative context. If Israelite scribes likewise accommodated Num 33:1–49 to a narrative source about the wilderness sojourn, we should see evidence of similar techniques. The process of abridgment posited by Cross for Num 33:1–49 and the wilderness narrative is not unlike the selective use Egyptian scribes made of entries from their daybooks, integrating them with other narrative materials to write campaign narratives. But the Egyptian scribes created formally and geographically coherent narratives out of their selections. If an Israelite redactor did use Num 33:1–49, he introduced a number of formal and geographical problems into the wilderness narrative that are not present in his source document.

Like the administrative documents I discussed in chap. 3, the itinerary in Num 33:1–49 lays out a route in which one stop is explicitly connected to the next by repetition of the place-name, and a single convention is used consistently throughout. A redactor seeking to create a coherent version of the wilderness narrative based on this itinerary would surely have benefited by copying the form of the notices just as it is, maintaining the consistency in style, and connecting the notices to one another even when using them selectively. Despite some failures to accommodate the person of the verbs, Tukulti-Ninurta II's scribe used a consistent convention throughout his Habur itinerary, and all of his notices are explicitly connected to one another by repetition of a place-name, just as they would have been in the administrative document from which he copied. We might expect the same if a redactor copied from Num 33:1–49, but we find notices in the wilderness narrative that use different conventions for the itinerary genre and that are not explicitly connected to one another.

Num 33:1–49 consistently displays a stereotyped formula for itinerary notices throughout, as illustrated by the first notice in Num 33:5: וַיִּסְעוּ בְנֵי־יִשְׂרָאֵל מֵרַעְמְסֵס וַיַּחֲנוּ בְּסֻכֹּת 'The Israelites set out from Ramses and camped at Sukkoth'. The verbs נסע and חנה are used in their narrative preterite forms, each followed by a place-name. Not all of the itinerary notices in the wilderness narrative, however, use this convention. The itinerary notices in Num 21:12–13a use מִשָּׁם 'from there', rather than repeating the place-name.[3]

Press, 1997); idem, "Matters of Space and Time in Exodus and Numbers," in *Theological Exegesis: Essays in Honor of Brevard S. Childs* (ed. C. Seitz and K. E. Greene-McCreight; Grand Rapids, MI: Eerdmans, 1999) 182–207.

3. G. W. Coats, "The Wilderness Itinerary," *CBQ* 34 (1972) 136. The same convention is used in Deut 10:6–7 as noted, for example, by G. B. Gray, *A Critical and Exegetical Commentary on Numbers* (ICC; New York: Scribner's, 1906) 280.

מִשָּׁם נָסָעוּ וַיַּחֲנוּ בְּנַחַל זָרֶד: מִשָּׁם נָסָעוּ וַיַּחֲנוּ מֵעֵבֶר אַרְנוֹן

From there they departed and camped at Wadi Zered. From there they departed and camped beyond the Arnon.

The author of these two notices has employed the same convention that we saw in the Middle Assyrian itinerary from Dur-Katlimmu:

ina ^{id}*Marirte*	At the river Marirte,
ibīat ištu ^{id}KI.MIN	they will stay overnight. From "ditto"
ina ^{uru}*Makrisi*	in Makrisi
ibīat ištu ^{uru}KI.MIN	they will stay overnight. From "ditto,"
ina ^{uru}*Napraṣi*	in Napraṣi,
ibīat	they will stay the night.

(DeZ 2521 lines 3–8)

The word מִשָּׁם in Num 21:12–13a functions just as KI.MIN does in this itinerary and is also comparable with the use of *st tn* 'this place' in Egyptian daybooks, as discussed in chap. 3. The author of Num 21:12–13a uses the perfect rather than the narrative preterite form in the departure clauses, because מִשָּׁם occurs at the front of the clause. The itinerary notices in Num 21:18b–20, on the other hand, use no verbs at all. The genre is indicated simply by repeating the place-names and using the preposition מִן.

וּמִמִּדְבָּר מַתָּנָה: וּמִמַּתָּנָה נַחֲלִיאֵל וּמִנַּחֲלִיאֵל בָּמוֹת: וּמִבָּמוֹת הַגַּיְא אֲשֶׁר בִּשְׂדֵה מוֹאָב רֹאשׁ הַפִּסְגָּה וְנִשְׁקָפָה עַל־פְּנֵי הַיְשִׁימֹן:

From Midbar to Mattanah. From Mattanah to Nahaliel. From Nahaliel to Bamoth. From Bamoth to the valley which is in the field of Moab, at the summit of Pisgah and overlooking Jeshimon.

This convention for writing an itinerary is very similar to the convention used in the letter from Shamshi-Adad to Kuwari at Shemshara:

. . . *ištu Zasli*	. . . from Zasli
ana Šegibbu ištu Šegibbu	to Shegibbu, from Shegibbu
ana Zikum ištu Zikum	to Zikum, from Zikum
ana Urau ištu Urau	to Urau, from Urau
ana Lutpiš ištu Lutpiš	to Lutpish, from Lutpish
ana mā[t] Ḫaburātim	to the land of Haburatim.

(SH 809 lines 54–59)

While this Akkadian itinerary uses both the prepositions *ištu* and *ana* to mark departure and arrival, a preposition (עַד or בְּ) for arrival is not needed in Hebrew, since the place-name functions simply as an accusative of direction. Num 21:12–13a and 18b–20, then, do use conventions for the itinerary with which we are quite familiar. But they do not use the *same* conventions used in Num 33:1–49 or in most of the rest of the wilderness narrative, for that matter. If the itinerary notices in the wilderness narrative are based on Num 33:1–49, the redactor compromised the coherence of the narrative by introducing new conventions and thus creating fractures in the itinerary chain that might prompt a reader, when she encounters a fracture of this sort, to wonder: Why the switch in form here?

If all of the itinerary notices in the wilderness narrative were taken from Num 33:1–49, the redactor also introduced some rather serious geographical problems. The wilderness narrative contains a number of double arrivals and departures that violate the linear character of the itinerary genre, run counter to our knowledge of how bodies move through space (one does not leave or arrive at a place twice), and are not present in Num 33:1–49. The Israelites arrive in Moab twice, once in Num 21:20 and again in Num 22:1, as I discussed already in chap. 2. They also arrive in the wilderness of Paran twice, once in Num 10:12 and again in Num 12:16. Furthermore, there are two departures from Egypt and two departures from Sinai, each with a different name for the place. The Israelites leave Egypt and head into the wilderness of Etham in Exod 13:20 but into the wilderness of Shur in Exod 15:22. Num 10:12 has the Israelites depart from the wilderness of Sinai, while they leave the mountain of Yahweh in Num 10:33.

There is also profound lack of clarity about the Israelites' route from Kadesh onward. We first encounter the Israelites at Kadesh in the spies episode (Num 13:26) *before they even arrive there* according to the itinerary notice in Num 20:1 and its counterpart in Num 33:36. The itinerary notice in Num 14:25 (which has no counterpart in Num 33:1–49) takes the Israelites away from Kadesh along the way of Yam Suf. The way of Yam Suf appears again in Num 21:4, where it takes the Israelites around Edom, but here the route conflicts with the series of itinerary notices in Num 21:10–20, which takes the Israelites into Transjordan around the south end of the Dead Sea, as the route in Num 33:37–49 appears to do as well.

Finally, if a redactor used Num 33:1–49 to structure the wilderness narrative, he has moved Yam Suf to a different location on the route. In the wilderness narrative, the Israelites camp at the sea (Exod 14:2) and, once they have crossed, Moses leads them away from it in Exod 15:22, where it is specifically called Yam Suf.

Numbers 33:7–11	Exodus 14:2; 15:22–23, 27; 16:1
[7] They set out from Etham and turned about toward Pi-hahiroth, which faces Baal-zephon, and they camped before Migdol.	[14:2] Speak to the Israelites so that they turn back and camp before Pi-hahiroth, between Migdol and the sea, before Baal-zephon. You should camp facing it, by the sea.
[8] They set out from Pene-hahiroth and passed through the sea into the wilderness.	
	[15:22] Then Moses caused Israel to set out from **Yam Suf**. They went out into the wilderness of Shur.
They made a three-day journey into the wilderness of Etham and camped at Marah.	They went for three days in the wilderness and found no water. [23a] They came to Marah.
[9] They set out from Marah and came to Elim.	[27a] They came to Elim
[10] They set out from Elim and encamped by **Yam Suf**.	[16:1a] They set out from Elim.
[11] They set out from **Yam Suf** and encamped in the wilderness of Sin.	The whole Israelite community came to the wilderness of Sin, which is between Elim and Sinai.

The sea crossing in the Numbers 33 itinerary is indicated in v. 8, but Yam Suf does not appear until vv. 10–11, *three stops later*. Why would a redactor create this and other geographical problems that are not present in the source document?

Explaining the formal and geographical problems in the itinerary notices scattered throughout wilderness narrative will occupy us throughout the remainder of this book. What we can already see at this point is that they are not the result of abridgment as proposed by Cross, particularly since his arguments for abridgment themselves do not stand up to close scrutiny. The parade example of abridgment, pointed out by both Cross and Graham I. Davies, is the use of לְמַסְעֵיהֶם 'their stages' in Exod 17:1. The stages are taken to refer to two specific sites, Dophkah and Alush in Num 33:12–14, which would have been omitted from the itinerary when it was used to structure the wilderness narrative because there were no episodes to go with them.[4] While abridgment

4. G. I. Davies, "Wilderness Itineraries and the Composition of the Pentateuch," 7; see also B. Jacob, *The Second Book of the Bible: Exodus* (trans. W. Jacob; Hoboken,

seems like a reasonable possibility in this case, many of the regional designations in the wilderness narrative in fact *do not* abridge a series of place-names from Numbers 33. The wilderness of Shur in Exod 15:22, for example, does not abbreviate anything from Numbers 33.[5] It is, rather, an alternative name for the wilderness of Etham in Num 33:8.

Cross also argued that the wilderness of Zin in Num 20:1 holds the spot of Zalmonah and Punon in Num 33:41–43.[6]

Numbers 33:36–43	*Numbers 20:1; 20:22; 21:4, 10*
[36] They set out from Ezion-geber and camped in the **wilderness of Zin**, that is, Kadesh.	[20:1a] The Israelites, the whole congregation, came to the **wilderness of Zin** in the first month, and the people stayed at Kadesh.
[37] They set out from Kadesh and camped at Mount Hor on the border of the land of Edom . . .	[20:22] They set out from Kadesh, and the Israelites, the whole congregation, came to Mount Hor.
[41] They set out from Mount Hor and camped at **Zalmonah.**	[21:4] They set out from Mount Hor by way of Yam Suf to go around the land of Edom.
[42] They set out from **Zalmonah** and camped at **Punon**.	
[43] They set out from **Punon** and camped at Oboth.	[21:10] The Israelites set out and camped at Oboth.

If the wilderness of Zin is an abbreviation for Zalmonah and Punon in Num 33:41–43, we would expect to see it in the wilderness narrative *after* Num 21:4, not in Num 20:1. Zalmonah and Punon appear after Mount Hor in Numbers 33, so the wilderness of Zin should come between the Israelites' departure from Mount Hor in Num 21:4 and their arrival in Oboth in v. 10 if it is an abridgment

NJ: Ktav, 1992) 512. Davies here fleshes out Martin Noth's insight that לְמַסְעֵיהֶם in Exod 17:1 "prompts the conjecture that in this context P may have found in some *Vorlage* still other station names which, up to the point of Rephidim, he found no need to cite" (*A History of Pentateuchal Traditions* [trans. B. W. Anderson; Englewood Cliffs, NJ: Prentice Hall, 1972] 225).

5. Num 33:8–9 takes the Israelites from Pi-hahiroth (Exod 14:2), to the wilderness of Etham (Exod 13:20), to Marah (Exod 15:23), and then to Elim (Exod 15:27); all of these place-names are in Exodus, so wilderness of Shur does not abbreviate Numbers 33 as Cross suggested (*Canaanite Myth*, 310).

6. English rendering of the place-names Sin (סִין), which refers to the wilderness east of the Egyptian border, and Zin (צִן), which refers to the region around Kadesh, echo the Hebrew spellings.

of these sites, which have no associated episodes. In fact, Num 20:1 places the wilderness of Zin at the same point in the journey as Num 33:36 does.[7]

The wilderness before Moab in Num 21:11 is, in Cross's view, an abbreviation for Dibon-gad, Almon-diblathaim, and the mountains of Abarim in Num 33:45–47.[8]

Numbers 33:44–48	*Numbers 21:11–13a, 16a, 18b–20; 22:1*
[44] They set out from Oboth and camped at Iye-abarim, in the territory of Moab. [45] They set out from Iyyim and camped at Dibon-gad. [46] They set out from Dibon-gad and camped at Almon-diblathaim. [47] They set out from Almon-diblathaim and camped in the hills of Abarim, before Nebo.	[21:11] They set out from Oboth and camped at Iye-abarim, in the **wilderness facing Moab to the east**. [12] From there they set out and camped at the Wadi Zered. [13] From there they set out and camped beyond the Arnon, that is, in the wilderness that extends from the territory of the Amorites. For the Arnon is the boundary of Moab, between Moab and the Amorites. [16a] And from there to Beer. . . . [18b] From Midbar to Mattanah. [19] From Mattanah to Nahaliel. From Nahaliel to Bamoth. [20] From Bamoth to the valley that is in the country of Moab, at the peak of Pisgah, overlooking the wasteland.
[48] They set out from the hills of Abarim and camped in the steppes of Moab, at the Jordan near Jericho.	[22:1] The Israelites then marched on and camped in the steppes of Moab, across the Jordan from Jericho.

The wilderness facing Moab to the east in Num 21:11b does not serve as a substitute for missing names; it specifies where the site of Iye-abarim is. In fact, it specifies a different location for Iye-abarim than the Numbers 33 itinerary does, since Num 33:44 situates it *in* Moab, while Num 21:11b situates it *east of* Moab. Moreover, both Numbers 33 and Numbers 21 continue with a list of sites in Transjordan—it is simply a *different* list of sites.

---

7. Despite Cross's argument that the wilderness of Zin in Num 20:1 substitutes for Zalmonah and Punon in Numbers 33 (ibid., 309), he did acknowledge its position in Num 33:36 at the same point it occurs in Num 20:1 (p. 315). Moreover, he elsewhere notes that it is the wilderness before Moab, not the wilderness of Zin, that substitutes for Zalmonah and Punon (p. 316 n. 81).

8. Ibid.

The wilderness of Paran, according to Cross, is meant to stand for the long string of place-names in Num 33:18b–35 that do not occur in the wilderness narrative.[9] As the following comparison shows, this suggestion works nicely for Num 12:16.

Numbers 33:16–36	*Numbers 10:12, 33; 11:35; 12:16; 20:1*
[16] They set out from the wilderness of Sinai	[10:12] The Israelites set out according to their stages from the wilderness of Sinai.
	The cloud came to rest in the **wilderness of Paran.**
	[10:33] They set out from the mountain of Yahweh on a three-day journey.
They camped at Kibroth-hattaavah.	
[17] They set out from Kibroth-hattaavah and camped at Hazeroth.	[11:35] From Kibroth-hattaavah, the people set out for Hazeroth.
[18] They set out from Hazeroth	[12:16] Afterward, the people set out from Hazeroth
and camped at Rithmah. [19] They set out from Rithmah and camped at Rimmon-perez....	and camped in the **wilderness of Paran.**
[34] They set out from Jotbath and camped at Abronah. [35] They set out from Abronah and camped at Ezion-geber.	
[36] They set out from Ezion-geber and encamped in the wilderness of Zin, that is, Kadesh.	[20:1] The Israelites—the whole congregation—arrived in the wilderness of Zin in the first month, and the people stayed at Kadesh.

But the wilderness of Paran is used in Num 10:12 as well, where it does not abridge anything. The names of Kibroth-hattaavah and Hazeroth that follow the departure from Sinai in Num 33:16–18 also occur in Num 11:35 and 12:16.

Use of Num 33:1–49 as a source document is thus *not* a plausible explanation for the presence of itinerary notices in the wilderness narrative: Cross's argument for abridgment of that source does not hold up, and we would have to assume that a redactor turned a source that is formally and geographically coherent into a narrative that is not, which would be at odds with the redactional

---

9. Ibid., 309, 314–15.

goal of bringing formal coherence to the disparate materials we find in the wilderness narrative. Moreover, it is not clear that Num 33:1–49 actually *is* a source document like those used by the Assyrian and Egyptian scribes discussed in chap. 4 to shape their narratives. While the *form* of Num 33:1–49 is more or less that of an administrative document, its *content* and social context, or *situation of address*, are not so clearly appropriate. Itineraries record the activities of merchants, small groups of workers, and diplomatic contingents as well as kings and their armies, not the movements of an entire ethnic group. Furthermore, as Davies has recognized, neither the situations that generated the need to report on a journey to a superior or provide instruction on a route to be taken (the reasons for which itineraries are typically written) nor the bureaucratic system within which they were produced likely existed in a wilderness period. Itineraries are also typically written by those who participated in the journey, so the notion that a later generation would write such a document as an account of a past event (a possible explanation for Num 33:1–49 as a record of a wilderness sojourn) does not fit with what we know about the typical production of itineraries.[10]

In the following pages, I will argue that we owe the present shape of the wilderness narrative not to use of a source document but to profoundly creative uses of the itinerary *genre*. Although Egyptian and Assyrian military narratives are highly ideological, scribes narrated past events in the service of this ideology. The fact that they turned to administrative documents as sources in at least some cases suggests that they balanced the desire to report with the desire to emplot. But the wilderness narrative is quite unlike standard forms of ancient Near Eastern historiography and even other Israelite historiography, all of which tends to be about kings and states.[11] Many of its episodes are foundational stories for Israel's legal, priestly, and prophetic institutions, and redaction-critical studies commonly understand its final shape to be, as Mark S. Smith states, a "foundational-story for rebuilding Judean society in the Persian period."[12] The itinerary notices are understood to shape a text that would speak to an audience concerned with reestablishing Israelite society after the

---

10. G. I. Davies, "The Wilderness Itineraries: A Comparative Study," *TynBul* 25 (1974) 79.

11. D. M. Carr, "The Rise of Torah," in *The Pentateuch as Torah: New Models for Understanding Its Promulgation and Acceptance* (ed. G. N. Knoppers and B. M. Levinson; Winona Lake, IN: Eisenbrauns, 2007) 48. For comparison of biblical and ancient Near Eastern historiographies, see J. Van Seters, *In Search of History: Historiography in the Ancient World and the Origins of Biblical History* (repr., Winona Lake, IN: Eisenbrauns, 1997).

12. M. S. Smith, *Pilgrimage Pattern*, 261.

return from exile by explaining its ancestral origins and the genesis of its social institutions. While the itinerary notices give the wilderness narrative a historiographical form, they are blended with material that is not typically historiographic—laws, ritual instructions, and narratives about getting water from a rock—creating a genre hybrid that is unprecedented in the ancient Near East.

The itinerary genre is used as a mode of emplotment to give *meaning* as well as formal coherence to this diverse collection of materials. (As we will see in chap. 6, fractures in the itinerary chain such as those discussed above are the result of revisions to the wilderness narrative.) Genre, as John Frow notes, shapes and guides the process of interpreting the meaning of a text.[13] Assyrian scribes used their source documents as modes of emplotment, and the itineraries gained an ideological dimension as they were repurposed not only to provide formal coherence to annals but also to convey the idea of mastery over territory. Yet the itinerary retains some of its character as a source document, particularly the strong link between form and content that had been necessary to achieve the pragmatic goals of administrative records. Using only the *genre* gives a scribe greater flexibility and leaves even more room for innovation. The genre can be used to provide formal coherence just as a source document can and certainly depicts the journey as being of a certain kind (for example, a military march rather than a flight of refugees). But the formal slots of character types, place-names, and date formulas can also be filled with content that is atypical for itineraries and can become vehicles for conveying ideology. Even as its norms are stretched in these ways, the itinerary genre still retains a connection to its typical cultural background, which is why we recognize the history-like character of the wilderness narrative even as we may also have a sense of its generic complexity.

From what cultural background would an ancient Israelite scribe have selected this element of repertoire, and why would he have chosen it to emplot the wilderness narrative? Because communal pilgrimage is an important element of corporate identity, M. S. Smith, following in the footsteps of Cross, has suggested that the itinerary notices depict the Israelites' journey through the wilderness as a pilgrimage. As Smith demonstrates, a number of elements in the exodus and wilderness narratives can be understood quite profitably in this context, including movement away from the profane (Egypt) toward the sacred (Mount Sinai), an audience with God that includes divine teaching, and particularly the three-day journey, which Smith suggests is the approximate travel time from Galilee to Jerusalem and became a trope indicating a pilgrimage

---

13. J. Frow, *Genre* (New Critical Idiom; London: Routledge, 2006) 10.

trip.[14] The idea of pilgrimage is especially prominent as Moses and Aaron request permission from Pharaoh to undertake a three-day journey into the wilderness to sacrifice to God, a ruse for escape from Egypt (Exod 3:18, 5:3, 8:23).

The role of the itinerary notices in depicting a pilgrimage, however, is problematic. As far as the itinerary notices are concerned, Mount Sinai is one stop on a *linear* journey from Egypt to Canaan. As William H. C. Propp has pointed out, a pilgrimage, properly speaking, would be a round trip to the mountain in the wilderness and back.[15] Although the Israelites used a three-day pilgrimage into the wilderness as an excuse to leave Egypt, the *itinerary notices* take them on a journey that has nothing to do with pilgrimage. Its ultimate goal is entry into Canaan, however important Sinai's function in the middle may be.

More importantly, pilgrimage does not fit the contexts we know to have prompted the production of itineraries, which were commercial, possibly civil, and certainly military. If there were a pilgrimage itinerary, we would expect it to be an official record of an organized pilgrimage. Martin Noth posits that just this sort of record might explain the place-names we find in Num 33:1–49 that occur nowhere else in the wilderness narrative.[16] But we have no evidence that the itinerary genre was used for this purpose in the ancient Near East. Although Smith has made a good case that the authors of the exodus and wilderness narratives drew upon repertoire related to pilgrimage, the fact that the itinerary genre is so well attested in the keeping of military records and the writing of military narratives mitigates against seeing the itinerary notices as having been selected from the background of pilgrimage. The comparative evidence discussed by G. I. Davies and revisited and expanded upon in this study suggests that a reader encountering the itinerary notices in the wilderness narrative would have read them instead against this military background.

---

14. M. S. Smith, *Pilgrimage Pattern*, 56–58, 100–107. On the three-day journey as a trope, see D. H. Aaron, *Etched in Stone: The Emergence of the Decalogue* (New York: T. & T. Clark, 2006) 48–49.

15. W. H. C. Propp, "Review of Mark S. Smith, *The Pilgrimage Pattern in Exodus*," *JQR* 89 (1999) 452–54.

16. M. Noth, "Der Wallfahrtsweg zum Sinai (Nu 33)," in *Aufsätze zur biblischen Landes- und Altertumskunde* (ed. H. W. Wolff; 2 vols.; Neukrichen-Vluyn: Neukirchener Verlag, 1971) 1.55–74. See also R. P. Knierim and G. W. Coats, *Numbers* (FOTL 4; Grand Rapids, MI: Eerdmans, 2005) 309–10. Noth's posited pilgrimage itinerary is often criticized on the grounds that, had there been regular pilgrimages to Mount Sinai or any other divine mountain in the wilderness, and especially if records of them had been kept, there would not be such lack of clarity in biblical literature about where Mount Sinai is; for example, E. W. Davies, *Numbers* (NCB; Grand Rapids, MI: Eerdmans, 1995) 342.

Itineraries are also found in early Greek historiography. John Van Seters turns to the Mediterranean world and finds a number of parallels in form and purpose between the Yahwistic version of the Torah and what he calls antiquarian historiography, a genre used by early Greek historians in the sixth–fourth centuries B.C.E., roughly the same time frame in which he understands the Yahwistic narrative to have been written. Like the Torah, antiquarian historiography is concerned with the origins of states, peoples, and tribes and serves as a prologue to national political history. Also like the Torah, it incorporates a diversity of other, smaller-scale genres such as folklore, myth, etiology, etymology, genealogy, and itinerary as it depicts eponymous ancestors migrating from one place to another. Thus, antiquarian historiography is what theorist Gérard Genette refers to as an archigenre.[17] Antiquarian historiography has the advantage of being able to account for the generic diversity of the wilderness narrative with a single genre label.

The case for antiquarian historiography as a generic influence on literature in the Torah is stronger for Genesis—which involves itineraries and genealogies as formal elements and the migration of individual eponymous ancestors as a theme—than it is for Exodus–Numbers. We find in the wilderness narrative a lengthy, more-or-less unified series of itinerary notices that are strongly military in character and, as Davies has shown, formally very close to the itinerary notices used in ancient Near Eastern administrative documents and military narratives.[18] Van Seters criticizes Davies's failure to consider antiquarian historiography as a possible genre for the Torah and explanation for the itinerary notices, but he does not make a case that antiquarian historiography is a *better* explanation that can also account for the combination of itinerary notices with date formulas and the depiction of the Israelites as an army on the march.[19] Indeed, these are not features of antiquarian historiography as Van Seters describes it. The problem of sustaining a theory that works well to explain Genesis into Exodus–Numbers is not new. Efforts to extend the classical Documentary sources into the exodus and wilderness narratives has generally produced less satisfying results, leading some scholars, following the work of Rolf Rendtorff, to argue that Genesis developed independently from Exodus–

---

17. G. Genette, "The Architext," in *Modern Genre Theory* (ed. D. Duff; London: Longman, 2000) 210–18; Van Seters developed his views on the Yahwist in *Prologue to History: The Yahwist as Historian in Genesis* (Louisville: Westminster John Knox, 1992); and *The Life of Moses: The Yahwist as Historian in Exodus–Numbers* (Louisville: Westminster John Knox, 1994).

18. G. I. Davies, "Wilderness Itineraries: A Comparative Study," 57–59.

19. For critique of Davies, see Van Seters, *Prologue to History*, 199–200; idem, *Life of Moses*, 162.

Numbers.[20] If they are correct, it would not be surprising to see different generic influences in the two bodies of literature.

What *can* account for the specific form and military character of the itinerary notices in the wilderness narrative is the influence of the Assyrian annals genre. Van Seters himself suggests that the Neo-Assyrian annals might be a genre analogue for the wilderness narrative, a suggestion he did not make for Genesis, but he does not pursue this suggestion in depth.[21] He is also not the only scholar to have observed the annalistic character of the wilderness narratives. George W. Coats notes, "in the same manner that a king recounts his exploits in a connected review of events at key places, so the narrator recounts God's exploits or Moses' unique leadership."[22] This similarity is also noted by Coats in his commentary on Numbers, published with Rolf P. Knierim, where the wilderness narrative is identified as a saga of a migrating sanctuary campaign, a genre label that nobly strives to account for the mix of features: a migrating people carrying a portable sanctuary that is described as an army on the march.[23] Coats and Knierim have beautifully described the literary goals of the wilderness narrative, but how genre was used to achieve them is another matter. The *campaign* element of their description captures the military flavor of the wilderness narrative created by the the form of the itinerary notices, its basic plot structure as a journey that ends in a battle, its method of reckoning time, and some of its character roles. These elements point to use of the *annals* genre as a mode of emplotment for the wilderness narrative.

The form of the itinerary notices themselves suggests that this element of repertoire was drawn from an Assyrian cultural background. Of all the conventions for the itinerary genre that we encountered in chap. 3, the itinerary notices in Num 33:1–49 and in the wilderness narrative employ the genre spe-

---

20. For historical overview and further bibliography, see T. C. Römer, "The Elusive Yahwist: A Short History of Research," in *A Farewell to the Yahwist? The Composition of the Pentateuch in Recent European Interpretation* (ed. T. B. Dozeman and K. Schmid; SBLSymS 34; Leiden: Brill, 2006) 9–27; and K. Schmid, *Genesis and the Moses Story: Israel's Dual Origins in the Hebrew Bible* (trans. J. D. Nogalski; Siphrut 3; Winona Lake, IN: Eisenbrauns, 2010) 1–49, 90–92.

21. Van Seters, *Life of Moses*, 163.

22. G. W. Coats, *Exodus 1–18* (FOTL 2A; Grand Rapids, MI: Eerdmans, 1999) 104–5; see also p. 91. Hans Jürgen Tertel also appeals to the Neo-Assyrian annals as an analogy for understanding the Torah. He focuses not on the genre of the wilderness narrative but on the way that the process of editing successive versions of the annals might serve as a control for understanding the redaction history of the Torah (*Text and Transmission: An Empirical Model for the Literary Development of Old Testament Narratives* [BZAW 221; Berlin: de Gruyter, 1994]).

23. Knierim and Coats, *Numbers*, 34.

cifically with the convention that we know from Assyrian administrative documents. This is evident, for example, in Num 21:10–11a:

וַיִּסְעוּ בְּנֵי יִשְׂרָאֵל וַיַּחֲנוּ בְּאֹבֹת: וַיִּסְעוּ מֵאֹבֹת וַיַּחֲנוּ בְּעִיֵּי הָעֲבָרִים

The Israelites departed and camped at Oboth. They departed from Oboth and camped at Iye-abarim.

Here the author has repeated the place-names and used the prepositions מִן and בְּ, akin to *ištu* and *ana* in cuneiform documents. The use of verb forms, however, is what ties this form most closely to the conventions used in the Assyrian examples. The report from Dur-Katlimmu uses *nasāḫu* to articulate the initial departure, which is cognate to נסע in Hebrew. The verb חנה, moreover, is a semantic equivalent to *biātu* 'to spend the night', used in the Neo-Assyrian Habur itineraries as well as the report from Dur-Katlimmu. As we saw in chap. 4, *biātu* also became a typical way to articulate a pause in movement in the ninth-century annals, under the influence of the itinerary genre.

The combination of these itinerary notices with date formulas points specifically to the Assyrian *annals* genre. Some of the date formulas in the wilderness narrative are associated with itinerary notices. Davies argues that the dates came from the same administrative document that the itinerary notices did.[24] Date formulas and itinerary notices do occur together in Egyptian daybooks, since a date formula is used to mark each entry in the log. But the the itinerary conventions used in the wilderness narrative correlate with Assyrian examples, not Egyptian. We should therefore be looking in an Assyrian rather than an Egyptian context for the background from which this repertoire was selected. Date formulas in cuneiform administrative documents, however, are found in headers or colophons; they are *not* used to account for the temporal progress of the journey as they are in the wilderness narrative. If time is marked in the itinerary itself, it is marked with a cardinal number indicating the length of stay at the spot; with an ordinal number noting the day of the journey as a whole, as in the Old Babylonian itineraries and the Neo-Assyrian itinerary (K. 4675+); or with the verb *biātu*, which indicates an overnight stay, as in the Middle Assyrian itinerary from Dur-Katlimmu (DeZ 2521). The combination of date formulas that mark the temporal progress of the journey with itinerary notices in an Assyrian context occurs *only* in the annals. In fact, the use of date formulas in the annals originated in experimentation with chronicles, as we saw in chap. 4, and is not related to itineraries at all.

---

24. G. I. Davies, "Wilderness Itineraries: A Comparative Study," 57.

Finally, key passages in the wilderness narrative depict the Israelites as an army. The itinerary genre is used in military, commercial, and civic contexts, so the Israelites could be cast as a group of traveling businessmen or as an army.[25] But their role as an army is made explicit throughout the narrative of the Israelites' departures from both Egypt (among the regulations for and observance of Pesah and *matsot*) and Sinai. The fact that the Israelites have just been referred to as צְבָאוֹת 'troops' in Exod 12:17 cues the reader to read the first itinerary notice in Exod 12:37 against a military, rather than a commercial or diplomatic background. Carol Meyers notes that the 600,000 men who set out from Ramses in 12:37 may be related to a military unit, identified as a group of 600 in Exod 14:7 and Judg 18:12, here multiplied by 1,000 in order to refer to an entire ethnic population.[26] The reference to the departure of Israel on the day of the festival as כָּל־צִבְאוֹת יְהוָה 'all the hosts of Yahweh' a few verses later in Exod 12:41 reinforces the military background of the itinerary notices. Finally, Exod 13:18 depicts the Israelites as departing from Egypt lined up in battle formations (חֲמֻשִׁים).[27]

---

25. Some of the evidence presented here for the effort to cast the Israelites as an army is also reviewed by B. E. Scolnic in order to demonstrate that מַסַּע in אֵלֶּה מַסְעֵי בְנֵי־יִשְׂרָאֵל(Num 33:1) is a specifically military term (*Theme and Context in Biblical Lists* [South Florida Studies in the History of Judaism 119; Atlanta: Scholars Press, 1995] 72–76). But comparative study of itineraries shows that, while נסע and *nasāḫu* are often used in a military context, they do not always convey a march to battle (as, for example, in the Dur-Katlimmu itinerary). Notably, מַסַּע is used in Gen 13:3 to describe the journeys of Abraham in a context that is not military at all. The term מַסַּע simply means 'stages', not specifically 'marches', as Scolnic argues. It is the *combination* of the term with a weapon-bearing army both in the wilderness narrative and in Num 33:1–49 that cues the reader to understand the stages as being part of a military rather than a commercial or diplomatic trip. The fact that Abraham travels with his chattel suggests a different context.

26. C. Meyers, *Exodus* (NCBC; Cambridge: Cambridge University Press, 2005) 100; see also N. Sarna, *Exodus* (JPS Torah Commentary; Philadelphia: Jewish Publication Society, 1991) 62, 245 n. 59. Efforts to understand this number in military terms often hinge on the interpretation of אֶלֶף as a military unit, following G. E. Mendenhall, who argued that אֶלֶף in the censuses does not mean 1,000 but refers to a tribal-military unit ("The Census Lists of Numbers 1 and 26," *JBL* 77 [1958] 52–66). A thorough review of this and other studies on the censuses can be found in D. T. Olson, *The Death of the Old and the Birth of the New: The Framework of the Book of Numbers and the Pentateuch* (BJS 71; Chico, CA: Scholars Press, 1985) 70–81; and P. J. Budd, *Numbers* (WBC 5; Waco, TX: Word, 1984) 7–8. It is most likely that אֶלֶף simply means 1,000 both in the censuses and in Exod 12:37 and, unlike אַלּוּף, does not in these cases refer to a social unit.

27. The word חֲמֻשִׁים is a term for social groups of 50 (see Exod 18:21; Deut 1:15), but it often has a specifically military tenor ("חמשׁ," *HALOT* 1.331). Its relationship with

The most aggressive effort to depict the Israelites as an army comes in the introduction to Numbers and culminates in the march away from Sinai that follows the itinerary notice in Num 10:11–12.[28] This effort in the early chapters of Numbers is a continuation of the description in Exodus; as Baruch A. Levine noted, the depiction of the Israelites as an army is a key "historiographic link" between the exodus and wilderness narratives.[29] The census in Numbers 1 is depicted as a military census. Only men of military age (כָּל־יֹצֵא צָבָא 'all who go out to war') are counted, and this expression is repeated for every tribe except the Levites throughout the entire census. The Israelite camp is depicted throughout Numbers 2 as a military camp with tribes camped as troops (צְבָאוֹת) around the Tabernacle.[30] Each camps with its own standard (אֹת). Although דֶּגֶל in Numbers 2 is typically understood as a synonym for אֹת and a reference to a standard, it is not clear that it actually means 'standard'. Instead, דִּגְלָא is used in fifth-century B.C.E. Aramaic ostraca from Egypt to refer to a mercenary unit that also functioned as an economic unit and was organized by ethnic group, with families of the soldiers living together in an enclave.[31] When the Israelites depart from Sinai, each division is led by its head, depicted as a military commander. Each leader is described in Numbers 10 as עַל־צָבָא 'in charge of the army', akin to the title of army commander (שַׂר־צָבָא) borne, for example, by Abner (1 Sam 26:5). Finally, the tribes depart in order, ending with Dan as the rear guard (מְאַסֵּף).

The annals genre, with its itinerary notices, provides the wilderness narrative with a coherent, unified formal structure. But it also provides conceptual coherence for the story by telling us what kind of story to read it *as*—in other words, what kind of *Gestalt* we should form and what expectations we should have about the story as we continue to read. The early itinerary notices and depiction of the Israelites as an army in Exodus help us envision the Israelites not as lost wanderers, refugees, or migrants but as an army on the march. We

---

efforts to depict the Israelites as an army has been noted noted by Sarna, *Exodus*, 69; and U. Cassuto, *A Commentary on the Book of Exodus* (trans. I. Abrahams. Jerusalem: Magnes, 1967) 156–57.

28. P. D. Miller, *The Divine Warrior in Early Israel* (HSM 5; Harvard: Harvard University Press, 1973) 161.

29. B. A. Levine, *Numbers 1–20: A New Translation with Introduction and Commentary* (AB 4A; New York: Doubleday, 1993) 126.

30. For the significant military overtones of this terminology, see "צָבָא," *HALOT* 2.994–97.

31. B. Porten, *Archives from Elephantine: Life of an Ancient Jewish Military Colony* (Berkeley: University of California Press, 1968) 29–35; B. A. Levine, *Numbers 1–20*, 147–48; "דֶּגֶל," *HALOT* 1.213.

expect them to head straight for their goal, and we expect the story to end in a conquest, and these expectations remain with us as we continue reading. When we encounter new elements—a sanctuary, laws, complaining, the miraculous procurement of food and water—we must somehow fit them into this formal and conceptual framework as we strive to understand the meaning of the narrative.

A Vision for Restoration

The wilderness narrative, as a story about nascent Israel marching through the desert with its portable shrine, is no typical annal. While the formal elements just discussed derive from the annals genre, much of the wilderness narrative's content is completely foreign to this genre. Annals consist of individual episodes just as the wilderness narrative does, but episodes in the annals relate battles or other activities such as the royal hunt that take place on military campaigns. Most of the episodes in the wilderness narrative, however, are not military at all. Only four are military in nature: the battle with Amalek (Exod 17:8–14), the spies episode (Numbers 13–14), the battle at Hormah (Num 21:1–3), and the conquest of Sihon and Og (Num 21:21–35). Although the Israelites are not combatants, the sea crossing (Exodus 14–15) also has some military overtones as the Egyptians "fight" Yahweh. The bulk of the narrative episodes deal with issues such as proper ritual observance (the instruction not to acquire food on Shabbat in Exodus 16), obedience as the basis for Israel's relationship with Yahweh (the rock/water contention in Exod 17:1b–7), legal procedures and judicial structure (the establishment of the judiciary in Exodus 18), prophecy and prophetic hierarchy (the episode in which Eldad and Medad prophesy in the camp and the challenge to Moses in Numbers 11–12), and priestly hierarchy (the Korah rebellion in Numbers 16–17), while significant parts of the wilderness narrative are not narrative at all but instead consist of law and ritual instruction. A portable sanctuary similar to the Tabernacle that the Israelites carry through the desert and around which they camp is also not a feature of any standard genre of ancient Near Eastern historiography. William Johnstone's understanding of the wilderness narrative as "the casting into quasi-historical narrative of shared commonplace institutions" only serves to highlight the fact that, although the wilderness narrative is annalistic in form, it is not a campaign narrative in substance.[32]

---

32. W. Johnstone, *Chronicles and Exodus: An Analogy and Its Application* (JSOTSup 275; Sheffield: Sheffield Academic Press, 1998) 164.

The wilderness narrative also differs from the annals genre in terms of who wrote it. Annals were produced by scribes in the employ of the Assyrian king who were responsible for creating royal propaganda. But the wilderness narrative, or at least the version of it shaped by itinerary notices, is typically thought to have been produced by scribes with a priestly orientation. The itinerary notices were once assigned to P because of their stereotypical formula and list-like character. This view was first articulated by Noth, and we continue to find it in the analyses of Cross and Smith, albeit implicitly in Smith's work insofar as he builds on Cross's understanding of the P redaction.[33] But these features are simply characteristic of the itinerary genre and would be present irrespective of the ideological leanings, compositional style, or literary goals of the author. Davies suggested that use of the itinerary notices should be attributed to a Deuteronomistic redaction because the apparent use of archival material and the interest in war are features shared with the Deuteronomistic History.[34] Van Seters's Yahwist could just as easily be responsible for choosing this mode of emplotment.

One factor indicates that it *was* the Priestly writer who emplotted the wilderness narrative as an annal: the itinerary notices, like the depictions of the Israelites as an army and the date formulas, are embedded in Priestly texts at key points in the narrative.[35] Some of the itinerary notices are loosely associated with their respective episodes. The Israelites' arrival at Rephidim in Exod 17:1, for example, occurs at the very beginning of an episode, and the episode would stand alone quite nicely without it. David Carr and Karel van der Toorn have noted that additions to and expansions of a previously existing text are frequently made at its borders, and itinerary notices that are positioned this way may frame previously existing material, as redaction-critical studies of the wilderness narrative (such as offered by Cross) argue.[36] While some itinerary notices may serve a redactional, or framing, function, other itinerary notices are deeply embedded in their respective narratives. Like the itinerary notices

---

33. E.g., M. Noth, *Exodus: A Commentary* (OTL; Philadelphia: Westminster, 1962) 127, 133; Cross, *Canaanite Myth*, 307–8; M. S. Smith, "Literary Arrangement," 35–36.

34. G. I. Davies, "Wilderness Itineraries: A Comparative Study," 80; idem, "Wilderness Itineraries and the Composition of the Pentateuch," 10–12.

35. A. Dillmann, *Die Bücher Exodus und Leviticus* (Kurzgefasstes exegetisches Handbuch zum Alten Testament 12; Leipzig: Hirzel, 1897) 71; see also S. R. Driver, *The Book of Exodus* (Cambridge Bible for Schools and Colleges; Cambridge: Cambridge University Press, 1918) 49, 95, 102.

36. D. M. Carr, *Writing on the Tablet of the Heart: Origins of Scripture and Literature* (Oxford: Oxford University Press, 2005) 39; K. van der Toorn, *Scribal Culture and the Making of the Hebrew Bible* (Cambridge: Harvard University Press, 2007) 128.

in Ashurnasirpal II's campaign to the land of Nirbu discussed in chap. 4, these itinerary notices cannot be extracted without unraveling the narrative and were probably composed as part of it.

Like the depictions of the Israelites as an army, itinerary notices are em-bedded in two texts that anchor the Priestly composition at key points in its plot: the Pesah/*matsot* narrative in which the Israelites depart from Egypt and the departure from Sinai. The notices in Exod 12:37 and 13:20, which bring the Israelites out of Egypt via Sukkoth and into the wilderness of Etham, are tied up in the middle of the Pesah/*matsot* narrative. The composition history of this passage is complex and difficult to pin down; one should not assume that the itinerary notices and all of the places within it where the Israelites are depicted as an army must come from the same compositional layer. Nonetheless, the annalistic elements do carry through the various reworkings of this passage. The itinerary notice in Exod 12:17, for example, associates the departure of the Israelite army with *matsot*, while Exod 12:51 associates it with Pesah. The de-piction of the Israelites as an army in Exod 12:17, 41, and 51 is characteristic of what is widely regarded to be a Priestly version of it, however the two obser-vances came to be combined.[37] The itinerary notice in Num 10:11–12, which has the Israelites depart from the wilderness of Sinai, is likewise embedded in the narrative at the beginning of Numbers, as Coats observes in his study of the wilderness itineraries.[38] Like the departure from Egypt, Numbers 1–10 may be made up of multiple layers, although in this case all are Priestly in character. That these two points anchor a broader Priestly composition is also suggested by the fact that we first encounter the Israelites explicitly identified as an army in Exod 6:26 and 7:4, in the Priestly version of Moses' call narrative, before we have even encountered an itinerary notice. This military depiction is notably absent in the non-Priestly version (Exodus 3–4).[39] Already in Moses' call, the

---

37. Exod 12:17, 41, and 51 are all in sections allotted to P by Noth, *Exodus*, 94–109. On the other hand, B. S. Childs assigns v. 17 to J and seems to leave 12:40–51 to P, as Noth does (Childs, *Book of Exodus: A Critical, Theological Commentary* [OTL; Philadelphia: Westminster, 1974] 184).

38. Coats, "Wilderness Itinerary," 145.

39. I use the term *non-Priestly* to refer to literature that preceded the Priestly ver-sion of the Torah because the authorship of that material remains a subject of signifi-cant debate, particularly in terms of its relationship to the Deuteronomistic History, the character and composition history of which is itself a subject of debate; see T. B. Dozeman, *Commentary on Exodus* (Eerdmans Critical Commentary; Grand Rapids, MI: Eerdmans, 2009) 39–41; and T. C. Römer, *The So-Called Deuteronomistic History: A Sociological, Historical and Literary Introduction* (London: T. & T. Clark, 2005).

Priestly author of this composition is shaping our vision of the Israelites' role in his version of the wilderness narrative.

If this Israelite "annal" is atypical in terms of its content and its authorship, it is even more atypical in its *purpose*. Assyrian annals are royal propaganda, designed to promote an image of the king as conqueror. This image of the king emerged when the image of the king as builder was no longer fully adequate to capture his activities as maintainer of cosmic order. The Priestly annalistic version of the wilderness narrative is also an ideological development designed to adapt to new circumstances, but it is a development of a very different kind. Tryggve N. D. Mettinger argues that the Priestly materials in the Torah present a picture of a mobile deity and a mobile sanctuary as a way of accounting for Yahweh's presence among the Israelites after the destruction of the Temple.[40] Preexilic Zion traditions conceptualized Yahweh's presence in the Temple as a king enthroned in his royal palace. The Temple was his dwelling, and he was referred to as יְהוָה צְבָאוֹת יֹשֵׁב הַכְּרֻבִים 'Yahweh of Hosts, who sits on the Cherubim'. This epithet encapsulates the image of Yahweh as a king sitting on a cherubim throne, typical of depictions of Semitic kings. While this image of Yahweh is aniconic, it also relates to the concept of the Temple as Yahweh's dwelling. Mettinger argues that the destruction of the Temple in 586 B.C.E. essentially dethroned Yahweh and led to a variety of efforts to reformulate Zion theology in response to this crisis.[41]

One of these efforts is articulated in the book of Ezekiel, particularly in the visions of the chariot throne in chaps. 1 and 8–10. This reformulation continues to depict Yahweh as present in the sanctuary, but he and the sanctuary—now the chariot throne—can *move*. Mettinger described this effort to reformulate the theology of Yahweh's presence as hermeneutical, because the scribe drew heavily on the imagery of the older Zion traditions even as he transformed them. The chariot throne, especially as described in chap. 10, is a mix of the cherubim throne image from the Zion traditions with the cloud from the theophanic tradition as well as wheels, which are a metonym for a chariot, in

---

40. T. N. D. Mettinger, *The Dethronement of Sabaoth: Studies in the Shem and Kabod Theologies* (ConBOT 18; Lund: CWK Gleerup, 1982) 80–97. See also idem, "The Name and the Glory: The Zion-Sabaoth Theology and Its Exilic Successors," *JNSL* 24 (1998) 13–18.

41. Idem, *Dethronement of Sabaoth*, 19–37; and, for a more detailed argument, idem, "YHWH SABAOTH: The Heavenly King on the Cherubim Throne," in *Studies in the Period of David and Solomon and Other Essays* (ed. T. Ishida; Winona Lake, IN: Eisenbrauns, 1982) 109–38. For a more in-depth study of royal imagery applied to God, see M. Z. Brettler, *God Is King: Understanding an Israelite Metaphor* (JSOTSup 76; Sheffield: Sheffield Academic Press, 1989).

order to make it mobile. The image of God as king is downplayed in favor of God as the king's *kavod* (כָּבוֹד). Here again, the author drew on Zion traditions such as Ps 24:7–10, where *kavod* is a divine attribute. But this term is used in Ezekiel to refer to God himself and, in some cases, to refer to the entire chariot throne. The scribe therefore combined elements of the Zion tradition with imagery from other traditions that aided in making the image of Yahweh's presence among the Israelites no longer dependent on the existence of the Temple.[42]

The Priestly wilderness narrative, according to Mettinger, takes essentially the same approach to the crisis as the chariot throne visions in Ezekiel: Yahweh's presence is depicted as the *kavod* in the now-mobile sanctuary. But the Priestly scribe developed a different picture of the mobile sanctuary than Ezekiel, mixing the image of the Temple as a מִשְׁכָּן, or 'Tabernacle', from the Zion tradition with various elements of the Tent of Meeting tradition in Exodus 33 and Numbers 11–12. (For the Temple as Yahweh's מִשְׁכָּן in the Zion traditions, see, for example, Ps 46:5; 84:2; 132:5, 7.) The Tent of Meeting (אֹהֶל מוֹעֵד) is outside the camp, functions as an oraculum rather than as a place for sacrifice, and Yahweh's presence in it is ad hoc—he descends upon it in a cloud when needed. The Priestly scribe fused the cloud with the *kavod* and transformed the temporary presence of the cloud over the Tent of Meeting into permanent presence in the Tabernacle in a variety of ways. He depicted public manifestations of the *kavod* as the cloud emanating from the Tabernacle rather than descending upon it. When the Tabernacle was finally set up, the *kavod* took its place in the Tabernacle just as Yahweh of Hosts took his place in the Temple in the Zion tradition (Exod 40:34–48 and 29:45–46; see Psalm 24). Finally, while Yahweh of Hosts sits (יֹשֵׁב) on his cherubim throne, the cloud/*kavod* dwells (שׁכֵן) in the Tabernacle. Although יֹשֵׁב is the typical verb used in the Zion traditions, evident from the epithet יְהוָה צְבָאוֹת יֹשֵׁב הַכְּרֻבִים 'Yahweh of Hosts Who Sits on the Cherubim', שׁכֵן is also used in the Zion traditions. The Priestly writer has simply emphasized שׁכֵן to move away from the now-problematic image of en-

---

42. Mettinger, *Dethronement of Sabaoth*, 97–111; idem, "Name and the Glory," 11–13. The shift in imagery and terminology that Mettinger points out may not be as extreme as he argued. According to Mettinger, the Deuteronomistic school advocated a similar reconceptualization of Yahweh's presence in texts such as Deuteronomy 4, which seem to relocate Yahweh to heaven. P. T. Vogt counters that there is still language in Deuteronomy 4 that indicates Yahweh's presence in the Temple; the shift is not an abstraction of Yahweh's presence so that he is understood to be absent but a shift in the way the Israelites experience Yahweh's presence, advocating this experience through *torah* (*Deuteronomic Theology and the Significance of Torah: A Reappraisal* [Winona Lake, IN: Eisenbrauns, 2006] 61, 118–35). In my view, Vogt does not fundamentally undercut Mettinger's argument but offers an appropriately subtler interpretation of the shift.

thronement.[43] The cloud that alights and makes its dwelling in the Tabernacle in order to lead the Israelites from one stop to another along the itinerary is, according to Mettinger, a fusion of images designed to maintain a plausible image of Yahweh's presence among the Israelites in exile.

Mettinger offers a convincing argument that the scribe who wrote the Priestly version of the wilderness narrative was dealing with an ideological problem raised by events of the (probably relatively recent) past, but I argue that he also had his eyes set on the future. The vision of return to Zion and reconstruction of both Temple and society in the land in Ezekiel 40–48 is framed, according to Mettinger, in the same *kavod* imagery found in the chariot throne visions at the beginning of the book.[44] The *kavod* enters the Temple by the east gate in Ezek 43:1–9, Yahweh is reestablished on his throne, and the gate is then blocked up to establish Yahweh's *permanent* presence. The Priestly version of the wilderness narrative has many of the same components as the prophetic vision in Ezekiel 40–48. Most notably, both contain blueprints for the Temple (Ezekiel 40–42; Exodus 25–31). Ezekiel envisions the future day when 'the *kavod* of Yahweh will fill the Temple' (וְהִנֵּה מָלֵא כְבוֹד־יְהוָה הַבָּיִת, Ezek 43:5). Exodus 35–40, however, narrates the construction of the Temple as well and concludes with the entrance of the *kavod* into the Tabernacle, just as in Ezek 43:1–9: 'the *kavod* of Yahweh filled the Tabernacle' (וּכְבוֹד יְהוָה מָלֵא אֶת־הַמִּשְׁכָּן, Exod 40:34). Ezekiel's vision for the restoration of the Temple was articulated as a prophetic vision, in which Yahweh brings the prophet בְּמַרְאוֹת אֱלֹהִים 'in visions of God' to the Temple Mount and gives him a tour of the ideally restored Temple, led by a man who shone like copper (Ezek 40:2–3). The Priestly version of the wilderness narrative, on the other hand, is articulated in history-like narrative. The authority for this vision of return is established *not* by casting it as a revelation from God but by retrojecting it into Israel's valorized prenational past. The wilderness narrative is a vision of how Israel will be after the exile cast as though this is how it had always been.

In addition to a reconstructed Temple, Israelites after the exile would also need a social structure and a calendar to govern their communal ritual activity. As E. Theodore Mullen and others have emphasized, these community-

---

43. Mettinger, *Dethronement of Sabaoth*, 80–97; idem, "Name and the Glory," 13–18. For an important refinement of Mettinger's work that recognizes that Ezekiel does not so much do away with enthronement theology as emphasize aspects of it that were more significant in exile, where Yahweh did not rule, see J. T. Strong, "God's *Kābôd*: The Presence of Yahweh in the Book of Ezekiel," in *The Book of Ezekiel: Theological and Anthropological Perspectives* (ed. M. S. Odell and J. T. Strong; SBLSymS 9; Atlanta: Society of Biblical Literature, 2000) 69–95.

44. Mettinger, *Dethronement of Sabaoth*, 108–9.

defining visions are motivated in part by the threat of social dissolution and particularly of assimilation.[45] The visions provide the structure perceived as necessary to maintain the culture. Ezek 45:1–8 and 47:13–48:35 offer an idealized social structure centered on the Temple in which each tribe as well as the prince has an alloted place, and Ezekiel 44 stipulates the roles of the priests and levites, who constitute the communal leadership. Ezek 45:9–46:24 offers some ritual instructions and a rudimentary calendar. The Priestly version of the wilderness narrative offers a vision for social structure and calendar as well, blending these elements with the annalistic mode of emplotment.

We find the Priestly vision for Israel's social structure, of course, in the early chapters of Numbers after the Tabernacle has been constructed and just before the Israelites leave Sinai.[46] Although the Israelites are strongly depicted here as an army, the notion that the Israelites actually came out of Egypt as an army does not sit comfortably with some commentators. Douglas K. Stuart is willing to accept that they might have been organized like an army but doubts that they had any military training, having been slaves in Egypt.[47] Alan Cole likewise notes: "The picture is not incorrect, so long as we do not interpret it in terms of a modern disciplined army. Every man was a soldier in an ancient 'horde' and no doubt every man in Israel had some weapon, even if only knife or sling."[48] Although John Durham recognizes that עַל־צִבְאֹתָם 'according to their troops' in Exod 6:26 is a military term, he suggests that in this context it actually refers to divisions of the population by tribe and clan. His uncertainty about the use of the term in these instances is further evident in the fact that he interprets it to have a double meaning in Exod 12:41, referring to both military units and the massive number of Israelites.[49] Umberto Cassuto contrasts the depiction of the Israelites as "hosts" in Exod 6:26 to their depiction elsewhere as slaves.[50] And Cross argues that a list of tribal officials, or נְשִׂיאִים, was used

---

45. E. T. Mullen Jr., *Ethnic Myths and Pentateuchal Foundations: A New Approach to the Formation of the Pentateuch* (Atlanta: Scholars Press, 1997) 64–66; K. L. Sparks, *Ethnicity and Identity in Ancient Israel: Prolegomena to the Study of Ethnic Sentiments and Their Expression in the Hebrew Bible* (Winona Lake, IN: Eisenbrauns, 1998) 285–319; Aaron, *Etched in Stone*, 44, 293–312.

46. Mullen, *Ethnic Myths*, 251–56.

47. D. K. Stuart, *Exodus* (NAC 2; Nashville: Broadman & Holman, 2006) 324.

48. A. Cole, *Exodus: An Introduction and Commentary* (Downers Grove, IL: InterVarsity, 1973) 88.

49. J. I. Durham, *Exodus* (WBC 3; Waco, TX: Word, 1987) 81, 173.

50. Cassuto, *Commentary on the Book of Exodus*, 88. He notes this throughout the commentary, whenever יְהוָה צְבָאוֹת is used, although he does not comment on the specifically military tenor of the term.

by P to create the census in Numbers 1, the military camps in Numbers 2, the tribal offerings in Numbers 7, and the departure of the military units from Sinai in Numbers 10.[51] We can see through the characterization of the Israelites as an army (a feature of the annals emplotment) to the social structure lying behind it that generally parallels the structure in Ezekiel 44, 47–48: tribes, schematically camped around the sanctuary, led by a priestly oligarchy.[52]

The blend of military terminology with elements of Israelite social structure is most evident in the description of the Levites, who are explicitly distinguished from the other Israelite "troops" and given their own census related not to military service but to service in the Tabernacle.[53] The term צָבָא is used in some cases (for example, Isa 40:2; Job 7:1, 10:17, 14:14) to refer to compulsory service generally, and the related verb is used for the service of women at the entrance to the sanctuary in Exod 38:8 and 1 Sam 2:22.[54] These uses are derived from its military use, which predominates in Numbers 1–10.[55] But in Numbers 4 it refers to *cultic* service. The typical expression for cultic service is לַעֲבֹד אֶת־עֲבֹדָה 'to perform service'; it is used not only in Numbers 4 and 8 alongside צָבָא but also throughout Numbers 3, in Num 7:5 and 16:9, and throughout Numbers 18.[56] The two expressions are combined into a single expression, צְבָא הָעֲבֹדָה, in Num 8:25, an example of what Levine refers to as the Priestly tendency to associate distinct terms with one another.[57] He suggests that צְבָא הָעֲבֹדָה is an effort to combine distinct traditions, but the combination may be better viewed as an effort by the Priestly scribe to blend elements of repertoire from two different backgrounds—the military terminology of the annals emplotment with Israelite social roles—as he shaped the characters in the wilderness narrative. He also

---

51. Cross, *Canaanite Myth*, 315, 321.

52. The differences in detail are not insignificant, of course, because Ezekiel has a Zadokite priesthood while Numbers has an Aaronide priesthood and the scheme for the tribal arrangement is different, but further pursuit of these issues is beyond the scope of this book. My intent is not to argue that the Priestly version of the wilderness narrative offers exactly the same vision as Ezekiel 40–48 or even to discuss possible relationships between the two but merely to note that they serve the same basic goals.

53. Knierim and Coats, *Numbers*, 29. See Num 4:1–4; compare Num 1:47–54 for the explicit distinction.

54. For commentators who understand צָבָא in this light in Numbers 4 and 8:25, see L. E. Binns, *The Book of Numbers* (London: Methuen, 1927) 21–22; N. H. Snaith, *Leviticus and Numbers* (Century Bible; London: Nelson, 1967) 194; B. A. Levine, *Numbers 1–20*, 279.

55. "צָבָא," *HALOT* 2.995; see also Budd, *Numbers*, 48.

56. Gray, *Critical and Exegetical Commentary on Numbers*, 33.

57. B. A. Levine, *Numbers 1–20*, 131. The combination in Num 8:25 was noted by Gray, *Critical and Exegetical Commentary on Numbers*, 82.

framed the age range for levitical service so it mirrors the age for military service and refers to the Levites as כָּל־בָּא לַצָּבָא 'all who come in for service', which is unique to Numbers 4 and mirrors the military expression כָּל־יֹצֵא צָבָא 'all who go out to war'.[58] The military flavor of the description of the Levites does not come from a distinct source or tradition but is part of an effort to emplot the wilderness narrative as an "annal." Priests do not feature in ancient Near Eastern military narratives, but soldiers do, so the scribe loosely characterized the priests as soldiers to fit their role in the mode of emplotment.

We find a similar blend of military and kinship terms in Numbers 1–2.[59] Just as the military imagery is artificially applied to levitical service in Numbers 4, so it is combined with the Israelite tribal structure here. In their march away from Sinai in Num 10:13–28, the Israelites are depicted strictly as a series of military camps departing in order under the direction of their respective commanders. But the description of these camps in Numbers 2, although each tribe is identified as a troop, has the Israelites camped לְבֵית אֲבֹתָם 'according to their ancestral houses', rather than לְצִבְאֹתָם 'according to their troops'. (Compare the header in Num 2:2 to that in Num 10:14.) While צָבָא is clearly a military term, בֵּית אָב is a kinship term.[60] The blend of military and kinship terminology is even more evident in the Numbers 1 census, where the same men who are identified explicitly as military commanders in Numbers 10 are identified each as a רֹאשׁ בֵּית־אָבֹת 'head of the ancestral house'. Although George Mendenhall argues that the census was originally a military census, this is by no means clear and requires reinterpreting אֶלֶף to refer to a military unit rather than its basic meaning of 1,000.[61] Whatever the origins of the census numbers, the combination of kinship with military terminology suggests the same type of blend we find in Numbers 4. Leaders of ancestral houses are not typical characters in an annal, but soldiers are. Casting the Israelite leaders as soldiers incorporates them into the mode of emplotment.

Participation in cultic ritual is just as important for membership in the community as knowing one's social place.[62] Mullen notes that Exodus 12–13

---

58. J. Sturdy, *Numbers* (CBC; Cambridge: Cambridge University Press, 1976) 37.

59. Knierim and Coats, *Numbers*, 44.

60. The term בֵּית אָב can refer to the "nuclear family, the extended family, or the lineage" and is smaller than a מִשְׁפָּחָה (K. van der Toorn, *Family Religion in Babylonia, Syria and Israel: Continuity and Change in the Forms of Religious Life* [Studies in the History and Culture of the Ancient Near East 7; Leiden: Brill, 1996] 195, 199). B. A. Levine cautions about the flexibility in use of the kinship terms, particularly בֵּית אָב and מִשְׁפָּחָה (*Numbers 1–20*, 131–33).

61. See n. 26 (p. 150) above.

62. Mullen, *Ethnic Myths*, 15–16.

Table 1. Dates in the Wilderness Narrative*

Exod 12:2, 6, 21–22, 41, 51 // Num 33:3	1/14–15/01 (Pesah)
Exod 16:1	**2/15/01 (Shabbat)**
Exod 19:1	**3/1/01 (Shavuot?)**
Exod 40:2, 17	1/1/02 (New Year)
Num 1:1, 18	2/1/02 (census)
Num 9:1, 3, 5, 11	1/1/02, 1/14/02, 2/14/02 (Pesah)
Num 10:11–12	**2/20/02 (departure from Sinai)**

*Dates are represented in this table as follows: month/day/year following the exodus.

depicts the departure from Egypt as the group's first collective observance of Pesah. This ritual is a new beginning for the community, because the month in which it occurs is emphatically the first: הַחֹדֶשׁ הַזֶּה לָכֶם רֹאשׁ חֳדָשִׁים רִאשׁוֹן הוּא לָכֶם לְחָדְשֵׁי הַשָּׁנָה 'You shall regard this month as the first of months; it shall be for you the first of the months of the year' (Exod 12:2). The community is defined by participation in this חֻקַּת עוֹלָם 'eternal statute' (Exod 12:14, 17). No foreigners are allowed to participate; if you are an outsider and you want to participate, you must become part of the group through circumcision (Exod 12:43–49). Those who peform the ritual improperly—for example, by consuming leaven—are cut off from the community (Exod 12:15, 19).[63]

Knowing when festivals such as Pesah are to be celebrated is particularly important to ensure that the entire community not only observes them and observes them properly but also observes them at the same and proper time. Ezek 45:18–25 offers a festival calendar consisting of purification of the Temple on the 1st day of the 1st month, or the New Year, Pesah on the 14th day of the 1st month, a seven-day festival of *matsot*, and another seven-day festival beginning on the 15th day of the 7th month. Ezek 46:1–3 also stipulates the opening of the Temple on the new moon and Shabbat, or the seventh day of the week on which no work is done. The Priestly version of the wilderness narrative also offers some reflections on matters of calendar. Apart from the various festival calendars in the wilderness narrative (for example, Exod 23:14–17, 34:18–24; Leviticus 23; Numbers 28–29), we find calendrical matters *written into the narrative itself.*

The date formulas in the annals genre provided the Priestly scribe with a vehicle for establishing a calendar. As Smith points out, the dates in the wilderness narrative are not linear but cyclical, marking out a liturgical year from the

---

63. Ibid., 208–9.

Table 2. Jaubert's 364-Day Calendar*

	months 1, 4, 7, 10	months 2, 5, 8, 11	months 3, 6, 9, 12
Fourth Day	1 8 15 22 29	6 13 20 27	4 11 18 25
Fifth Day	2 9 16 23 30	7 14 21 28	5 12 19 26
Sixth Day	3 10 17 24	1 8 15 22 29	6 13 20 27
Seventh Day	4 11 18 25	2 9 16 23 30	7 14 21 28
First Day	5 12 19 26	3 10 17 24	1 8 15 22 29
Second Day	6 13 20 27	4 11 18 25	2 9 16 23 30
Third Day	7 14 21 28	5 12 19 26	3 10 17 24 31

*Reprinted with permission, from A. Jaubert, *The Date of the Last Supper* (Staten Island, NY: Alba, 1965) 27.

Pesah associated with the departure from Egypt to the first and second Pesah after the Tabernacle was constructed, shown in table 1.[64] The Priestly version of the wilderness narrative is focused on the construction of the Tabernacle, dated to the New Year in Exod 40:2, 17, just as Ezek 45:18 is focused on its purification. This temporal setting continues in Num 7:1, where the first offerings are brought "on the day Moses set up the Tabernacle," and in Num 9:1–5, where the Israelites offer the Pesah sacrifice in the first month after the construction of the Tabernacle. Their stay in the wilderness of Sinai extends into the second month to accommodate a second Pesah for those on a journey or for those who are suffering corpse contamination until the cloud assumes its presence over the Tabernacle, and the Israelites finally depart from the wilderness of Sinai in Num 10:11–12.[65] Although the scribe used the annals *form*, the *content* expresses his Priestly ideological concerns.

---

64. M. S. Smith, *The Memoirs of God: History, Memory, and the Experience of the Divine in Ancient Israel* (Minneapolis: Fortress, 2004) 81; idem, *Pilgrimage Pattern*, 290–98. Other scholars have also pointed out the liturgical nature of some of the dates; see Sturdy, *Numbers*, 13, 76–77; Olson, *Death of the Old*, 95–96; W. W. Lee, *Punishment and Forgiveness in Israel's Migratory Campaign* (Grand Rapids, MI: Eerdmans, 2003) 90.

65. The dates in Num 1:1, 18 put the census out of chronological order. One way of addressing the problem is to see Num 7:1 and 9:1 as flashbacks or efforts to date these activities to their proper times once the date in 1:1 had already become part of the structure of Numbers. The second-month context indicated in Num 1:1 is then resumed in Num 10:11; see Sturdy, *Numbers*, 56, 70, 76; J. Milgrom, *Numbers* (JPS Torah Commentary; Philadelphia: Jewish Publication Society, 1990) 67; T. R. Ashley, *The Book of Numbers* (NICOT; Grand Rapids, MI: Eerdmans, 1993) 47, 192; M. R. Hauge, *The Descent from the Mountain: Narrative Patterns in Exodus 19–40* (JSOTSup 323; Sheffield: Sheffield Academic Press, 2001) 213–16, esp. p. 213 n. 47; Lee, *Punishment and Forgiveness*, 77–81. But

We see the importance of calendars in later priestly texts such as the Astronomical Book of *1 Enoch* (no later than the third century B.C.E.), *Jubilees* (mid-second century B.C.E.), and various calendrical texts from Qumran. As James C. VanderKam has put it, these calendars are "written records of the way in which God had ordered his creation," and the calendar in the Astronomical Book is given by divine revelation mediated by the angel Uriel.[66] The Priestly version of the wilderness narrative quite likely stands within this broader priestly tradition of using the 364-day ideal solar calendar to set the liturgical year. Although the Torah is not as systematic in its use of this calendar as *Jubilees* is, two factors do point to its use. First, D. Barthélemy suggested in 1952 that the 364-day ideal calendar year as construed by *Jubilees* began on the fourth day of the week, noting that the sun, which regulates the calendar according to *Jub.* 2:8–10, was created along with the moon and stars on the fourth day just as they are in Gen 1:14.[67] The basis for determining the calendar is thus written into the creation of the cosmos in the Priestly version of the Torah as well as in *Jubilees*.

Second, traces of this calendar are evident elsewhere in the Torah as well. Based on Barthélemy's suggestion about *Jubilees*, Annie Jaubert in 1965 argued that each 13-week season is made up of two 30-day months plus one 31-day month, as shown in table 2.[68] If the calendar begins on the fourth day of the

---

the second-month departure in Num 10:11–12 more readily relates to second Pesah, not to the census. Because the entire series cited above, except for Num 1:1, 18, is a coherent liturgical year, I favor understanding the date in Num 1:1 as the oddity, a view also held by B. A. Levine, *Numbers 1–20*, 295.

66. J. C. VanderKam, *Calendars in the Dead Sea Scrolls: Measuring Time* (Literature of the Dead Sea Scrolls; London: Routledge, 1998) 110. See also A. Jaubert, *The Date of the Last Supper* (Staten Island, NY: Alba, 1965) 17; and R. T. Beckwith, *Calendar and Chronology, Jewish and Christian: Biblical, Intertestamental and Patristic Studies* (Leiden: Brill, 2001) 94.

67. D. Barthélemy, "Notes en marge de publication récentes sur les manuscrits de Qumran," *RB* 59 (1952) 199–203. Gen 1:14 has the 'lights' (מְאֹרֹת) in general determine the calendar, while *Jub.* 2:8–10 specifies that only the sun serves this function. While the calendrical texts from Qumran and the Astronomical Book of *1 Enoch* correlate lunar and solar calendars, *Jubilees* rejects use of a lunar calendar altogether (VanderKam, *Calendars in the Dead Sea Scrolls*, 17–27, 74). This anti-lunar polemic is quite possibly due to adoption of the lunar Seleucid calendar for the Temple cult during the mid-second century B.C.E. (VanderKam, *Calendars in the Dead Sea Scrolls*, 111–6; idem, "Calendrical Texts and the Origins of the Dead Sea Scroll Community," in *Methods of Investigation of the Dead Sea Scrolls and the Khirbet Qumran Site: Present Realities and Future Prospects* [ed. M. O. Wise et al.; Annals of the New York Academy of Sciences 722; New York: New York Academy of Sciences, 1994] 384–85).

68. This calendar is conveniently laid out in Jaubert, *Date of the Last Supper*, 27; and (even easier to work with) VanderKam, *Calendars in the Dead Sea Scrolls*, 55.

week, as Barthélemy suggested, we can know the day of the week on which festivals took place, and Jaubert argued that no festival takes place on the seventh day, or Shabbat, and also that none of the patriarchs travel on Shabbat in *Jubilees*. Jaubert maintained that the same is true for the Priestly material in the Torah, noting in particular that the Israelites depart from the wilderness of Sinai on 2/20/02 in Num 10:11–12, which works out to be the fourth day of the week, and in Num 10:33 the ark travels three days to rest on the seventh day.[69] While the three-day journey is clearly a literary trope, as is commonly recognized, Jaubert's argument suggests that it is also taken literally here so that it fits within the ideal calendar and has the ark rest on Shabbat.

While other details of Jaubert's discussion of calendrical matters have not held up to scrutiny, her basic argument about the use of a 364-day solar calendar remains tenable, even though it is sometimes looked upon with suspicion.[70] Her contention about its use in the Priestly version of the Torah has been challenged most recently by Roger T. Beckwith, who argues that this ideal calendar must have been invented under Greek influence by the author of the Astronomical Book, the earliest text unquestionably to use it. One reason it cannot have been inherited from the Bible as Jaubert suggested, according to Beckwith, is that the Essenes were meticulous about rest on Shabbat to the point of questioning whether even priestly service was permitted, a degree of meticulousness not found in biblical literature.[71] But rest on Shabbat *is* strongly emphasized in the Torah, and its authority is rooted both in creation and the deliverance from Egypt. While Priestly authors of biblical literature indeed do not go as far as to question their own service, there is sufficient seriousness about Shabbat rest to have motivated use of such a calendar.

Beckwith's second argument against the idea that the 364-day ideal solar calendar is used in the Torah is that one must look very hard to find it. He suggests that the Essenes "found" it hidden there as an act of exegesis.[72] It is certainly neither the only nor the most prominent calendrical system assumed in biblical literature. The lunar calendar is much more prominent, as the month

---

69. Jaubert, *Date of the Last Supper*, 33–35. Jaubert also makes the argument here that Wednesday, Friday, and Sunday are significant days in the Israelite calendar. While it remains true that no dated travel or activity falls on the seventh day, this particular element of her argument does not hold; see J. C. VanderKam, "The Origin, Character, and Early History of the 364-Day Calendar: A Reassessment of Jaubert's Hypothesis," *CBQ* 41 (1979) 399–401.

70. See discussion in VanderKam, "Origin, Character, and Early History," 390–411; idem, *Calendars in the Dead Sea Scrolls*.

71. Beckwith, *Calendar and Chronology*, 105.

72. Ibid., 104.

is typically referred to as יֶרַח, which is also the word for 'moon', and Ps 104:19 suggests that, while the day may be determined by the sun, it is the moon that establishes the cultic festivals.[73] The flood narrative, furthermore, seems to presume a different solar calendar, since Gen 7:24 indicates that the flood lasted for 150 days. The date formulas here cover five months, which would last 30 days each and presumably be part of a 360-day solar year.[74] But, as Beckwith admits, use of two other calendars does not necessarily preclude use of the 364-day ideal solar calendar as well.[75] Although the latter calendar may not be systematically laid out in or dominate the Bible, it stands to reason that it was purposefully used if it explains the lack of narratives dated to the seventh day and, furthermore, if it explains otherwise apparently arbitrary dates in the wilderness narrative. As Jeffrey Cooley notes: "it would be very difficult to give an explanation of the calendar used by the priestly source that does not utilize [Jaubert's] reconstruction."[76]

Use of this ideal solar calendar explains the apparently arbitrary date in Exod 16:1, where the itinerary notice has the Israelites arriving in the wilderness of Sin on the 15th day of the 2nd month after their departure from Egypt, which takes place in the 1st month of the year and is associated with Pesah. Although many commentators understand the date in Exod 16:1 simply to reflect the amount of time passed after the Israelites left Egypt and otherwise to serve no function in the narrative, the purposeful use of date formulas for cultic observances elsewhere in the wilderness narrative should leave us unsatisfied with this explanation.[77] In fact, 2/15 is a quite significant and appropriate temporal setting for the manna episode, the main theme of which is Shabbat observance, because it falls on the *sixth day* in the 364-day ideal solar calendar (see table 2). In other words, the Israelites arrive right before Shabbat, just in time for the episode to take place. On the day they arrive, the sixth day of the week (2/15), they receive instructions about how to observe Shabbat and proceed to gather a double portion. Most of them rest on the next day, the seventh,

---

73. Ibid., 99. He also points to Ps 89:37, where the moon is a "faithful witness," but the moon here occurs alongside the sun, and they are witnesses to the endurance of the Davidic line, so the specific function of the sun and moon in determining the calendar are not at all clear here.

74. However, the date formulas consist of 1 year plus 11 days, and the 11 days may be the difference between a 354-day lunar year and a full 365-day solar year; see VanderKam, *Calendars in the Dead Sea Scrolls*, 4–5.

75. Beckwith, *Calendar and Chronology*, 99–102.

76. J. L. Cooley, *Poetic Astronomy in the Ancient Near East and Hebrew Bible* (Ph.D. diss., Hebrew Union College–Jewish Institute of Religion, 2006) 285.

77. E.g., Noth, *Exodus*, 133.

subsisting on the extra manna and quail that they had gathered the previous day. The individuals who disobeyed the instructions and went out to gather on the next day—on Shabbat—provide an opportunity to reiterate the lesson.[78] The 2/15 date is meaningful within this complaint episode only if we presume use of the 364-day ideal calendar.[79]

Other dates in this calendar could have been used for the Shabbat episode, because any sixth day would be equally appropriate. But the second month seems most appropriate given the fact that this is one of the first episodes after the departure from Egypt and the first opportunity to illustrate proper observance of Shabbat. Like Pesah, it is a group-defining observance or ethnic marker. Shabbat is construed in a variety of ways in biblical literature, most notably in the Decalogues as a commemoration of deliverance from Egypt and in Exod 31:12–17 as a commemoration of creation. Ezek 20:20 construes it as a defining symbol of the relationship between Yahweh and Israel: וְאֶת־שַׁבְּתוֹתַי קַדֵּשׁוּ וְהָיוּ לְאוֹת בֵּינִי וּבֵינֵיכֶם לָדַעַת כִּי אֲנִי יְהוָה אֱלֹהֵיכֶם 'Sanctify my Sabbaths, for they are a sign between you and me so that [you] may know that I am Yahweh, your God'. Desecration of Shabbat is considered a breach of covenant.[80] This view of Shabbat's role in maintaining the relationship between Yahweh and

---

78. This chronology cannot be pushed too hard through the episode. Moses responds to the Israelites' complaint presumably on the 15th (sixth day of the week), but the manna arrives only with the dew on the following morning, which would have the Israelites gathering their double portion on the seventh day and resting on the eighth, obviously a day off kilter. But the gathering on the next morning, after the dew, is simply a function of the way the Israelites receive "bread" in the wilderness. F. S. Bodenheimer pointed out that manna (Arabic *mann*) is a flaky substance that appears early in the morning after the dew ("The Manna of Sinai," *BA* 10 [1947] 2–6). The author of this complaint episode appears to have drawn on his knowledge of the desert environment to create the narrative; however, the circumstances of it—the fact that manna comes only after dew and must therefore be collected the next morning—do not *quite* fit the temporal setting. This should be thought of simply as a problematic blend of repertoire; see the discussion of other problematic blends in chap. 6.

79. P. Guillaume interprets the date in Exod 16:1 to be the date of the beginning of *matsot* before the reference to *matsot* was added in Exod 13:3–10; when the earlier reference was added, the date in Exod 16:1 was pushed back a month to make room for it. His association between manna and *matsot* seems to be predicated on manna's being a substitute for *matsot* until the Israelites enter the land and have grain in Josh 5:10–12 (*Land and Calendar: The Priestly Document from Genesis 1 to Joshua 18* [LHBOTS 391; New York: T. & T. Clark, 2009] 91–94). This explanation seems odd and unecessarily complex given that the ritual observance of concern in the manna episode is *Shabbat*, not *matsot*.

80. Sparks, *Ethnicity and Identity*, 304–5; Aaron, *Etched in Stone*, 301–4.

Israel is situated in the Priestly version of the wilderness narrative with the blueprints and instructions for the construction of the Temple. Here, failure to observe Shabbat properly by abstaining from work—a חֻקַּת עוֹלָם just like Pesah—will result in being cut off from the community (Exod 31:12–17).

Although the 364-day ideal solar calendar is used in Priestly narrative material in the Torah, it is not systematically worked out there, as it is in *Jubilees*. M. S. Smith suggests that the date associated with the itinerary notice in Exod 19:1, which brings the Israelites into the wilderness of Sinai in the third month, may be an effort to associate the Sinai lawgiving with Shavuot.[81] Given the overall cultic nature of the dates in the wilderness narrative, it is likely that this date is also not accidental. Nevertheless, Smith's suggestion is quite problematic, because there is no clear reference to the association between Shavuot and the revelation at Sinai before the third century C.E., and Shavuot remained a harvest festival (firstfruits, or הַג הַקָּצִיר, as in Exod 23:16, called חַג שָׁבֻעֹת in Exod 34:22) into the Amoraic period (third–fifth centuries C.E.).[82] Moreover, *Jubilees* associates Shavuot, or firstfruits, with a whole variety of biblical events in addition to the Sinai covenant, including Jacob's covenant with Laban, God's covenants with Abraham and Jacob, and particularly the Noachide covenant. As Beckwith puts it, Shavuot in *Jubilees* is the "occasion of all covenants."[83]

If the date in Exod 19:1 is a reference to Shavuot, or firstfruits, the lack of a specific day in the third month may reflect the fact that the date of Shavuot and the narrative event with which it was associated was still flexible when the Torah was taking shape, as it remained for many centuries. Lev 23:15–21 stipulates that firstfruits is to be celebrated 50 days after the waving of the omer, which is מִמָּחֳרַת הַשַּׁבָּת 'the day after Shabbat'. But the date of firstfruits is difficult to calculate on this basis because, as Michael Fishbane discusses in detail, it is not clear just what *shabbat* refers to in the expression מִמָּחֳרַת הַשַּׁבָּת.[84] Josh 5:10–12 interprets it as the Pesah festival itself. The Israelites cross the Jordan on th 10th day of the 1st month in Josh 4:19, the same day that the Israelites were instructed to prepare for Pesah in Exod 12:3, and then observe Pesah on the 14th day of the 1st month in Josh 5:10. Josh 5:11 specifies that the Israelites

---

81. M. S. Smith, *Pilgrimage Pattern*, 62–65.

82. L. Jacobs, "Shavuot," *EncJud* 18.422; J. L. Rubenstein, *The History of Sukkot in the Second Temple and Rabbinic Periods* (BJS 302; Atlanta: Scholars Press, 1995) 315–16; see also pp. 2, 4, 289–90 n. 44.

83. Beckwith, *Calendar and Chronology*, 111. See also J. Morgenstern, "The Calendar of the Book of Jubilees: Its Origin and Its Character," *VT* 5 (1955) 56–57.

84. M. Fishbane, *Biblical Interpretation in Ancient Israel* (Oxford: Clarendon, 1985) 145–47.

ate parched grain (along with unleavened bread appropriate for *matsot*) מִמָּחֳרַת הַפֶּסַח 'on the day after Pesaḥ'. Fishbane argues that מִמָּחֳרַת הַפֶּסַח is an interpretation of מִמָּחֳרַת הַשַּׁבָּת in Lev 23:15 and reflects the use of *shabbat* to refer to the mid-month observance on a lunar calendar, like the Mesopotamian *šapattu* and the occurrence of major Israelite festivals on the 15th of the month.[85] *Jubilees*, on the other hand, interprets *shabbat* in מִמָּחֳרַת הַשַּׁבָּת as the 7th day of the week in the context of a 364-day ideal solar calendar. *Jubilees* fixes firstfruits on the 15th day of the 3rd month (see *Jub.* 15:1, 16:3, 44:1–4). As Jaubert argued, 50 days prior to 3/15 is 1/26 in the ideal 364-day solar calendar, which is indeed the day after Shabbat, understood as the 7th day of the week, since 1/26 occurs on the 1st day of the week (see table 2).[86] *Jubilees*, however, is only one effort to fix the date and not necessarily a normative one, given the fact that the date remains a subject of significant debate in postbiblical literature.

Because the 364-day calendar is ideal, it would eventually cease to coordinate with natural phenomena, particularly the seasons, and would require some method of intercalation in order to make it usable. Beckwith backs away from his argument that the author of the Astronomical Book invented this calendar and suggests that it must have been invented earlier because the author of the Astronomical Book discusses the disjunction between natural phenomena and the ideal calendar, blaming failure to maintain the ideal calendar on sinful humans and deceitful angels who did not guide the heavenly bodies properly. He notes that this calendar may have originated in an earlier edition of *1 Enoch*, a different book that is no longer extant, or an oral tradition, preferring the first option.[87] Although the Priestly version of the wilderness narrative does not fully work out such an ideal calendar, as later sources do, its ability to explain the 2/15 arrival in Exod 16:1 as well as other chronological peculiarities in Priestly literature in the Torah suggests that it was used nonetheless. Moreover, the need for intercalation would not have been immediate in the context of a *vision* for return to Zion and restoration of the Temple. While it would be purely speculative to assert that the Priestly author of the wilderness narrative invented the 364-day ideal solar calendar, its use fits nicely in this context, making the Torah, rather than a hypothetical earlier edition of *1 Enoch*, a more likely inspiration for the more worked-out version of it in later priestly literature.

---

85. Ibid., 149–51.
86. Jaubert, *Date of the Last Supper*, 22–27.
87. Beckwith, *Calendar and Chronology*, 109–10.

Yahweh as King

The date formulas are not the only formal feature of the annals genre used by the Priestly author of the wilderness narrative to convey his ideological content. The annals genre is typically used to glorify the king as victor in battle, maintainer of the empire, and leader of the army. Although his purpose is not to write royal propaganda, the Priestly author also glorifies a king who leads his army back to Zion. While the Israelites play the role of the army, the cloud that covers the Tabernacle plays the role of the king. [88]

וַיְהִי בַּשָּׁנָה הַשֵּׁנִית בַּחֹדֶשׁ הַשֵּׁנִי בְּעֶשְׂרִים בַּחֹדֶשׁ נַעֲלָה הֶעָנָן מֵעַל מִשְׁכַּן הָעֵדֻת׃
וַיִּסְעוּ בְנֵי־יִשְׂרָאֵל לְמַסְעֵיהֶם מִמִּדְבַּר סִינָי וַיִּשְׁכֹּן הֶעָנָן בְּמִדְבַּר פָּארָן׃

In the second year, in the second month, on the twentieth of the month, the cloud lifted off the Tabernacle of the *edut*, and the Israelites departed according to their stages from the wilderness of Sinai. The cloud then settled in the wilderness of Paran. (Num 10:11–12)

The Israelites are the subject of most of the itinerary notices in the wilderness narrative, but they depart from Sinai *in response to* the movement of the cloud, a symbol of Yahweh's presence. The Israelites, in the role of the army, are led by Yahweh, in the role of the king.

The annals form is used and even altered in order to express *kavod* ideology, because the scribe changed the stereotypical itinerary verbs accordingly. The cloud does not depart (נסע) and camp (חנה) according to the typical itinerary form but lifts off (עלה) and settles or assumes its dwelling (שכן). [89] The Akkadian cognate *šakānu* is used frequently in the Habur itineraries and throughout the ninth-century annals to articulate arrival in the expression *issakan bēde* 'he pitched camp and spent the night', which makes it possible that this verb is a feature of the itinerary genre. But שכן is also the Priestly scribe's verb of choice to articulate divine presence in the sanctuary and more likely a way in which the standard form of itinerary notices in the annals genre was altered to accommodate its combination with the cloud. The author of the

---

88. Scolnic (*Theme and Context*, 82) notes the parallel between Yahweh and the royal subject of the annals but not the particularly Priestly character of Yahweh's depiction here.

89. Coats observes that the cloud as the subject and the verb שכן vary "radically from all the other examples in the chain" of itinerary notices and attributes this variation to the special relationship that this itinerary notice has with its narrative context ("Wilderness Itinerary," 137). See also Sturdy, *Numbers*, 73. For this use of שכן, see, for example, Exod 40:38 (cloud, and 1 Kgs 8:12 for Yahweh's dwelling within the cloud); Exod 24:16 (כבוד); Isa 8:18 (Zion); Ezek 43:7 (the Temple).

wilderness narrative has thus blended the roles of king and deity in the annals. While the king leads the Assyrian army, he does so *ina tukulti Aššur bēli rabê bēliya u urigalli ālik muḫḫiya* 'with the help of Ashur, the great lord, my lord, and the divine standard that goes before me' (e.g., A.0.101.1 ii 25–26). Yahweh, the deity himself, acts as leader of the Israelite army.

The blend of divine and royal roles in the characterization of Yahweh is actually evident throughout the entire composition structured by the itinerary notices in Exod 16:1, 17:1, 19:2; and Num 10:11–12. The Assyrian king sets out on campaign at the command of Ashur:

> *ina līme* ᵐᵈ*Šamaš-nūrī ina qibit* ᵈ*Aššur bēli rabê bēliya ina* ⁱᵗⁱ*Iyyar* UD.13. KAM *ištu* ᵘʳᵘ*Kalḫi attumuš*

> In the eponymy of Shamash-nuri, by the command of Ashur, the great lord, my lord, on the thirteenth day of Iyyar, I departed from Calah. (A.0.101.1 iii 92–93)

The Israelite army likewise moves by the command of its divine king. Numbers 9–10 is devoted to establishing the cloud over the Tabernacle as Israel's guide for moving and stopping, determining the stages of its journey (לְמַסְעֵיהֶם) according to the command of Yahweh (עַל־פִּי יְהוָה). This text presumes the construction of the Tabernacle described in Exodus 25–31 and 35–40, where we also find the concept of the Tabernacle as Israel's guide on the route articulated in Exod 40:34–38. While the sanctuary does not exist in the chronology of the narrative until the end of Exodus, the author incorporates the idea of a divinely directed march even into its earlier stages by using the phrase עַל־פִּי יְהוָה, which is dominant in Numbers 9–10 alongside the cloud. Unlike the cloud, however, this phrase is not anachronistic prior to the sanctuary's construction, as in Exod 17:1: וַיִּסְעוּ כָּל־עֲדַת בְּנֵי־יִשְׂרָאֵל מִמִּדְבַּר־סִין לְמַסְעֵיהֶם עַל־פִּי יְהוָה 'The entire congregation of Israelites set out from the wilderness of Sin by their stages *at the command of Yahweh*'.[90] Use of לְמַסְעֵיהֶם here is not, as Davies argues, an abbreviation for Dophkah and Alush in Num 33:12–14.[91] Rather, it articulates the concept of regular, measured movements directed by Yahweh in order to

---

90. In the wilderness narrative, פִּי יְהוָה has a limited range of uses, all Priestly. Num 3:16, 39, 51; 4:37, 41, 45, 49 have a divinely directed census, while Exod 17:1; Num 9:18, 20, 23; 10:13 use it for a divinely-directed wilderness itinerary (see also Num 13:3; 14:41; and 33:2, 38, where this idea is picked up). Otherwise it is used to identify oracular decisions, as in the cases of the blasphemer (Lev 24:12) and Zelophehad's daughters (Num 36:5).

91. G. I. Davies, "Wilderness Itineraries and the Composition of the Pentateuch," 7.

convey the notion of God's direction of Israel via the Tabernacle, even before (in terms of the narrative progression) it was built.

The date formulas are a formal slot in the annals genre that is filled with Priestly ideological content, and the role of king in this mode of emplotment is significant for the Priestly scribe's image of Yahweh. Royal imagery, as Mettinger discusses, is prominent in preexilic Zion theology but was downplayed in favor of other elements of the tradition in order to deemphasize enthronement. Yahweh is depicted as a ruler and military leader in Ezek 20:33–34, where the Israelites' return to Zion is cast as a second exodus and Yahweh as the king who brings them out of exile בְּיָד חֲזָקָה וּבִזְרוֹעַ נְטוּיָה 'with a strong hand and an outstretched arm' in order to judge them in the wilderness. But royal imagery is otherwise virtually absent in Ezekiel, and the name יְהוָה צְבָאוֹת never occurs in that corpus. Royal imagery is, however, prevalent in Zechariah 1–8 and Deutero-Isaiah, where יְהוָה צְבָאוֹת is consistently used to refer to Yahweh.[92] In these texts, not only do we find the image of Yahweh as king to be prominent, but the vision of this king's return to Zion along with his people is also informed by *military* imagery. Although we find this imagery in a variety of texts, Isa 52:7–12 is a very clear example:

^{7} מַה־נָּאווּ עַל־הֶהָרִים רַגְלֵי מְבַשֵּׂר
מַשְׁמִיעַ שָׁלוֹם מְבַשֵּׂר טוֹב מַשְׁמִיעַ יְשׁוּעָה
אֹמֵר לְצִיּוֹן מָלַךְ אֱלֹהָיִךְ:
^{8} קוֹל צֹפַיִךְ נָשְׂאוּ קוֹל יַחְדָּו יְרַנֵּנוּ
כִּי עַיִן בְּעַיִן יִרְאוּ בְּשׁוּב יְהוָה צִיּוֹן:
^{9} פִּצְחוּ רַנְּנוּ יַחְדָּו חָרְבוֹת יְרוּשָׁלָםִ
כִּי־נִחַם יְהוָה עַמּוֹ גָּאַל יְרוּשָׁלָםִ:
^{10} חָשַׂף יְהוָה אֶת־זְרוֹעַ קָדְשׁוֹ לְעֵינֵי כָּל־הַגּוֹיִם
וְרָאוּ כָּל־אַפְסֵי־אָרֶץ אֵת יְשׁוּעַת אֱלֹהֵינוּ: ס
^{11} סוּרוּ סוּרוּ צְאוּ מִשָּׁם טָמֵא אַל־תִּגָּעוּ
צְאוּ מִתּוֹכָהּ הִבָּרוּ נֹשְׂאֵי כְּלֵי יְהוָה:
^{12} כִּי לֹא בְחִפָּזוֹן תֵּצֵאוּ וּבִמְנוּסָה לֹא תֵלֵכוּן
כִּי־הֹלֵךְ לִפְנֵיכֶם יְהוָה וּמְאַסִּפְכֶם אֱלֹהֵי יִשְׂרָאֵל: ס

^{7} How delightful on the mountains are the footsteps of the herald
Announcing peace, heralding good tidings, announcing salvation,
Saying to Zion, "Your God reigns!"
^{8} Hark! Your watchmen raise their voices, as one they shout for joy,
For every eye shall see when Yahweh returns to Zion.
^{9} Be happy! Together shout for joy, O ruins of Jerusalem!
For Yahweh has comforted his people, has redeemed Jerusalem.

---

92. Mettinger, *Dethronement of Sabaoth*, 112.

¹⁰ Yahweh has bared his holy arm in sight of all the nations,
And all the ends of the earth have seen the salvation of our God.
¹¹ Turn, turn, get out of there! Touch nothing unclean.
Go out from its midst. Purify yourselves, you who bear the vessels of Yahweh!
¹² You will not even depart in haste, in flight you will not leave,
For Yahweh is marching before you; the God of Israel is your rear guard.

Yahweh is depicted here not only as a king but as the military commander of the Israelites on their way back to Jerusalem from Babylon.[93] The image of Yahweh baring his arm in v. 10 may be an expression of royal military might, as is his role as Israel's rear guard (מְאַסֵּף) in v. 12.[94] The כְּבוֹד יְהוָה likewise serves as Israel's rear guard in Isa 58:8.[95] Yahweh as a military leader is also depicted in Isa 43:17, where he is הַמּוֹצִיא רֶכֶב וָסוּס חַיִל וְעִזּוּז 'the one who brings out chariot and horse, army and warrior'. While Isaiah 52 contains no explicit image of Israel as an army, this characterization is implicit in the image of Yahweh as a military commander, and we find it explicitly articulated in Zech 10:3–7, where the Israelites are compared with soldiers (גִבֹּרִים) and cast as Yahweh's bow (קֶשֶׁת מִלְחָמָה).

Why would a Priestly scribe use the *annals genre* to emplot his vision for Israel's return to Zion and restoration of Israel's Temple, society, and cult? The annals genre is a perfect literary framework not only to return to the royal imagery of the Zion tradition as Zechariah and Deutero-Isaiah do but also to cast Yahweh as a king leading his Israelite army as they "bear the vessels of Yahweh" back to Zion.[96] I suggest that this is how the wilderness narrative became a saga of a migrating sanctuary campaign. The imagery is royal and military, but the objective is the restoration of Israel's cult back in Zion. In fact, one might suggest that the use of צָבָא in the wilderness narrative to describe the Israelites as an army rather than other terms for army such as חַיִל may have been a deliberate play on the title יְהוָה צְבָאוֹת, an effort to depict the *Israelites* as

---

93. For the Babylonian context of literature in Deutero-Isaiah, see J. L. McKenzie, *Second Isaiah* (AB 20; Garden City, NY: Doubleday, 1986) xxiv–xxx. This passage draws on language from the enthronement Psalms, as in the expression מָלַךְ אֱלֹהָיִךְ, understood as a cultic refrain, as in Ps 97:1; see R. N. Whybray, *Isaiah 40–66* (NCB; London: Oliphants, 1975) 167; McKenzie, *Second Isaiah*, 124.

94. For discussion of the possibly related expression "outstretched arm" in biblical and Egyptian contexts, see J. K. Hoffmeier, "The Arm of God versus the Arm of Pharaoh in the Exodus Narratives," *Bib* 67 (1986) 378–87.

95. The word יַאַסְפֶךָ in Isa 58:8 should be repointed to יְאַסְפֶךָ based on similarity with Isa 52:12; see "אסף," *HALOT* 1.74. For the military nature of מְאַסֵּף, see Josh 6:9, 13.

96. For recognition that the depiction of the Israelites as an army even in the Priestly call narrative anticipates conquest, see Stuart, *Exodus*, 179.

Yahweh's "hosts" despite the fact that this term usually refers to Yahweh's heavenly entourage.[97] Retrojecting this vision of restoration into Israel's valorized prenational period—in which Israel ostensibly carries the *original* sanctuary into the land—establishes its authority. The epic past, according to Mikhail Bakhtin, has authority by virtue of the fact that it is already complete and is not open to question or revision, but this does not mean that epic fails to address contemporary concerns. Epic is similar to prophecy in that it looks ahead to a future but different in that it depicts this future as having already been sealed in the past—and has all the more authority for it.[98]

The connection between the imagery in Isaiah 52 and the exodus narrative is commonly noted, and the return from exile in Isaiah 52, like the vision of return in Ezekiel 20, is typically understood as a second exodus. Commentators have pointed to the use of חִפָּזוֹן, which occurs elsewhere only in Exod 12:11 and Deut 16:3, as evidence that Isaiah 52 is dependent on the exodus narrative.[99] While use of this word suggests a relationship between the two texts, however, it does not imply a particular *direction* of dependence. Interpreters of Isaiah 52 as a second exodus assume that Deutero-Isaiah was written later than the wilderness narrative, or at the very least, *read* it as though it were later, because it comes later in the canon. We must be careful of falling into this trap and should instead think very carefully and cautiously about the intertextual relationships. They can be very difficult to define with certainty and, in this case, may be rather complicated.

We can think through some possible intertextual relationships by noting that Isa 52:12 contrasts a flight from Babylon with a measured, triumphant, proud march. Commentators have noted that the measured *march* back to Zion from Babylon is quite different from the *flight* from Egypt expressed with חִפָּזוֹן in Exod 12:11 and Deut 16:3 and interpret Isa 52:12 as a deliberate effort to contrast the return from exile with the hurried exodus.[100] The exodus narrative in the form we now have it, however, contains *both*, because the itinerary

---

97. Mettinger argues that this expression refers to the divine council, which is sometimes described in military terms, although other suggestions have been proposed ("YHWH SABAOTH," 109–11, 123–28). Cole notes: "No doubt the thought passes readily from the 'armies of Israel' to the heavenly armies, equally at God's disposal" (*Exodus*, 88).

98. M. Bakhtin, "Epic and Novel: Toward a Methodology for the Study of the Novel," in *The Dialogic Imagination: Four Essays* (ed. M. Holquist; trans. C. Emerson and M. Holquist; University of Texas Press Slavic Series 1; Austin: University of Texas Press, 1981) 13–18, 31.

99. Whybray, *Isaiah 40–66*, 168; McKenzie, *Second Isaiah*, 124.

100. Whybray, *Isaiah 40–66*, 168; McKenzie, *Second Isaiah*, 124.

notices convey the idea of a military march. One possibility is that the author of Isaiah 52 knew a wilderness narrative with both flight and march and made reference to both here. One problem with this approach is that these two modes of travel—fleeing and marching—are very different from one another. The juxtaposition of these two ideas in Exodus 12–13 is in fact a bit confusing: Did they flee Egypt in the middle of the night? (Exod 12:11, 29–36; note particularly the emphasis on nighttime observance in v. 42: ‏הוּא־הַלַּיְלָה הַזֶּה לַיהוָה שִׁמֻּרִים לְכָל־‎ ‏בְּנֵי יִשְׂרָאֵל לְדֹרֹתָם‎). Or did they march out, possibly during the day? (Exod 12:37, 13:20; note the lack of emphasis on nighttime in 13:3–4: ‏זָכוֹר אֶת־הַיּוֹם הַזֶּה אֲשֶׁר‎ ‏יְצָאתֶם מִמִּצְרַיִם‎).

A second possibility is that Isaiah 52 is not alluding to the exodus narrative at all. Flight and march may be used as generic types of movement without *any* literary baggage. A group of exiles surely has direct experience with marching armies and the need to flee a village or a city. We could, therefore, also understand the contrast between flight and march made here as a constrast between the way they left Judah when the Babylonians attacked it and the way they will return.

But there is also a third option. The author of Isaiah 52 might indeed be casting the return to Zion as a second exodus, but the exodus narrative he knew was *not yet cast as a march*, only as a flight from Egypt. If so, he contrasted the departure from Babylon with the escape from Egypt by depicting it as a triumphal march. This, in turn, may have inspired a Priestly writer to *rewrite* the exodus and wilderness narratives to depict just such a triumphal march in *narrative* rather than poetic form. The annals genre, with its itinerary notices, is a perfect mode of emplotment not only for supplying the character roles of king and army but also for articulating a stop-by-stop march, *even if* the main goal is not battle, as would be typical for an annal, but ultimately to set up the sanctuary in Zion. This third option involves a rather dynamic intertextual relationship between these two pieces of literature.

The Priestly version of the wilderness narrative, a vision for the restoration of the cult as the center of Israelite society, does not necessarily tell the same story as the previous version. Redaction-critical approaches undertaken within the Documentary Hypothesis paradigm, however, generally assume that the itinerary notices and the narrative sources they structure *do* tell the same story. Cross argues that the P redactor used itinerary notices from Num 33:1–49 in the wilderness narrative only in cases where the combined JE source or P narrative had a corresponding episode.[101] Davies, likewise, argues that the geographical

---

101. Cross, *Canaanite Myth*, 308.

framework for the wilderness narrative was already in the episodes before a redactor introduced the itinerary notices, which simply added a "military flavour" to the narrative.[102] This view stems from the assumption that the source documents, whatever their differences, all reflect the same historical events or the same collection of traditions. Noth's *Grundlage*, the hypothetical apotheosis of an oral stage of tradition-historical development and the basis for all four written source documents, is one manifestation of this assumption within the Documentary Hypothesis paradigm.[103] Another is Gerhard von Rad's view that a historical "creed" formed the basis for successive recitals of Israel's *Heilsgeschichte*, however much its external form varied from one version to the next.[104]

Johnstone, in *Chronicles and Exodus: An Analogy and Its Application*, follows Erhard Blum in making a case for a much more profound Priestly recasting of the wilderness narrative that did not merely add a different flavor but changed its entire shape. Johnstone, like Cross, understands Num 33:1–49 to be the blueprint for the Priestly version of the wilderness narrative, and he relies on the introduction to Deuteronomy to understand the shape of the pre-Priestly version.[105] As we have now seen, Num 33:1–49 was *not* the blueprint for the Priestly version. Rather, the Priestly author reemplotted the wilderness narrative as an "annal" in order to make it read as the Israelites' return to Zion from exile. Rather than look to a blueprint for the pre-Priestly version, as Johnstone does, I suggest that Meir Sternberg offers a better approach to discerning what the pre-Priestly version of the wilderness narrative looked like when he notes that "the task of decomposition calls for the most sensitive response to the arts of composition."[106] In the paragraphs that follow, I will explore what we can learn about the pre-Priestly version by looking at the way the Priestly writer combined his own material with previously existing material to create a coherent blend.

How, without a blueprint, do we know what the elements of preexisting text are? Like the march out of Egypt versus the flight out of Egypt, certain elements of the Priestly version create dissonance with other parts of the narrative as it stands because the combination violates something about the way

---

102. G. I. Davies, "Wilderness Itineraries and the Composition of the Pentateuch," 9.

103. Noth, *History of Pentateuchal Traditions*, 38–41.

104. G. von Rad, "The Form-Critical Problem of the Hexateuch," *The Problem of the Hexateuch and Other Essays* (London: SCM, 1984) 3.

105. Johnstone, *Chronicles and Exodus*, 242–80.

106. M. Sternberg, *The Poetics of Biblical Narrative: Ideological Literature and the Drama of Reading* (ed. R. M. Polzin; Indiana Literary Biblical Series; Bloomington: Indiana University Press, 1985) 16.

repertoire works in its background contexts. Just as trash cans are not a place where you put items to save them (to bring to mind again Mark Turner and Gilles Fauconnier's parade example of a problematic blend from chap. 2), people do not march and flee at the same time; some formal features are associated with the itinerary genre while others are not, and certain ideological positions are incompatible. When we encounter this sort of horizon in the text, we must negotiate the way it fits with the theme or the consistent picture of the text that we have already built in our reading process so far. Iser argues that the author constructs cues in the text to help the reader negotiate these spots and build a *Gestalt* of the text that accounts for them. But consistency-building always sets some possibilities of meaning to the side that nonetheless remain in the text. We can negotiate the dissonance by harmonizing or ignoring it, but we can also choose to pay attention to the dissonance.[107] It is at such points that we can see the techniques used by the Priestly writer to make the blend of his material and pre-Priestly material read as much as possible as a coherent whole. I refrain here from offering a reconstruction of the entire pre-Priestly wilderness narrative, because my main goal is to elucidate how the Priestly writer used the itinerary notices to guide the reading process at such points of dissonance. The two examples I am about to discuss are those that I perceive to be the clearest and that illustrate the technique of structuring theme and horizon.

The first itinerary notice in Exod 12:37, especially as it is combined with an active effort to depict the Israelites as an army, establishes a theme for the wilderness narrative. The theme involves not only the formal features of itinerary notices but also an entire set of expectations based on the way the itinerary and annals genres are used in their background contexts. What kind of narrative is this? How will it progress? How will it end? Assuming a reader recognizes the genre and the background context from which it was selected—which we now can—she need read no further than וַיִּסְעוּ בְנֵי־יִשְׂרָאֵל מֵרַעְמְסֵס סֻכֹּתָה 'The Israelites set out from Ramses to Succoth' to know that she should read this narrative as a campaign, that it is likely to progress stop by stop in a linear fashion, that it will probably end in a battle, and that she will encounter formulaic statements just like this one many more times as the Israelites progress on their journey.

As the Israelites arrive at Marah in Exod 15:23, however, the reader encounters an atypical expression for their movement: וַיָּבֹאוּ מָרָתָה 'they came to Marah'. She encounters the same again for their arrival at Elim in Exod 15:27:

---

107. W. Iser, *The Act of Reading: A Theory of Aesthetic Response* (Baltimore: Johns Hopkins University Press, 1978) 126. Iser does not deal with composite texts that were the product of multiple authors, but his ideas can be applied to help us understand this characteristic of the Torah.

וַיָּבֹאוּ אֵילִמָה'they came to Elim'. Instead of the stereotypical arrival formula with חנה and departure formula with נסע—characteristic of the itinerary genre as it is used in Assyrian annals, in the preceding itinerary notices in Exod 12:37 and 13:20, and throughout the itinerary in Num 33:1–49—she finds no departure formula and, consequently, no repetition of the place-name to connect Marah and Elim explicitly. Moreover, the arrival is articulated with the verb בוא. Being a new form, apparently of an itinerary notice, these constitute a horizon. On one level, they are statements of movement toward and arrival at a place, and one might not think twice about them. On another level, the itinerary genre is very formulaic. Whatever convention is established in an itinerary is carried consistently through the document to its very end, whether that be the form with חנה and נסע characteristic of the Habur campaigns, or a place-name preceded by the number of days at the stop, as in the Old Babylonian itineraries. The itinerary notices in the theme so far have been in the form of חנה and נסע. Are Exod 15:23 and 27 *really* itinerary notices?

Coats understands בוא simply as a variant of חנה in the itinerary formula.[108] But, while בוא certainly articulates movement to a place, it is not characteristic of the itinerary genre. Its semantic equivalent in Akkadian, *erēbu*, is not used in any administrative document discussed in chap. 3, nor is it an element of the Habur itineraries that are incorporated into the ninth-century annals. We do see *erēbu* used in the Neo-Assyrian annals, but it is a feature of the annals that has been *combined with* the itinerary genre in order to accommodate the itinerary to the narrative context. The verb *erēbu* is used when the king enters difficult mountain passes, a stereotypical expression characteristic of the annals, just as other stereotypical expressions have a broad range of verbs for movement, including *alāku* 'to go', *ṣabātu* 'to head for', *ebēru* 'to cross', *elû* 'to go up', and *redû* 'to continue on', as well as *erēbu*. As we saw in chap. 4, the combination of the formulaic itinerary verbs *biātu*, *šakānu*, and *namāšu* with these other general verbs for movement that are not part of the itinerary genre reflects the accommodation of the itinerary genre to the annals genre as the itineraries became part of the effort to narrate movement to the battle site. The same is true of Exod 15:23 and 27; while these two expressions do convey movement, the author does not use features of the *itinerary genre specifically* to convey it.[109]

---

108. Coats, "Wilderness Itinerary," 137.

109. Coats, Davies, and Walsh all identify the arrivals at Marah and Elim as itinerary notices; see Coats, "Wilderness Itinerary," 135; G. I. Davies, "Wilderness Itineraries and the Composition of the Pentateuch," 2; J. T. Walsh, "From Egypt to Moab: A Source Critical Analysis of the Wilderness Itinerary," *CBQ* 39 (1977) 21.

Table 3. Itinerary Notices in the Priestly "Annal"

Exod 12:37	וַיִּסְעוּ בְנֵי־יִשְׂרָאֵל מֵרַעְמְסֵס סֻכֹּתָה	The Israelites departed from Ramses to Succoth.
Exod 13:20	וַיִּסְעוּ מִסֻּכֹּת וַיַּחֲנוּ בְאֵתָם בִּקְצֵה הַמִּדְבָּר׃	They departed from Succoth and camped at Etham at the edge of the wilderness.
Exod 16:1a	וַיִּסְעוּ מֵאֵילִם וַיָּבֹאוּ כָּל־עֲדַת בְּנֵי־יִשְׂרָאֵל אֶל־מִדְבַּר־סִין אֲשֶׁר בֵּין־אֵילִם וּבֵין סִינָי	They departed from Elim. The whole congregation of Israelites came to the wilderness of Sin, which is between Elim and Sinai.
Exod 17:1	וַיִּסְעוּ כָּל־עֲדַת בְּנֵי־יִשְׂרָאֵל מִמִּדְבַּר־סִין לְמַסְעֵיהֶם עַל־פִּי יְהוָה וַיַּחֲנוּ בִּרְפִידִים	The whole congregation of Israelites departed from the wilderness of Sin according to their stages by the command of Yahweh, and they camped at Rephidim.
Exod 19:2	וַיִּסְעוּ מֵרְפִידִים וַיָּבֹאוּ מִדְבַּר סִינַי וַיַּחֲנוּ בַּמִּדְבָּר	They departed from Rephidim, came to the wildernes of Sinai, and camped in the wilderness.
Num 10:12	וַיִּסְעוּ בְנֵי־יִשְׂרָאֵל לְמַסְעֵיהֶם מִמִּדְבַּר סִינָי וַיִּשְׁכֹּן הֶעָנָן בְּמִדְבַּר פָּארָן׃	The Israelites departed according to their stages from the wilderness of Sinai, and the cloud settled in the wilderness of Paran.
Num 20:1	וַיָּבֹאוּ בְנֵי־יִשְׂרָאֵל כָּל־הָעֵדָה מִדְבַּר־צִן בַּחֹדֶשׁ הָרִאשׁוֹן וַיֵּשֶׁב הָעָם בְּקָדֵשׁ׃	The Israelites, the whole congregation, arrived in the wilderness of Zin in the first month, and the people stayed at Kadesh.
Num 20:22	וַיִּסְעוּ מִקָּדֵשׁ וַיָּבֹאוּ בְנֵי־יִשְׂרָאֵל כָּל־הָעֵדָה הֹר הָהָר׃	They set out from Kadesh and the Israelites, the whole congregation, arrived at Mount Hor.
Num 21:10	וַיִּסְעוּ בְּנֵי יִשְׂרָאֵל וַיַּחֲנוּ בְּאֹבֹת׃	The Israelites set out and camped at Oboth.
Num 21:11	וַיִּסְעוּ מֵאֹבֹת וַיַּחֲנוּ בְּעִיֵּי הָעֲבָרִים	They set out from Oboth and camped at Iye-abarim.

If a reader notices that the arrivals at Marah and Elim do not actually employ the itinerary genre, Exod 15:23 and 27 *alone* may not cue him to invoke his knowledge of the military background of the itinerary genre or view the Israelites as an army on campaign. But the Priestly author has integrated these verses into his chain of itinerary notices so that they *read as* part of the chain. The next itinerary notice returns to the theme:

וַיִּסְעוּ מֵאֵילִם וַיָּבֹאוּ כָּל־עֲדַת בְּנֵי־יִשְׂרָאֵל אֶל־מִדְבַּר־סִין אֲשֶׁר בֵּין־אֵילִם וּבֵין סִינָי

They set out from Elim, and the whole congregation of Israelites came to
the wilderness of Sin, which is between Elim and Sinai. (Exod 16:1)

This return to theme prompts the reader to process the new horizon of the
arrivals at Marah and Elim as part of the itinerary chain that has the Israelites
headed for Sinai. Even though they do not use the itinerary genre, they become
part of the reader's *Gestalt* of the narrative as an itinerary. But Exod 16:1 is not
quite a return to theme. Just as Tukulti-Ninurta II's scribe blended the elements
of the source document for the king's Habur campaign with features of the
annals genre in order to make it read coherently as part of the narrative, the
Priestly author has here adapted the stereotypical form of the itinerary notice
so that the arrivals at Marah and Elim read better as part of the chain.

He accomplished this in two ways. First, although there is no departure
formula for Marah that would connect Marah and Elim, he created one for
Elim to connect it explicitly to the wilderness of Sin. He strengthened this connection with the relative clause אֲשֶׁר בֵּין־אֵילִם וּבֵין סִינָי 'which is between Elim
and Sinai', a type of clause that is not typical of the uses of the itinerary genre
in the wilderness narrative.[110] By strengthening the connection between Elim,
the wilderness of Sin, *and* Sinai, the Priestly author created an apparent unity to
the episodes that are structured by this itinerary chain. Second, he substituted
בוא for the typical חנה to articulate the arrival in the wilderness of Sin, creating
a blended form of itinerary notice. In fact, a number of the itinerary notices in
the wilderness narrative after this point use the verb בוא. Exod 19:2 uses it in
addition to חנה, while Num 20:1 and 20:22 use it in place of the formulaic חנה
in the arrival notice (see also Exod 16:1). This blended form of itinerary notice
thus extends through the entire series of itinerary notices from the departure
from Egypt nearly to the entry into Canaan in the wilderness narrative as it
now stands, as shown in table 3 (p. 178). In fact, although this series does not
stretch as far as the expected conquest of the whole land in the book of Joshua,
we do find a battle—the conquest of Hormah at the beginning of Numbers 21—

---

110. It occurs elsewhere only in Exod 14:2. T. B. Dozeman views this clause as a
stylistic trait of P and part of a P effort in Exod 14:2, 16:1–2, and 17:1a to shift the setting of the manna episode from Elim (its original setting in the pre-P version, in his
view) to the wilderness of Sin and reconnect with the pre-P arrival at Rephidim (17:1b)
(*Commentary on Exodus*, 380–81). This analysis is untenable because it breaks up an
otherwise-coherent itinerary notice with arrival and departure formula (Exod 17:1) and
connects a proper itinerary notice (Exod 17:1) with a travel notice that does not use the
stereotypical form of itinerary genre that is used elsewhere throughout the wilderness
narrative (Exod 15:27).

near the end of this series of itinerary notices. This series of notices constitutes the basic structure of the Priestly annalistic version of the wilderness narrative. There are clearly fractures in this series, where one notice is not explicitly connected to the next. These occur between Exod 13:20 and 16:1, between Num 10:12 and 20:1, and between Num 20:22 and 21:10. Yet, despite these fractures, the same blended form of itinerary notice is used throughout. This blended form is the new theme.

The arrivals at Marah and Elim, I suggest, were part of the pre-Priestly wilderness narrative. Just as the Israelites flee rather than march out of Egypt in the pre-Priestly version of the exodus narrative, the reader encounters their arrival at these first desert stops, where they find water and palms, with no notion in the text that they are an army on a military march. There is a dissonance in form between the stops at Marah and Elim and the typical itinerary notices used prior to them. But the Priestly author cued the reader to negotiate this dissonance by making the horizon—the stops at Marah and Elim—read as part of the theme. He recontextualized these two stops in the context of a much more extensive itinerary cast specifically as an "annal." He blended the stereotypical itinerary form with the verb from these arrivals and created an explicit connection between the stop at Elim and his itinerary chain in an effort to make the narrative read as a coherent whole even though it was written in different stages.

The rock/water episode in Exod 17:1b–7 and the establishment of a judiciary in Exodus 18 constitute another important horizon in the wilderness narrative. While the horizon at the Marah and Elim stops was a matter of dissonance in genre, here the dissonance is geographical; the geography of Exodus 17–18 is confusing at best. These two episodes are also the only ones that have glaringly problematic relationships with their respective itinerary notices. A number of the itinerary notices are integrated nicely with the narratives they structure. The Israelites' departure from Ramses in Exod 12:37 fits the setting of the Egyptian sojourn as it is otherwise articulated in Exod 1:11 as well as in Gen 47:11. Mount Hor is not only the arrival point in Num 20:22 but is mentioned a number of times in the account of Aaron's death. Although the specific setting of the manna/quail narrative in the wilderness of Sin supplied by the itinerary notice in Exod 16:1 does not carry through the episode, there is nothing in the episode to contradict it. However, the rock/water episode in Exod 17:1b–7 is set at Massah and Meribah, and the rock is further identified with Horeb, while the itinerary notice indicates arrival at a place called Rephidim.[111] Moreover, and

---

111. Coats misses this problem when he states, "insofar as the itinerary chain is concerned, all the narratives arranged between particular itinerary formulas have their

perhaps even more jarring, the setting of Exodus 18 at the mountain of God, if not also the setting of Exod 17:1b–7 at Horeb, anticipates the Israelites' arrival at the mountain in Exod 19:2b, where it is called Sinai.[112] This geographical sequence violates knowledge of the way bodies move through space: a person cannot arrive at a place before she gets there. Here we encounter the same problem that confronts us with the double arrival in Moab in Numbers 21–22.

One solution to the problematic geography of these two episodes is to argue that they were moved to their present positions in the narrative from elsewhere. This solution is particularly common for Exodus 18, because Deut 1:9–18 situates the episode in which the judges are appointed just before the Israelites *leave* Horeb, leading commentators with a variety of approaches to composition history to suppose that it was once located in Numbers 10.[113] Johnstone offers a similar argument to explain the geographical conflict caused by the rock/water episode in Exod 17:1b–7. As part of his effort to show how the Priestly writer created a narrative centered on Sinai, he argues that the scribe moved the rock/water episode from an original location between Num 11:3 and 4 but "kept references to it" in Numbers 20.[114] But Numbers 20, while it certainly uses the rock/water plot structure, is a separate story with a distinct purpose and cannot be reduced to "references" to a now-relocated episode.[115] Moreover, as Propp points out, the geographical confusion created by these sorts of alleged moves is just as problematic as understanding these episodes to belong right where they are.[116] The question of how and why the geographical confusion came to be is still unresolved.

---

setting at the destination noted in the lead itinerary" and went on to note that Exod 17:8–16 are set at Rephidim like Exod 17:1, passing over the setting in vv. 2–7, which certainly does not correspond to v. 1 (Coats, "Wilderness Itinerary," 147).

112. The problem with Exodus 18 is thoroughly articulated by D. A. Glatt, who surveys the key medieval rabbinic sources that discuss the problem as well as modern scholarship (*Chronological Displacement in Biblical and Related Literatures* [SBLDS 139; Atlanta: Scholars Press, 1993] 152–54). For a succinct summary of the problem generated by Horeb in Exod 17:6 vis-à-vis Sinai in Exodus 19, see Cole, *Exodus*, 135.

113. Driver, *Book of Exodus*, 162; J. Van Seters, "Etiology in the Moses Tradition: The Case of Exodus 18," *HAR* 9 (1985) 355; Van Seters, *Life of Moses*, 208–19; Johnstone, *Chronicles and Exodus*, 26, 147, 266. This type of solution to the problem is not new to modern critical scholarship; for citation of Ibn Ezra's solution, see Sarna, *Exodus*, 97.

114. Johnstone, *Chronicles and Exodus*, 255–57; quotation from p. 257.

115. On the rock/water plot structure and the distinct uses of the motif in Exodus 17 and Numbers 20, see Aaron, *Etched in Stone*, 203–9.

116. W. H. C. Propp, *Exodus 1–18: A New Translation with Introduction and Commentary* (AB 2; New York: Doubleday, 1999) 627–28.

Geographical dissonance is not the only problem. We also find ideological dissonance here. While the Priestly writer, like Zechariah 1–8 and Deutero-Isaiah, retains the image of Yahweh as king from the Zion traditions, his depiction is, like the *kavod* imagery in Ezekiel, still a response to the no-longer-tenable idea that Yahweh dwells in a fixed location. However, the rock/water episode and the appointment of judges assume that Yahweh dwells in a fixed location. Horeb and the mountain of God are clearly not the Temple Mount, as they are located in the wilderness, and these two episodes do not express enthronement theology. Yet they are understood as the place where Yahweh *lives*, where one goes to find Yahweh, just as the Temple Mount is in the Zion traditions. The idea of the divine mountain as the residence of the deity, the place where humans meet the gods in theophanies, and the locus of a banquet such as we find in Exodus 18 is rooted in the Canaanite complex of religious ideas and, as Mettinger points out, the Zion tradition is informed by this same imagery.[117] Thus the setting(s) of Exod 17:1b–7 and Exodus 18 invoke an idea similar to the idea that was understood by our Priestly writer to be problematic in the absence of a Temple.

The Priestly author cued us to negotiate this geographical and ideological dissonance by instructing us to neutralize—effectively to ignore—the settings of these episodes. He did so by the way he related them to the by-now-dominant itinerary theme just as he did for the arrivals at Marah and Elim. Both episodes occur between the following two itinerary notices:

וַיִּסְעוּ כָּל־עֲדַת בְּנֵי־יִשְׂרָאֵל מִמִּדְבַּר־סִין לְמַסְעֵיהֶם עַל־פִּי יְהוָה וַיַּחֲנוּ בִּרְפִידִים

The whole congregation of Israelites departed from the wilderness of Sin according to their stages by the command of Yahweh, and they camped at Rephidim. (Exod 17:1)

וַיִּסְעוּ מֵרְפִידִים וַיָּבֹאוּ מִדְבַּר סִינַי וַיַּחֲנוּ בַּמִּדְבָּר

They departed from Rephidim, came to the wilderness of Sinai, and camped in the wilderness. (Exod 19:2)

The Priestly author used these itinerary notices to establish a new setting for these episodes. The conflict in setting between Rephidim in the Exod 17:1 itinerary notice and the setting of the rock/water episode in vv. 1b–7 at Massah, Meribah, and Horeb has suggested to a number of commentators that the two

---

117. R. J. Clifford, *The Cosmic Mountain in Canaan and the Old Testament* (Cambridge: Harvard University Press, 1972) 1–8, 34–97; Mettinger, "YHWH SABAOTH," 121–22. See also Noth (*Exodus*, 148), who points out some of these features, notably the offering of sacrifices.

were not written by the same author but are artificially related to one another.[118] Exodus 18 also appears to be set at Rephidim, since it has no itinerary notice of its own.[119] From the dominant perspective in the narrative, these episodes read as though they take place at Rephidim, even though their actual settings are at Horeb and the mountain of God, respectively. Just as he adapted a number of itinerary notices to include בוא as a way to integrate the arrivals at Marah and Elim into his narrative, the Priestly author might have chosen to make Horeb and the mountain of God stops on the itinerary. But he did not do so because, as names for a fixed abode of Yahweh, they run counter to his image of Yahweh's presence in a movable Tabernacle.

These itinerary notices not only establish a new setting for Exodus 17–18 but also distinguish them from the Sinai pericope that follows. Smith as well as Ranier Albertz argue that the itinerary notice in Exod 19:2 was added by a redactor in order to make it appear as though the Israelites arrive in a new place for the theophany and lawgiving at Mount Sinai. Smith argues that its purpose is to distinguish the non-Priestly material in Exodus 17–18 from the Priestly material beginning in Exodus 19, while Albertz argues that the separation is meant to distance the mountain of God from Midian and neutralize as much as possible the idea that a foreigner influenced Israel's cult and social structure.[120] Their insight that the Exod 19:2 itinerary notice serves to marginalize the preceding episodes is very important, but its purpose is to neutralize the idea that Yahweh dwells in a fixed spot.

There is, of course, one glaring problem with the understanding I have offered here. Exodus 19 and the chapters that follow contain what we now think of as the paradigmatic mountain theophany scene. Interestingly, this scene is missing from the wilderness itinerary in Num 33:1–49. Given the importance of the theophany and lawgiving at Mount Sinai in the wilderness narrative as we now have it, we might expect to find a note about it, akin to the brief statements

---

118. E.g., ibid., 138.

119. Driver, *Book of Exodus*, 162.

120. M. S. Smith, *Pilgrimage Pattern*, 189, 230, 234; R. Albertz, *A History of Israelite Religion in the Old Testament Period* (2 vols.; trans. J. Bowden; OTL; Louisville: Westminster John Knox, 1994) 1.53; F. V. Winnett, *The Mosaic Tradition* (Toronto: University of Toronto Press, 1949) 60–62. For review of the idea that Exodus 18 and other passages involving law or the Midianites/Kenites were originally part of a tradition centered at Kadesh, see J. Blenkinsopp, *The Pentateuch: An Introduction to the First Five Books of the Bible* (ABRL; New York: Doubleday, 1992) 138. On the position of Exodus 18 vis-à-vis Exodus 19 as an indication of anti-Midianite polemic, see also Cross, who argues that it belongs with the Sinai tradition but was "forced" into the material set at Rephidim by P (*Canaanite Myth*, 311).

about the departure from Egypt (Num 33:3–4) and Aaron's death (Num 33:38–39), but it goes unmentioned. Even the Israelites' passing by the king of Arad (Num 33:40) merits mention over the lawgiving at Mount Sinai. Num 33:15–16, which relates the itinerary stop at Sinai, refers to the *wilderness* of Sinai, and the notion of a *mountain* of any significance in the middle of the wilderness sojourn is altogether missing from Numbers 33. Even more curious is that Exod 19:2 and Num 10:11–12, which relate the departure and arrival at Sinai, also neglect the mountain setting of the Sinai pericope as we now have it; they call the place *wilderness* of Sinai, rather than *Mount* Sinai just as Num 33:1–49 does. How is an effort to downplay the mountain setting of Exodus 17–18 plausible for the Sinai pericope, given the prominence of its mountain setting in our current version of the wilderness narrative? I will address this question in chap. 6.

Chapter 6

The Routes of the
Wilderness Sojourn:
Itineraries and Composition History

Criticism comes easier than craftsmanship.
—Pliny the Elder

A well-crafted narrative is a pleasure to read. Roland Barthes, in *The Pleasure of the Text*, discusses two different ways to enjoy reading. *Readerly* pleasure is pleasure taken in a more-or-less passive reading of a text focused on processing the narrative as a whole, understanding the meaning and significance of the text. *Writerly* pleasure, on the other hand, is pleasure taken in more active and analytical reading of a text focused on understanding how it was written, appreciating the artistry that went into its composition.[1] The difference is easy to grasp if you imagine standing a distance away from a Monet, noting the effect it has on you, and then coming up close to see how the artist used brush strokes, texture, and color to *create* the effect it had on you when you were farther away from it.

Even when we are focused on the readerly pleasure of processing the narrative as a whole, at times we stumble on a feature of the text—a horizon—that causes us to pause because it is not immediately clear to us how this feature fits with what we have read so far. Historical critics navigate these sorts of horizons in a writerly fashion, looking for clues about the diachronic development of the text. Many scholars have expressed frustration with historical criticism because it seems at times to focus more on deconstructing a narrative than explaining how it manages to work as a whole, even though composite. Brian Peckham captures this frustration well when he says:

---

1. R. Barthes, *The Pleasure of the Text* (trans. R. Miller; New York: Hill and Wang, 1975).

185

In its heyday the historical-critical method was renowned for its ability to detect sources and the work of redactors. As time passed, it was
criticized for its excesses and omissions, for its obsession with attributing
every conceivable inconcinnity to some intrusive hand, for its unscrupu-
lous fragmentation of a perfectly good text in its search for a hypothetical
original, and for its benign neglect of the secondary material and of the
editorial processes that produced the books.[2]

Historical critics have sometimes been too quick to jump in with a diachronic
solution to what may be a synchronic problem. Iser argues that creating and
resolving horizons is the way an author develops a narrative. Horizons that
are tensions within a well-constructed narrative are productive and eventually
are either resolved or left in such a way as to contribute to its meaning. The
influence of New Criticism on biblical studies has turned our attention to the
literary craftsmanship of ancient Israelite scribes and provided an important
corrective to the excesses of which Peckham speaks.

Nevertheless, some horizons are truly *fractures* in a text—places where
the narrative just does not work optimally. Sometimes the problem lies not in
the text but in our own faulty or unexplored assumptions about what the text
ought to be, such as when a commentator deems that a point in the narrative
does not read as smoothly as he or she might like. But we are warranted in seeing a fracture when something in the text grates against shared context gained
from in-depth study of ancient culture. We should stop to question the different forms of the itinerary genre in Num 21:12–13a, which takes the Israelites
past Wadi Zered and Wadi Arnon, and Num 21:18b–20, which takes them past
Bamoth to Pisgah in Moab, because the itineraries we know *from antiquity*
do not change form in the middle. Outright conflicts in the text itself are also
likely to be fractures. We should wonder whether something is amiss when
Yam Suf is the sea that the Israelites cross to leave Egypt in Exod 15:22 but is a
place three stops beyond that sea in Num 33:10–11. Finally, our assessment of
these sorts of fractures is also warranted when a text violates basic constraints
of human experience that we can reasonably presume the ancient Israelites to
have experienced just as we do. Since people cannot be in two places at once,
we should wonder whether a scribe really meant to depict the Israelites' going
both around and through Moab at the same time or whether this difficulty is a
casualty of the composition process. Fractures such as these make the narrative
sometimes less and sometimes more difficult to read as a coherent whole, and

---

2. B. Peckham, "Writing and Editing," in *Fortunate the Eyes That See: Essays in
Honor of David Noel Freedman in Celebration of His Seventieth Birthday* (ed. A. Beck
et al.; Grand Rapids, MI: Eerdmans, 1995) 364.

it is reasonable to consider the presence of such a horizon as a sign of compositional problems.

Various methods of historical criticism have been used to explain these fractures in the wilderness itinerary, points at which the chain of itinerary notices lacks coherence. They usually employ a standard of coherence that is external to the specific text under consideration, be it a single event presumed to lie behind the narrative, a consistent style or theme that is assumed to characterize one source, or even another biblical text. Despite the insights they offer, the key studies briefly reviewed here fall short because they sometimes fail to explain the fractures we actually encounter as we read, or they even disturb the coherence we *do* encounter in the text.

George W. Coats thought that a coherent, unified story of the Israelites' journey lay at the beginning of the wilderness narrative's transmission history. He understood the itinerary notices as the framework used to organize various traditions about the journey and give them an "impression of unity" as they were combined and took shape as a single narrative during an oral stage of development. The fractures in the chain resulted from corruption during this process. Coats did note the fractures we actually encounter as we read, but his analysis of the way they came about is no longer tenable.[3] For example, he argued that the double arrival in the wilderness of Paran (Num 10:12 and 12:16) reflects two different developments of the itinerary tradition that have been conflated in Numbers 11–12: one with the route Sinai → Kibroth-hattaavah → Hazeroth → Zin, reflected in Numbers 33; and the other with the route Sinai → Paran, reflected in Num 10:12.[4] But he did not articulate the process by which they emerged or what the originally unified tradition might have looked like. He simply assumed that there was a unified itinerary chain at some level of tradition history and explained away the disunity in its present form without actually articulating a plausible and coherent tradition-historical process through which the disunity came about. We now know that itineraries were not oral tradition but written administrative documents. Moreover, recent studies of the relationship between orality and writing in antiquity such as Susan Niditch's *Oral World and Written Word* and David Carr's *Writing on the Tablet of the Heart* suggest that the assumptions on which classic tradition-historical criticism is based, particularly an oral stage of transmission followed by a separate written stage, must be rethought.[5]

---

3. G. W. Coats, "The Wilderness Itinerary," *CBQ* 34 (1972) 138 (see pp. 138–40 for discussion of fractures).

4. Ibid., 140.

5. S. Niditch, *Oral World and Written Word: Ancient Israelite Literature* (Library of Ancient Israel; Louisville: Westminster John Knox, 1996); D. M. Carr, *Writing on the*

Jerome T. Walsh's source-critical study of the itinerary notices sought to explain the composition history of the itinerary chain by grouping the notices into different stylistic categories. Although he did not assume the classical sources (J, E, P, and D) or stylistic criteria (for example, different names for the deity) characteristic of the Documentary Hypothesis, Walsh did isolate three distinct itinerary chains on the basis of stylistic concerns unique to itinerary notices. The first chain is very formulaic, with consistent use of verbs (וַיִּסְעוּ for departure and וַיַּחֲנוּ for arrival) and concern with specific stations rather than routes. Chain I is most like Num 33:1–49. The second uses a greater variety of verb forms and place designations (for example, regional names and roads in addition to specific sites) and includes chronological notices. Chain II is the furthest removed from the style of Num 33:1–49. The notices in the third chain are not all connected to one another, represent a variety of stylistic types, and may instead represent a fragment of a chain. Chain III is most similar to Deut 10:6–7.[6]

While Walsh certainly found one way of dividing the itinerary notices into different types, his approach sheds no light on the fractures we actually encounter in the itinerary chain as we read. For example, it does not help us understand why the itinerary notices in Numbers 21 shift from chain I (Num 21:10–11a) to chain III (Num 21:12–13a, 18b–20) or how we navigate this shift as we read. It also does not explain how the chain reads as a coherent whole in spite of this stylistic shift. In fact, Walsh broke up itinerary notices that are explicitly connected to one another by repetition of a place-name, such as Exod 16:1 (chain II) and 17:1 (chain I), which one should surely attribute to a single source or version. Indeed, Graham I. Davies insists that short coherent sections, or strings, of the itinerary chain that are consistent in form and/or connected to one another by repetition of the place-name such as Exod 16:1 and 17:1 should be treated as coherent compositional units rather than being divided up into separate sources.[7] In so doing, Davies avoids the problem of breaking up the coherence *that is already present in the text* in order to find

---

Tablet of the Heart: Origins of Scripture and Literature (Oxford: Oxford University Press, 2005). The use of memes that float through a culture in literary and other representations is a very promising way to rethink it, and here I am indebted to the approach taken by D. H. Aaron, *Etched in Stone: The Emergence of the Decalogue* (New York: T. & T. Clark, 2006) 171–75.

6. J. T. Walsh, "From Egypt to Moab: A Source Critical Analysis of the Wilderness Itinerary," *CBQ* 39 (1977) 20–33.

7. See G. I. Davies, *The Wilderness Itineraries in the Old Testament* (Ph.D. diss., University of Cambridge, 1975) 62, 64 for a summary of the strings.

a coherence that fits a set of lexical or stylistic criteria. One could say that an approach such as Walsh's is criticism without a view toward craftsmanship. In its search for coherence, it takes the text apart without also considering how it already does hang together.

Redaction criticism has fared better because it focuses on understanding the editorial processes that produced the form of the Torah that we now encounter when we read it. The coherent strings of itinerary notices, such as the chain that includes Exod 16:1, 17:1, 19:2; and Num 10:12 and takes the Israelites from Elim to Sinai and on to the wilderness of Paran (see table 3, p. 178), remain intact in the redactional analyses of G. I. Davies and William Johnstone. [8] But both Davies and Johnstone assigned the various strings to a redactional layer that matches the structure of the journey in Num 33:1–49, which they viewed as a blueprint for what the redactor was trying to create. Thus virtually all of the itinerary notices in the wilderness narrative are understood as being part of the *same* chain. This analysis keeps the strings of connected itinerary notices intact, but it also leaves unexplained the fractures that we encounter as we read the wilderness narrative. Num 33:1–49 does not contain these fractures; all of its itinerary notices use the same formulaic language, and each notice is connected to the previous by repeating the place-name of the arrival site as the new departure site. While the *structure* of the wilderness narrative with its itineraries is much like the structure in Num 33:1–49, it lacks the actual *coherence* present there. Despite the improvements that redaction criticism has made in our understanding of the itinerary notices, we are still left without a satisfactory explanation for the fractures that we encounter in the chain as we read the wilderness narrative. Such an explanation should shed light on the way those fractures came about *and* help us to navigate them as we read.

Peckham describes the editing of biblical materials as a hermeneutical activity. Editing, in his view, involves not just weaving together previously existing materials but reinterpreting them:

> Interpretation is a complete rewriting of the whole original text that consists in bracketing and omitting some parts, emphasizing others, and substituting different narrative, dramatic, or logical developments to situate the original in a new or contemporary setting. [9]

---

8. Idem, "The Wilderness Itineraries and the Composition of the Pentateuch," *VT* 33 (1983) 1–13; W. Johnstone, *Chronicles and Exodus: An Analogy and Its Application* (JSOTSup 275; Sheffield: Sheffield Academic Press, 1998).

9. Peckham, "Writing and Editing," 365.

When a text is rewritten in this way, interpretation adds something to the tradition because the two are combined, creating a dynamic between the tradition and its reinterpretation in the same text. [10] We can see the relationship between old and new, between *traditum* and *traditio*, where the two were not well integrated. Peckham noted that we can detect revisions where elements of the text are partial, contrary, abrupt, or without clear relevance to the narrative. [11] We may have limited insight into the shape of the pre-Priestly wilderness narrative (*traditum*). But, as discussed at the end of chap. 5, we can see parts of it through the Priestly version (*traditio*) into which it has been incorporated, where movement is indicated without using the itinerary genre, where the geography is problematic, and where incompatible views about Yahweh are juxtaposed with one another.

As the tradition develops, however, the *traditio* becomes the new *traditum* and is itself subject to reinterpretation and revision. When the Priestly author chose the annals genre as a mode of emplotment for the wilderness narrative, he established what kind of narrative it was, how it ended, what the character roles were, and how it was structured. The Priestly version became the new *traditum*; the string of itinerary notices shown in table 3 (p. 178) create a dominant theme for the narrative and constitute its basic structure. But table 3 is not a comprehensive list of the itinerary notices in the wilderness narrative. Since the Priestly author introduced itinerary notices into the wilderness narrative for the first time as part of his "annal," other notices that make use of the basic features of the itinerary genre—נסע, חנה, and place-names—must be dependent on it. When we encounter a fracture in the chain of itinerary notices, such as the different conventions used in Num 21:12–13a and 18b–20, we should understand it to mark a place where the Priestly version of the wilderness narrative was itself revised. The new revisions, as I will discuss below, were integrated into the Priestly *traditum* by linking them to its dominant itinerary structure. The purpose of doing this was to make the new revisions read as part of a single journey—the *traditio* as though it were part and parcel of the *traditum*.

But craftsmanship is not always so easy. The scribes who shaped the wilderness narrative had to contend with the challenge of how to integrate material that did not always quite fit. The *traditio* was not always integrated seamlessly, which is good for us from the standpoint of criticism because it is the fractures that allow us to see that revision took place. In fact, as we will see, the revisions *could not* always have been integrated seamlessly. We might think of fractures in the itinerary chain as sacrifices made in the interest of creating an optimally

---

10. Carr, *Writing on the Tablet*, 45–46.
11. Peckham, "Writing and Editing," 370, 377.

(although not always perfectly) functional blend. As I discussed in chap. 2, the consituent parts of a blend must sometimes be stretched, and compromises must be made in order for the blend to work. Even if these itinerary notices could not be fitted seamlessly into the chain, the scribes did tie into the expectation that an itinerary depicts coherent, linear, goal-directed movement. A reader has this expecation if the itinerary genre is something she knows, an element of repertoire that she shares with the author. Although we are quite removed from the author's immediate context, study of cultural remains has helped us develop—or at least approximate—a shared repertoire that enables us to follow the author's cues. Even when we encounter an itinerary notice that has a different form or is not explicitly connected to the notices that precede and follow, we do still recognize the itinerary genre at work, and this helps us form a *Gestalt* of the itinerary chain that includes even these aberrant notices. The scribes thus *created* the very "impression of unity" to which Coats refers.[12]

Fractures in the itinerary chain can therefore be understood *both* to create an impression of unity in the text *and* to point to disunity in the text due to diachronic development. Wolfgang Iser notes that part of the reading process involves accepting the illusion of the text, making differences disappear. When we read more passively, we experience the readerly pleasure of the illusion of a coherent itinerary chain. Of course, the illusion can also be broken: "[T]he broken illusion makes transparent what it pretended to be, the seemingly eradicated difference reasserts itself."[13] When we read more analytically, breaking the illusion, the workings of the text begin to show themselves, and we experience the writerly pleasure of figuring out the puzzle of how the text was written. John Barton has characterized historical criticism as "more the search for coherence and unity than a desire to carry out textual archaeology."[14] Ideally, we do not deconstruct the text at fractures simply for the sake of analysis but out of a pleasure in understanding how a scribe made the text the way it is and how it functions as a coherent whole in spite of its fractures.

A number of stray itinerary notices throughout the wilderness narrative are not accounted for in the Priestly version of it. We could try to fit all of these into another layer of composition, a new version of the wilderness narrative that encompasses the whole scope of it. Pentateuchal criticism has tended to work in these sorts of broad strokes, assuming that sources or major redactions

---

12. Coats, "Wilderness Itinerary," 138.

13. W. Iser, *The Fictive and the Imaginary: Charting Literary Anthropology* (Baltimore: Johns Hopkins University Press, 1993) 262.

14. J. Barton, *The Nature of Biblical Criticism* (Louisville: Westminster John Knox, 2007) 44.

extend from exodus (or creation) to conquest, be it Julius Wellhausen's J, E, and P sources; John Van Seters's Yahwistic version; or Erhard Blum's *D-Komposition* and *P-Komposition*. Because there is no stylistic consistency among the remaining itinerary notices and no external blueprint for positing such a compositional layer, I would like to try a different approach that begins with the simple experience of encountering these fractures as we read the text in its present form and uses the analytical tools I laid out in chap. 2 to make sense of them. When we encounter a new convention for the itinerary genre, for example, the first question we might naturally ask is: "Why the switch in form?" The next questions we should ask, to help us answer the first, are: "What are the author's literary goals *here*, at this very point in the text?" and "How did he blend elements of repertoire in the text in order to achieve them?"

The answers to these questions will vary from one fracture in the itinerary chain to another. The goals, tools, and techniques used by a scribe at one point in the narrative may not be the same as those used at another point in the narrative, so we must ask these questions anew at each fracture in the itinerary chain. Budding mechanics learn how to make small appliances, bicycles, and automobile engines by taking them apart and putting them back together. The process reveals what the different pieces are, how each part is fastened to the next (not always with the same fastener), and how the item works. Our task here is to understand how texts, composed out of disparate materials, work. Rather than fragmenting based on an assumed principle, we are best served to work backward from the whole, doing historical criticism by studying the composition process and thus understanding the techniques by which the whole was put together.

Two itinerary notices that turn out to serve the same set of literary goals may be considered part of a single revision. But, as we will see, a *number* of different revisions were made to the Priestly version of the wilderness narrative, each limited in scope. Karel van der Toorn has outlined a number of techniques that scribes used to shape texts including transcription, invention, compilation, expansion, adoption, and integration.[15] As I argued at the end of chap. 5 and as is commonly held in pentateuchal criticism, the Priestly version of the wilderness narrative is itself an expansion of a previous version of the wilderness narrative. The revisions I am about to discuss involve (1) compilations, in which scribes created an anthology by bringing disparate bodies of literature together, and (2) expansions designed to change the shape of the wilderness narrative in various ways.

---

15. K. van der Toorn, *Scribal Culture and the Making of the Hebrew Bible* (Cambridge: Harvard University Press, 2007) 109–42.

Yairah Amit has described biblical literature as the remains of a culture trying to shape itself. In it, we find the efforts of multiple writers, often with different views on Israel's identity and Yahweh's presence in its midst, to impact the shape of Israelite society and life.[16] Each revision to the wilderness narrative that we will consider has its own purpose, whether compositional or ideological. It is unclear how the Torah served power interests, especially in a context in which the Israelites were without a king and subsumed in an imperial social structure, whether Babylonian or Persian. On the other hand, whatever the political and social influence of different groups of Israelite scribes may have been, control of *ideas* during the emergence of what would become Israel's defining body of literature was important as Israelite scribes envisioned their society renewed in the land.

Around Edom (Numbers 14:25, 21:4)

Although the Priestly version of the wilderness narrative is a vision for the restoration of Israel's Temple, society, and cult, its annalistic character leads one to expect that it will end in a battle. Just like the date formulas and the roles of king and army, the typical ending is a feature of the mode of emplotment that needs to be filled. While the wholesale conquest of Canaan as depicted in the book of Joshua is the obvious candidate for such a battle, we already encounter an Israelite defeat of the Canaanites in Num 21:1–3.

וַיִּשְׁמַע הַכְּנַעֲנִי מֶלֶךְ־עֲרָד יֹשֵׁב הַנֶּגֶב כִּי בָּא יִשְׂרָאֵל דֶּרֶךְ הָאֲתָרִים וַיִּלָּחֶם בְּיִשְׂרָאֵל
וַיִּשְׁבְּ | מִמֶּנּוּ שֶׁבִי: וַיִּדַּר יִשְׂרָאֵל נֶדֶר לַיהוָה וַיֹּאמַר אִם־נָתֹן תִּתֵּן אֶת־הָעָם הַזֶּה בְּיָדִי
וְהַחֲרַמְתִּי אֶת־עָרֵיהֶם: וַיִּשְׁמַע יְהוָה בְּקוֹל יִשְׂרָאֵל וַיִּתֵּן אֶת־הַכְּנַעֲנִי וַיַּחֲרֵם אֶתְהֶם
וְאֶת־עָרֵיהֶם וַיִּקְרָא שֵׁם־הַמָּקוֹם חָרְמָה:

The Canaanite, the king of Arad, who lived in the Negev (indeed, Israel was coming by the way of Atharim) fought with Israel and took captives from them. Israel made a vow to Yahweh and said, "If you hand this people over to me, I will proscribe their towns." Yahweh responded to Israel and handed over the Canaanites. [Israel] proscribed them and their towns and named the place Hormah.

This little battle episode constitutes a horizon in the context of the itinerary notices that precede and follow it. It is preceded by the Israelites' arrival at Mount Hor in Num 20:22 (וַיִּסְעוּ מִקָּדֵשׁ וַיָּבֹאוּ בְנֵי־יִשְׂרָאֵל כָּל־הָעֵדָה הֹר הָהָר) 'They set

---

16. Y. Amit, *Hidden Polemics in Biblical Narrative* (trans. J. Chipman; Biblical Interpretation Series 25; Leiden: Brill, 2000) 3–4.

out from Kadesh, and the Israelites, the whole congregation, arrived at Mount Hor') and the episode in which Aaron dies there. The next itinerary notice occurs in Num 21:4 and notes the Israelites' departure *not from Hormah* but from Mount Hor: וַיִּסְעוּ מֵהֹר הָהָר דֶּרֶךְ יַם־סוּף לִסְבֹב אֶת־אֶרֶץ אֱדוֹם 'They set out from Mount Hor by way of Yam Suf in order to go around the land of Edom'. Although the itinerary notice following the battle has the Israelites leaving Mount Hor, Num 21:1 has the Israelites *already en route* from there, heading along the way of Atharim, the route on which the king of Arad finds them.

How are we to negotiate this horizon and make sense of the little battle episode in Num 21:1–3 in its present context? Had the author of the itinerary notice in Num 21:4 made *Hormah* the departure point, we would read the successful battle as part of the itinerary. Instead, he repeated the place-name הֹר הָהָר 'Mount Hor', explicitly connecting to the preceding Priestly notice in Num 20:22. There is effectively no stop at Hormah on the itinerary. Since the itinerary genre is the dominant theme for the wilderness narrative, once we have read the Israelites' arrival at Mount Hor in Num 20:22, we are anticipating their departure from that spot, which comes in Num 21:4. Thus the battle at Hormah can easily slip under the reader's radar. Just as the author of the Priestly version instructed the reader to downplay the episodes in Exodus 17–18 that are set at Horeb and the mountain of God, which are contrary to his vision of Yahweh in a movable sanctuary (see chap. 5, pp. 180–183), so this scribe marginalized the Hormah episode by *not* including it in an itinerary notice. Using this compositional technique, the author cued the reader to ignore the battle at Hormah and continue reading as though the Israelites were still a long way from conquest.

Although Num 21:4 picks up the place-name from Num 20:22 and uses the same convention for the itinerary genre as the Priestly itinerary notices (see table 3, p. 178), it is an atypical itnerary notice because it identifies the *route* the Israelites took from Mount Hor rather than using a typical arrival notice with חנה to identify the next campsite. The itinerary genre, as it is used in both administrative documents and military narratives, tends to use the names of specific places rather than the names of routes. Even when an itinerary is written to define a route, as in the letter from Shemshara discussed in chap. 3, this is typically done by articulating key points along the route. This same route name, the way of Yam Suf, is used in another atypical itinerary notice, Yahweh's command to the Israelites in Num 14:25: מָחָר פְּנוּ וּסְעוּ לָכֶם הַמִּדְבָּר דֶּרֶךְ יַם־סוּף 'Tomorrow, turn and set out into the wilderness on the way of Yam Suf'.[17] Use

---

17. Coats, Davies, and Walsh exclude Num 14:25 from their lists of itinerary notices because it uses a route name and is framed as a command, despite the fact that Exod 14:2 is also framed as a command yet is included in their discussions (Coats, "Wilderness Itinerary," 135–36; Davies, "Wilderness Itineraries in the Old Testament,"

of the same route name suggests that Num 14:25 may be part of the same revision as Num 21:4, part of the effort to marginalize the Hormah episode in Num 21:1–3.[18]

The spies episode, which includes the itinerary notice in Num 14:25, establishes a theme for which direction the Israelites are headed when they leave Kadesh, and this theme is picked up and reinforced in Num 21:4. Our *Gestalt* of which direction the Israelites are traveling is thus well established long before we ever encounter the battle at Hormah in Num 21:1–3. The Israelites reconnoiter the land, presumably in preparation for taking possession of it from Kadesh, but are afraid of being overcome by the natives (Num 13:31–33). Yahweh punishes their lack of faith by delaying entry into the land until the next generation (Num 14:20–37). Their punishment involves a deliberate *alteration* of the route, articulated explicitly in the Num 14:25 itinerary notice by the use of פנה alongside the typical itinerary verb נסע. When paired with another verb, פנה often indicates a shift in focus or a change of direction (see Exod 10:6; 32:15; Num 21:33; Deut 9:15; 10:5; Josh 22:4; Judg 18:21, 26; 20:45, 47; 1 Kgs 10:13; 2 Kgs 5:12).[19] Had the Israelites not been afraid and taken possession of the land, their direction of travel would have been north from Kadesh, *the same general direction* suggested by their encounter with the king of Arad in Num 21:1–3, as shown on the map in fig. 7 (p. 197). We do not know for sure where the way of Atharim (Num 21:1) is, but the Israelites must have moved north from Kadesh, where they were also camped prior to their conquest of Hormah (Num 20:1), and into Canaan in order to go anywhere near Arad.[20]

62, 64; Walsh, "From Egypt to Moab," 21, 25–26). Although commands are not used for itinerary notices in annals, the use of imperatives is not out of place in the itinerary genre more broadly. As we saw in chap. 3, itineraries are sometimes framed as commands or instructions, especially in letters. More importantly, use of the verb נסע and a place-name cues the reader to read this command as part of the series of itinerary notices that has structured the narrative so far, despite its difference from the convention used in the Priestly version.

18. For the idea that these two notices are related to one another in an effort to indicate that the Israelites went around Edom, see V. Fritz, *Israel in der Wüste: Traditionsgeschichtliche Untersuchung der Wüstenüberlieferung des Jahwisten* (Marburger Theologische Studien 7; Marburg: Elwert, 1970). But Fritz frames this insight in terms of the Documentary Hypothesis (these are assigned to J), so he does not acknowledge the possibility that they may be a *separate* effort to shift the route of the itinerary, as I am arguing here.

19. The change from northern to southern direction is explicitly noted by G. B. Gray, *A Critical and Exegetical Commentary on Numbers* (ICC; New York: Scribner's, 1906) 160.

20. Num 21:1 is the only reference to the way of Atharim in the Bible, so it is difficult for us today to determine where exactly it was in antiquity, except that it went

The change in direction takes the Israelites south from Kadesh, away from Canaan rather than north into it. The route name in these itinerary notices, the way of Yam Suf, is ambiguous in the context of the exodus and wilderness narratives because Yam Suf appears to be in two different places in the ancient Israelites' mental map. According to the poem in Exod 15:4 and the itinerary notice in Exod 15:22, Yam Suf is back in the Nile Delta, the sea the Israelites crossed in order to leave Egypt. (Other references to Yam Suf as the site of the sea crossing include Deut 11:4; Josh 2:10; 4:23; 24:6; Judg 11:6; Pss 106:7, 9, 22; 136:13, 15; and Neh 9:9.) But everywhere else Yam Suf is mentioned in the Hebrew Bible, it refers either to the Gulf of Aqaba/Eilat or the Gulf of Suez. [21] Uses of the term to refer to the Gulf of Aqaba/Eilat include Exod 23:31, which articulates Israel's east-to-west extent using as reference points the sea of the Philistines (that is, the Mediterranean) and Yam Suf; 1 Kgs 9:26, which has Solomon's fleet docked at Ezion-geber on the shore of Yam Suf; and Jer 49:21, which uses it in the context of an oracle concerning Edom's destruction (see also Num 14:25; 21:4; Deut 1:40, 2:1). Num 33:10–11 most likely uses the term to refer to the Gulf of Suez, because it situates this stop on the itinerary after Elim, three stops after the sea crossing. [22] The use of Yam Suf everywhere except references to the sea crossing, then, is similar to the use of Red Sea in Classical sources and suggests that the Septuagint translation of יָם סוּף as ἡ Ἐρυθρὴ Θάλασσα may be roughly equivalent to the use of this term by biblical writers. [23]

---

north from Kadesh. Aharoni et al. suggested that it might be Nahal Avdat, which runs from Avdat to Beer Hafir and is the shortest route from Kadesh northward ("The Ancient Desert Agriculture of the Negev V: An Israelite Agricultural Settlement at Ramat Matred," *IEJ* 10 [1960] 24, 103–4; see also Y. Aharoni, "Forerunners of the Limes: Iron Age Fortresses in the Negev," *IEJ* 17 [1967] 11–13).

21. M. Noth, *Numbers: A Commentary* (trans. J. D. Martin; OTL; Philadelphia: Westminster, 1968) 110.

22. Many commentators understand Yam Suf in Num 33:10–11 to refer to the sea that the Israelites crossed but believe that its location became conflated at a tradition-historical stage of development (Noth, *Numbers*, 244) or an effort to shift the route (and thus the location of the sea event) on the part of the author of Num 33:1–49 (J. Van Seters, *The Life of Moses: The Yahwist as Historian in Exodus–Numbers* [Louisville: Westminster John Knox, 1994] 155). A simpler solution is to understand Yam Suf in Num 33:10–11 as a reference to what we today call the Gulf of Suez and an instance of reference repair. See discussion on pp. 249–252.

23. N. H. Snaith, "יָם סוּף: The Sea of Reeds: The Red Sea," *VT* 15 (1965) 395; Noth, *Numbers*, 110; G. I. Davies, *The Way of the Wilderness: A Geographical Study of the Wilderness Itineraries in the Old Testament* (Cambridge: Cambridge University Press, 1979) 70–74.

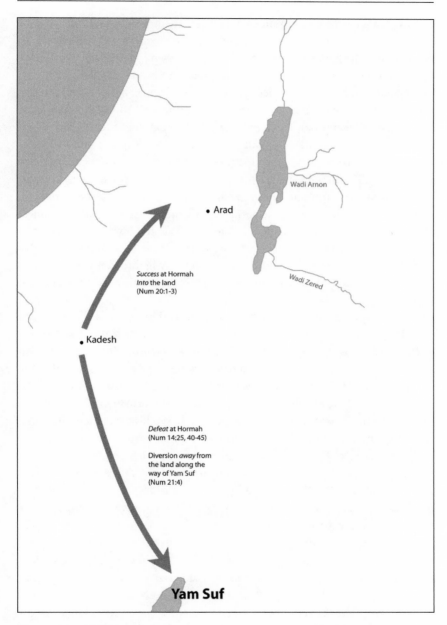

Fig. 7. Around Edom.

In Num 21:4, the way of Yam Suf takes the Israelites around Edom, which is east and south of Kadesh, so Yam Suf here must refer to the Gulf of Aqaba/Eilat, not a place in the Egyptian Delta. Num 14:25 already has the reader envisioning the Israelites on this route southeast from Kadesh toward Yam Suf (see fig. 7). This *Gestalt* is formed in the spies episode, seven chapters before the successful battle at Hormah in Num 21:1–3, as the command/itinerary notice in Num 14:25 and the events that prompt it *counteract* the idea that the Israelites conquered Canaan from the south. This *Gestalt* sets up the reader's expectations of what is to come in the narrative: the Israelites are heading around Edom and have not yet successfully entered Canaan. It is only reinforced by Moses' unsuccessful request for passage through Edom in Num 20:8–14 and the itinerary notice in Num 21:4, which has them continuing on this route. The successful conquest of Hormah in Num 21:1–3, then, challenges this *Gestalt*, forcing the reader to decide how to make sense of this little battle episode. The itinerary notices provide a cue: skip over it. While we *can* effectively ignore it, it is nonetheless still present in the narrative, a window onto the diachronic development of the narrative.

Establishing a *Gestalt* for the Israelites' direction of travel that does not include Hormah is not the only way the scribe who made this revision countered the idea that the Israelites conquered any land from the south. He also established the battle at Hormah as a failure rather than a success. Reading the narrative as it stands, by the time we get to the *successful* Hormah episode in Num 21:1–3, we have already encountered a *defeat* at Hormah in Num 14:39–45, a battle that the Israelites lose because they disobey Yahweh's command to turn and head south on the way of Yam Suf, and they go north anyway. Coats and Rolf P. Knierim note that the defeat at Hormah, which concludes the spies episode, "stands as a bitter irony in comparison to the reference to the same place in Num 21:3."[24] When we read the spies episode, this defeat at Hormah becomes part of our *Gestalt* for the progress of the narrative and only helps us neutralize the sucessful conquest of Canaan from the south when we finally encounter it in Num 21:1–3.

A number of commentators have understood the successful battle at Hormah and the defeat at Hormah as two separate events. Won Lee attempted to see the two episodes in a cause-effect relationship, the Numbers 21 episode as a case of revenge for the actions in Numbers 14. Num 21:2 has Israel make a vow to Yahweh, and Lee sees this vow as a "reaction to the initial defeat" in Numbers

---

24. R. P. Knierim and G. W. Coats, *Numbers* (FOTL 4; Grand Rapids, MI: Eerdmans, 2005) 188.

14.[25] But this explanation is not satisfactory because the the vow in Num 21:2 is a direct response to the captives taken by the king of Arad. It is revenge, but the reason is given right in Numbers 21, so we need not look to another text to find it. J. Maxwell Miller strove to resolve the relationship between the two episodes by positing a chain of historical events that he understood the episodes to narrate. He argued that the conquest of Hormah in Num 21:1–3 took place first. Later, in the episode narrated in Num 14:39–45, the Israelites are chased back to Hormah, which they had already conquered. But how was the chronological relationship between these two events reversed in the narrative as we now have it? This problem is particularly acute because Miller assigned both episodes to a single source document, J.[26] The reversal in order can therefore not be understood as the result of redactional activity assuming the Documentary Hypothesis model; one would have to posit that it happened at an oral stage of tradition-historical development.

Baruch A. Levine viewed the two episodes as doublets, not separate events, each belonging to a different source document. Using the standard Documentary Hypothesis paradigm, Levine argued that Num 21:1–3 must be P, and therefore later than the JE Hormah episode in Numbers 14, because the encounter with the king of Arad is mentioned in Num 33:40, which is also P.[27] He understood P to have rewritten the Hormah episode in Numbers 14 in order to reverse the significance of חֵרֶם as 'defeat' in Numbers 14, where it serves as a folk etymology for *Hormah* as it also does in Numbers 21.[28] But this argument is problematic because the name *Hormah* is explained only in *Numbers 21*, not Numbers 14. The name Hormah for the battle site in Numbers 21 derives from the vow the Israelites made after some of their men were captured. The same etiology for Hormah is invoked in Judg 1:17, where Zephath was renamed Hormah because Judah and Simeon proscribed it: וַיַּחֲרִימוּ אוֹתָהּ וַיִּקְרָא אֶת־שֵׁם־הָעִיר

---

25. W. W. Lee, *Punishment and Forgiveness in Israel's Migratory Campaign* (Grand Rapids, MI: Eerdmans, 2003) 252.

26. J. M. Miller, "The Israelite Occupation of Canaan," in *Israelite and Judean History* (ed. J. H. Hayes and J. M. Miller; Philadelphia: Westminster, 1977) 224–25. E. Auerbach offered a similar argument that the southern tribes went into Canaan from the south (Num 21:1–3 and, he argued, Judg 1:7). Because it was against Moses' will, this tradition was marginalized in the narrative in favor of conquest from the east led by Moses. Auerbach did not, however, explain how these two divergent historical traditions ended up in the same text (*Moses* [Detroit: Wayne State University Press, 1975] 159–63).

27. B. A. Levine, *Numbers 1–20: A New Translation with Introduction and Commentary* (AB 4A; New York: Doubleday, 1993) 60–61; idem, *Numbers 21–36: A New Translation with Introduction and Commentary* (AB 4B; New York: Doubleday, 2000) 79.

28. Ibid., 85.

חָרְמָה. In fact, Num 14:39–45 does not explain the origin of the name Hormah, evident in the fact that the author does not make use of the etiological form as Num 21:3 and Judg 1:17 do.[29]

We should instead view the Hormah battle in Num 14:39–45 as a rewrite of Num 21:1–3. The reference to Hormah in Num 14:45 (עַד־הַחָרְמָה 'as far as Hormah') is not actually a place-name or an etiology for it but rather a *word-play* on the name. The definite article suggests that עַד־הַחָרְמָה is being used as a common noun in this context. It certainly resonates with the place-name Hormah, but its basic reading here as a common noun is 'unto defeat' or 'to utter destruction'.[30] Through this wordplay, this double reading, the author turns the successful battle at Hormah—the place where Israel vowed to proscribe all the Canaanite towns according to Num 21:1–3—into a defeat. This wordplay depends on the root חרם as the basis for the Hormah etiology as it is established in Num 21:1–3 but serves the simple goal of turning the Israelite victory over the Canaanites from the south into a defeat.

Why is the scribe who made this revision to the wilderness narrative so adamant that the Israelites did not conquer any of Canaan from the south? And where do the Israelites go if not north into Canaan? The itinerary notices in Num 14:25 and 21:4 do not tell us. They indicate only the route the Israelites take from Kadesh—the way of Yam Suf—and this place-name is never picked up by another itinerary notice that might tell us where they went next. But the geography of the spies episode, where the new theme is established, does. Commentators have generally recognized that Israel symbolically lays claim to the whole of Canaan as its tribal representatives reconnoiter it.[31] Rather than articulate a number of specific sites at which the spies stop, the scribe summarized the extent of their mission with the expression "from the wilderness of Zin to Lebo-hamath," a trope frequently used to refer to the whole land (1 Kgs 8:65 // 2 Chr 7:8, 2 Kgs 14:25, Amos 6:14, 1 Chr 13:5). Lebo-hamath always marks the northern extent, while the southern extent is flexible. Although this trope is not associated with a specific concept of the extent of the whole land, its

---

29. On etiological form, see B. O. Long, *The Problem of Etiological Narrative in the Old Testament* (BZAW 108; Berlin: Alfred Töpelmann, 1968).

30. B. A. Levine, *Numbers 1–20*, 372. For the view that עַד־הַחָרְמָה presumes Num 21:1–3, see L. A. Axelsson, *The Lord Rose up from Seir: Studies in the History and Traditions of the Negev and Southern Judah* (trans. F. H. Cryer; ConBOT 25; Lund: Almqvist & Wiksell, 1987) 135–36.

31. J. Simons notes that the spies episode is a "promissory text" (*The Geographical and Topographical Texts of the Old Testament: A Concise Commentary in XXXII Chapters* [Leiden: Brill, 1959] 96, 98); see also J. Milgrom, *Numbers* (The JPS Torah Commentary; Philadelphia: Jewish Publication Society, 1990) 100.

combination with other place-names here in the spies episode indicates that the author had the tribal allotments in Joshua 13–19 in mind. The setting of the spies episode at Kadesh on the edge of the wilderness of Zin resonates with the role that this place-name plays as the southern boundary of Canaan in Josh 15:1–4's boundary list. Num 13:26 has Kadesh situated in the wilderness of Paran, but the spies depart from the *wilderness of Zin* in 13:21, reflecting the same association between Kadesh and the wilderness of Zin that we see not only in Josh 15:1–3 but also in Num 27:4 and Deut 32:1. Likewise, the pairing of Rehob with Lebo-hamath, which occurs only in Num 13:21, resonates with the role of Rehob as a key site at the northern extent of the tribal list of Asher (Josh 19:28), the northernmost tribe.[32] The author's selection of place-names for the setting of the spies episode indicates that his preferred alternative to conquest of Canaan from the south is conquest from the east *as depicted in the book of Joshua*.

This alternative should be understood in literary rather than historical terms. Whatever historical circumstances may inform the spies episode and the tribal allotments in Joshua, the function of the place-names in the spies episode is to bridge two disparate bodies of literature by foreshadowing the setting of Joshua in the geography of the spies episode. The Israelites are still in the wilderness, far from taking up residence in Canaan, when they reconnoiter it in Numbers 13–14. But the framing of the geographical extent of their mission as the extreme northern and southern boundaries of their future tribal allotments as they are articulated in Joshua anticipates an ending in which they finally do take up residence within those boundaries. As Levine notes, the successful entry into Canaan from the south in Num 21:1–3 "[flies] in the face of the Transjordanian expedition" and conquest from the east as depicted in Joshua.[33] It was apparently, however, already in the wilderness narrative when material in Joshua was connected to material in the Torah. Rather than omit it, our scribe sought to neutralize the conflict between the *traditum* and the *traditio* by influencing how we read the composite narrative.

The connection between the spies episode and the tribal allotments in Joshua 13–19 is further strengthened by verbal correspondences between Numbers 13–14 and Josh 14:6–15, where Caleb approaches Joshua to request that he make good on Yahweh's promise of the land he trod as a reward for his loyalty (Num 14:24). This promise is reiterated in the version of the spies episode at the beginning of Deuteronomy (Deut 1:36), and many commentators understand

---

32. Z. Kallai, *Historical Geography of the Bible: The Tribal Territories of Israel* (Leiden: Brill, 1986) 432.

33. B. A. Levine, *Numbers 21–36*, 83.

Joshua 14, coupled with this Deuteronomistic version of the spies episode, as an effort to incorporate the tribal allotments into the Deuteronomistic History.[34] Elie Assis, however, noted an important relationship between Joshua 14 and the spies episode in Numbers 13–14. In Josh 14:12, near the end of his appeal to Joshua to make good on Moses' promise of the land he traversed, Caleb states, אוּלַי יְהוָה אוֹתִי וְהוֹרַשְׁתִּים 'If only Yahweh is with me, I will dispossess them'. This exclamation picks up two key phrases from the version of the spies episode in Numbers 13–14, both from segments of the narrative where Caleb encourages the Israelites: וַיהוָה אִתָּנוּ 'Yahweh is with us' (Num 14:49) and וְיָרַשְׁנוּ אֹתָהּ 'We will dispossess it' (Num 13:30).[35] These expressions do not occur in Deuteronomy's version of the spies episode. In other words, Josh 14:6–15 connects not to Deuteronomy 1, but to Numbers 13–14. The connection between the geography of Numbers 13–14 and Joshua 13–19, this verbal correspondence, the revision of the Hormah episode as a defeat rather than a success, and the itinerary notices that shift the route south away from Canaan work together to incorporate Joshua as a new, more comprehensive conquest to end the annalistic wilderness narrative.

In the discussion over whether Martin Noth's Tetrateuch actually existed as an independent text, commentators juggle the expectation of an imminent ending created by Moses' final scene in Num 27:12–23 and the need for a conquest, which does not come until Joshua.[36] In light of the work of Rolf

---

34. E.g., M. Noth, *A History of Pentateuchal Traditions* (trans. B. W. Anderson; Englewood Cliffs, NJ: Prentice Hall, 1972) 131; idem, *The Deuteronomistic History* (JSOTSup 15; Sheffield: JSOT Press, 1981) 15, 28–29, 39; A. D. H. Mayes, *The Story of Israel between Settlement and Exile: A Redactional Study of the Deuteronomistic History* (London: SCM, 1983) 55; Van Seters, *Life of Moses*, 377; E. T. Mullen Jr., *Ethnic Myths and Pentateuchal Foundations: A New Approach to the Formation of the Pentateuch* (Atlanta: Scholars Press, 1997) 297 (who, however, questions the dependence on Joshua 15); M. N. van der Meer, *Formulation and Reformulation: The Redaction of the Book of Joshua in the Light of the Oldest Textual Witnesses* (VTSup 102; Leiden: Brill, 2004) 124–25, 153 n. 131.

35. E. Assis, "'How long are you slack to go into the land?' (Jos. XVIII 3): Ideal and Reality in the Distribution Descriptions in Joshua XIII–XIX," *VT* 53 (2003) 17–18.

36. Some commentators address this issue on the assumption that the Pentateuch in its current shape is a unity, explaining the similarity between Deuteronomy 34 and Num 27:12–23 as a "repetitive resumption" that simply serves to remind the reader where the story left off before Moses' lawgiving and testament (for example, Milgrom, *Numbers*, 233). The standard view among scholars who take a historical-critical approach is that Numbers 27 originally had a narrative of Moses' death that was truncated by the redactor who connected the Pentateuch and the Deuteronomistic History; see Noth, *Numbers*, 4–10, 213. A related view holds that Moses' death was moved to the end of Deuteronomy for the inclusion of that book alone; see Gray, *Critical and Exegetical*

Rendtorff, who has argued strongly for the independence of the primeval and patriarchal traditions in Genesis from other blocks of material in the Penta-teuch, we can no longer speak so clearly of a Tetrateuch.[37] But, although re-visions such as this one have obscured the ending of the Priestly wilderness narrative in such a way that its shape can no longer be discerned in its specifics, it is reasonable to suggest that the successful Hormah episode in Num 21:1–3 is the conquest narrative for a Priestly version that ended in Numbers, the battle in which an "annal" should end.[38] We need not look to Joshua for a conquest of Canaan despite the fact that it now dominates the literature in its present shape. In fact, the battle at Hormah in Num 21:1–3 is less a story of how a specific site was named than it is an expression of the successful conquest of Canaan in general, undertaken from the south. The scribe uses synecdoche to depict the conquest of Canaan *on the whole* in terms of a specific battle at Hormah. The Israelites fight a specific battle with the king of Arad, but the outcome of this specific battle—presumably the rescue of the captive Israelites and success in the battle—is never related. Instead, the story focuses on how Israel proscribed (וַיַּחֲרֵם, the basis for חָרְמָה) the Canaanites and their towns *in general* in fulfill-ment of their vow. The brief conquest may not seem satisfactory in comparison with Joshua, but we should remember that writing a campaign narrative was not the Priestly writer's primary goal. Although the Hormah episode satisfies the expectation that an "annal" will end in a battle, the writer used the annals genre *not* for its typical use to depict a conquest but to craft a vision of the Is-raelites' marching back to Zion with the vessels of Yahweh.

Commentary on Numbers, 399; A. G. Auld, *Joshua, Moses and the Land: Tetrateuch—Pentateuch—Hexateuch in a Generation since 1938* (Edinburgh: T. & T. Clark, 1980) 72. Finally, some understand Deuteronomy 34 to be D rather than P, so P never had a nar-rative of Moses' death; P ended in Numbers 27, and it did not have a conquest either; see B. A. Levine, *Numbers 21–36*, 354; J. Blenkinsopp, *Sage, Priest, Prophet: Religious and Intellectual Leadership in Ancient Israel* (Library of Ancient Israel; Louisville: Westmin-ster John Knox, 1995) 105, 109. For an overview of the problem of where P ends, see J. Ska, *Introduction to Reading the Pentateuch* (trans. P. Dominique; Winona Lake, IN: Eisenbrauns, 2006) 147–51.

37. R. Rendtorff, *The Problem of the Process of Transmission in the Pentateuch* (trans. J. J. Scullion; JSOTSup 89; Sheffield: JSOT Press, 1990).

38. G. W. Coats illustrates the confusion created by this revision. Adopting a tra-dition-historical approach, he argues that the Hormah conquest in Num 21:1–3 is really a wilderness tradition because the Israelites have not yet entered Canaan, although he acknowledges that it may have been a conquest tradition at one point in its development ("Conquest Traditions in the Wilderness Theme," *JBL* 95 [1976] 177–90).

Transjordan (Numbers 21:10–20, 22:1)

Few sections of the Torah may be as frustrating to read as Numbers 21. We may experience little readerly pleasure as we are confronted with different conventions for the itinerary genre and, far more challenging, the "geographical hodgepodge," as J. Miller calls it, that makes it profoundly difficult to read this text as a coherent whole.[39] There is, of course, the problem of whether the Israelites are going around or through Moab. But there are other hurdles as well. Is the plateau north of the Arnon *Moab*? Or is it *Amorite* territory? The conquest of Sihon and Og (Num 21:21–32) would have us think it is Amorite, but the Balaam narrative that follows it in chap. 22 clearly takes place in Moab, and the itinerary notice in Num 21:20 situates the Israelites in Moab already, before they even encounter Sihon. Furthermore, the Israelites arrive in Moab *twice*—once in Num 21:20 and again in Num 22:1. Such a time-space warp is not characteristic of itineraries, which convey forward, linear movement from one place to the next.

Numbers 21 has always been a particular problem for the classical Documentary Hypothesis, because it is difficult to use the criteria of divine names and distinctive styles to separate sources here. Scholars have frequently turned to geography as an aid in sorting out the composition history. Wellhausen assumed that the authors of various source documents knew and represented the political geographies of the respective historical periods in which they wrote and divided Numbers 20–21 into sources on this basis. J, which narrates the conquest of Sihon, was written during the monarchy, when the Israelites would have encountered various nations in Transjordan, while P, like Numbers 33, depicts Transjordan as a *tabula rasa*, through which the Israelites pass without conflict.[40]

An alternative view was adopted by Noth and Van Seters, who understood Numbers 21 as a sort of tradition-historical vacuum, a place where pieces from

---

39. J. M. Miller, "The Israelite Journey through (around) Moab and Moabite Toponymy," *JBL* 108 (1989) 577–95.

40. J. Wellhausen, *Die Composition des Hexateuchs und der historischen Bücher des Alten Testaments* (3rd ed.; Berlin: Reimer, 1899) 108–9, 181–82. For an overview of geography's role in historical criticism, see T. B. Dozeman, "Geography and Ideology in the Wilderness Journey from Kadesh through the Transjordan," in *Abschied vom Jahwisten: Die Komposition des Hexateuch in der jüngsten Diskussion* (ed. J. C. Gertz, K. Schmid, and M. Witte; BZAW 315; Berlin: de Gruyter, 2002) 176; idem, "Biblical Geography and Critical Spatial Studies," in *Constructions of Space I: Theory, Geography, and Narrative* (ed. J. L. Berquist and C. V. Camp; LHBOTS 481; New York: T. & T. Clark, 2007) 100–102.

the Numbers 33 itinerary, the Balaam narrative, Deuteronomy, and Judges were cobbled together to create a literary connection between the pentateuchal material and the Deuteronomistic History. [41] In their view, the geography in Numbers 21 is a hodgepodge because it was drawn from traditional material without regard to physical geography. According to this view, the resulting route is a conflation of various texts with different concepts of the route through Transjordan. Deuteronomy 2–3 takes the Israelites through both Edom and Moab, and the Israelites approach Sihon and Og from the south. Num 21:12–13 conflates this *through* route with the route *around* Edom and Moab articulated in Judg 11:16–22, where they approach Sihon and Og from the east. [42]

Numbers 21 *is* transitional, as Noth and Van Seters argued, since it acts as a bridge between the wilderness narrative and other pieces of literature at the end of Numbers and beyond. But I would like to offer a different way of thinking about how it came to be this way. The different conventions for the itinerary genre in Num 21:12–13a and 18b–20 point to two different post-Priestly revisions that involve compilation. They show us how scribes created an anthology of ancient Israelite literature. A third revision involves an expansion that addresses an issue of ideological concern. The geography of Numbers 21 is, as Noth thought, dependent on other literary traditions. But, rather than resulting from an effort to fill a gap in the traditions, the place-names aid the process of anthologizing by bridging the settings of originally disparate pieces of literature. The scribes' use of genre helps us identify the revisions, but we will not be able to understand the *purposes* of these revisions without considering how they used geographical repertoire—routes and place-names—as well.

We should begin by considering *to what* the scribes who revised this narrative added their revisions. The itinerary notices in Num 21:10–11a use the same convention for the itinerary genre found throughout the Priestly string of itinerary notices and are likely part of the same composition (see table 3, p. 178).

---

41. Noth, *Numbers*, 159–60. For a more detailed exposition of the argument, see idem, "Nu 21 als Glied der 'Hexateuch'-Erzählung," in *Aufsätze zur biblischen Landes- und Altertumskunde* (ed. H. W. Wolff; 2 vols.; Neukirchen-Vluyn: Neukirchener Verlag, 1971) 1.84–91. For an excellent summary of Noth's contribution to scholarship on this passage, considered in context, see Dozeman, "Geography and Ideology," 179–82; idem, "Biblical Geography," 100–102.

42. J. Van Seters, "The Conquest of Sihon's Kingdom: A Literary Examination," *JBL* 91 (1972) 182–97; idem, *The Life of Moses*, 159–63, 383–404. Note that Van Seters did not commit to whether the the Sihon and Og episodes should be attributed to a specific author or redactor in 1972, while in 1994 he assigned them to the Yahwist.

וַיִּסְעוּ בְּנֵי יִשְׂרָאֵל וַיַּחֲנוּ בְּאֹבֹת: וַיִּסְעוּ מֵאֹבֹת וַיַּחֲנוּ בְּעִיֵּי הָעֲבָרִים

The Israelites set out and camped at Oboth. They set out from Oboth and camped at Iye-abarim.

Num 21:10–11a may be one of the last preserved pieces of the Priestly Tetrateuch. The little battle episode in Num 21:1–3 easily passes notice in the larger scheme of a Pentateuch with Deuteronomy at the end of it (or a Hexateuch with Joshua at the end of it). But, as I suggested above, it may once have been part of the denouement of the Tetrateuch. The itinerary notices in Num 21:10–11a may have moved the Israelites to whatever episode came next.

The change in form of the itinerary genre in Num 21:12–13a is a clue to one of the revisions of this text. But it is really the place-names used here that tell us about the revision.

מִשָּׁם נָסָעוּ וַיַּחֲנוּ בְּנַחַל זָרֶד: מִשָּׁם נָסָעוּ וַיַּחֲנוּ מֵעֵבֶר אַרְנוֹן

From there they departed and camped at Wadi Zered. From there they departed and camped beyond the Arnon.

Place-names are an element of repertoire that an author can use to influence the reader's process of consistency-building. When the scribe chose place-names for the setting of the spies episode that were significant in the tribal allotments in Joshua, he created an intertextual relationship between these two texts that served to connect them. As it so happens, we know where Wadi Zered and Wadi Arnon are on the ground (see fig. 8); we share this repertoire with ancient Israelite scribes. But more important for our purposes is where these place-names are used in other biblical literature. We do not need to look far. The introduction to Deuteronomy uses these names in its retrospective of the Israelites' journey through the wilderness. The itinerary notices in Num 21:12–13a, then, are one part of what is surely a much more extensive revision, the purpose of which was to *connect Deuteronomy to the end of Numbers*. Incorporating Deuteronomy as the new ending of the wilderness narrative required a change of setting, because Deuteronomy takes place in the plains of Moab, not south of Canaan. The scribe extended the itinerary that was already present in the text that he was revising in order to move the Israelites from southern Canaan into Transjordan. And he used place-names from Deuteronomy's version of the trip through Transjordan as the stops on this route in order to anticipate the specific setting of this text.

We now have the tools to understand Num 21:18b–20, where we find yet another form of the itinerary genre—one without any verbs at all.

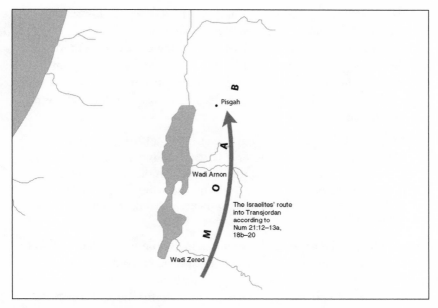

Fig. 8. The Route into Moab.

וּמִמִּדְבָּר מַתָּנָה: וּמִמַּתָּנָה נַחֲלִיאֵל וּמִנַּחֲלִיאֵל בָּמוֹת: וּמִבָּמוֹת הַגַּיְא אֲשֶׁר בִּשְׂדֵה
מוֹאָב רֹאשׁ הַפִּסְגָּה וְנִשְׁקָפָה עַל־פְּנֵי הַיְשִׁימֹן:

From Midbar to Mattanah. From Mattanah to Nahaliel. From Nahaliel to Bamoth. From Bamoth to the valley that is in the field of Moab, at the summit of Pisgah and overlooking Jeshimon.

Since we expect that a scribe would not switch conventions mid-text, an expectation grounded in our experience with itineraries in chaps. 3–4, it is reasonable to think that this itinerary notice points to a distinct revision made by a different scribe from the scribe responsible for Num 21:12–13a, or at least on a different occasion. This new scribe also used two elements of repertoire—the itinerary genre and place-names—to integrate an addition to the anthology. Again, we can recognize what the addition is from the place-names that were used to anticipate the setting. Bamoth, Pisgah, and Yeshimon are place-names found in the Balaam narrative, which occurs in the next chapter and of course takes place on the Moabite plateau (see Num 22:41; 23:14, 28).[43] Here again, the

---

43. Noth, *Numbers*, 159–60.

itinerary genre was used to extend the Israelites' journey, in this case *to incorporate the Balaam episode into the wilderness narrative.*

The fact that each of these scribes happened to use a different form of the itinerary genre is lucky for us, as it alerts us to the revisions. Peckham argues that authors who made revisions to biblical narrative purposefully left traces of their work, particularly by using the techniques of repetition and reversion to integrate additions.

> Editing was always marked and meant to be noticed.... Marking an editorial change preserved the original, left it in its place in the development of literary and historical traditions, and let the editorial contribution to those traditions stand out and be understood in its relationship to the original and to the developing tradition that the original text had inspired.[44]

These scribes, in theory, could have chosen to use the same convention as the Priestly chain of notices, just as the author of Num 21:4 did, but, for whatever reason, they did not. The author of Num 21:18b–20 did not even connect his string of itinerary notices to the preceding text. His first notice is וּמִמִּדְבָּר מַתָּנָה 'From Midbar to Mattanah'. If מִדְבָּר is in fact a proper noun rather than the common noun for 'wilderness', the place is not mentioned before this. But the author of the itinerary notices in Num 21:12–13a did at least make an explicit connection, using מִשָּׁם 'from there'.[45] Perhaps the effort to make only the most minimal connection reflects carelessness. If Peckham is right, however, these scribes may have sought to mark their revisions by deliberately using a different convention. If so, they intended for us to notice the dynamic between *traditum* and *traditio*. Use of the itinerary genre nonetheless aids our ability to build a coherent *Gestalt* of this text as an itinerary in spite of indications that it is a *composite* text. Genre and geography are not merely cues to the composition history of the passage. They also, perhaps ironically, *help* us read it as a whole.

---

44. Peckham, "Writing and Editing," 382–83.

45. Van Seters argues that vv. 12–13 are part of the Yahwistic composition and that מִשָּׁם connects them not to the itinerary notices in vv. 10–11, which are part of a "late erudite expansion" based on Numbers 33, but to the complaint episode in Num 21:4b–9 (*Life of Moses*, 159). But there is no specific place-name in the complaint episode about the bronze serpent to which שָׁם might refer. The episode is set simply בַּדֶּרֶךְ 'on the way', referring to the *route* name דֶּרֶךְ יַם־סוּף 'way of Yam Suf' given in the itinerary notice in Num 21:4. The word מִשָּׁם is better understood to pick up the preceding place-name Iye-abarim in Num 21:11a, as it does in the administrative documents we studied in chap. 3 that use this convention.

These two revisions created very little problem for the coherence of the growing anthology. It is a clear itinerary despite the different forms, and, so far, the Israelites' route appears to go north through Transjordan straight into the Moabite plateau (see fig. 8). It is the *third* revision to Numbers 21 that wreaked all the geographical havoc, including the confusion between Moab and Amorite territory, the confusion about whether the Israelites went around or through Moab, and the double arrival in Moab. Before we look at the mechanics of how this revision was made, I will first consider its purpose. This revision is an expansion concerning an ideological matter. This ideological matter has to do with *land*.

As I just discussed, Num 21:18b–20 takes the Israelites into Moab for the Balaam episode. Here, they are in *foreign* territory. Indeed, they are in territory that, according to Deut 2:9, the Israelites are not supposed to touch because Yahweh has assigned it to the descendants of Lot. We see the same idea reflected in Numbers 34, which delineates the extent of the promised land—and it does not include anything in Transjordan. Yet Num 21:21–35 narrates the *conquest* of this territory by the Israelites! We are here confronted with differing views about the extent of Israel's rightful territory. A scribe who thought that the Transjordanian plateau ought to be accounted for as *Israelite* territory revised the wilderness narrative in order to include a conquest narrative for it.

The scribe who did this was confronted by the problem of a text with an already quite full trek through Transjordan. The revisions that helped incorporate Deuteronomy and the Balaam narrative into the growing anthology create relatively minimal problems in reading the text. Both Carr and van der Toorn note that expansions of a text tend to occur at its borders (that is, its beginning or end), and it may be that the relative ease of blending these pieces of literature together is due to the fact that new additions were incorporated into the end of the wilderness narrative. [46] But the scribe responsible for this third revision of Numbers 21 was working with a text in which the Israelites are already in the territory to be conquered, and it is ruled by a foreigner and called Moab. In order to create a truly coherent narrative, this scribe would have had to omit Num 21:18b–20 and also the Balaam narrative. Clearly he did not do that. Instead, he strove as best he could to influence the way the text would be read, including cues encouraging the reader to privilege his version of the story.

First, the scribe added glosses in Num 21:11b and 13b that shift the Israelites' route so that it runs *around* Moab to the east rather than *through* it, as shown in fig. 9. The glosses are underlined here.

---

46. Carr, *Writing on the Tablet*, 39; van der Toorn, *Scribal Culture*, 128.

וַיִּסְעוּ מֵאֹבֹת וַיַּחֲנוּ בְּעִיֵּי הָעֲבָרִים בַּמִּדְבָּר אֲשֶׁר עַל־פְּנֵי מוֹאָב מִמִּזְרַח הַשָּׁמֶשׁ:
מִשָּׁם נָסָעוּ וַיַּחֲנוּ בְּנַחַל זָרֶד: מִשָּׁם נָסָעוּ וַיַּחֲנוּ מֵעֵבֶר אַרְנוֹן אֲשֶׁר בַּמִּדְבָּר הַיֹּצֵא
מִגְּבוּל הָאֱמֹרִי . . . וּמִמִּדְבָּר מַתָּנָה: וּמִמַּתָּנָה נַחֲלִיאֵל וּמִנַּחֲלִיאֵל בָּמוֹת: וּמִבָּמוֹת
הַגַּיְא אֲשֶׁר בִּשְׂדֵה מוֹאָב רֹאשׁ הַפִּסְגָּה וְנִשְׁקָפָה עַל־פְּנֵי הַיְשִׁימֹן:

They set out from Oboth and camped at Iye-abarim, in the wilderness
that faces Moab to the east. From there they set out and camped at Wadi
Zered. From there they set out and camped beyond the Arnon, which is in
the wilderness extending from the border of the Amorites. . . . From Midbar to Mattanah. From Mattanah to Nahaliel. From Nahaliel to Bamoth.
From Bamoth to the valley that is in the plain of Moab at the summit of
Pisgah, looking out over the wasteland. (Num 21:11–13, 18b–20)[47]

Michael Fishbane discusses a variety of particles, such as הוּא, אֶת, and זֶה, that
mark explicative scribal glosses. While he does not include relative clauses in
his discussion, v. 13b functions much like the examples he gives of instances in
which the particle does not have a precise referent.[48] The clause in v. 11b clearly
modifies Iye-abarim, giving it a location east of Moab. But the clause in v. 13b, a
relative clause marked by אֲשֶׁר, has no clear referent because the specific campsite beyond the Arnon is not given. Its function, then, is not to explain the location of a place. Rather, it simply works with v. 11b to shift the Israelites' route to
the east. If the reader builds a *Gestalt* of the narrative with the Israelites going
this way, she might not notice that they are heading straight north into Moab
in other verses that she is about to read. Verses 18b–20, the end of the itinerary,
explicitly bring the Israelites into the northern part of *Moab*. As Miller notes,
this designation for the region is consistent with other biblical texts such as
Isaiah 15, in which Moab is understood to extend as far north as Heshbon and
to include sites in the plateau such as Nebo.[49]

If we bracket out these two glosses, we are left with the route north *through*
Transjordan across Wadi Zered and Wadi Arnon and into the Moabite plateau,

---

47. I have omitted the justification of Sihon's southern border and the well song
in vv. 14–18a. As will become apparent from my argument below, the justification of
Sihon's southern border is likely an addition to the itinerary. Moreover, the place-names
in this text are problematic, and detailed discussion of it and the Song at the Well do not
add to the present argument. For discussion of these issues, see B. A. Levine, *Numbers
21–36*, 91–98.

48. M. Fishbane, *Biblical Interpretation in Ancient Israel* (Oxford: Clarendon, 1985)
44–55. See in particular his discussion of הוּא פַרְעֹה וְכָל־הֲמוֹנֹה in Ezek 31:18b and זֶה סִינַי
in Ps 68:9, both of which have ambiguous referents, as בַּמִּדְבָּר הַיֹּצֵא מִגְּבוּל הָאֱמֹרִי does in
Num 21:13b. For treatment of this type of editorial addition, see also Peckham, "Writing
and Editing," 371–77 on deictic repetition.

49. Miller, "Israelite Journey," 578, 587.

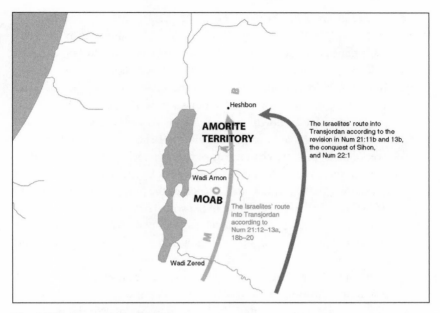

Fig. 9. The Route around Moab.

shown in fig. 8, which brings the Israelites to the settings of Deuteronomy and the Balaam narrative. Davies argues that these two clauses are "harmonizing additions" to the Num 21:10–20 itinerary. He subscribes to the general approach of Noth and Van Seters, that Numbers 21 in its present form conflates the wilderness routes that we find in other texts such as Judges 11. But, where Van Seters and Miller saw a text by a single scribe whose geography is a conflation of the geography in Deuteronomy 2–3 and Judges 11, Davies thinks that Numbers 21 originally had a route that went strictly through Moab, similar to the route that we find in Deut 2:1–23. And these glosses were *added* to harmonize this route with the one in Judges 11, which goes around both Edom and Moab.[50]

The function of these glosses, however, is not to harmonize the routes around and through Transjordan that we find in Deuteronomy 2–3 and Judges 11, as Davies suggests, because the route is not the only thing that these two clauses shift. They also limit Moab to the territory *south* of the Arnon and

---

50. G. I. Davies, "Wilderness Itineraries and the Composition of the Pentateuch," 10–11. H. Seebass also sees Num 21:11b as a gloss based on Deut 2:8 and Judg 11:18 ("Edom und seine Umgehang nach Numeri XX–XXI: Zu Num XXI 10–13," *VT* 47 [1997] 255–62).

make territory *north* of the Arnon Amorite: אֲשֶׁר בַּמִּדְבָּר הַיֹּצֵא מִגְּבוּל הָאֱמֹרִי כִּי
אַרְנוֹן גְּבוּל מוֹאָב בֵּין מוֹאָב וּבֵין הָאֱמֹרִי (Num 21:13b). Why Amorite? In Deut 2:9,
Israelites are not to conquer territory that has been assigned to Lot, and this
includes Moab. But Amorites, while certainly a known ethnic group, function
in the Torah as part of a trope referring to the previous inhabitants of land
promised to Israel. As such, Amorite territory is perfectly permissible to conquer.[51] Casting the plateau north of the Arnon as an Amorite kingdom ruled
by Sihon rather than a Moabite kingdom ruled by Balak (as in the Balaam episode) serves to make this stretch of territory part of Israel's promised land, land
that *can* be conquered, despite the fact that it is not included in texts such as
Numbers 34 or Ezekiel 48, which offer a vision of the promised land limited to
Cisjordan.[52] The author of this revision to the wilderness narrative, then, shifts
both the Israelites' route and the political geography of Transjordan in order
to incorporate the plateau north of the Arnon into Israel's promised land and
to include a conquest narrative for it, as the land promised in Cisjordan has in
the book of Joshua.[53] The circumvention of Moab, then, is this scribe's way of
introducing a new episode and a new land ideology into the wilderness narrative. What is really "circumvented" is the previous version of the narrative,
which has the Israelites moving straight north into Moab. The resulting text is
a literary palimpsest.

The glosses in Num 21:11b and 13b serve to integrate this revision into the
itinerary structure on the front end, while the itinerary notice in Num 22:1,
which has the Israelites arrive again in Moab (having already arrived there in
Num 21:18b–20), integrates it into the previously existing text on the back end.
The Amorite conquest narrative and the Balaam narrative are *alternative* accounts of Israel's activity on the Transjordanian plateau. However, they must
read as though they are consecutive episodes in a single narrative with a linear
plot. The scribe added the Amorite conquest narrative *between* the Israelites'

---

51. J. Van Seters, "The Terms 'Amorite' and 'Hittite' in the Old Testament," *VT* 22
(1972) 64–81.

52. M. Weippert, "The Israelite 'Conquest' and the Evidence from Transjordan,"
in *Symposia Celebrating the Seventy-Fifth Anniversary of the Founding of the American
Schools of Oriental Research (1900–1975)* (Zion Research Foundation Occasional Publications 1–2; Cambridge, MA: American Schools of Oriental Research, 1979) 22. For an
excellent overview of Transjordan's status in land promised to Israel, see M. Weinfeld,
"The Extent of the Promised Land: The Status of the Transjordan," in *Das Land Israel
in biblischer Zeit* (ed. G. Strecker; GTA 25; Göttingen: Vandenhoeck & Ruprecht, 1983)
59–75.

53. The Sihon and Og episodes are seen by some as an addition to the wilderness
narrative; for example, Weippert, "Israelite 'Conquest,'" 23.

arrival in Moab for the Balaam narrative in v. 20 and the Balaam narrative itself beginning in chap. 22. This meant that he needed to create a bridge back to the Balaam episode in order to restore the linear character of the narrative. So, once the conquest was finished, the scribe wrote an itinerary notice in 22:1 that had the Israelites arrive (again) in Moab for the Balaam episode.[54] The statement in 22:2 that Balak saw what Israel did to the Amorites is also part of this effort to reintegrate, while the Balaam narrative proper begins in 22:3.[55]

It is probably fair to say that Numbers 21 offers a great deal more writerly pleasure than readerly pleasure. This third revision does *not* make for an optimally functional narrative; indeed, it is "pressed to the limits of what is readable."[56] The double arrival in Moab creates a wrinkle in time and space, violating the norms of the itinerary genre. Elements of the itinerary chain are also at odds with one another. The problem with using the trash can on the computer desktop to eject a disk, in Mark Turner and Gilles Fauconnier's example discussed in chap. 2, is that the trash can then takes on two conflicting functions in the blend, because it is used both to save and to delete. Here the itinerary genre is used for two conflicting functions: to take the Israelites through Moab *and* around it to the east. An additional problem is that we have to read all of the place-names in Numbers 21 as though they are located not in Moab but in the wilderness *east of* Moab. This means that we must read their stop at Bamoth and their camp near Pisgah and Jeshimon in vv. 19–20 as though they are still in the wilderness. But we can share the ancient Israelites' mental map enough to know that this is not where they are. Bamoth, Pisgah, and Jeshimon are *in the Moabite plateau* in the Balaam narrative. Pisgah in Deuteronomy is a site from which Moses can see Cisjordan, just across the Jordan from Jericho. Moreover, Josh 12:3 and 13:20 locate Pisgah, not in the wilderness, but as part of

---

54. This incongruity in the text is reflected in interesting ways in the work of a number of key commentators. M. Lagrange notes that, in order to maintain the text as it is, one must assume that Moses traversed Sihon's territory before asking permission to go through it ("L'Itinéraire des Israélites du pays de Gessen aux bords du Jourdain," *RB* 9 [1900] 67). Gray notes that, when the Israelites reach Pisgah in Num 21:20, they are still apparently outside the land, having not yet conquered the Amorites (*Critical and Exegetical Commentary on Numbers*, 280). G. Smith asserts that the journey to the plains of Moab described in Num 21:18–20 must have come after the battle with Sihon (*The Historical Geography of the Holy Land* [1894; repr. Jerusalem: Ariel, 1974] 380–82).

55. See B. A. Levine, *Numbers 21–36*, 139, 143.

56. G. von Rad, "The Form-Critical Problem of the Hexateuch," *The Problem of the Hexateuch and Other Essays* (London: SCM, 1984) 2. This expression applied to the entire Hexateuch, as von Rad does, strikes me as hyperbole, but it is quite apt for Numbers 21.

territory conquered under Moses' leadership and assigned to the Reubenites. The revision also grates against basic bodily experience because one cannot go around and through a place at the same time. Between the glosses in Num 21:11b and 13b and the itinerary notice in Num 22:1, this scribe integrated his revision *as best he could* into a narrative that did not *really* allow room for it. In the process, he made the geographical mess that now confronts and frustrates us when we try to make some coherent sense of Numbers 21. While the reading process may be quite frustrating, it does tell us something about the work of these scribes. They tended not to excise passages from the text when they revised, no matter how much they conflicted with what they were trying to write, but worked their revisions into the *traditum* as they copied it.

The conflated final form of Numbers 21, then, is not due to a single scribe's dependence on the Numbers 33 itinerary, Deuteronomy, and Judges but is the result of a series of purposeful revisions to the wilderness narrative, made to read plausibly (although less so than some of the other revisions I have discussed) within the previously existing narrative framework through the use of itinerary notices. Noth understands the phrase הַגַּיְא אֲשֶׁר בִּשְׂדֵה מוֹאָב 'the valley that is in the plain of Moab' in Num 21:20 to draw also on Deut 3:27 and 34:1, 6, where the plains of Moab are mentioned as the setting for Moses' last speech, and thus bring the Balaam narrative *and* Deuteronomy into the same literary orbit.[57] But, as we have now seen, the incorporation of Deuteronomy was accomplished in part via the change in setting created by Num 21:12–13a, a different revision to the Priestly wilderness narrative than the revision involving Num 21:18b–20, because the two use different conventions for the itinerary genre. Moreover, if Num 21:20 were dependent on Deuteronomy 34, we might expect Moab to be called עַרְבוֹת מוֹאָב rather than שְׂדֵה מוֹאָב, since the first term is used frequently in Deuteronomy 34, while the second is not used there at all.

It is actually Deuteronomy 34, not Num 21:18b–20, that pulls together place-names from a variety of different texts. While the setting of Deuteronomy 34 is the Moabite plateau, the mix of specific names used to refer to the plateau and towns within it suggests an effort to make the Num 21:10–20 itinerary, Deuteronomy, the Balaam narrative, and other material at the end of Numbers read, in hindsight, as part of one coherent narrative with a common setting despite the diversity of literature anthologized here. In addition to עַרְבוֹת מוֹאָב, Deut 34:5–6 refers to the plateau as אֶרֶץ מוֹאָב, resonating with the use of this particular term for Moab in the introduction and conclusion to Deuteronomy, including the previous installment of Moses' final scene in chap. 32 (Deut 1:5;

---

57. Noth, *Numbers*, 159–60.

28:69; 32:49; 34:5–6; see Judg 11:15, 18; Jer 48:24, 33).[58] Deut 34:6 also pulls in Beth-peor from the setting of the Balaam narrative (Num 23:38) as well as the historical prologue to Deuteronomy (Deut 3:29) and the lawgiving itself (Deut 4:46). (Use of Beth-peor here may also resonate with the Peor incident at Shittim in Num 25:18; note references to it in Num 31:16, Josh 22:17, and Ps 106:28.) Furthermore, Deut 34:1 identifies Mount Nebo as the summit of the Pisgah range. The summit of Pisgah is mentioned in Num 21:20 as the site from which Moses views the land, but the summit is specifically called Mount Nebo only in Deut 32:49, suggesting that Deuteronomy 34 is drawing on the names used for this site in *both* texts.

The author of Deuteronomy 34 used theme and horizon to prompt the reader to build a coherent picture of the narrative. As we read through the ending of Numbers and into and through Deuteronomy, we are constantly negotiating the setting of the story because of the variety of place-names used. When we have read through the Numbers 21 itinerary and reach the Balaam narrative, we understand that names such as Bamoth and Pisgah and Jeshimon in the itinerary helped us move to the setting of the narrative that we are currently reading. When we get to Deuteronomy 34, however, and encounter Moses viewing the land from Pisgah, we renegotiate the meaning of Num 21:20 as a whole, understanding this itinerary—with the hindsight provided by Deuteronomy 34—not simply to have brought us to the story of Balaam but also to have been the setting for the whole stretch of narrative since then, including Deuteronomy and its version of Moses' final scene at Mount Nebo. Having engaged in this consistency-building process, we have ideally created a coherent *Gestalt* of the narrative in our brains with, in effect, a single setting from the end of the Numbers 21 itinerary to the end of Deuteronomy.

Sea Crossing (Exodus 14:2, 15:22a)

The double arrival in Moab is not the first wrinkle in the linear space-time continuum of the itinerary that we encounter in the wilderness narrative. After the redemption of the Israelite firstborn and observance of the first Pesah in the Priestly version of the wilderness narrative, the Israelites arrive בְאֵתָם בִּקְצֵה הַמִּדְבָּר 'at Etham, at the edge of the wilderness' in Exod 13:20 (מִדְבַּר אֵתָם in Num 33:8), poised finally to depart from Egypt. But the itinerary notice in

---

58. This distribution in use is noted by J. E. Harvey, *Retelling the Torah: The Deuteronomistic Historian's Use of Tetrateuchal Narratives* (JSOTSup 403; London: T. & T. Clark, 2004) 23.

Exod 14:20 has them alter their route and eventually enter the wilderness in Exod 15:22a *after the sea crossing* rather than immediately after Pesah. Here the wilderness also goes by a different name, מִדְבַּר־שׁוּר 'wilderness of Shur'. Like the double arrival in Moab in Num 21:20 and 22:1, this double arrival in the wilderness in Exod 13:20 and 15:22a points to a revision of the wilderness narrative, a *traditio* incorporated into its *traditum* by means of itinerary notices.

Each departure into the wilderness follows a different event: Pesah and the sea crossing, respectively. An important issue for tradition-historical and source-critical scholarship on the exodus narrative has been deciding which one of these should be understood as the paradigmatic redemption event. When Yahweh is referred to as the one אֲשֶׁר הוֹצֵאתִיךָ מֵאֶרֶץ מִצְרַיִם 'who brought you out from the land of Egypt', the epithet does not specify how Yahweh accomplished this task, whether by saving the Israelite firstborn or by splitting the sea in two. Brevard S. Childs, for example, argues that J, to which source he ascribes the itinerary notices in Exod 12:37 and 13:20, understood *Pesah* as the redemption scene and situated the sea crossing with the wilderness traditions. P, on the other hand, understood the *sea crossing* as the redemption scene, a role that resulted from influence by the Jordan crossing (now in Joshua 3–4) at some point in the narrative's tradition history.[59] The two source documents, J and P, thus reflect different stages of tradition-historical growth, according to Childs.

The supplementary model of composition history that I have been using here, however, understands developments of the tradition such as these to take place through revisions of previously existing text. I have been arguing that such revisions to the wilderness narrative were crafted to be read as part of it by integrating them into the itinerary framework. Here we find no exception. The arrival in the wilderness of Shur after the sea crossing in Exod 15:22a is not really an arrival, but another departure.

---

59. B. S. Childs has argued that the redemption scene shifted through the course of the tradition history from the plagues to the sea crossing; see "Deuteronomic Formulae of the Exodus Traditions," in *Hebräische Wortforschung: Festschrift zum 80. Geburtstag von Walter Baumgartner* (VTSup 16; Leiden: Brill, 1967) 30–39; idem, *Book of Exodus: A Critical, Theological Commentary* (OTL; Philadelphia: Westminster, 1974) 193–94, 223. For more in-depth discussion of tradition history for this passage, see idem, "A Traditio-Historical Study of the Reed Sea Tradition," *VT* 20 (1970) 406–18; G. W. Coats, "History and Theology in the Sea Tradition," *ST* 29 (1975) 53–62; idem, "The Sea Tradition in the Wilderness Theme: A Review," *JSOT* 12 (1979) 2–8. For focus on the role of the Jordan crossing in the tradition-historical development, see T. B. Dozeman, "The Yam-sûp in the Exodus and the Crossing of the Jordan River," *CBQ* 58 (1996) 407–16.

וַיַּסַּע מֹשֶׁה אֶת־יִשְׂרָאֵל מִיַּם־סוּף וַיֵּצְאוּ אֶל־מִדְבַּר־שׁוּר

Moses caused Israel to set out from Yam Suf, and they went out into the wilderness of Shur.

The itinerary notice begins with the typical departure formula with נסע, but the next clause uses יצא 'to go out' in lieu of the typical arrival notice with חנה. Coats argues that this clause must be seen as an arrival anyway; otherwise the itinerary notice would be incomplete, containing two departures without an arrival.[60] His expectation is clearly conditioned by the conventions used by the Priestly writer, which involve both departure and arrival. But the verb used here, יצא, nonetheless expresses *departure*, not arrival and, furthermore, is not found in any other itinerary notices. Just as the Priestly scribe changed the arrival verb in Num 10:12 from the typical חנה to שכן in order to accommodate use of the cloud as subject, so this author changed the typical itinerary verb to convey his purpose. As Volkmar Fritz notes, יצא comes from the trope אֲשֶׁר הוֹצֵאתִיךָ מֵאֶרֶץ מִצְרַיִם (see Exod 20:2, and other places), which refers to the paradigmatic exodus event, even if it does not specify which one.[61] Use of this verb with the departure from the sea makes it clear that, for this author, the sea crossing is the one.

The itinerary notices for the Priestly version of the departure from Egypt, Exod 12:37 and 13:20, are embedded in the Pesah narrative and clearly associate the departure from Egypt with the plague of the firstborn and observance of that holiday. The revision that culminates in 15:22a and departure associated with the sea crossing is facilitated on its front end by a turn in the route.

דַּבֵּר אֶל־בְּנֵי יִשְׂרָאֵל וְיָשֻׁבוּ וְיַחֲנוּ לִפְנֵי פִּי הַחִירֹת בֵּין מִגְדֹּל וּבֵין הַיָּם לִפְנֵי בַּעַל צְפֹן נִכְחוֹ תַחֲנוּ עַל־הַיָּם

Speak to the Israelites so that they turn and camp before Pi-hahiroth, between Migdol and the sea, before Baal-zephon. You should camp opposite it, beside the sea.

---

60. G. W. Coats, *Rebellion in the Wilderness: The Murmuring Motif in the Wilderness Traditions of the Old Testament* (Nashville: Abingdon, 1968) 47. Note also idem, "Wilderness Itinerary," 137, 150–51, where Coats treats יצא alongside חנה and בוא as an arrival verb, albeit an atypical one, despite the fact that it expresses departure.

61. The connection between יצא in Exod 15:22 and this trope is pointed out by Fritz, *Israel in der Wüste*, 38. Coats attempts to counter Fritz's connection with the departure-from-Egypt trope by pointing out that יצא is used to note departure in an itinerary in Gen 14:8 ("Wilderness Itinerary," 151). But the fact that it is a second depature notice here and the fact of the exodus context in my view outweigh Coats's concern.

Like Num 14:25, this itinerary notice is framed as a command, and it likewise alters the route, bringing the Israelites to an appropriate setting for a sea crossing.[62] Yahweh commands Moses to "speak to the Israelites so that they *turn* [שוב] and camp" in the area near the sea defined by the places mentioned in the verse. The word שוב clearly articulates a change in direction, and people can certainly make turns en route. But *description* of the twists and turns in a route is not the aim of the itinerary genre, which simply outlines the stops in linear fashion. The equivalents of שוב in Akkadian and Egyptian are never used in examples of the itinerary genre.[63] Even if a trip such as the journey described in the Old Babylonian itineraries involved a bend or change in direction, the route would still be articulated as linear, using the formulaic conventions. The use of שוב, like the use of פנה in Num 14:25, is a sign that the author of this itinerary notice has shifted the route as it was articulated in the Priestly version in order to facilitate a revision that would identify the sea crossing as Yahweh's miraculous act of deliverance.

The Mountain of Yahweh (Exodus 19:2b, Numbers 10:33)

The narrative and legal materials in Exodus 19–Numbers 10 in the present form of the Torah consist of an extended revelation from Yahweh set on a *mountain* somewhere in the Sinai Peninsula. Reference to this mountain is altogether missing from the itinerary in Num 33:1–49, and the scribe who wrote the Priestly version of the wilderness narrative chose to refer to the *wilderness* of Sinai rather than Mount Sinai in the itinerary notices in Exod 19:2a and

---

62. Ibid., 138; Walsh, "From Egypt to Moab," 21. W. H. C. Propp sees this note as part of the P sea crossing narrative rather than an element of the redaction, because it does not use נסע (*Exodus 1–18: A New Translation with Introduction and Commentary* [AB 2; New York: Doubleday, 1999] 461, 477). He follows Cross's view of the role of itinerary notices in the P redaction (Propp, *Exodus 19–40: A New Translation with Introduction and Commentary* [AB 2A; New York: Doubleday, 2006] 141). For the view that Exod 14:2 changes the route to bring the Israelites to the sea, see M. Noth, *Exodus: A Commentary* (OTL; Philadelphia: Westminster, 1962) 109; and, for fuller argument, idem, "Der Schauplatz des Meereswunders," in *Aufsätze zur biblischen Landes- und Altertumskunde* (ed. H. W. Wolff; 2 vols.; Neukirchen-Vluyn: Neukirchener Verlag, 1971) 1.102–10.

63. Coats argues that שוב *is* a verb characteristic of the itinerary genre, pointing to its use in Gen 14:17 ("Wilderness Itinerary," 151). But, while Genesis 14 narrates a military campaign, the formulaic verbs נסע and חנה characteristic of the itinerary genre as it is used here are entirely absent there.

Num 10:11–12. He made this choice, as I argued at the end of chap. 5, in order
to downplay the mountain setting of the rock/water episode in Exod 17:1b–7
and the appointment of judges in Exodus 18, because the idea that Yahweh lives
in a fixed spot runs counter to his image of Yahweh in a movable sanctuary,
a reconceptualization of Zion theology in response to the destruction of the
Temple and exile. How is such an effort plausible for the Sinai pericope given
the prominence of Exodus 19's mountain setting in our current version of the
wilderness narrative?

While the Priestly itinerary notices in Exod 19:1–2a and Num 10:11–12 have
the Israelites arrive at and depart from the *wilderness* of Sinai, we find a second
departure notice in Num 10:33–34 that describes them as leaving the *mountain*
of Yahweh.

וַיִּסְעוּ מֵהַר יְהוָה דֶּרֶךְ שְׁלֹשֶׁת יָמִים וַאֲרוֹן בְּרִית־יְהוָה נֹסֵעַ לִפְנֵיהֶם דֶּרֶךְ שְׁלֹשֶׁת
יָמִים לָתוּר לָהֶם מְנוּחָה: וַעֲנַן יְהוָה עֲלֵיהֶם יוֹמָם בְּנָסְעָם מִן־הַמַּחֲנֶה:

> They set out from the mountain of Yahweh on a three-day journey, and
> the ark of the covenant of Yahweh went ahead of them on a three-day
> journey to seek out a resting place for them. The cloud of Yahweh was
> above them by day as they departed from the camp.

Like the double arrival in Moab in Num 21:20 and 22:1 as well as the double
departure from Egypt into the wilderness in Exod 13:20 and 15:22a, this double
departure from Sinai should be understood as pointing to a development of the
traditum made through revision to the Priestly wilderness narrative.

In addition to a double departure, we find a double arrival at Sinai. The difference in setting between wilderness in Num 10:11–12 and mountain in Num
10:33 is matched by the double arrival at Sinai.[64] The Priestly itinerary notice
in Exod 19:2a has the Israelites camp in the wilderness of Sinai (וַיָּבֹאוּ מִדְבַּר סִינַי
וַיַּחֲנוּ בַּמִּדְבָּר). Verse 2b repeats the arrival notice with חנה but has them camp
more specifically at the mountain (וַיִּחַן־שָׁם יִשְׂרָאֵל נֶגֶד הָהָר). The double arrival
and departure from Sinai are commonly recognized in both source-critical and
redaction-critical studies. The arrival at and departure from the *mountain* in
Exod 19:2b and Num 10:33 are typically understood to come earlier in the composition history, whether they are assigned to an earlier source document (J or
JE) or an earlier version of the narrative (the Deuteronomistic version in the
supplementary model adopted by Johnstone). The arrival and departure from
the *wilderness* of Sinai in Exod 19:2a and Num 10:11–12 are typically understood to recontextualize the mountain episode by providing a broader regional

---

64. Walsh, "From Egypt to Moab," 23–24.

designation for the place and assigned to P by advocates of the Documentary Hypothesis, while Johnstone also assigns them to his Priestly version.[65] One important problem that this approach does not solve is that Exodus 17 and 18, apart from the itinerary notices that contextualize them at Rephidim, also have mountain settings, and they are also typically considered pre-Priestly. By this reconstruction of the composition history, the Israelites arrive at the mountain twice *in the same version of the narrative.*[66]

The arrival at the mountain should instead be understood as *later* in the process of composition history, and we can see how the double arrival was added. As Van Seters notes, the arrival at the mountain in Exod 19:2b cannot be earlier than v. 2a, as many commentators argue, because it uses the pronoun שָׁם, which could not have stood alone without a referent. Its referent is the wilderness in v. 2a: וַיָּבֹאוּ מִדְבַּר סִינַי וַיַּחֲנוּ בַּמִּדְבָּר 'They arrived in the wilderness of Sinai and camped in the wilderness'. Van Seters consequently views the whole of v. 2 as a unity and understands it to have been written by the Yahwist.[67] This explanation makes sense in terms of the *arrival* at Sinai. We could understand v. 2b simply to specify further the location as the mountain, although we might be bothered by the fact that the verb (וַיַּחֲנוּ) in Exod 19:2a and its subject (בְּנֵי־יִשְׂרָאֵל [Exod 19:1]) are plural, while the verb (וַיִּחַן) and its subject (יִשְׂרָאֵל) in 19:2b are singular. We should be bothered by these differences, since the idea that Exod 19:2a and b come from the same hand is not as likely in light of the *departure* from Sinai, where the double departure notices are clearly distinct from one another.[68]

In his effort to solve the problem of a referent for שָׁם by assigning both Exod 19:2a and b to the Yahwist, Van Seters has split up the itinerary notices

---

65. Noth, *Numbers,* 76–77, 157; Coats, "Wilderness Itinerary," 146; F. M. Cross, *Canaanite Myth and Hebrew Epic: Essays in the History of the Religion of Israel* (Cambridge: Harvard University Press, 1973) 315; Van Seters, *Life of Moses,* 156; Johnstone, *Chronicles and Exodus,* 40–41, 259, 267.

66. For examples of this problem, see T. Booij, "Mountain and Theophany in the Sinai Narrative," *Bib* 65 (1984) 17; T. B. Dozeman, *God on the Mountain: A Study of Redaction, Theology, and Canon in Exodus 19–24* (SBLMS 37; Atlanta: Scholars Press, 1989) 20, 92–93, 123–25.

67. Van Seters, *Life of Moses,* 153–64.

68. Whether assigned to different documentary sources, different itinerary chains, or different redactional levels, the connections between Exod 19:2a and Num 10:12, on the one hand, and Exod 19:2b and Num 10:33, on the other, are commonly recognized. For source-critical approaches that connect Exod 19:2b with Num 10:33, see G. I. Davies, "Wilderness Itineraries in the Old Testament," 64, 85; Walsh, "From Egypt to Moab," 23. Van Seters sees both verses as part of J's history (*Life of Moses,* 156, 249), while Johnstone sees both as part of the D composition (*Chronicles and Exodus,* 259, 267).

in Exod 19:2a and Num 10:11–12, since he assigned the latter to P and the former to the Yahwist.[69] But these should not be split up, because they are explicitly connected to one another by repetition of the place-name מִדְבַּר סִינָי 'wilderness of Sinai'. Moreover, the notice in Exod 19:2a is explicitly connected to the previous notices in Exod 17:1, since it repeats the place-name Rephidim from there, and 16:1, where the expression בֵּין־אֵילִם וּבֵין סִינַי 'between Elim and Sinai' ties together this whole section of the itinerary into a coherent textual unit. This whole string of notices, as I argued in chap. 5, belongs to the Priestly version, the first to make use of the itinerary genre as part of an effort to emplot the wilderness narrative as an "annal." Additional uses of the itinerary genre in all of the examples we have studied here reflect efforts to incorporate revisions into the Priestly *traditum*. While Exod 19:2b, with its pronoun שָׁם, cannot be earlier than 19:2a, it can be an *addition* to it and, along with the departure from the mountain in Num 10:33, point to a revision of the Sinai pericope. By selecting a mountain setting for Exod 19:2b and the place-name הַר יְהוָה 'mountain of Yahweh' for the departure in Num 10:33, the author of this revision reintroduced the mountain setting that the Priestly author had marginalized. The Priestly writer could marginalize the mountain setting of Exod 17:1b–7 and Exodus 18 by using the name מִדְבַּר סִינָי 'wilderness of Sinai' without causing severe geographical confusion in the narrative because the *mountain* setting that is so prominent at the beginning of the Sinai pericope had not yet attained the prominence that it now has.

This revision to the Priestly version of the wilderness narrative may be related to the incorporation of the Decalogue scenes into the Torah. Detailed consideration of the composition history of the Sinai pericope is quite beyond the scope of our focus on how the authors of the wilderness narrative used the itinerary genre and place-names. But it is worth briefly noting how the argument I have made here about the itinerary notices may fit with other scholarship on the Decalogue. A number of commentators have argued that some elements of the Sinai pericope were latecomers to pentateuchal narrative. Frank Crüsemann, for example, has suggested that the Priestly construction of the sanctuary and cultic law was included in the Sinai narrative before the Decalogue, and David H. Aaron has argued that the Decalogue scenes are a relatively late development in the composition history of the Torah.[70] I suggest

---

69. Van Seters, *Life of Moses*, 156–57, 249.

70. F. Crüsemann, *The Torah: Theology and Social History of Old Testament Law* (trans. A. W. Mahnke; Edinburgh: T. & T. Clark, 1989) 49; Aaron, *Etched in Stone*. See also E. W. Nicholson, *Exodus and Sinai in History and Tradition* (Growing Points in Theology; Richmond, VA: John Knox, 1973) 74–77.

that the itinerary notices in Exod 19:2b and Num 10:33 may shed some light on how those scenes were incorporated into the wilderness narrative. It is important to note that I am *not* advocating a return to the idea that the entire Sinai pericope was a separate element of tradition, combined only late in a tradition-historical development, as advocated, for example, by Gerhard von Rad.[71] I recognize, with the general thrust of recent scholarship, that it has a very complex composition history and seek here only to make one small contribution to this discussion.

The doublet itinerary notices not only allowed the scribe to reintroduce a mountain setting but also provided him an opportunity to recast the role of the king in this "annal." While the cloud/*kavod* fills this role in Num 10:11–12, Num 10:34 indicates that Israel's next campsite is determined not by where the cloud settles but by the אֲרוֹן בְּרִית־יְהוָה 'ark of the covenant of Yahweh' in its role as a battle standard (see 1 Samuel 3–7).[72] The cloud is still present in Num 10:34, but it simply *accompanies* the army, relegated from its position as the subject of the narrative in Num 10:11–12 to a circumstantial clause in v. 34. Lee sees no incompatibility between the cloud in Num 10:12 and the ark of the covenant in Num 10:33, since both are signs of Yahweh's leadership and serve to guide the Israelites in the wilderness. But the fact that they function similarly in the Israelites' journey does not mean that they are mere variants of one another.[73] The ark represents Yahweh's presence in two ways, both in its use as a battle standard, where it reflects the typical ancient Near Eastern practice of a city god preceding the army into battle, and in its cherubim features, which resonate with the typical imagery of a royal throne.[74] The idea that the ark leads the Israelites in battle is not new here, but it is *refreshed* here with the ark, specifically called אֲרוֹן בְּרִית־יְהוָה, transformed from its role as an icon of Yahweh's presence to a box for the Decalogue tablets.[75] This term for the ark is notably used in

---

71. Von Rad, "Form-Critical Problem."

72. For the ark as battle standard, see P. D. Miller, *The Divine Warrior in Early Israel* (HSM 5; Cambridge: Harvard University Press, 1973) 157–59.

73. Lee, *Punishment and Forgiveness*, 125–26. For the view that the cloud and ark are incompatible variants, see Auerbach, *Moses*, 113.

74. For royal imagery connected with the ark, see C. L. Seow, *Myth, Drama, and the Politics of David's Dance* (HSM 44; Cambridge: Harvard University Press, 1989) 104–36, 143.

75. D. H. Aaron, *Biblical Ambiguities: Metaphor, Semantics, and Divine Imagery* (Leiden: Brill, 2002) 164–65, 170–79. If Num 10:33 is understood as being earlier than Num 10:11–12, as it often is, the reference to אֲרוֹן בְּרִית־יְהוָה in v. 33 must be understood as a Deuteronomistic gloss; see, for example, Noth, *Numbers*, 78; Dozeman, *God on the Mountain*, 20.

1 Kgs 8:9, where the author categorically insists that Yahweh is *not* present in the ark and that the ark contains *only* the covenant tablets. This transformation of the ark's role, like the cloud/*kavod*, moves away from a more literal construal of Yahweh's presence among the Israelites.[76] While the ark retains a vestige of its function as a battle standard at the end of Numbers 10, the *covenant*, in the ark that carries it, is now Israel's guide through the wilderness—or, in terms of the character roles of the annals genre used to emplot the wilderness narrative, Israel's king.[77]

Mikhail Bakhtin's thoughts on epic as finished and inaccessible to the past were framed in contrast to the modern novel, which he viewed as open and dynamic, a "genre in the making." The novel, according to Bakhtin, has no fixed framework but is characterized by the creative fusion of other genres and dialogue among various perspectives.[78] Although it presents a valorized, epic past, the wilderness narrative was far from ossified, as Bakhtin thought epic to be. The scribes who shaped it, as we have now seen, made profoundly creative use of genre, blending features of law and ritual instruction, saga, and prophecy with standard ancient Near Eastern historiographical genres. We also find dialogue in the various revisions that changed its shape. But this is not the kind of open, unfinished dialogue that Bakhtin thought to be characteristic of the novel. Different scribes sought to make their mark on this community-defining body of literature during the process of its emergence, definitively changing its shape. But they did so by recontextualizing the *traditum*, retaining alternate perspectives even while seeking to impose new ones. This dialogue is about the control of ideas as a newly reemergent Israel strove to reshape itself as a culture.

Numbers 33:1–49 and Its Relationship with the Wilderness Narrative

Having now studied the itinerary genre as it is used in various ancient Near Eastern contexts as well as by the authors of the wilderness narrative, we are in a position to understand that Num 33:1–49 could not have been the

---

76. Aaron, *Biblical Ambiguities*, 167, 178.

77. For the role of law in the absence of a king, see Aaron, *Etched in Stone*, 166–68, 182–84.

78. M. Bakhtin, "Epic and Novel: Toward a Methodology for the Study of the Novel," in *The Dialogic Imagination: Four Essays* (ed. M. Holquist; trans. C. Emerson and M. Holquist; University of Texas Press Slavic Series 1; Austin: University of Texas Press, 1981) 3–40.

source for the itinerary notices in the wilderness narrative. Itinerary notices were first introduced into the wilderness narrative alongside date formulas, a depiction of the Israelites as an army, and Yahweh in the role of the king by a Priestly author who was using the *annals* genre as a mode of emplotment, not incorporating an administrative document. The fractures in the itinerary chain are not the result of adaptation but were created by a number of revisions to this Priestly version. While the itinerary in Num 33:1–49 reads like a report, it is, as Van Seters argues, not a report in substance.[79] It is, rather, a summary of the entire wilderness narrative, more or less complete.[80]

A. Graeme Auld has argued that the material at the end of Numbers is dependent on Deuteronomy and Joshua as well as the wilderness narrative.[81] The itinerary in Num 33:1–49 is no exception. Its dependence on a variety of materials, including revisions to the wilderness narrative and the materials anthologized by means of these revisions suggests that it is later than and dependent upon a composite wilderness narrative. Num 33:7–8, for example, has the place-names Pi-hahiroth, Baal-zephon, and Migdol, found also in the Exod 14:2 itinerary notice, which shifts the route of the Priestly wilderness narrative in order to incorporate the sea crossing into the itinerary. Likewise, Num 33:47–48 has a double arrival in Moab just like Num 21:20 and 22:1. Num 33:48 picks up nearly the exact wording from Num 22:1, giving בְּעַרְבֹת מוֹאָב עַל יַרְדֵּן יְרֵחוֹ 'in the steppes of Moab at the Jordan near Jericho' as the next campsite after הָרֵי הָעֲבָרִים לִפְנֵי נְבוֹ 'the hills of Abarim, before Nebo' (Num 33:47). But the combination of Abarim and Nebo does not come from Num 21:20, the itinerary notice that precedes Num 22:1 in the wilderness narrative. It comes instead from Deut 32:49, suggesting that Deuteronomy has already been incorporated into the wilderness narrative. The long list of place-names between the wilderness of Sinai and Kadesh in Num 33:16–36 also suggests a relationship with

---

79. Van Seters, *Life of Moses*, 153–64.

80. For the observation that Numbers 33 may be based on a more or less complete form of the wilderness narrative, see T. R. Ashley, who points this out in order to draw attention to the difficulties with the Documentary Hypothesis, although his preferred alternative is to treat the text as a unified whole rather than address its compositeness in a more satisfactory manner (*The Book of Numbers* [NICOT; Grand Rapids, MI: Eerdmans, 1993] 624–25).

81. Auld, *Joshua, Moses and the Land*, 105, 116. See also G. N. Knoppers, "Establishing the Rule of Law? The Composition Num 33,50–56 and the Relationships among the Pentateuch, the Hexateuch and the Deuteronomistic History," in *Das Deuteronomium zwischen Pentateuch und Deuteronomistischen Geschichtswerk* (ed. E. Otto and R. Achenbach; FRLANT 206; Göttingen: Vandenhoeck & Ruprecht, 2004) 135–54.

Deuteronomy, because some of these names appear in Deut 1:1 and 10:6–7.[82] The final itinerary notice in Num 33:49, which has the Israelites camped from Beth-jeshimoth to Abel-shittim, draws these place-names from Joshua. Beth-jeshimoth appears in the conquest and allotment of land in Transjordan as it is outlined in Joshua 12–13 (see Josh 12:3 and 13:20). Shittim is the campsite from which the spies depart for Jericho in Josh 2:1 and from which the Israelites depart to cross the Jordan in Josh 3:1 (see also Mic 6:5). The Numbers 33 itinerary pulls the settings of a variety of now-anthologized literatures together in order to create a composite whole.

This "report," despite the genre, is not neutral. It offers a definitive version of the wilderness sojourn that corrects it back to the shape of the Priestly wilderness narrative as much as possible. The priestly character of Numbers 33 is commonly recognized, whether it is viewed as the source for the notices in the wilderness narrative or a later composition based on the narrative. In some cases, commentators argue that it is priestly because it is a list, because of its style, or, in Cross's case, because it has a round number of stops.[83] Davies rightly counteracts these arguments on the grounds that the style is simply a feature of the itinerary genre.[84] But the character of the short notes in this

---

82. There is no consensus about the direction of dependence here, and I cannot resolve this issue in the present context. N. H. Snaith sees the Numbers 33 itinerary as being dependent on Deuteronomy for the place-names (*Leviticus and Numbers* [The Century Bible; London: Nelson, 1967] 337). T. B. Dozeman, however, sees Deuteronomy as being dependent on the Numbers 33 itinerary ("The Book of Numbers: Introduction, Commentary, and Reflections," in *The New Interpreter's Bible* [ed. L. E. Keck; 4 vols.; Nashville: Abingdon, 1998] 4.254). M. Weinfeld sees Deut 10:6–7 as being independent from Num 33:1–49 because the place-names are in a different order, and these verses locate Aaron's death differently (*Deuteronomy 1–11* [AB 5; New York: Doubleday, 1991] 419). R. D. Nelson notes the relationship but does not offer a specific view on the direction of dependence (*Deuteronomy: A Commentary* [OTL; Louisville: Westminster John Knox, 2002] 120 n. 1, 128).

83. For the argument from style, see B. E. Scolnic, who seems not to have taken adequate account of Davies's form-critical study (*Theme and Context in Biblical Lists* [South Florida Studies in the History of Judaism 119; Atlanta: Scholars Press, 1995] 113–16). Cross (*Canaanite Myth*, 309) must *omit* two stations in order to get to the round number of 40 names from the 42 that are actually in the list. The idea of 40 stops corresponding with the 40 years of the wilderness sojourn (the chronology according to Num 14:34) goes at least as far back as Wellhausen, who makes no mention that there are actually 42 (*Composition des Hexateuchs*, 181).

84. G. I. Davies, "Wilderness Itineraries in the Old Testament," 47–58. Davies actually argues that the priestly character is not a feature of the list itself but a redaction of it, in which it acquired its pseudonarrative form due to the use of narrative preterites

itinerary offers reliable clues.[85] The focus on Aaron's death in Num 33:38–40, which includes a date formula and his age, features missing from any other account, in itself suggests a priestly point of view. Moreover, the author used מִדְבַּר סִינַי 'wilderness of Sinai' as the place-name in Num 33:15–16 just as in Exod 19:2a and Num 10:11–12 rather than the mountain of God, Horeb, or the mountain of Yahweh in line with the Priestly image of Yahweh present *not* on a mountain but as the *kavod* in a movable Tabernacle.

Num 33:3–4 also associates the departure from Egypt with Pesah rather than the sea crossing, just as it is in the Priestly version of the wilderness narrative. While the author of the Numbers 33 itinerary accounted for the arrival at the sea in Exod 14:2, he omitted Exod 15:22. This omission allowed him to deemphasize the role of the sea crossing as the paradigmatic redemption scene, suggested by the use of יצא in that notice. Instead, he reinstated the Priestly view, associating the departure from Egypt with Pesah, actually dating it to the 15th day of the 1st month. Exodus 12–13 does not indicate anything taking place on the 15th day and, in fact, presents a rather ambiguous picture of the time that the Israelites left. That it was not necessarily the next day is evident from sections that depict the Israelites eating the offering in a hurry, all ready to leave (Exod 12:29–32, 39). Departure on the 15th day of the 1st month in Num 33:3–4 depends on Josh 5:10–11, which, as I discussed in chap. 5, interprets הַשַּׁבָּת of מִמָּחֳרַת הַשַּׁבָּת in Lev 23:15 as the Pesah festival itself, indicating that the Israelites began to eat parched grain מִמָּחֳרַת הַפֶּסַח.[86] The scribe further emphasized their departure immediately after Pesah by noting that the Egyptians were still burying their dead while the Israelites were leaving, a detail that is not in Exodus 12–13 at all. And he used the wilderness of Etham rather than the wilderness of Shur in Num 33:8 as the region into which they departed, correcting the route back to the route articulated in Exod 12:37 and 13:20, even though he accounted for the stop at the sea.[87]

Finally, while the covenant at Sinai merits no note, the encounter with the king of Arad does, and these notices further indicate that Numbers 33 reflects a priestly view of the wilderness sojourn. Scolnic argues that the author of Num 33:1–49 included a note about the victory over the king of Arad because this

---

and notices that correspond to those in the narrative that he assigns to P (idem, "Wilderness Itineraries and the Composition of the Pentateuch," 6).

85. As suggested already by Lagrange, "L'Itinéraire des Israélites," 65.

86. M. Fishbane understands the author of Josh 5:10–11 to have drawn on Num 33:1–49 (*Biblical Interpretation*, 148 n. 16), but the direction of dependence should be reversed given the general dependence of Numbers 33 on the wilderness narrative more broadly.

87. Scolnic, *Theme and Context*, 77–80.

episode is an instance of "God's mercy on the Israelites," a pattern that governs the notes included in the Numbers 33 itinerary, according to Scolnic.[88] But this pattern does not pan out, because many other wilderness episodes that could be understood as instances of God's mercy, such as the manna and quail in Exodus 16, go unmentioned. Moreover, the Hormah episode in Num 21:1–3 referenced here is not an instance of mercy but victory in battle awarded in response to Israel's vow. The reference to the king of Arad is better understood as a nod to the Priestly wilderness narrative that ended south of Canaan. The author of the Numbers 33 itinerary had to contend with a narrative of Israel's wilderness sojourn and conquest that included Deuteronomy and Joshua and the conquest of Transjordan. It was no longer plausible to recast the narrative so that the Israelites conquer Canaan from the south. Num 33:40 states that the king of Arad notes the Israelites as they were approaching. The allusion to Num 21:1–3 is clear in the designation of the king of Arad as מֶלֶךְ עֲרָד וְהוּא־יֹשֵׁב בַּנֶּגֶב הַכְּנַעֲנִי 'the king of Arad—he dwells in the Canaanite Negev', which picks up nearly the exact wording of Num 21:1. But there is no stop at Hormah and no battle. Instead the king simply *hears about* their approach. As we have seen, the Hormah episode, so short to begin with, had been marginalized in such a way that it nearly escapes notice in the wilderness narrative as it now stands. But this modified reference to the otherwise insignificant little episode reveals the author's priestly interests and, moreover, his motive to correct the shape of wilderness narrative as much as possible back to what it was prior to the various revisions.

The author of the Numbers 33 itinerary was particularly concerned that his version of the wilderness narrative be read as the authoritative one, because he established a header for the document in which he claimed divine authority for it. The itinerary is depicted as not just any report but a report that Moses wrote at Yahweh's direction: וַיִּכְתֹּב מֹשֶׁה אֶת־מוֹצָאֵיהֶם לְמַסְעֵיהֶם עַל־פִּי יְהֹוָה 'Moses wrote their departures, according to their stages at the command of Yahweh' (Num 33:2). Scolnic highlights an ambiguity in the syntax of this sentence when he considers whether עַל־פִּי יְהֹוָה refers to the stages of the Israelites' journey, as it does in the wilderness narrative where it is also associated with לְמַסְעֵיהֶם, or to Moses' composition of the list, which could then be understood like his dictation of Yahweh's commands in Exod 24:4.[89] There is no way to resolve this ambiguity decisively, but the function of the statement is nonetheless to claim authority for *this* account of the journey through the wilderness.

---

88. Ibid., 90.
89. Ibid., 76–77.

The author also established authority for this version of the wilderness sojourn by casting it as an official report. Verisimilitude or accuracy is a key expectation of the itinerary genre when it is used to make a report, because a report cannot properly function as such if it is not accurate. Although the purpose of Num 33:1–49 is not to make a report any more than the Priestly scribe's purpose in using the annals genre was to write a campaign narrative, use of the report form conveys authority about the content. As Van Seters and Benjamin Edidin Scolnic have already argued, the purpose for using this genre is to provide a definitive, apparently neutral, official-looking, coherent and unified version of the wilderness sojourn.[90] As we have seen, the itinerary chain in the wilderness narrative as it stands is not actually unified but shows the seams created where a number of different revisions were worked into the narrative. In order to create this sort of document based on the wilderness narrative, the author used various compositional techniques to create a coherent, unified itinerary out of what gives only the *impression* of unity in the wilderness narrative.

First, he changed verbs that are not narrative preterites in the wilderness narrative into narrative preterites, creating a uniform style that is consistent with the convention used in the Priestly version of the wilderness narrative. This is clearest in his treatment of the arrival at the sea in Exod 14:2, where he omitted the imperative דַּבֵּר and changed the indirect jussives into narrative preterites.

דַּבֵּר אֶל־בְּנֵי יִשְׂרָאֵל וְיָשֻׁבוּ וְיַחֲנוּ לִפְנֵי פִּי הַחִירֹת בֵּין מִגְדֹּל וּבֵין הַיָּם לִפְנֵי בַּעַל צְפֹן נִכְחוֹ תַחֲנוּ עַל־הַיָּם

Speak to the Israelites so that they turn and camp before Pi-hahiroth, between Migdol and the sea, before Baal-zephon. They should camp opposite it alongside the sea. (Exod 14:2)

וַיִּסְעוּ מֵאֵתָם וַיָּשָׁב עַל־פִּי הַחִירֹת אֲשֶׁר עַל־פְּנֵי בַּעַל צְפוֹן וַיַּחֲנוּ לִפְנֵי מִגְדֹּל

They set out from Etham, turned to Pi-hahiroth, which is before Baal-zephon, and camped before Migdol. (Num 33:7)

This concern for uniformity of convention is manifest throughout the itinerary, because the author also changed the perfects in Num 11:35 (// Num 33:17) and 12:16a (// Num 33:18) into narrative preterites.

Second, he reduced the verbs as much as possible to נסע and חנה, which are characteristic of the itinerary genre. He did not, for example, eliminate שׁוב in

---

90. See the summary of their views in chap. 1. Ironically, Knierim and Coats suggest that Num 33:1–49 is an itinerary list comparable to the annals (*Numbers*, 309).

Exod 14:2, evident in the passages just cited. But he did omit בוא in most of the places where it occurs, replacing it with the formulaic חנה, as in the following example:

וַיָּבֹאוּ כָּל־עֲדַת בְּנֵי־יִשְׂרָאֵל אֶל־מִדְבַּר־סִין אֲשֶׁר בֵּין־אֵילִם וּבֵין סִינָי
וַיִּסְעוּ כָּל־עֲדַת בְּנֵי־יִשְׂרָאֵל מִמִּדְבַּר־סִין לְמַסְעֵיהֶם עַל־פִּי יְהוָה

> The whole congregation of the Israelites came to the wilderness of Sin, which is between Elim and Sinai.
>
> The whole congregation of the Israelites set out from the wilderness of Sin on their stages according to the command of Yahweh. (Exod 16:1a, 17:1a)

וַיַּחֲנוּ בְּמִדְבַּר־סִין: וַיִּסְעוּ מִמִּדְבַּר־סִין

> They camped in the wilderness of Sin. They set out from the wilderness of Sin. (Num 33:11b–12a)

The author also included an entire arrival formula with וַיַּחֲנוּ where the accusative of direction is used in the wilderness narrative to note arrival, such as the arrivals at Succoth in Exod 12:37a (// Num 33:5) and the arrival at Hazeroth in Num 11:35 (// Num 33:17).

The author of Numbers 33 also omitted all of the subjects and phrases such as לְמַסְעֵיהֶם עַל־פִּי יְהוָה or בֵּין־אֵילִם וּבֵין סִינָי, which are not typical of itineraries that function as reports.[91] This effort makes the itinerary notices read more like a report. Reports such as the Old Babylonian itinerary do contain notes of this sort, but they point to noteworthy occurrences along the route rather than relating place-names to one another or identifying the guide of the journey. As I noted above, the author of Num 33:1–49 used this feature of the itinerary genre as it is used in reports in order to convey his particular view of the wilderness sojourn, but anything that did not contribute to this purpose was excised in order to give the impression of neutrality and objectivity characteristic of reports.

Finally, in addition to creating an itinerary form that is consistent and apparently objective, the author of Num 33:1–49 also created explicit connections between notices where there are fractures in the narratives. We can see this in Num 33:7, cited above, which does not merely incorporate Exod 14:2 but also connects it explicitly to Etham, the arrival point in Exod 13:20. It is also evident in the author's handling of Numbers 10–11.

---

91. See also the following passages in Numbers for omission of subjects: Num 10:12a // 33:16a; 11:35 // 33:17; 12:16 // 33:18; 21:10 // 33:43; 22:1 // 33:48. Note also the omission of the date formula from 20:1a // 33:36 and the temporal expression אַחַר from Num 12:16 // 33:18.

וַיִּסְעוּ בְנֵי־יִשְׂרָאֵל לְמַסְעֵיהֶם מִמִּדְבַּר סִינָי וַיִּשְׁכֹּן הֶעָנָן בְּמִדְבַּר פָּארָן:
וַיִּסְעוּ מֵהַר יְהֹוָה דֶּרֶךְ שְׁלֹשֶׁת יָמִים
מִקִּבְרוֹת הַתַּאֲוָה נָסְעוּ הָעָם חֲצֵרוֹת

The Israelites set out on their stages from the wilderness of Sinai, and
the cloud settled in the wilderness of Paran.
They set out from the mountain of Yahweh on a three-day journey.
From Kibroth-hattaavah, the people set out for Hazeroth. (Num 10:12,
33; 11:35)

וַיִּסְעוּ מִמִּדְבַּר סִינָי וַיַּחֲנוּ בְּקִבְרֹת הַתַּאֲוָה: וַיִּסְעוּ מִקִּבְרֹת הַתַּאֲוָה וַיַּחֲנוּ בַּחֲצֵרֹת:

They set out from the wilderness of Sinai and camped at Kibroth-
hattaavah. They set out from Kibroth-hattaavah and camped at Hazeroth.
(Num 33:16–17)

Here the author of Num 33:1–49 omitted not only the subjects and extraneous
phrases such as לְמַסְעֵיהֶם but also the arrival in the wilderness of Paran in Num
10:12 and the second departure from Sinai in Num 10:33. He then created an explicit connection between the wilderness of Sinai and Kibroth-hattaavah. The
fractures that offer clues to the composition history of the wilderness narrative
have here been obscured so that this account of the wilderness sojourn does
not appear to be the composite that it actually is.

If the form of the report was not enough, the header in Num 33:1 tells
us how to read it. Davies argues that אֵלֶּה in the header אֵלֶּה מַסְעֵי בְנֵי־יִשְׂרָאֵל
is characteristic of an archival document, just as אֵלֶּה marks a variety of lists
within biblical narrative, including land allotments and genealogies.[92] Because
they mark reportage, broadly speaking, these statements lend a degree of authority to what follows, but their key function is to influence the way we read
the following material by assigning it a genre label. Although these headers
certainly cue the reader to read the following text as a list, the use of one does
not necessarily mean that what follows actually *is*. The אֵלֶּה headers are also
used in other places in biblical literature, where they may not point to the inclusion of an archival document. Ezra 7:11 introduces the text of a letter that
may be an actual letter from an archive, but its authenticity is questioned, and

92. G. I. Davies, "Wilderness Itineraries: A Comparative Study," 48–49; see also
Scolnic, *Theme and Context*, 77. For the land allotments thus marked, see Josh 13:32,
14:1; 1 Chr 6:39. For discussion of the genealogies as lists that were incorporated into the
Pentateuch by P, see Cross, *Canaanite Myth*, 301–7.

some commentators regard it as fictional.[93] Deut 1:1 introduces the entire book of Deuteronomy, which is clearly not an archival document. Although Cross understands the אֵלֶּה תּוֹלְדֹת headers to be derived from a genealogical list, he acknowledges that a number of the headings do not actually begin genealogies.[94] Indeed, the אֵלֶּה תּוֹלְדֹת header in Gen 37:2 is not followed by a genealogy at all but by the Joseph story. This use of אֵלֶּה תּוֹלְדֹת simply cues the reader to read the Joseph story as part of the genealogical structure of Genesis. The clause אֵלֶּה מַסְעֵי בְנֵי־יִשְׂרָאֵל likewise cues the reader to read the following text as a report, reinforcing the form used, even though in content it is not.

We have seen throughout this chapter that a variety of authors revised the wilderness narrative in order to have an effect on its shape. It is fair to assume that, if the author of the Numbers 33 itinerary could have made substantive additions to the wilderness narrative that would have met his goals, he likewise would have. Instead, he wrote a *separate* definitive version in the form of a report. Included at the end of Numbers, it appears to have little impact on how the preceding narrative is read. The same header that colors our reading of the itinerary in Num 33:1 (אֵלֶּה מַסְעֵי בְנֵי־יִשְׂרָאֵל לְצִבְאֹתָם) 'these are the stages of the Israelites, according to their troops') also appears in Num 10:28, between the two accounts of the departure from Sinai articulated by the itinerary notices in Num 10:11–12 and 10:33, respectively. This position for a *header* is rather peculiar. It is often viewed as a colophon to the list of personal names indicating the marching order as the Israelites leave Sinai with the Tabernacle at the center. If read this way, however, מַסְעֵי בְנֵי־יִשְׂרָאֵל must be translated 'deployments' to refer back to the text it summarizes.[95] But, just as this header colors our reading of the itinerary in Numbers 33, so in this context it may color our reading of the wilderness journey yet to come.

I suggest that the "header" in Num 10:28 may have been included here by the author of Numbers 33 as the effort he *could* make in order to influence the reading within the wilderness narrative itself. The "header" in this position in Num 10:28, by this view, sets up a connection that the reader can pick up when she gets to Numbers 33 and encounters the very same header there. Thinking back to the previous time she saw it, she will make the connection between Numbers 33 and the wilderness narrative and merge the two versions of the journey in her mind, allowing this more recent one, of Yahweh through the

---

93. See discussion with further bibliography in F. C. Fensham, *The Books of Ezra and Nehemiah* (NICOT; Grand Rapids, MI: Eerdmans, 1982) 103–4.

94. Cross, *Canaanite Myth*, 301–4.

95. B. A. Levine, *Numbers 1–20*, 308; Ashley, *Book of Numbers*, 194.

hand of Moses, to define her perception of the wilderness sojourn as a whole. One might consider the views of Cross, Davies, Smith, Johnstone, and others who read Num 33:1–49 as the clearest, most authoritative version of the wilderness narrative and strive to explain the function of the wilderness itineraries with reference to it as evidence that this effort was successful.[96]

96. Scolnic, *Theme and Context*, 99–100.

Chapter 7

Places in the Wilderness: Geography as Artistry

Before it can ever be a repose for the senses, landscape is a work of the mind.
Its scenery is built up from strata of memory as from layers of rock.
—Simon Schama

Whether an administrative document or an origin narrative, a text takes *shape* through a scribe's sometimes quite typical and sometimes profoundly creative use of genre. Selecting and foregrounding elements of social, historical, and geographical repertoire from the real world help a text take *place*. An author creates a discourse world in the text no matter what type of document he is writing; as Paul Werth noted, "all situations must be represented in the minds of the participants, whether they refer to the real world, to memory, or to imagination."[1] How geography is used in a text depends on the author's goals, which also influence his use of genre.[2] The places named in the reports and letters discussed in chap. 3 must all be locatable and on a traceable route in order for one of these itineraries to serve the pragmatic goal of its author, whether to report or to give instructions. Both Egyptian and Assyrian scribes extended the norms of the itinerary genre as they used it to shape the military narratives discussed in chap. 4. These narratives met the needs of a new rhetorical situation, but their authors strove to report as well as emplot. Although the itinerary genre was used creatively and took on ideological significance in these contexts, in many cases a source document was adapted for use in the narrative, so we can reasonably expect the geography of these texts to involve locatable places on a single, coherent route as well.

---

1. P. Werth, "How to Build a World (in a lot less than six days, and using only what's in your head)," in *New Essays in Deixis: Discourse, Narrative, Literature* (ed. K. Green; Costerus New Series 103; Amsterdam: Rodopi, 1995) 64.

2. L. Lutwack, *The Role of Place in Literature* (Syracuse, NY: Syracuse University Press, 1984) 34.

The itinerary in Num 33:1–49 *looks like* an administrative document, not unlike the documents discussed in chap. 3. On the face of it, we should expect it to relate locatable places along a coherent and travelable route as reports typically must in order to achieve their pragmatic goals. We might understandably try to identify the route, turning to historical geography and extrabiblical textual evidence to help. Charles R. Krahmalkov claims to have found evidence of just such a route through Transjordan in sections of Thutmose III's Palestine List (1479–1425 B.C.E.) and a list from the reign of Ramesses II (1279–1212 B.C.E.).[3] When combined, Krahmalkov argues, these lists reflect a map that corresponds to the section of the Numbers 33 itinerary that relates the journey from Iyyim through Moab to the Jordan (vv. 44–49), and they prove that Num 33:1–49 is the same type of text as the Palestine lists.[4] The pertinent section of Thutmose III's list is given in table 4 with Krahmalkov's biblical identifications juxtaposed.[5]

Krahmalkov's interpretation of these lists and their relationship to Numbers 33 is problematic. He reads the list as a route running from south to north around the south end of the Dead Sea and into Transjordan that parallels the Israelites' wilderness journey. Donald Redford, on the other hand, reads the list as a route that runs in the opposite direction—from *north to south*, from Damascus to Kerak. One's understanding of the direction of the route hinges on interpretation of *Ybr* (##90, 92, 99). Redford follows William Foxwell Albright's analysis of *Ybr* as meaning 'river' or 'stream' in light of the Arabic cognate *wābil* and reads these as references to wadis Jabbok (#90), Arnon (#92), and Zered (#99), respectively.[6] Krahmalkov, on the other hand, interprets *Ybr* (#99) as the biblical Abel, corresponding to the Israelites' final campsite

---

3. In terms of their form, these are simply lists of place-names rather than itineraries. Like many similar lists of names, their nature is debated, but it seems likely that the list of names does mark out a route. Redford argues that the lists were composed from daybooks used by Egyptian couriers in the fifteenth century B.C.E. ("A Bronze Age Itinerary in Transjordan [Nos. 89–101 of Thutmose III's List of Asiatic Toponymš," JSSEA 12 [1982] 55–74).

4. C. R. Krahmalkov, "Exodus Itinerary Confirmed by Egyptian Evidence," *BAR* 20/5 (1994) 54–62, 79.

5. Excerpt of Thutmose III's Palestine List from E. J. van der Steen, *Tribes and Territories in Transition* (OLA 130; Leuven: Peeters, 2004) 11–12; for the full list, see J. Simons, *Handbook for the Study of Egyptian Topographical Lists Relating to Western Asia* (Leiden: Brill, 1937) 109–24 and background on pp. 27–38; for the biblical associations, see Krahmalkov, "Exodus Itinerary," 57.

6. Redford, "Bronze Age Itinerary," 55–74 (esp. pp. 64, 74); W. F. Albright, *The Vocalization of the Egyptian Syllabic Orthography* (AOS 5; New Haven, CT: American Oriental Society, 1934) 39.

**Table 4. Excerpt from Thutmose III's Palestine List
with Comparisons with Numbers 33**

89	*Hykrym*	
90	*Ybr*	
91	*Utra'a*	
92	*Ybr*	
93	*Kntwt*	
94	*Mkrpwt*	
95	*ʿyn*	Iyyim
96	*Krmn*	
97	*Btiy3*	
98	*Tpwn*	Dibon
99	*Ybr*	Abel
100	*Yrwtw*	Jordan
101	*Hrkr*	

at Abel-shittim according to Num 33:49. This leaves one wondering how he understands the other two references to *Ybr*, on which he does not comment. Although some of Redford's identifications of individual sites have generated debate, his overall interpretation of the list is generally, if tentatively, accepted.[7] The identifications of *Utra'a* (#91) with Edrei and *Tpwn* (#98) with Dibon were accepted in key works on historical geography even before Redford published his analysis of the list and strengthen his reading of it as running from north to

---

7. The lists were once understood to reflect administrative districts in the Egyptian province of Canaan. Y. Aharoni, for example, viewed some of the names as a group of sites in Upper Galilee (*The Land of the Bible: A Historical Geography* [rev. ed.; trans. A. F. Rainey; Philadelphia: Westminster, 1979] 158, 164). N. Naʾaman recognizes that Redford's theory is a possibility but is very skeptical about the idea that the lists were compiled using daybooks because some of the names in Canaan do not occur in geographical order, and other Egyptian topographical lists were not composed using itineraries ("The Hurrians and the End of the Middle Bronze Age in Palestine," *Levant* 26 [1994] 184 n. 7). K. A. Kitchen prefers Redford's interpretation, with caution ("The Egyptian Evidence on Ancient Jordan," in *Early Edom and Moab: The Beginning of the Iron Age in Southern Jordan* [ed. P. Bienkowski; Oxford: J. R. Collis, 1992] 25). One challenge is the lack of evidence for Late Bronze Age occupation at some of the sites that Redford identifies with names in the list, but criticism of the theory usually involves positing other possible locations rather than questioning the whole line of interpretation; see overview in van der Steen, *Tribes and Territories*, 12.

south. Krahmalkov's interpretation of the list is thus untenable.[8] By Redford's
reading, ʿyn (#95) requires a site *even north of Dibon* and cannot be the biblical
Iyyim, which comes before (and would therefore be south of) Dibon on the
route into Transjordan from the Negev in Numbers 33.

Krahmalkov's attempt to understand the geography of Num 33:1–49 with
reference to Egyptian topographical lists was prompted by what turns out to
be an inadequate understanding of the way its author used genre. As discussed
in chaps. 5 and 6, the Israelite scribes who shaped the wilderness narrative *and*
the itinerary in Num 33:1–49 used the itinerary genre for reasons that have
nothing to do with reporting or writing military narrative. Although its formal
literary framework is that of an annal, the Priestly version of the story of the
Israelites' sojourn through the wilderness breaks with the other conventions of
that genre. Its focus is not primarily battle but the restoration of Israel's Temple,
land, and cult. Its main character is a deity rather than a king, and its purpose
is not to promote the deeds of those in power but to envision the shape of
Israelite culture after the return from exile and give this vision authority by
setting it in Israel's distant past. The Numbers 33 itinerary restored this Priestly
version of the wilderness narrative as much as possible after various revisions
had changed its compositional and ideological shape, using the itinerary genre
to make the Priestly writer's version read like—and have the authority of—a
report. Num 33:1–49 may look like an administrative document, but it is not
one in substance. Krahmalkov *classifies* the genre of Num 33:1–49 perfectly. But
if we stop at classification and fail to ask, "How does genre *shape* this text?" we
may miss a great deal of the text's meaning and risk misunderstanding its use
of geography.

---

8. Redford, "Bronze Age Itinerary," 60–61. For interpretation of #91 and #98
prior to Redford, see J. Simons, *The Geographical and Topographical Texts of the Old
Testament: A Concise Commentary in XXXII Chapters* (Leiden: Brill, 1959) 198; and
Aharoni, *Land of the Bible*, 150. See also Z. A. Kafafi, "Egyptian Topographical Lists of
the Late Bronze Age on Jordan (East Bank)," *BN* 29 (1985) 19; J. M. Miller, "Moab and
the Moabites," in *Studies in the Mesha Inscription and Moab* (ed. A. Dearman; Archaeology and Biblical Studies 2; Atlanta: Scholars Press, 1989) 15; J. M. Miller, *Archaeological
Survey of the Kerak Plateau* (American Schools of Oriental Research Archaeological
Reports 1; Atlanta: Scholars Press, 1991) 8. Kitchen notes that Semitic *b* usually does not
correspond to Egyptian *p*, so we would not expect Dibon to be *tpn*, but he does note *b/p*
variation in other names in the list, and Byblos is a clear case of *b/p* variation, as it is *gbl*
in Semitic but *kpn* in Egyptian ("Egyptian Evidence," 25). In an earlier article, he does
not question the linguistic correspondence, even though he questions which Dibon it
might be, suggesting a Judahite Dibon in Neh 11:25 rather than Dibon in Transjordan
("Some New Light on the Asiatic Wars of Ramesses II," *JEA* 50 [1964] 55).

Composition of this generative literature involved selecting and fore-grounding cultural repertoire of all sorts in order to shape both Israel's literature and its reemerging culture out of pieces of its past. These include Israel's social structure, law, ritual calendar, divine imagery, previous versions of Israel's traditions, and standard administrative and historiographical genres shared with or, in the case of the annals, borrowed from other ancient Near Eastern cultures.[9] The writers also used geography in service of their literary goals. We would make a mistake to think that the setting of the wilderness narrative must be the stuff of fantasy because its authors did not seek to report as well as emplot. In fact, we know that it was not. Places like Ramses and Kadesh are identifiable to us today, and they were a real part of the world of the ancient scribes, be it the world contemporary with them or the world of the past that remained with them in memory. Creative uses of the itinerary genre simply loosen the typical constraints on the use of geography that are operative in its primary administrative contexts and even in its secondary historiographical contexts. The authors of the wilderness narrative and the itinerary in Num 33:1–49 had a great deal more latitude in their use of geography, just as they did in their use of the itinerary genre. Instead of simply looking for correspondence between a text and the world outside it, we should consider that place-names are foregrounded in the text *as elements of the scribe's cultural repertoire* and blended with other elements of repertoire to achieve the scribe's literary goals. In this way, we can better understand not only how the text was composed but also how realia played a role in shaping it.

Delta Geography

In his work on poetics, Benjamin Harshav notes that narratives are frequently anchored in some external frame of reference, such as a historical time and place, early in their development in order for the narrator to set up a discourse world. Harshav calls this technique *referential grounding*.[10] The wilderness narrative is grounded in the geography of the first two itinerary notices, which are embedded in the end of the exodus narrative. Archaeology and Egyptian texts provide us with access to the potential for shared context

---

9. For the idea that shared culture comprises elements of one's own culture, borrowed elements taken on as one's own, and invented elements, see E. T. Mullen Jr., *Ethnic Myths and Pentateuchal Foundations: A New Approach to the Formation of the Pentateuch* (Atlanta: Scholars Press, 1997) 70.

10. B. Harshav, *Explorations in Poetics* (Stanford. CA: Stanford University Press, 2007) 134.

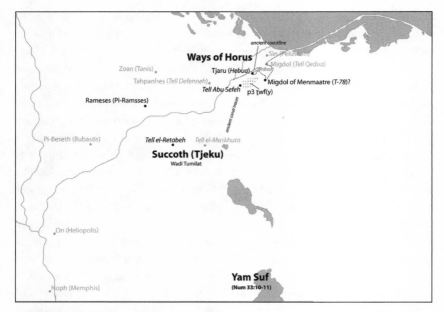

Fig. 10. The Egyptian Delta.

that we need in order to understand how the scribes used geography to provide a setting for the narrative.

The first two itinerary notices in the Priestly version of the wilderness narrative (Exod 12:37 and 13:20) articulate the departure from Ramses, past Succoth, and on to Etham at the edge of the wilderness (see fig. 10). Succoth is a Hebrew rendering of the Egyptian name Tjeku (*Tkw*). In Egyptian texts, the term usually refers to the entire region of Wadi Tumilat, a defended frontier area with manned forts that controlled traffic going in and out of Egypt, but the term is also used to refer to a fortress town within it.[11] Etham seems to relate to the deity Atum; temples and place-names attest to his worship in this

---

11. E. Morris, *The Architecture of Imperialism: Military Bases and the Evolution of Foreign Policy in Egypt's New Kingdom* (Problem der Ägyptologie 22; Leiden: Brill, 2005) 212, 382–83. For cases where the name is applied to the fortress town in Wadi Tumilat, see J. K. Hoffmeier, *Ancient Israel in Sinai: The Evidence for the Authenticity of the Wilderness Tradition* (Oxford: Oxford University Press, 2005) 65–66. For discussion of the determinatives that identify the type of place Tjeku is, see J. Van Seters, "The Geography of the Exodus," in *The Land That I Will Show You: Essays on the History and Archaeology of the Ancient Near East in Honour of J. Maxwell Miller* (ed. J. A. Dearman and M. P. Graham; JSOTSup 343; Sheffield: Sheffield Academic Press, 2001) 259; Hoffmeier, *Ancient Israel in Sinai*, 65–66.

region.[12] Wadi Tumilat was one of two main traffic areas in and out of Egypt in antiquity and remains so today. As is well known, Papyrus Anastasi V, a model letter from Dynasty XIX (1295–1188 B.C.E.), relates an effort by an Egyptian official to track down two workers who left Egypt via the region of Tjeku.[13] People also came into Egypt through Tjeku; Papyrus Anastasi VI famously refers to the Shasu tribes of Edom who came in from the Sinai Peninsula to water their flocks.[14]

While Exod 12:37 and 13:20 take the Israelites out of Egypt via Tjeku, Exod 14:2 brings them to the Ways of Horus, לִפְנֵי פִּי הַחִירֹת בֵּין מִגְדֹּל וּבֵין הַיָּם לִפְנֵי בַּעַל צְפֹן 'before Pi-hahiroth, between Migdol and the sea, before Baal-zephon'. The Ways of Horus (*wȝwt ḥr*), also shown on the map (fig. 10), is the other main traffic area in and out of Egypt; the name refers to the northern frontier region and the military road extending from this area across the northern Sinai Peninsula and into the Levantine coastal region.[15] The region included a number of sites and a system of canals that controlled access to Egypt and defended its frontier. Migdol, evident from its name, is a fortress. Pi-hahiroth (פִּי הַחִירֹת) refers to a canal near the *pȝ š ḥr*, or Lake of Horus, known to Israelite scribes as Shihor (Josh 13:3, Isa 23:3, 1 Chr 13:5). Papyrus Anastasi III refers to just such a place as it celebrates the resources of the royal estate at Pi-Ramesses: "The Lake of Horus has salt, the Canal (*pȝ ḥw-jr*) has natron. Its ships set out and dock, and the food of sustenance is in it every day."[16] And, since this area is right on the ancient coastline, as shown in fig. 10, the most obvious candidate for a sea is the Mediterranean, which appears to have extended slightly inland as the Shihor.

---

12. Ibid., 69.

13. "A Report of Escaped Laborers," trans. J. P. Allen (*COS* 1.4).

14. "A Report of Bedouin," trans. J. P. Allen (*COS* 3.5). Van Seters describes Bedouin coming into Wadi Tumilat with flocks to camp near the excavations at Tell el-Maskhuta in the 1970s and 1980s ("Geography of the Exodus," 270–71).

15. J. K. Hoffmeier, "'The Walls of the Ruler' in Egyptian Literature and the Archaeological Record: Investigating Egypt's Eastern Frontier in the Bronze Age," *BASOR* 343 (2006) 9–10. The route is mentioned in Papyrus Anastasi I ("The Craft of the Scribe," trans. J. P. Allen [*COS* 3.2] 27.2) and depicted in a relief in the Hypostyle Hall at Karnak from the reign of Seti I, where its main stops are also given as captions. For a thorough study of these sources, see A. H. Gardiner, "The Ancient Military Road between Egypt and Palestine," *JEA* 6 (1920) 99–116. For archaeological exploration of the route, see E. Oren, "The 'Ways of Horus' in North Sinai," in *Egypt, Israel, Sinai: Archaeological and Historical Relationships in the Biblical Period* (ed. A. F. Rainey; Tel Aviv: Tel Aviv University Press, 1987) 69–120; and review of Oren's synthesis combined with his own excavation results in Hoffmeier, *Ancient Israel in Sinai*, 95–96, esp. p. 62 fig. 1, 65 fig. 2.

16. "Praise of Pi-Ramessu," trans. J. P. Allen (*COS* 3.3); see discussion in Hoffmeier, *Ancient Israel in Sinai*, 105–7.

The referential grounding of the wilderness narrative in a place—the Egyptian Delta—is much clearer than its grounding in a historical time period, which has been a subject of significant debate. Scholars typically assume that the Israelite scribes supplied a setting for their narratives using the geography of the time in which they were writing. Julius Wellhausen took this approach, and it is typical among scholars who work with the Documentary Hypothesis. [17] We can obtain a sense of the ancient Israelites' mental map of the Delta in the sixth century B.C.E., when the Priestly version of the wilderness narrative is commonly understood to have been written, from oracles and narratives in Jeremiah and Ezekiel that have to do with Egypt. The author of Ezekiel 30 envisioned the destruction of Egypt by Nebuchadnezzar, which was attempted in 601 B.C.E., as a *complete* destruction including Pathros (Upper Egypt) as well as the Delta, from Migdol to Syene (Ezek 30:6; see also 29:10). But the geography of the Delta in Ezek 30:13–19 is especially detailed; it includes Zoan (Tanis), Sin (Pelusium), Noph (Memphis), On (Heliopolis), Pi-Beseth (Bubastis), and Tahpanhes (Tell Defenneh). This mental map is depicted by the gray place-names in fig. 10, with the geography of the exodus narrative superimposed upon it.

Judahites likely acquired this map based on their experience living in the area from the late seventh century B.C.E. onward. [18] According to Jeremiah 41–43, Johanan, son of Kareah, and a contingent of army officers fled to Egypt in fear of the Babylonians after Gedaliah was assassinated, despite Jeremiah's protestations. According to Jer 43:7, they went to Tahpanhes, one of four major military garrisons in the Delta along with Migdol and Noph. (Tell el-Maskhuta was another garrison site in this period.) These garrisons were inhabited by Phoenician, Greek, and Judahite mercenaries, craftsmen, and traders, evident

---

17. For example, M. Haran argues that the authors of J, E, and P no longer knew the route taken during the wilderness sojourn but re-created it using places and routes from the times in which they were writing ("Exodus, The," in *The Interpreter's Dictionary of the Bible Supplementary Volume* [Nashville: Abingdon, 1976] 308). See reviews in T. B. Dozeman, "Geography and Ideology in the Wilderness Journey from Kadesh through the Transjordan," in *Abschied vom Jahwisten: Die Komposition des Hexateuch in der jüngsten Diskussion* (ed. J. C. Gertz, K. Schmid, and M. Witte; BZAW 315; Berlin: de Gruyter, 2002) 173–90; idem, "Biblical Geography and Critical Spatial Studies," in *Constructions of Space I: Theory, Geography, and Narrative* (ed. J. L. Berquist and C. V. Camp; LHBOTS 481; New York: T. & T. Clark, 2007) 87–108. For scholars who see this as sixth-century geography, see D. B. Redford, "Exodus I 11," *VT* 13 (1963) 401–18; idem, "An Egyptological Perspective on the Exodus Narrative," in *Egypt, Israel, Sinai: Archaeological and Historical Relationships in the Biblical Period* (ed. A. F. Rainey; Tel Aviv: Tel Aviv University Press, 1987) 137–62; Van Seters, "Geography of the Exodus," 255–77.

18. E. Oren, "Migdol: A New Fortress on the Edge of the Eastern Nile Delta," *BASOR* 256 (1984) 31–32.

in the mix of material culture found at sites such as Tell Qedua (Migdol) and Tell Defenneh (Tahpanhes).[19] The oracles in Jer 44:1–30 and 46:14–24 are addressed to Judahites living in Migdol, Tahpanhes, and Noph, and an Aramaic papyrus contains a letter sent to Elephantine from a Judahite at the Migdol garrison.[20] The Judahite community in Egypt after 586 B.C.E. was apparently prominent enough to be addressed in Jer 24:8 as on a par with the remnant community in Jerusalem.

But this is not the picture of the Delta that we find in the exodus narrative. Our textual and archaeological sources for understanding the place-names in these first few itinerary notices come principally from Dynasty XIX (1295–1188 B.C.E.). In addition to the Anastasi Papyri mentioned above, the Ways of Horus is depicted notably in the battle reliefs of Seti I (1294–1279 B.C.E.) from Karnak. The military road begins at Tjaru, passes through the Dwelling of the Lion and Migdol, and extends out into the northern Sinai Peninsula (see fig. 10).[21] Migdol here refers to the *migdol*, or fortress, of Menmaatre, the praenomen (throne name) of Seti I. This last fortress before the desert is also mentioned in the funerary Temple of Ramesses III (1186–1154 B.C.E.) at Medinet Habu as the place to which the pharaoh returned after his battle with the Sea Peoples; there it is named Migdol of Ramesses, suggesting that each pharaoh would rename it after himself.[22]

Many of the place-names mentioned in the itinerary notices in Exod 12:37a, 13:20, 14:2, and 15:22 could refer to sites in the Egyptian Delta in either the Late Period (747–525 B.C.E.), the time frame in which the Priestly version of the wilderness narrative was most likely written, or Dynasty XIX, prior to Israel's first emergence as a nation and the period that many scholars consider a plausible date for the exodus as a historical event. As shown in fig. 10, there was a major fortress in Wadi Tumilat during both periods, at Tell el-Retabeh during the New Kingdom and Tell el-Maskhuta during the Late Period.[23] Atum was

---

19. Ibid.; E. Stern, *Archaeology of the Land of the Bible: The Assyrian, Babylonian, and Persian Periods (732–332 B.C.E.)* (ABRL; New York: Doubleday, 2001) 223–24. See also the discussion in B. Porten, *Archives from Elephantine: Life of an Ancient Jewish Military Colony* (Berkeley: University of California Press, 1968) 8–13.

20. Oren, "Migdol," 33.

21. See Gardiner, "Ancient Military Road," for discussion, drawings, and bibliography.

22. Hoffmeier, *Ancient Israel in Sinai*, 103–14.

23. Redford, "Egyptological Perspective," 140; C. A. Redmount, "The Wadi Tumilat and the 'Canal of the Pharaohs'," *JNES* 54 (1995) 127–35; J. K. Hoffmeier *Israel in Egypt: The Evidence for the Authenticity of the Exodus Tradition* (New York: Oxford University Press, 1996) 180; Van Seters, "Geography of the Exodus," 261–62; Hoffmeier,

also worshiped throughout the region in both periods.[24] Migdol could refer to the Migdol of Menmaatre as a station on the Ways of Horus during the New Kingdom, but there is also a Migdol located at Tell Qedua, where Judahites lived and worked in the seventh–sixth centuries B.C.E.[25]

One place-name that does *not* fit in a sixth-century map of the Egyptian Delta is Ramses, the site from which the Israelites initially depart in Exod 12:37, because it had not existed for centuries by the Late Period. The location of Pi-Ramesses was hotly debated during much of the twentieth century, but it is now clearly identified with Qantir. This site served as the capital of the Delta following Ramesses II's battle at Qadesh, but it was abandoned in the mid-eleventh century, probably when the Pelusiac branch of the Nile near Qantir shifted farther north and the waterways that had sustained it silted up. At this point, a new capital was established at Tanis using material quarried from the old site, and Tanis remained a strategic city in the Delta into the Late Period.[26] It was prominent enough in the ancient Israelites' mental map of the Delta that the author of Psalm 78 (vv. 12, 43) used *Tanis*, not the places referred to in Exodus, as the setting for his recital of the signs and wonders that Yahweh performed before the Egyptians.

If we continue with the assumption that the Israelite scribes set their narratives using the geography of the time in which they were writing, the use of Ramses as the initial departure site would mean that the wilderness narrative

Ancient Israel in Sinai, 60; J. S. Holladay Jr., *Cities of the Delta, Part III: Tell el-Maskhuta. Preliminary Report on the Wadi Tumilat Project, 1978–1979* (American Research Center in Egypt Reports 6; Malibu, CA: Undena, 1982).

24. Hoffmeier, *Ancient Israel in Sinai*, 69.

25. For the New Kingdom Migdol, see J. K. Hoffmeier, "The North Sinai Archaeological Project's Excavations at Tell el-Borg (Sinai): An Example of the 'New' Biblical Archaeology," in *The Future of Biblical Archaeology: Reassessing Methodologies and Assumptions* (ed. J. K. Hoffmeier and A. Millard; Grand Rapids, MI: Eerdmans, 2004) 63–65; B. E. Scolnic, "A New Working Hypothesis for the Identification of Migdol," in ibid., 91–120; Hoffmeier, *Ancient Israel in Sinai*, 97–102. For the Late Period Migdol, see Oren, "Migdol," 7–44; Hoffmeier, *Ancient Israel in Sinai*, 95–96, and pp. 62 fig. 1, 65 fig. 2.

26. See review of the discussion in ibid., 57. For further resources on Qantir, see J. Van Seters, *The Hyksos: A New Investigation* (New Haven, CT: Yale University Press, 1966) 128–37; M. Bietak, *Avaris and Piramesse: Archaeological Exploration in the Eastern Nile Delta* (Oxford: Oxford University Press, 1981) 229–31; idem, "Comments on the 'Exodus'," in *Egypt, Israel, Sinai: Archaeological and Historical Relationships in the Biblical Period* (ed. A. F. Rainey; Tel Aviv: Tel Aviv University Press, 1987) 164; D. B. Redford, *Egypt, Canaan, and Israel in Ancient Times* (Princeton: Princeton University Press, 1992) 185; Hoffmeier, *Israel in Egypt*, 117–19; Van Seters, "Geography of the Exodus," 264–65; Hoffmeier, *Ancient Israel in Sinai*, 53–54; idem, "Out of Egypt: The Archaeological Context of the Exodus," *BAR* 33/1 (2007) 36–37.

was written in the *second millennium* B.C.E. or consists of oral tradition extending back that far. James K. Hoffmeier asks why, if the writers of the exodus narrative lived in the sixth century B.C.E., would they not have set it in Tanis as the author of Psalm 78 did? His answer is that the authors of the exodus and wilderness narratives lived not in the sixth century but at some point in the thirteenth–twelfth centuries, when Pi-Ramesses was the capital of the Delta. [27] But the efforts of Hoffmeier to date the exodus narrative to the thirteenth–twelfth centuries and John Van Seters to date it to the sixth century on the basis of geography *both* fall short because the assumption that drives this approach is faulty. [28] Although a writer can certainly select repertoire from the environment in which he lives, the time in which he lives is not what drives his *use* of it. He selects and foregrounds a place-name, like any other element of repertoire, based on his *literary goals*.

You are currently reading a narrative written in the early twenty-first century C.E. about texts written at least 2,600 years ago, about an environment that has changed significantly (note the difference between the ancient coastline and the modern coastline in fig. 10), and about material culture of which we would have little or no awareness were it not for archaeological excavation. Granted, my goals are very different from the goals of the Israelite scribes who shaped the wilderness narrative, and the constraints on my use of data are certainly tighter. The point is simply this: a writer can use any repertoire he or she happens to *know* in order to shape a narrative. It need not be directly and physically accessible, because knowledge of place—even the places to which a writer has direct physical access—is in the brain. A mental map can include much more than just the locations of contemporary places. It involves social and political aspects of place, sacred or symbolic aspects, movement, sensory experience of place, and—important in this case—memory and absence in a landscape. [29] The absence of Pi-Ramesses as an inhabited site in the sixth

---

27. Idem, *Ancient Israel in Sinai*, 56–57; see also K. A. Kitchen, *On the Reliability of the Old Testament* (Grand Rapids, MI: Eerdmans, 2003) 256.

28. Van Seters, "The Geography of the Exodus." This assumption has been made most recently by R. Gmirkin, who proposes that his third-century B.C.E. date for the composition of the Torah can be "tested by analysis of the geographical references in the biblical account" (*Berossus and Genesis, Manetho and Exodus: Hellenistic Histories and the Date of the Pentateuch* [LHBOTS 433; New York: T. & T. Clark, 2006] 222). This test runs aground particularly on his discussion of Ramses, since he recognizes its identification with Qantir but fails to discuss the date of the site or the shift of the capital to Tanis (p. 225).

29. P. Bienkowski, "The Wadi Arabah: Meanings in a contested landscape," in *Crossing the Rift: Resources, routes, settlement patterns and interaction in the Wadi*

century need not mean that it had been forgotten. In fact, providing a setting for the wilderness narrative that is grounded in references to a historical place and time *prior to Israel's emergence as a nation the first time* is critical to the Priestly author's effort to retroject into the past his vision of Israel's restoration after the exile as though it had always been so.

The author of Psalm 78 did not share this literary goal. He offered a poetic recital of Yahweh's great deeds in which the specific geographical setting plays a minor role. Using Tanis as a setting may have functioned simply to help its audience grasp the significance of the message for the world in which they lived. Despite the referential grounding of the exodus narrative at a point in the distant past, many of the places would have also been on some level recognizable to an ancient Israelite who knew the geography of the Delta in the sixth century. Migdol moved, and the fortress in Tjeku is at a different site. But there *is* a Tjeku and a Migdol in the sixth-century Delta just as there was in the Delta of the distant past. The geography of the exodus narrative may have served both to provide a setting for the narrative in the distant past and also to make it recognizable to a sixth-century audience so that they might be able to relate its message to their own world.

How could an ancient Israelite scribe in the mid–late sixth century have known about the landscape of the Delta more than half a millennium earlier? Although the capital of the Delta had long ago moved to Tanis when the Priestly version of the wilderness narrative was written, Pi-Ramesses remained part of the landscape of memory well into the first millennium. The name is known from a few texts in the first millennium, including the Onomasticon of Amenemope (Dynasties XXI and XX, 1188–945 B.C.E.).[30] The latter includes a list of place-names that seems to run through the Delta from south to north. It lists both Pi-Ramesses and Tanis, suggesting that the list may be a historical composite.[31] Shishak (945–924 B.C.E.) revived one of the names of Pi-Ramesses when he set up his residence in the area of the eastern Delta as a base for his Asiatic campaign; this move was part of an effort to cast himself in the image of his imperial predecessor.[32] Cults to the gods of Ramesses operated at Tanis and Bubastis into the mid-first millennium B.C.E.[33]

Arabah (ed. P. Bienkowski and K. Galor; Levant Supplementary Series 3; Oxford: Oxbow, 2006) 17.

30. Redford, "Exodus I 11," 409–10.

31. A. H. Gardiner, "The Delta Residence of the Ramessides," *JEA* 5 (1918) 198–99.

32. Redford, *Egypt, Canaan, and Israel*, 314–15; Van Seters, "Geography of the Exodus," 265.

33. Kitchen, *On the Reliability*, 256.

Some have objected to the possibility that Pi-Ramesses could have been known especially to an Israelite writer centuries later by rightly pointing out that foreigners would not have had access to the Ramesses cult.[34] But even a foreigner would not have needed such specific access in order to have the general knowledge that the current capital of the Delta is Tanis, that it used to be located at Pi-Ramesses, and that it moved a long time ago. In fact, Israelite scribes seem to have had just this general knowledge. Num 13:22 states that Hebron was founded seven years prior to Zoan (צֹעַן), a Hebrew transcription of the Egyptian name for Tanis (*D^cnt*). Various suggestions have been made about what the purpose of this statement in the context of the spies episode might be. Tanis was once thought to refer to the Hyksos (1674–1553 B.C.E.) capital of Avaris, but we now know that Tanis was founded much too late for that. Nadav Na'aman has proposed that a scribe meant to emphasize the antiquity of Hebron as the royal seat of the Israelite monarchy by comparing it with Tanis.[35] The immediate function of this statement, however, is simply to give the spies episode the same referential grounding established by use of Pi-Ramesses in the initial itinerary notice (Exod 12:37). Here the scribe does so more transparently. Tanis is the capital of the Delta as far as a sixth-century audience is concerned. Telling the reader that Hebron was founded seven years (a sufficiently long time) before Tanis tells him that the spies narrative—indeed, the whole wilderness narrative—takes place not *now*, but *in the distant past*, before the present landscape came to be.

The use of geography in both Exod 12:37 and Num 13:22 to ground the wilderness narrative in the distant past suggests that the Israelites did have some general knowledge of ancient history. And they would not necessarily have needed access to a foreign cult to know it. While the information we have about how Ramesses functioned in the first millennium B.C.E. is indeed limited to a few obscure references, the impression that Pharaoh made on the imperial image of Egypt suggests that his cultural impact probably remained much more influential. A modern analogy can be found in the city of St. Paul, Minnesota, which was called Pig's Eye two centuries ago. Few living there today think that they live in Pig's Eye, but the old name of the city lives on in various

---

34. Ibid.; Hoffmeier, *Ancient Israel in Sinai*, 56–57.

35. N. Na'aman, "'Hebron Was Built Seven Years before Zoan in Egypt' (Numbers XIII 22)," *VT* 31 (1981) 490–91. His suggestion is interesting but problematic. He assumes that the writer pulls the seven years from 2 Kgs 2:11, which states that David reigned for seven years in Hebron before moving the capital to Jerusalem, and he assumes a chronological synchronism between Tanis and Jerusalem. But there is no other evidence that Israelite scribes made this sort of synchronism.

manifestations (such as the name of a microbrewing company), and these manifestations generate even the most general knowledge of the city's past.[36]

Archaeology can be important for interpreting texts. The Priestly author's
literary goals are evident from his use of genre and from intertextual connections that we can make with other extant Israelite literature. So we do not need
geography to help us determine them in this case. However, if we did not know
where Pi-Ramesses was (as, in fact, we did not until relatively recently) or that
it was not occupied at the time the wilderness narrative was written, it would
be difficult to know how the scribe used geography to help him achieve those
literary goals. The literary analysis I offered in chaps. 5–6 already made it clear
that the Priestly author aimed to set his vision for restoration in Israel's epic
past. But how did he establish it as a narrative that takes place *in the past*? The
answer to this question has to do with setting. And we can understand how
the scribe set the the narrative only because archaeology enables us to us piece
together enough potential for shared context to allow us to satisfy the referents
of the place-names in the text.

We must be careful, however, not to allow realia alone to *determine* our
interpretation of text. Tjeku and the Ways of Horus, the two main routes out
of Egypt, appear to have been connected by a canal system, shown in fig. 10,
which served in part to defend the eastern frontier. Only traces of it can now be
determined using remains of embankments, aerial photographs, and satellite
imaging, but it once connected Wadi Tumilat with the Mediterranean.[37] Hoffmeier suggests that the Israelites may have traveled along this defensive system
from Succoth and Etham toward the sea.[38] As I argued in chap. 6, however,
the double departure into the wilderness, once into the wilderness of Etham
in Exod 13:20 and a second time into the wilderness of Shur in Exod 15:22,
points to a revision of the wilderness narrative. It may be tempting to argue
that, because the geography is coherent, the text must be a unity and relate a

---

36. For a concise explanation of how cultural information is transmitted in this
way, framed in the context of biblical studies, see the discussion of memes in D. H.
Aaron, *Etched in Stone: The Emergence of the Decalogue* (New York: T. & T. Clark, 2006)
171–75. L. B. Couroyer suggests that the chariot battle at the sea in Exodus 14 was inspired by the external temple reliefs of the battle of Qadesh ("L'Exode et la Bataille de
Qadesh," *RB* 97 [1990] 321–58). Whether he is correct or not, his argument illustrates
this type of diffuse cultural influence.

37. A. Sneh, T. Weissbrod, and I. Perath, "Evidence for an Ancient Egyptian Frontier Canal," *American Scientist* 63 (1975) 542–48; Oren, "Migdol," 9; see an overview of
this work in the context of Delta geography more broadly in Hoffmeier, *Israel in Egypt*,
166–69, fig. 17; idem, *Ancient Israel in Sinai*, 72.

38. Ibid., 71–73.

single, coherent journey. But we must pay attention to literary issues as well. The Israelites' turn northward toward the Mediterranean coast is expressed with שׁוב, which violates the linear character of the itinerary genre. Whatever the actual shape of the route, however many turns or bends in it there may be, the itinerary genre depicts movement in linear fashion through space and time. Were the text a unity, we would expect to see consistent use only of the formulaic itinerary verbs נסע and חנה. We cannot allow realia to override genre constraints but should consider topographical and literary issues *in tandem* as we interpret this text. Both the topography and the literary issues can be accounted for if we understand the author of the itinerary notices in Exod 14:2 and 15:22 simply to have maintained the temporal and geographical setting established in Exod 12:37a and 13:20 but took the people out of Egypt via the Ways of Horus instead of Tjeku. Unlike Tjeku, the Ways of Horus is near a sea.

Yam Suf

The itinerary notice in Exod 14:2 brings the Israelites to a specific setting appropriate for a sea crossing, although it *names* everything but the sea itself: Migdol, Pi-hahiroth, Baal-zephon. A number of scholars understand the sea crossing originally to have been a mythical battle between Yahweh and the Sea (a character, not a place) that was historicized by turning the Sea into a real geographical place. Bernard Batto, for example, argues that P historicized a mythological Yam Suf, or 'sea of extinction', by telescoping the sea event and the stop at the real Yam Suf in Num 33:10–11 into the same event in the narrative.[39] Carola Kloos avoids the questionable understanding of Yam Suf as 'sea of extinction' by suggesting that the mythological character was just Yam, or Sea, and was historicized by being named Yam Suf.[40] Where is the real Yam Suf?

In every biblical text apart from passages about the sea crossing, Yam Suf refers to one of the northern arms of the Red Sea, either the Gulf of Eilat/Aqaba or the Gulf of Suez (see fig. 7, p. 197, and fig. 10, p. 238).[41] But Migdol and Pi-hahiroth are not near this Yam Suf. When the sea crossing is at issue, Yam Suf must refer to a place in the Egyptian Delta. Although the sea is not named in Exod 14:2, the Mediterranean, typically called יָם פְּלִשְׁתִּים 'Sea of the Philistines'

---

39. B. F. Batto, "The Reed Sea: Requiescat in Pace," *JBL* 102 (1983) 29. The translation 'sea of extinction' or 'sea at the end of the land' originated with N. H. Snaith, "יָם סוּף: The Sea of Reeds: The Red Sea," *VT* 15 (1965) 395–98.

40. C. Kloos, *Yhwh's Combat with the Sea: A Canaanite Tradition in the Religion of Ancient Israel* (Amsterdam: van Oorschot, 1986) 156–57, 171–90.

41. See pp. 196–198 for discussion.

or הַיָּם הַגָּדוֹל 'Great Sea' is the closest sea in the ancient Israelites' mental map as we know it from the Hebrew Bible and quite possibly the sea that יָם would have immediately evoked in the mind of a reader. Of course, one would not have crossed the Mediterranean on the way out of Egypt along the Ways of Horus, and the most likely candidate for a Yam Suf in the Delta is *pꜣ ṯwf(y)* 'the papyrus marsh(es)'. Shown in fig. 10, *pꜣ ṯwf(y)* refers to a specific reed marsh in the northeastern Egyptian Delta known to have supplied the royal estate at Pi-Ramesses with rushes and fish, just as the Lake of Horus (Shihor) and the Canal (*pꜣ ḥw-jr* or פִּי הַחִירֹת) supply it with salt and natron.[42]

The linguistic similarity between Hebrew יַם־סוּף and Egyptian *pꜣ ṯwf(y)* is commonly noted. It is not fully clear whether יַם־סוּף is a direct rendering of *pꜣ ṯwf(y)*, and *ṯwf* and סוּף may have a common Semitic origin.[43] The word סוּף is at least a semantic equivalent of *ṯwf*, since both mean 'reed'. But, as John Currid noted, יָם does not render the Egyptian definite article (*pꜣ*) in any way.[44] The Israelites transcribed Egyptian *pꜣ* (definite article) and *pr* or *pi* ('house') as פִּי, evident from the rendering of *pꜣ ḥw-jr* as פִּי הַחִירֹת (Exod 14:2) and *Pi-Baste(t)* as פִּי־בֶסֶת (Ezek 30:17). If the author of Exod 15:22, who referred to the sea that the Israelites crossed as Yam Suf, simply meant to refer to *pꜣ ṯwf(y)*, we might

---

42. "Praise of Pi-Ramessu," trans. J. P. Allen (*COS* 3.3). The Onomasticon of Amenemope also locates *pꜣ ṯwf(y)* in this area; see discussion in J. K. Hoffmeier and S. O. Moshier, "New Paleo-Environmental Evidence from North Sinai to Complement Manfred Bietak's Map of the Eastern Delta and Some Historical Implications," in *Time-lines: Studies in Honour of Manfred Bietak* (3 vols.; ed. E. Czerny et al.; OLA 149; Leuven: Peeters, 2006) 2.171–73. For discussion of Papyrus Anastasi VIII, which speaks of fish coming from this area, see S. I. Groll, "The Historical Background to the Exodus: Papyrus Anastasi VIII," in *Études Égyptologiques et bibliques à la memoire du Père B. Couroyer* (CahRB 36; Paris: Gabalda, 1997) 109–14; and S. I. Groll, "The Egyptian Background of the Exodus and the Crossing of the Reed Sea: A New Reading of Papyrus Anastasi VIII," in *Jerusalem Studies in Egyptology* (ed. I. Shirun-Grumach; Ägypten und Altes Testament 40; Wiesbaden: Harrassowitz, 1998) 173–92. J. P. Allen translates *pꜣ ṯwf(y)* 'papyrus marshes', a common noun ("Praise of Pi-Ramessu" [*COS* 3.3]).

43. W. A. Ward, "The Semitic Biconsonantal Root *sp* and the Common Origin of Egyptian *čwf* and Hebrew *sûp*: 'Marsh(-Plant),'" *VT* 24 (1974) 339–49; M. Vervenne, "The Lexeme סוּף (*sûph*) and the Phrase יַם סוּף (*yam sûph*): A Brief Reflection on the Etymology and Semantics of a Key Word in the Hebrew Exodus Tradition," in *Migration and Emigration within the Ancient Near East: Festschrift E. Lipiński* (ed. K. van Lerberghe and A. Schoors; OLA 65; Leuven: Peeters, 1995) 403–29, esp. pp. 419–22; Y. Muchiki, *Egyptian Proper Names and Loanwords in North-West Semitic* (SBLDS 173; Atlanta: Society of Biblical Literature, 1999) 252.

44. J. D. Currid, *Ancient Egypt and the Old Testament* (Grand Rapids, MI: Baker, 1997) 135.

expect to see פִּי סוּף or פִּי הַסּוּף rather than יַם־סוּף.[45] How did the site of the sea crossing come to be called *Yam* Suf? I suggest that יַם־סוּף, when it refers to the sea crossing, is a hybrid name, the result of an effort in Exod 15:22a to associate Exod 14:2's unnamed sea (יָם) with *pȝ ṭwf(y)*, locating the sea more specifically within the geographical background of the northern Delta already articulated in Exod 14:2, and at a place that would be directly on this route out of Egypt. [46] The contrived character of the association is apparent in the fact that a papyrus marsh, however suitably located on a route out of Egypt, is not really a sea. [47]

In his contribution to the effort to understand Yam Suf, Marc Vervenne states that "we must take account of the fact that the place-names in the Sea Narrative function on a literary level far more than a geographical one." [48] But a place-name can have a literary use *and* be tied to a real geographical background. When a writer refers to a real place that has a set location in the mental map he shares with his readers (that is, when both the writer and the reader know where it is), he is constrained to use it with this referent or risk causing confusion. The effort to localize the sea crossing at a specific place in the Egyptian Delta by calling it Yam Suf created just this sort of confusion. If a reader who knows the typical referent of Yam Suf as the gulfs of Suez and Eilat/Aqaba is reading about Yahweh's great deeds at Yam Suf in Psalm 106, she would likely suspend disbelief. It is clear to her that the author means to refer to the Egyptian Delta (especially if she happens to know about *pȝ ṭwf*[*y*]), and he uses only this setting consistently throughout the text, so there are no internal conflicts. The use of Yam Suf to refer to a place in the Egyptian Delta in the context of the wilderness narrative is another matter, because it conflicts with the use of Yam Suf later on in the story to refer to a completely different place. If we try to read Yam Suf in Num 14:25 and 21:4 as though it refers to a place in the Egyptian Delta, the ensuing trip around Edom and into Transjordan makes no sense, and the Israelites appear to be heading back to Egypt. To return to Mark

---

45. Vervenne, "Lexeme סוּף (*sûph*)," 428.

46. How the reference to Yam Suf in Exod 15:3 plays a role in the selection of this place-name for the itinerary notice in Exod 15:22a is important but beyond the scope of this study. If the poem is archaic, the Priestly scribe quite likely pulled the name from here. If it is not (despite the archaic linguistic features), then we would need to consider whether the composition of this song might have played a role in the revision that I refer to here and discuss in more detail on pp. 215–218. For recent reflections and bibliography on the problem of the date of the Song at the Sea, see B. D. Russell, *The Song of the Sea: The Date of Composition and Influence of Exodus 15:1–21* (Studies in Biblical Literature 101; New York: Peter Lang, 2007).

47. Batto, "Reed Sea," 30.

48. Vervenne, "Lexeme סוּף (*sûph*)," 427.

Turner and Gilles Fauconnier's optimality principles, discussed in chap. 2, the use of Yam Suf in the wilderness narrative to refer to two different places created a conflict in the blend.

Van Seters rejects the possibility that Yam Suf could have been used to refer to two different places in the same narrative.[49] But linguists recognize that speakers sometimes do introduce confusion in conversation. When a reference is not clear or conflicts with a listener's knowledge base, the listener may have to resort to repair strategies such as asking for clarification, guessing what the referent is, or simply ignoring it. Speakers may also note the problem and repair it.[50] Put differently, even when geography is used in the service of literary goals, writers are still constrained by shared knowledge of where the place actually is or is commonly thought to be. If a place violates this shared knowledge, the reference may generate tension or confusion. It seems that ancient scribes felt the same tension as Van Seters does because we find two instances of *reference repair* related to Yam Suf that came about as the wilderness narrative was revised.

The first is in Num 33:10–11. It is clear that the scribe was reading a version of the wilderness narrative in which the sea crossing has its specific location in the Delta because Num 33:7–8 mentions the conglomeration of place-names Pi-hahiroth, Baal-zephon, and Migdol, accounting for the Israelites' arrival at the sea in Exod 14:2. But he omitted Exod 15:22, which refers to the sea specifically as Yam Suf. Instead, he used the name Yam Suf as its own stop on the itinerary in Num 33:10–11, *three stops after* the Israelites had already passed through the sea and after they had already gone by Marah and Elim. Yam Suf here does not refer to $p\beta$ $twf(y)$ or the sea that the Israelites crossed because the sea crossing is already specified in Num 33:7–8. As shown in fig. 10, it refers instead to what we now call the Gulf of Suez, the western arm of the body of water otherwise referred to in the wilderness narrative as Yam Suf. So, in addition to correcting the wilderness itinerary back as much as possible to the Priestly version and using a consistent convention for the itinerary genre throughout, the author of Numbers 33 also repaired the referent of Yam Suf.

The second instance of reference repair is back in Exod 13:17–19. This passage is a relative latecomer in the composition history of the Torah. Its key

---

49. Van Seters, "Geography of the Exodus," 272.

50. H. H. Clark, *Using Language* (Cambridge: Cambridge University Press, 1996) 284–85; R. Jackendoff, *Foundations of Language: Brain, Meaning, Grammar, Evolution* (Oxford: Oxford University Press, 2002) 325.

function, according to Rolf Rendtorff, is to connect this body of literature to the patriarchal narratives, evident in the reference here to the Joseph story.[51]

וַיְהִי בְּשַׁלַּח פַּרְעֹה אֶת־הָעָם וְלֹא־נָחָם אֱלֹהִים דֶּרֶךְ אֶרֶץ פְּלִשְׁתִּים כִּי קָרוֹב הוּא כִּי אָמַר אֱלֹהִים פֶּן־יִנָּחֵם הָעָם בִּרְאֹתָם מִלְחָמָה וְשָׁבוּ מִצְרָיְמָה: וַיַּסֵּב אֱלֹהִים אֶת־הָעָם דֶּרֶךְ הַמִּדְבָּר יַם־סוּף וַחֲמֻשִׁים עָלוּ בְנֵי־יִשְׂרָאֵל מֵאֶרֶץ מִצְרָיִם: וַיִּקַּח מֹשֶׁה אֶת־עַצְמוֹת יוֹסֵף עִמּוֹ כִּי הַשְׁבֵּעַ הִשְׁבִּיעַ אֶת־בְּנֵי יִשְׂרָאֵל לֵאמֹר פָּקֹד יִפְקֹד אֱלֹהִים אֶתְכֶם וְהַעֲלִיתֶם אֶת־עַצְמֹתַי מִזֶּה אִתְּכֶם:

> When Pharaoh sent the people away, God did not lead them by the way of the Philistines, although it was closer, for God thought, "Lest the people experience regret when they see war and return to Egypt." So God led the people around by way of the wilderness of Yam Suf. Now, the Israelites went up armed from the land of Egypt. And Moses took Joseph's bones with him, for he had made the Israelites promise as follows: "God will in fact take note of you, and you will bring my bones up with you from there."

This passage indicates that the Israelites did *not* follow the military road that they would have traveled had they left Egypt via the Ways of Horus after crossing the sea from the northern Delta where *pʒ ṯwf(y)* is, as the upcoming itinerary notices in Exod 14:2 and 15:22 suggest that they did. Instead, the author of this passage corrects the route back toward the more southerly route implied by the itinerary notices in Exod 12:37a and 13:20. In so doing, the author also uses Yam Suf with its normal referent. The similarity of the name דֶּרֶךְ הַמִּדְבָּר יַם־סוּף 'way of the wilderness of Yam Suf' to דֶּרֶךְ יַם־סוּף 'way of Yam Suf' in Num 14:25 and 21:4 suggests that this author wants the reader to envision the Israelites heading southeast across the Sinai Peninsula toward the Gulf of Aqaba/Eilat instead of along the northern military route.

Why repair the reference *here*, before the Israelites even get to the sea? As we saw in chap. 6, the author of Num 14:25 established a theme for which direction the Israelites are headed from Kadesh long before the Israelites actually arrive there according to the itinerary notice in Num 20:1. By the time the reader arrives at Numbers 20–21, then, she has already established a *Gestalt* for the wilderness narrative that has the Israelites going south from Kadesh rather north into Canaan. This *Gestalt* colors her reading of Numbers 20–21 and predisposes her to ignore the Israelites' successful foray into Canaan in Num 21:1–3

---

51. R. Rendtorff, *The Problem of the Process of Transmission in the Pentateuch* (trans. J. J. Scullion; JSOTSup 89; Sheffield: JSOT Press, 1990) 97; and, more recently, K. Schmid, *Genesis and the Moses Story: Israel's Dual Origins in the Hebrew Bible* (Sifrut 3; Winona Lake, IN: Eisenbrauns, 2010) 50–55, 193–97, 214–16.

even before she reads these texts. The author of Exod 13:17–19 likewise established a theme for which way the Israelites go out of Egypt before they actually depart into the wilderness, attempting to influence the reader's *Gestalt* against the northern route before she even reads it.

The artificiality of this effort is quite evident. The scribe must take the Israelites away from the problematic referent for Yam Suf and have them head toward the same Yam Suf referred to elsewhere in the wilderness narrative. To do this, he gives the potential for encountering war as a reason for the diversion away from the military route. While this reason does accomplish the goal of reference repair, the scribe must sacrifice some plausibility vis-à-vis the annalistic character of the wilderness narrative, given that the Priestly scribe has already cast the Israelites as an enormous *army*.

Kadesh

A basic *temporal* setting for the spies episode is established, as I discussed above, with the statement in Num 13:22 that Hebron was built seven years before Zoan (Tanis). Its *geographical* setting, however, is established with a quite complex use of the place-name Kadesh. Numbers 13–14 calls for a setting outside the promised land, at an appropriate place from which the Israelites can launch an excursion into it while they remain camped in the wilderness. Kadesh is an important oasis on the road network in the Negev during a variety of periods, so its geographical position makes it an ideal setting for this narrative. Its settlement history is another matter. The central Negev is settled during Middle Bronze I/Intermediate Bronze (2200–2000 B.C.E.), which is followed by a settlement gap that extends through the Late Bronze Age (ca. 1500–1150 B.C.E.).[52] According to Rudolph Cohen, the excavator of Kadesh, "no artifacts or structures were found which could be assigned to the time of the Exodus."[53] This settlement gap has been a problem for scholars who are looking for a single historical and geographical setting for the narratives in Exodus–Joshua. This sort of search is based on the assumption that the authors' goals are historiographical, like the goals of the Egyptian scribes who wrote the Poem and

---

52. R. Cohen, *Ancient Settlement of the Central Negev*, vol. 1: *The Chalcolithic Period, the Early Bronze Age, and the Middle Bronze Age I* (IAA Report 6; Jerusalem: Israel Antiquities Authority, 1999); R. Cohen and R. Cohen-Amin, *Ancient Settlement of the Negev Highlands*, vol. 2: *The Iron Age and the Persian Period* (IAA Report 20; Jerusalem: Israel Antiquities Authority, 2004).

53. R. Cohen, *Kadesh-barnea: A Fortress from the Time of the Judahite Kingdom* (Jerusalem: Israel Museum, 1983) xix.

Bulletin versions of the battle at Qadesh in Syria discussed in chap. 4. However ideologically motivated, their goal was to relate a single event that took place at a single point in time, and they were quite constrained in their use of data.

While the statement about Hebron establishes a temporal setting consistent with that established at the beginning of the itinerary chain in Exodus, the use of Kadesh does not maintain this temporal setting. The wilderness narrative is ostensibly a story of Israel's past, but this story is not a history. It is a vision for the future set in *valorized* rather than historical time, and its authors did not, as David H. Aaron put it, "insist upon the same principles of temporality and consistency" that we would expect to find in an administrative document or a standard historiographical narrative.[54] While a setting in the distant past was key at the *beginning* of the wilderness narrative in order to ground it referentially, the scribes apparently did not feel the need to maintain that same setting consistently, since they drew geographical repertoire from other historical contexts as it served their literary goals. Kadesh suited the geographical needs for a setting very well, since it was outside the land. But the scribe had to turn to his mental map of the Negev *in the sixth century* B.C.E. for this geographical repertoire.

There is some debate about just where the southern border of Judah was in the late seventh–early sixth centuries B.C.E., and some scholars think it extended far enough south to *include* Kadesh and incorporated local nomadic populations living in the central Negev.[55] Kadesh may indeed have been a Judahite site in this period, since the pottery and small finds at the site are mainly Judahite, alongside some Negebite ware made by the local desert population.[56] But the area of the central Negev between Kadesh and the string of fortresses in the Beersheva region, shown on the map (fig. 11, p. 254), is very sparsely settled in this period. The only known sites are Kadesh, Kuntillet ʿAjrud, and

---

54. Aaron, *Etched in Stone*, 323.

55. E.g., Z. Meshel, "The 'Aharoni Fortress' near Quseima and the 'Israelite Fortresses' in the Negev," *BASOR* 294 (1994) 39–67; Y. Levin, "The Southern Frontier of *Yehud* and the Creation of Idumea," in *A Time of Change: Judah and Its Neighbours in the Persian and Early Hellenistic Periods* (ed. Y. Levin; Library of Second Temple Studies 65; London: T. & T. Clark, 2007) 240; L. M. Zucconi, "From the Wilderness of Zin alongside Edom: Edomite Territory in the Eastern Negev during the Eighth–Sixth Centuries B.C.E.," in *Milk and Honey: Essays on Ancient Israel and the Bible in Appreciation of the Judaic Studies Program at the University of California, San Diego* (ed. S. Malena and D. Miano; Winona Lake, IN: Eisenbrauns, 2007) 241.

56. Cohen, *Kadesh-barnea*, xii–xiv; G. Barkay, "The Iron Age II–III," in *The Archaeology of Ancient Israel* (ed. A. Ben-Tor; trans. R. Greenberg; New Haven, CT: Yale University Press, 1992) 341.

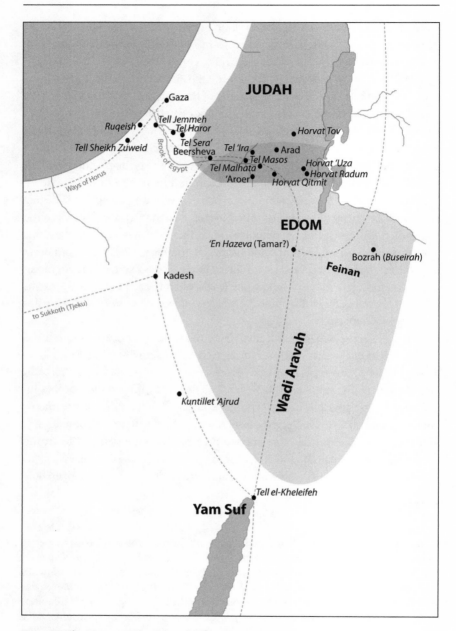

Fig. 11. The Negev in the 8th–6th Centuries B.C.E.

Tell el-Kheleifeh.[57] The political frontier of Judah is instead marked by fortress sites such as Horvat ʿUza, Horvat Radum, Horvat Tov, Arad, Tel ʿIra, Tel Masos, Tel Malhata, ʿAroer, and Beersheva. Fortresses of this sort covered the entire Kingdom of Judah, along the Dead Sea and throughout the central hill country; according to Gabriel Barkay, "they appear to have been within the ken of one another, so that news could be conveyed by signal fires."[58] The entire complex speaks to a centralized planning effort. Assuming Kadesh was controlled by Judah during this period, it would have been outside the land and served to control communication and trade along the variety of routes that converge at Kadesh.[59]

It is rarely explicit why scholars interpret Kadesh as being the southern extent of Judahite territory in the late seventh–early sixth centuries B.C.E. rather than simply being part of an effort to control a route. In an article on the relationship between Edom and Judah at this time, Laura Zucconi laid bare a possible assumption: She took the boundaries of the land articulated in Num 34:3–5 and Josh 15:1–4, which are classically attributed to P, to reflect the geopolitical circumstances of the eighth–sixth centuries when this source document took shape.[60] But the textual development of the tribal allotments in Joshua 13–19 is quite complex, and boundary descriptions such as Josh 15:1–4 should be understood as distinct from town lists such as Josh 15:21–32, which enumerates the towns in the southernmost part of Judah on the frontier with Edom.[61] Naʾaman instead placed the tribal allotments in the late seventh–early sixth centuries B.C.E., because they dovetail not only with the archaeological distribution of sites at this time but also with other biblical references to territory within Judah during Josiah's reign, place-names mentioned in ostraca, and the distribution of rosette-stamped jar handles, usually taken to indicate the extent of Judahite administrative control under Josiah.[62]

---

57. A. Mazar, *Archaeology of the Land of the Bible, 10,000–586 B.C.E.* (ABRL; New York: Doubleday, 1990) 444; Barkay, "Iron Age," 344; M. Haiman, "The 10th Century B.C. Settlement of the Negev Highlands and Iron Age Rural Palestine," in *The Rural Landscape of Ancient Israel* (ed. A. M. Maeir, S. Dar, and Z. Safrai; BAR International Series 1121; Oxford: Archaeopress, 2003) 77.

58. Barkay, "Iron Age," 344.

59. A. Mazar, *Archaeology of the Land of the Bible*, 444, 451; Stern, *Archaeology of the Land of the Bible*, 151.

60. Zucconi, "From the Wilderness of Zin," 253–54.

61. For a taste of the complexities, see A. G. Auld, *Joshua, Moses and the Land: Tetrateuch—Pentateuch—Hexateuch in a Generation since 1938* (Edinburgh: T. & T. Clark, 1980) 52–71.

62. N. Naʾaman, "The Kingdom of Judah under Josiah," *TA* 18 (1991) 24.

The area south of this frontier is best understood as contested, not controlled as a *territorial* province by anyone, and its archaeological record in the eighth–sixth centuries B.C.E. is best explained in terms of commercial activity.[63] Control of the routes through this area was important because it meant control of trade in copper and spices between the Arabian Peninsula, Egypt, Transjordan, and the Levantine coast—and thus wealth. The Assyrians were particularly interested in this area after Tiglath-pileser III's capture of Gaza in 734 B.C.E.[64] This interest is borne out in the archaeological record, since there is evidence of Assyrian presence in the form of military forts at Tell Sheikh Zuweid, Tell Jemmeh, Tel Haror, and Tel Seraʿ; an Assyrian *kāru*, or port, at Ruqeish; and Assyrian-style architecture at Buseirah.[65] Naʾaman offers a working hypothesis that the Assyrians, not the Judahites, were responsible for building the eighth-century B.C.E. fortress at Kadesh since it was outside the boundary of Judah proper at the time.[66] There has since been an effort to discern a coherent Assyrian construction program in fortresses having a similar architectural plan, such as Tell el-Kheleifeh, ʿEn Hazevah, and even Kuntillet ʿAjrud.[67] As long ago as 1967, Yohanan Aharoni noted the similarity between

63. Zucconi, "From the Wilderness of Zin," 250.

64. E. A. Knauf, "Edom: The Social and Economic History," in *You Shall Not Abhor an Edomite for He Is Your Brother: Edom and Seir in History and Tradition* (ed. D. V. Edelman; Archaeology and Biblical Studies 3; Atlanta: Scholars Press, 1995) 93–94; L. Singer-Avitz, "Beersheba: A Gateway Community in Southern Arabian Long-Distance Trade in the Eighth Century B.C.E.," *TA* 26 (1999) 3–74.

65. R. Reich, "Palaces and Residencies in the Iron Age," in *The Architecture of Ancient Israel from the Prehistoric to the Persian Periods* (ed. A. Kempinski and R. Reich; Jerusalem: Israel Exploration Society, 1992) 219–22; E. Oren, "Ethnicity and Regional Archaeology: The Western Negev under Assyrian Rule," in *Biblical Archaeology Today, 1990: Proceedings of the Second International Congress on Biblical Archaeology, Jerusalem, June–July 1990* (ed. A. Biran and J. Aviram; Jerusalem: Israel Exploration Society, 1993) 104; N. Naʾaman, "An Assyrian Residence at Ramat Raḥel?" *TA* 28 (2001) 262; E. Stern, *Archaeology of the Land of the Bible*, 25–29.

66. Naʾaman, "Kingdom of Judah," 48–49. D. Ussishkin accepts this idea ("The Rectangular Fortress at Kadesh-Barnea," *IEJ* 45 [1995] 126).

67. Naʾaman, "Assyrian Residence," 267–70. Including Kuntillet ʿAjrud in this program means redating the site, since it is is typically dated to the ninth–early eighth centuries—too early to have been built by the Assyrians (A. Mazar, *Archaeology of the Land of the Bible*, 449). L. Singer-Avitz has redated the pottery at the site to the eighth–seventh centuries ("The Date of Kuntillet ʿAjrud." *TA* 33 [2006] 196–228), but not without controversy; see L. Freud, "The Date of Kuntillet ʿAjrud: A Reply to Lilly Singer-Avitz," *TA* 35 (2008) 169–74; L. Singer-Avitz, "The Date of Kuntillet ʿAjrud: A Rejoinder," *TA* 36 (2009) 110–19. D. Ussishkin rightly notes that we must take into account

fortresses with towers such as the fortress at Kadesh and the shape of Assyrian camps as depicted in reliefs. [68] If the Assyrians did not build these, it seems that whoever did was influenced by Assyrian-style architecture.

Even if Judahites did not build the fortress at Kadesh at their own behest, they certainly lived and worked there. At least until Esarhaddon's campaign to Egypt in 671 B.C.E., Assyrian practice was to enlist the cooperation and even help of local populations to build and administer its provincial areas. Assyrians often installed a *qīpu*, or administrator, at a provincial outpost, and this individual was in some cases a local. Sargon (721–705 B.C.E.), for example, put the local sheikh of Laban in charge of resettled population in the area near the Brook of Egypt, and Siruatti the Me'unite and Idibi'ilu served similar roles under Tiglath-pileser III (744–727 B.C.E.). Because of their relationship with the Assyrians, these locals became economically and politically more powerful, albeit under the Assyrian umbrella. [69] The strong Judahite character of the small finds at Kadesh along with Israelite items found at the site could indicate that this particular outpost was controlled by Judahites who benefited from cooperation with the Assyrians. [70]

Whether it represents a Judahite effort to control trade or Judahite cooperation with the Assyrians in management of the trade network, Kadesh sat *outside* Judahite territory proper and was at the confluence of numerous routes in the region at the time when the Priestly version of the wilderness narrative and its various revisions were probably written, given that the Priestly version is a narrative vision for the return from exile. Roads in this region are difficult to trace in antiquity, because they were not paved or otherwise marked. But they can be reconstructed based on settlement patterns, topography, models

---

the unique cultic character of the site as a factor in our interpretation of it ("Rectangular Fortress," 127). Besides its cultic character, the site is unique in its mix of Judahite and Israelite material culture (and language, in its inscriptions) and its lack of Negebite pottery, suggesting that the site was not used by local nomadic groups; see A. Mazar, *Archaeology of the Land of the Bible*, 446–50; and Barkay, "Iron Age," 341. These characteristics lend credence to the idea that Kuntillet ʿAjrud was an Israelite/Judahite pilgrimage site or roadside shrine and was not primarily involved in the trade network.

68. Y. Aharoni, "Forerunners of the Limes: Iron Age Fortresses in the Negev," *IEJ* 17 (1967) 14.

69. I. Ephʿal, *The Ancient Arabs: Nomads on the Borders of the Fertile Crescent, 9th–5th Centuries B.C.* (Jerusalem: Magnes, 1982) 93–94, 99; Naʾaman, "Assyrian Residence," 269–70; idem, "The Boundary System and Political Status of Gaza under the Assyrian Empire," *ZDPV* 120 (2004) 62–64.

70. Singer-Avitz, "Date of Kuntillet ʿAjrud," 13; I. Finkelstein, "Horvat Qitmit and the Southern Trade in the Late Iron Age II," *ZDPV* 108 (1992) 164.

from later periods, and references in texts.[71] The main routes are indicated in fig. 11 (p. 254). The major route in this network runs from Gaza, through the Beersheva valley, to the Red Sea (Yam Suf) via Kadesh, and on into the Arabian Peninsula; it was the main artery for international communication and trade.[72] The way of Yam Suf in Num 14:25 and 21:4 is almost certainly a reference to this route. The Beersheva valley is also connected to the fortress at ʿEn Hazevah, from which one can travel down Wadi Aravah to connect with the route into the Arabian Peninsula or across the Aravah and into Transjordan via Bozrah (Buseirah).[73] The area between ʿEn Hazevah on the west side of Wadi Aravah and Wadi Faynan on the east was likely a main crossing point because it is relatively level and there are water sources on both sides.[74] Finally, the network connects to Egypt by either the Ways of Horus or a route that runs from Beersheva to Wadi Tumilat (Tjeku, or Succoth), passing near Kadesh.[75] Kadesh is a critical oasis in this network of routes because it has one of the largest springs in the region.[76] As such, Kadesh is an appropriate setting not only for a story about providing water for the people (Num 20:1–13) but also for a successful

---

71. D. A. Dorsey, *The Roads and Highways of Ancient Israel* (Baltimore: Johns Hopkins University Press, 1991) 52–56; A. M. Smith, "Pathways, Roadways, and Highways: Networks of Communication and Exchange in Wadi Arabah," *NEA* 68 (2005) 180–89.

72. G. I. Davies, *The Way of the Wilderness: A Geographical Study of the Wilderness Itineraries in the Old Testament* (Cambridge: Cambridge University Press, 1979) 77; I. Finkelstein, *Living on the Fringe: The Archaeology and History of the Negev, Sinai and Neighbouring Regions in the Bronze and Iron Ages* (Monographs in Mediterranean Archaeology 6; Sheffield: Sheffield Academic Press, 1995) 149.

73. B. MacDonald, "The Hinterland of Busayra," in *Busayra: Excavations by Crystal-M. Bennett 1971–1980* (British Academy Monographs in Archaeology; Oxford: Oxford University Press, 2002) 52; P. Bienkowski, *Busayra: Excavations by Crystal-M. Bennett 1971–1980* (British Academy Monographs in Archaeology 13; Oxford: Oxford University Press, 2002) 37–39; B. MacDonald, "The southern Ghors and north-east Arabah: Resources, sites and routes," in *Crossing the Rift: Resources, routes, settlement patterns and interaction in the Wadi Arabah* (ed. P. Bienkowski and K. Galor; Levant Supplementary Series 3; Oxford: Oxbow, 2006) 85.

74. P. Bienkowski and E. van der Steen, "Tribes, Trade, and Towns: A Framework for the Late Iron Age in Southern Jordan and the Negev," *BASOR* 323 (2001) 36; Bienkowski, *Busayra*, 39, 478; idem, "Wadi Arabah," 8; H. J. Bruins, "Desert environment and geoarchaeology of the Wadi Arabah," in *Crossing the Rift: Resources, routes, settlement patterns and interaction in the Wadi Arabah* (ed. P. Bienkowski and K. Galor; Levant Supplementary Series 3; Oxford: Oxbow, 2006) 29; MacDonald, "Southern Ghors," 86–87.

75. G. I. Davies, *Way of the Wilderness*, 77.

76. Y. Aharoni, "Kadesh-Barnea and Mount Sinai," in *God's Wilderness: Discoveries in Sinai* (London: Thames and Hudson, 1961) 121.

campaign *into* the land (Num 21:1–3)—or for an unsucessful one in which the disobedient Israelites are punished by being forced to travel *away from* the land (Num 14:40–45, 21:4).

The route south from Kadesh would, in the late seventh–early sixth centuries B.C.E., also have taken one around Edom (Num 20:14–21, 21:4). Edom has often been understood as being limited to Transjordan because Wadi Aravah—a large rift valley—is viewed as a natural boundary. But it has become increasingly clear that the rift valley did not inhibit the movement of people and culture from east to west at all; in fact, our perception of it as a territorial boundary may be more influenced by its modern status as a political border than anything else.[77] Egyptian texts from the thirteenth century B.C.E. speak of the Shasu of Edom moving west across the Aravah as a subsistence strategy, coming even to Egypt to water their herds.[78] In the eleventh–tenth centuries and then beginning again in the seventh century B.C.E., copper from the Faynan region was transported across the Aravah, an important factor in international trade.[79] As Assyrian control of the trade network loosened toward the middle or end of the seventh century, Edomites had impetus to become more directly involved in commercial activity west of the Aravah.

Archaeologically, we find an increase in Edomite material culture in the central and northern Negev during this period. Its extent is depicted in fig. 11 (p. 262). Edomites probably settled at Horvat Qitmit and ʿEn Hazevah, given the presence of shrines whose figurines may be Edomite in character. These are often interpreted as roadside shrines, used primarily by travelers, but the presence of locally made Edomite pottery as well as pottery made in Transjordan suggests that Edomites also lived in the area.[80] There is also a strong presence of Edomite material culture at sites such as Tel Malhata and Horvat ʿUza that are typically thought to be Judahite. Judahite clay figurines, *šql* and *nsf* weights, and a rosette seal impression were found at Tel Malhata alongside an Edomite figurine like those found at Horvat Qitmit and ʿEn Hazevah and

---

77. Bienkowski, "Wadi Arabah," 22–23.

78. Zucconi, "From the Wilderness of Zin," 250–51.

79. Knauf, "Edom," 111–13.

80. I. Beit-Arieh, "The Edomite Shrine at Ḥorvat Qitmit in the Judean Negev: Preliminary Excavation Report," *TA* 18 (1991) 114; idem, "The Edomites in Cisjordan," in *You Shall Not Abhor an Edomite for He Is Your Brother: Edom and Seir in History and Tradition* (ed. D. V. Edelman; Archaeology and Biblical Studies 3; Atlanta: Scholars Press, 1995) 36; R. Cohen and Y. Yisrael, *On the Road to Edom: Discoveries from ʿEn Hazeva* (Jerusalem: Israel Museum, 1995) 10–11; Zucconi, "From the Wilderness of Zin," 250–51.

a large quantity of Edomite pottery.[81] The Edomite material at Horvat ʿUza includes an ostracon with an instruction to deliver grain that begins with a blessing in the name of the Edomite deity Qos and is written in an idiosyncratic Edomite script.[82] Edomite material has also been found at Tel Masos, Tel ʿIra, ʿAroer, Arad, and Horvat Radum along the southern Judahite frontier as well as at Kadesh.[83]

The problem is how to interpret these finds. Some argue that they speak to Edomite territorial expansion into the Negev and encroachment on Judah.[84] Proponents of this view cite letter 24 from Arad, which discusses the transfer of men from Kinah to Ramat-Negev "lest the Edomites should come there," and clearly speaks to a potential Edomite threat. In light of this letter, the fortresses at Horvat Tov, Arad, Horvat ʿUza, and Horvat Radum—two of which may be the Kinah and Ramat-Negev mentioned in the Arad letter—are sometimes interpreted as efforts to protect Judah from Edomite incursions.[85] Ephraim Stern is thus inclined to interpret the Edomite ostracon at Horvat ʿUza as "authentic historical evidence that the fort fell into the hands of the Edomites."[86] The mix of Judahite and Edomite culture at sites such as Tel Malhata, however, may be better interpreted as evidence of cultural interpenetration in a frontier area. It is important to remember that what is key in this region at this time is control of the *routes*, and direct territorial annexation is not the only way to accomplish this goal; it seems that not even the Assyrians annexed this territory. It should perhaps not be surprising to see evidence of both cultural mixing and contention between Judah and Edom, which were left to fill the vacuum after the Assyrians withdrew.[87] The term *Edom* need not refer to a geographically or

---

81. Beit-Arieh, "Edomites in Cisjordan," 37; E. Stern, *Archaeology of the Land of the Bible*, 155–56.

82. D. S. Vanderhooft, "The Edomite Dialect and Script: A Review of the Evidence," in *You Shall Not Abhor an Edomite for He Is Your Brother: Edom and Seir in History and Tradition* (ed. D. V. Edelman; Archaeology and Biblical Studies 3; Atlanta: Scholars Press, 1995) 137–57.

83. Beit-Arieh, "Edomites in Cisjordan," 33, 37–38; E. Stern, *Archaeology of the Land of the Bible*, 155.

84. E.g., Beit-Arieh, "Edomites in Cisjordan," 36, 38; Zucconi, "From the Wilderness of Zin," 241, 246–49.

85. Beit-Arieh, "Edomites in Cisjordan," 35; Bienkowski and van der Steen, "Tribes, Trade, and Towns," 24, 26. For the possibility that Horvat ʿUza is Kinah, also mentioned in the Negev town list in Josh 15:21–32, see Naʾaman, "Kingdom of Judah," 30.

86. E. Stern, *Archaeology of the Land of the Bible*, 154.

87. For interpretation of the Edomite finds in the central Negev as evidence of greater Arabian involvement in commercial activity, see E. Mazar, "Edomite Pottery at the End of the Iron Age," *IEJ* 35 (1985) 268–69.

politically bounded space.[88] Whether Edomite material culture in the central Negev was due to political factors, cultural interpenetration, or some of both, it was a strong enough presence for the area to be thought of as Edom. Thus a mental map of the geopolitics of the Negev in this period is also a suitable background against which to imagine the Israelites going around Edom.

The immediate context of the wilderness narrative required a setting for the spies episode that was *outside* the land, but the goal of having the Israelites reconnoiter the entire promised land and anticipate the book of Joshua where they finally take up residence in that land required Kadesh to be *inside* the land. Kadesh is inside the land in the descriptions of the southern boundary of the promised land in Josh 15:1–4 (not outside it as implied by the Judah town list in Josh 15:21–32), which the author of the spies episode anticipates. The boundaries in Num 34:3–4 and Ezek 47:19 and 48:28 also include Kadesh *within* the land. These boundaries are idealized, and are presented particularly in Ezekiel as a vision for restoration of the land as well as the Temple.

Kadesh's place as the southernmost extremity of this idealized mental map of the promised land appears to have been a powerful element of cultural repertoire. We find it used to articulate the southern extent of Joshua's conquests, as summarized in Josh 10:40–43 and in the patriarchal narratives. In his study of the itineraries in the Abraham cycle, K. A. Deurloo suggests that Abraham's travels from one sanctuary to another serve to define the land promised to him and his progeny in Genesis 12. Kadesh is used in two key narratives to articulate the southern extent of this land. First, Sarai banishes Hagar to Beer-lahai-roi in Genesis 16, and it is only here that Ishmael is born. Beer-lahai-roi, according to Gen 16:14, is situated "between Kadesh and Bered." Kadesh here serves to indicate that Ishmael, who is a threat to the line of progeny promised to Abram and Sarai, was born outside the promised land.[89] Second, the sister/wife episode in Genesis 20 constitutes a threat to both land and progeny as Abraham travels to Gerar, located "between Kadesh and Shur" (Gen 20:1), not only creating a threat to the promise of progeny by lending his wife to a foreigner but also by putting his claim to the land in temporary hiatus by leaving it.[90]

---

88. Zucconi speaks only of *geographically* bounded territory and argues for Edomite territorial domination in the Negev and a boundary with Judah ("From the Wilderness of Zin," 243–44), but her argument applies equally to *politically* bounded territory.

89. On Hagar as introducing a threat of specifically Egyptian origin for Israel, see F. V. Greifenhagen, *Egypt on the Pentateuch's Ideological Map: Constructing Biblical Israel's Identity* (JSOTSup 361; London: Sheffield Academic Press, 2002) 31–33.

90. K. A. Deurloo, "Narrative Geography in the Abraham Cycle," in *In Quest of the Past: Studies on Israelite Religion, Literature, and Prophetism* (OtSt 26; Leiden: Brill,

A Kadesh understood to be *inside* the promised land served the literary goal of anticipating Joshua as an ending to the wilderness narrative. But the author was juggling two literary goals, since he also had to set the episode *outside* the land, leaving the Israelites still in the wilderness. Kallai notes this geographical conflict in the wilderness narrative when studying Moses' request for passage through Edom (Num 20:14–21): "It is obvious that there is an internal contradiction between Kadesh-barnea as a station in the wandering on the way to Canaan, and as an area at the extremity of the Land of Canaan, but within it."[91] The scribe achieved both literary goals with a single setting, Kadesh, by creating a temporal and geographical palimpsest: he superimposed a map of the central Negev during his own time (in which Kadesh was *outside* the land) on a map of the southern boundary of the idealized land (in which Kadesh was just *inside* the land). Both mental maps could have been carried around in the brain simultaneously, giving a place like Kadesh a very rich set of associations. The temporal setting of the spies episode also has a third dimension because the scribe juggled a third literary goal of setting it in the same temporal context as the departure from Egypt, although this is accomplished with the reference to the founding of Hebron in Num 13:22.

The palimpsest may also involve superimposing mental maps of the Negev in different historical periods. Kallai understands the boundary lists (including Josh 15:1–4) to be idealized but also to incorporate pieces of Israel's past. While the town lists for Judah reflect the geography of the eighth–sixth centuries B.C.E. (see fig. 11), the boundary lists may be rooted in the geographical reality at the time of the early Israelite monarchy. Kallai's argument rests principally on comparison with other biblical texts such as David's census in 2 Sam 24:1–9 and the list of Solomon's prefects in 1 Kings 4, which Kallai held to provide accurate information about the extent of Israelite territory at the time.[92] As shown on the map in fig. 12, however, there is also a "striking similarity"

1990) 53; see also J. Ska, *Introduction to Reading the Pentateuch* (trans. P. Dominique; Winona Lake, IN: Eisenbrauns, 2006) 25.

91. Z. Kallai, "The Southern Border of the Land of Israel: Pattern and Application," in *Biblical Historiography and Historical Geography: Collection of Studies* (BEATAJ 44; Frankfurt am Main: Peter Lang, 1998) 216.

92. Z. Kallai, "The United Monarchy of Israel: A Focal Point in Israelite Historiography," *IEJ* 27 (1977) 103–9; idem, *Historical Geography of the Bible: The Tribal Territories of Israel* (Leiden: Brill, 1986). See also N. Naʾaman, *Borders and Districts in Biblical Historiography* (Jerusalem Biblical Studies 4; Jerusalem, 1986) 80–101. This argument is not unproblematic, because neither text clearly indicates area south of the Beersheva valley as part of the land, even as the boundary texts put the southern limit of the land at Kadesh. To explain this, Kallai posits that the limits of the remaining land in Joshua 13

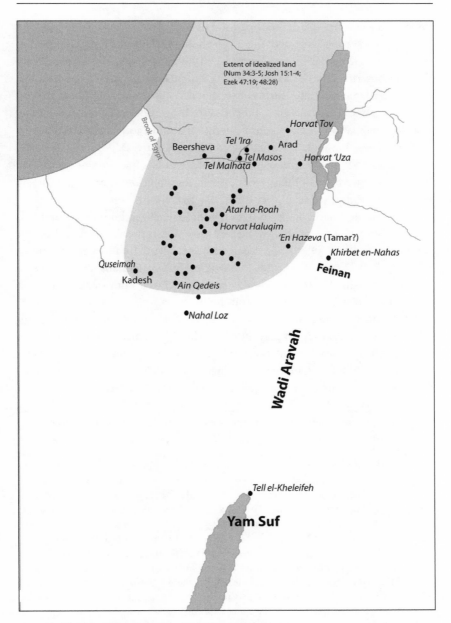

Fig. 12. The Negev in the 11th–10th Centuries B.C.E.

between these boundary descriptions and the distribution of settlements in the northern and central Negev in the eleventh–tenth centuries B.C.E., the period during which the Israelite state emerged.[93] Unlike the sparse settlement during the eighth–sixth centuries B.C.E., the Negev highlands contain 50 or more permanent settlements at sites such as Beersheva, Tel Malhata, Tel Masos, Tel ʿIra, Arad, Horvat Tov, Horvat ʿUza, ʿEn Hazevah, ʿAin Qedeis, Kadesh, Quseimah, Atar ha-Roah, and Horvat Haluqim, along with about 300 smaller settlements that are often—but not always—grouped around a fortress.[94] *If* these idealized boundaries do have some basis in the memory of Israel's first emergence as a nation, what we have in the spies episode, geographically speaking, is Israel's present, superimposed on a piece of its past, as a vision for its future.

Sorting out the relationship between these idealized boundaries and historical reality is not easy. The traditional view is that these sites were built by the early Israelite state as a defense against the Egyptians and were destroyed by Shishak.[95] They were built at strategic places; Quseimah, for example, is situated on a summit that overlooks the junction of a number of routes and would have been "an excellent lookout point" from which to monitor traffic.[96] The sites, being on high outcrops in a desert region, are not ideal and contain relatively few finds; only 60 percent of the rooms had any evidence of occupation. This has led some to interpret the sites as military outposts, the purpose of which was to house temporary contingents of soliders and serve as a refuge for people in the surrounding settlements during times of danger, although it

---

and Judges 1 are informed by the extent of Canaan at the end of the Late Bronze Age, viewed as an ideal eventually to be filled.

93. Cohen, *Kadesh-barnea*, xi.

94. Aharoni, "Forerunners of the Limes"; Cohen, *Kadesh-barnea*, ix–xi; Cohen and Yisrael, *On the Road*, 17, 34; Bienkowski and van der Steen, "Tribes, Trade, and Towns," 24; Haiman, "10th Century B.C. Settlement," 71–72; A. Mazar, "The Spade and the Text: The Interaction between Archaeology and Israelite History Relating to the Tenth–Ninth Centuries BCE," in *Understanding the History of Israel* (ed. H. G. M. Williamson; Proceedings of the British Academy 143; Oxford: Oxford University Press, 2007) 151. T. E. Levy et al. include Tell el-Kheleifeh on this list because the recent discovery of an eleventh–ninth-century settlement at Khirbet en-Nahas warrants a reassessment of the eighth-century date for the settlement there ("Lowland Edom and the High and Low Chronologies: Edomite state formation, the Bible and recent archaeological research in southern Jordan," in *The Bible and Radiocarbon Dating: Archaeology, Text and Science* [ed. T. E. Levy and T. Higham; London: Equinox, 2005] 138–39, 147).

95. Z. Herzog, "Enclosed Settlements in the Negeb and the Wilderness of Beersheba," *BASOR* 250 (1983) 41–49; Cohen and Yisrael, *On the Road to Edom*, 34; Haiman, "10th Century B.C. Settlement."

96. Meshel, "'Aharoni Fortress'," 39.

has led others to the conclusion that the sites were simply abandoned rather than destroyed by Shishak.[97]

Archaeologically, however, it is not clear who was responsible for building these sites.[98] The enclosures themselves have been compared to enclosures at sites farther north, suggesting that the central Negev sites may be related to the emergent Israelite polity and point to an extension of its southern frontier, but these northern parallels are two centuries later than the central Negev sites in question, and thus they provide a weak argument for southern expansion in the eleventh–tenth centuries B.C.E.[99] The enclosure at Izbet Sartah would also be a northern parallel in the appropriate period, but it and other sites like it in the western Galilee, Ephraim, and the Judean Desert are commonly attributed to sedentarization rather than state formation.[100] There also does not seem to be an overall logic for the placement of these sites, which one might expect if they were a centralized planning effort, so it is not clear whether their strategic function served a centralized power or local interests.[101] Indeed, the settlement pattern may be best explained as a local sedentarization process. The circular shape of the architecture is similar to bedouin tent encampments, suggesting a pastoralist population that established a more permanent settlement.[102] While some sites similar to Quseimah certainly appear to have a strategic function, many sites are also situated where land could be made suitable for agriculture—near wadis where dry farming could be sustained even in this marginal climate by winter flood water and surface runoff—and many have rock-hewn cisterns for collecting water. Terracing, silos, and threshing floors point directly

97. Haiman, "10th Century B.C. Settlement," 72–73; but Meshel also points out that there is no evidence of widespread destruction of the sites ("'Aharoni Fortress'," 57, 60).

98. Ibid., 39; T. E. Levy and M. Najjar, "Some Thoughts on Khirbet en-Nahas, Edom, Biblical History and Anthropology: A Response to Israel Finkelstein," *TA* 33 (2006) 10–12.

99. A. Mazar, "Iron Age Fortresses in the Judean Hills," *PEQ* 114 (1982) 97; Meshel, "Aharoni Fortress," 57–58; Haiman, "10th Century B.C. Settlement," 75–76; Cohen and Cohen-Amin, *Ancient Settlement*, 11*.

100. I. Finkelstein, *'Izbet Ṣarṭah: An Early Iron Age Site near Rosh Haʿayin, Israel* (BAR International Series 299; Oxford: British Archaeological Reports, 1986) 106–9, 116–17; idem, *The Archaeology of the Israelite Settlement* (Jerusalem: Israel Exploration Society, 1988) 238–50.

101. Meshel, "'Aharoni Fortress'," 57–58.

102. I. Finkelstein, "The Iron Age 'Fortresses' of the Negev Highlands: Sedentarization of the Nomads," *TA* 11 (1984) 189–209; idem, "Arabian Trade and Socio-Political Conditions in the Negev in the Twelfth–Eleventh Centuries B.C.E.," *JNES* 47 (1988) 241–52. See also Cohen and Cohen-Amin, *Ancient Settlement*, 9*–10*, although they entertains other possible explanations as well.

to agricultural activity at these sites, and the southern limit of the settlement pattern is also, in terms of climate and ecology, roughly the southern limit of sustainable agriculture.[103] All of the sites have locally made Negebite pottery, which suggests that their inhabitants may have been locals.

Explaining the Negev highlands sites in terms of a sedentarization process need not be incompatible with political and economic activity in the region. As Amihai Mazar has noted, locals may have built settlements around sites established by more-organized social groups, "finding sources of income in this new neighborhood."[104] Recent excavation in the Faynan region has made it clear that copper mining, processing, and trade was an important economic factor in southern Transjordan and the Negev during this period. Copper mining in this region was an active part of the Early Bronze Age (3200–2200 B.C.E.) economy, but copper came into the Near East from Cyprus during the Late Bronze Age. The collapse of that trade network created renewed opportunity for the Faynan region in the early Iron Age, when the Negev highland settlements appear.[105] Most of the copper from this region during the Early Bronze Age was shipped across the Aravah valley and west toward the Levantine coast rather than east into the Transjordanian plateau, and the same appears to have been true in the early Iron Age as well.[106] The fortress at Khirbet en-Nahas, a key site in the Faynan region during this period, may thus be connected to other desert fortresses in the Negev such as Arad, Horvat ʿUza, Tel ʿIra, ʿAin Qedeis, and Kadesh as well as to Tell el-Kheleifeh on the coast of the Red Sea (Yam Suf), if its occupation turns out to date to Iron IIA and not only the eighth cen-

103. Meshel, "Aharoni Fortress," 57–58; D. Eitam, "The Settlement of Nomadic Tribes in the Negeb Highlands during the 11th Century B.C.," in *Society and Economy in the Eastern Mediterranean (c. 1500–1000 B.C.)* (ed. M. Heltzer and E. Lipiński; OLA 23; Leuven: Peeters, 1988) 313–40; Cohen and Cohen-Amin, *Ancient Settlements*, 10*–11*.

104. A. Mazar, "Spade and the Text," 151. See also Meshel, "Aharoni Fortress," 54–57; Cohen and Cohen-Amin, *Ancient Settlements*, 8*; and especially Haiman ("10th Century B.C. Settlement," 76), who notes that transhumants tend not to settle on their own initiative but near established permanent settlements.

105. T. E. Levy and M. Najjar, "Ancient Metal Production and Social Change in Southern Jordan: The Edom Lowlands Regional Authority Project and Hope for a UNESCO World Heritage Site in Faynan," in *Crossing Jordan: North American Contributions to the Archaeology of Jordan* (ed. T. E. Levy et al.; London: Equinox, 2007) 100.

106. I. Finkelstein, "Khirbet en-Nahas, Edom and Biblical History," *TA* 32 (2005) 120; A. Hauptmann, "Mining archaeology and archaeometallurgy in the Wadi Arabah: The mining districts of Faynan and Timna," in *Crossing the Rift: Resources, routes, settlement patterns and interaction in the Wadi Arabah* (ed. P. Bienkowski and K. Galor; Levant Supplementary Series 3; Oxford: Oxbow, 2006) 125–33.

tury B.C.E.[107] The fortress at ʿEn Hazevah, which is directly across the Aravah from the Faynan region, would have connected Khirbet en-Nahas with the western routes toward the Levantine coast.[108] Mazar notes that the impetus to build the Negev highland sites "must have been economic, perhaps related to the vast copper smelting activity at Faynan."[109] While this seems an important factor for interpreting the Negev highland sites, however, there is no positive evidence for their role in copper trade, and it is not clear that they are located in such a fashion that they are best interpreted as way stations along roads.[110]

The date of the Negev highland sites is a critical element for answering the questions Who built them? and Why? At many of the sites, as at Quseimah, ceramic chronology does not allow a more precise date than the eleventh–tenth centuries B.C.E.[111] The early side of this range makes them too early to have been established by the Israelite monarchy. Archaeologists have thus had to rely on their understanding of the function and origin of these sites to interpret them: those who see them as the result of a local sedentarization process tend to date them to the early end of this range, while those who see them as having been established by the Israelite monarchy date them to the later end.[112] The stratigraphy of Khirbet en-Nahas, at the heart of the Faynan region, along with radiocarbon (14C) dates from this and other sites in the region offer some hope of sorting out this situation. Copper production in the Faynan region ranges from the twelfth or mid-eleventh to the ninth centuries B.C.E. based on 14C dates.[113] The main building at Khirbet en-Nahas has two phases: the first phase dates to the twelfth–eleventh centuries and the second to

---

107. Aharoni, "Forerunners of the Limes"; Levy et al., "Lowland Edom," 138–39, 147.

108. Ibid., 139; A. Mazar, "Spade and the Text," 151.

109. Ibid.

110. Meshel, "Aharoni Fortress," 57–59.

111. Ibid., 53.

112. H. J. Bruins and J. van der Plicht. "Desert Settlement through the Iron Age: Radiocarbon dates from Sinai and the Negev Highlands," in *The Bible and Radiocarbon Dating: Archaeology, Text and Science* (ed. T. E. Levy and T. Higham; London: Equinox, 2005) 350.

113. T. E. Levy et al., "Reassessing the chronology of Biblical Edom: New excavations and 14C dates from Khirbet en-Nahas (Jordan)," *Antiquity* 78 (2004) 869–71; I. Finkelstein and E. Piasetzky, "Radiocarbon and the History of Copper Production at Khirbet en-Nahas," *TA* 35 (2008) 86. For a mid-eleventh-century start date, see T. E. Levy et al., "High-precision radiocarbon dating and historical biblical archaeology in southern Jordan," *Proceedings of the National Academy of Science* 105 (2008) 16464.

the tenth–ninth centuries B.C.E.[114] The second phase involves a gatehouse and other public/administrative buildings at Khirbet en-Nahas, suggesting a more concerted administrative control, and there is also occupation from the tenth through seventh centuries B.C.E. at Rujm Hamra Ifdan.[115] Tenth–ninth-century occuption in the Faynan region may connect with the fortresses in the Negev highlands; the most recent consensus on their chronology is that they were a "chronologically homogenous phenomenon" dating to Iron IIA (1000–800 B.C.E.).[116] If so, the Negev highland sites *may* be connected to a strengthened effort to transport copper to the west during this period.

Nevertheless, it is not clear who controlled this economic enterprise, which means that it remains unclear who is responsible for constructing the Negev highland sites. The Faynan region produced approximately 100,000 tons of copper slag (about 10,000 tons of actual metal) during the Iron Age.[117] Piotr Bienkowski and Eveline van der Steen note that "[t]he huge scale of the operations must have required considerable organization."[118] Until recently, it seemed that there were no settlements associated with the evidence for mining activity in the Faynan region, but excavation of Khirbet en-Nahas has demonstrated direct control over the activities in the region. But by whom? The settlement at Khirbet en-Nahas may suggest that Edom developed as an economic and political power significantly earlier than previously thought, spurred by the development of copper in the early Iron Age.[119] Edomite sites in the highlands, such as Buseirah and Tawilan, do not appear until the eighth century B.C.E. under Assyrian influence, but the earlier settlement in the lowland region at sites such as Khirbet en-Nahas and Rujm Hamra Ifdan suggests that Edom may have developed in the lowlands prior to Assyrian involvement in the region and spread to the highlands later in the Iron Age.[120] The Faynan region

114. Levy et al., "Reassessing the chronology," 876; Levy and Najjar, "Ancient Metal Production," 101.

115. Levy et al., "High-precision radiocarbon dating," 16464–65.

116. A. Gilboa et al., "Notes on Iron IIA 14C Dates from Tell el-Qudeirat (Kadesh Barnea)," *TA* 36 (2009) 89. But see the radiocarbon dates given by Bruins and van der Plicht, which put the elliptical fortress at Kadesh in the eleventh century at the latest, making it (and perhaps the other elliptical buildings in the Negev as well) contemporary with the *first* phase of occupation at Khirbet en-Nahas ("Desert Settlement," 355–57).

117. Levy and Najjar, "Ancient Metal Production," 99.

118. Bienkowski and van der Steen, "Tribes, Trade, and Towns," 23; see also Levy et al., "Lowland Edom."

119. Levy et al., "Lowland Edom," 158.

120. Bienkowski and van der Steen, "Tribes, Trade, and Towns," 23; Levy et al., "Lowland Edom," 131; Levy and Najjar, "Some Thoughts on Khirbet en-Nahas," 11–12; Levy et al., "High-precision radiocarbon dating."

could also, however, have been controlled by the Israelites. Israel Finkelstein points out that Israel would have had a natural interest in expanding southward to "eliminate the threat to its southern fringes and to take over the Arabian trade."[121] Thomas Levy acknowledges that the fortress at Khirbet en-Nahas could also have been constructed by the Israelites, which may be reflected in the statement that David placed garrisons in Edom (2 Sam 8:14).[122] This system might have been controlled by a local chiefdom, centered either locally in the Faynan region or at Tel Masos.[123]

The landscape we investigate archaeologically is not merely a container, something separate from and determinative of human activity. Rather, the physical environment is shaped by naming, building, and using it—activities that are bound up with cultural values, identity, imagination, memory, and ideas—and it, in turn, shapes the people who live in it. Landscape, then, is a site of interaction between humans and the environment.[124] Because landscape is shaped in part by human thoughts and intentions, there is a sense in which we can *read* the archaeological record. But it does not speak directly, as an informant from antiquity would if we had one; we must infer human thoughts and intentions.[125] We can do well with considering how natural adaptation and

---

121. Finkelstein suggests that the Israelites may have taken over control of the copper trade as it was managed in the previous phase (by local tribes centered on Tel Masos, in his view) ("Arabian Trade," 250). Finkelstein and Piasetzky connect this phase not only to the rise of Israel and Damascus but also to an Egyptian effort (by Shishak) to take over copper trade ("Radiocarbon and the History of Copper," 89–90).

122. Levy et al., "Lowland Edom," 158–59; Levy and Najjar, "Some Thoughts on Khirbet en-Nahas," 11–12; see also A. Mazar, "Spade and the Text," 151. Finkelstein understands the claim in 2 Sam 8:14 that David established garrisons in *all Edom* to mean throughout the Negev ("Arabian Trade," 251).

123. Ibid., 249; idem, "Khirbet en-Nahas," 122–23.

124. Discussion of the way perceptions, attitudes, and values influence our interaction with physical environment is a constant theme in Yi-Fu Tuan's work but was first and most clearly articulated by him in *Topophilia: A Study of Environmental Perception, Attitudes, and Values* (Englewood Cliffs, NJ: Prentice-Hall, 1974) 4. See also idem, *Space and Place: The Perspective of Experience* (Minneapolis: University of Minnesota Press, 1977); and idem, "Language and the Making of Place: A Narrative-Descriptive Approach," *Annals of the Association of American Geographers* 81 (1991) 684–96.

125. C. Renfrew, "Problems in the modelling of socio-cultural systems," *European Journal of Operational Research* 30 (1987) 179; idem and P. Bahn, *Archaeology: Theories, Methods, and Practice* (2nd ed.; London: Thames and Hudson, 1991) 370. Because archaeological remains are sometimes shaped by ideas and values, some archaeologists have explored how they might be *read*, not altogether unlike a text, to yield insight into "past ways of thought" (C. Renfrew, "Towards a cognitive archaeology," in *The ancient mind: Elements of cognitive archaeology* [ed. C. Renfrew and E. B. Zubrow; Cambridge:

economic factors may have influenced the settlement pattern we find in the
Negev highlands, but ethnic and historical factors are much more difficult to
identify in the archaeological record. Colin Renfrew and Paul Bahn have emphasized the importance of texts, when available, to strengthen or call into
question what we infer from material remains.[126] Nicholas Postgate uses an
example of Mesopotamian human and animal figurines buried in the same
deposit *but with different functions* to show that archaeological context alone
may not always give us enough information to interpret the finds properly.[127]

The challenge with a text, according to Renfrew and Bahn, is that we must
first understand what conventions it follows or what bias it may have before
we can use it to help us interpret the archaeological record. The same challenge confronts us when using pictorial art such as reliefs or paintings: "The
rules and conventions for depictions on a flat surface will vary from culture to
culture, and require detailed study in each case."[128] The effort to understand
how a text relates to archaeological finds must go well beyond a simple assessment. We can take a text to be something other than what it really is based on
a superficial genre classification. We also can dismiss too quickly the idea that
a text has any relationship to realia because it is literary or ideological. Over

---

Cambridge University Press, 1994] 3). This hermeneutical approach has been controversial among archaeologists, partly because archaeology came into its own as a scientific
discipline by adopting scientific methods (a movement called the New Archaeology)
to describe the material culture itself and rejecting "undisciplined" and "speculative"
efforts to imagine what ancient people might have been thinking when they made the
artifacts. Questions of what ancient people thought were set aside because of doubt that
we can access human cognition and culture through the archaeological record the way
that ethnographers can through their informants (L. Binford, "Data, Relativism, and
Archaeological Science," *Man* 22 [1987] 391–404). Nevertheless, artifacts are shaped by
human ideas and activity, and questions about how the archaeological record can shed
light on past ways of thought should be considered fair game as long as we pursue
answers to them with methodological rigor and disciplined self-reflection about our
methods of inference and our interpretations.

126. Renfrew and Bahn, *Archaeology*, 384–86; see also K. V. Flannery and J. Mar-
cus, who contrast the aceramic Neolithic as a poor period in which to do cognitive
archaeology with New Kingdom Egypt as a good period because there is a wealth of
data from the latter that is absent from the former; the data include, among other things,
many texts ("Cognitive Archaeology," in *Contemporary Archaeology in Theory* [ed.
R. Preucel and I. Hodder; Oxford: Blackwell, 1996] 360–61).

127. J. N. Postgate, "Text and figure in ancient Mesopotamia: Match and mis-
match," in *The ancient mind: Elements of cognitive archaeology* (ed. C. Renfrew and E. B.
Zubrow; Cambridge: Cambridge University Press, 1994) 176–84.

128. Renfrew and Bahn use decorum in Egyptian art to illustrate the problem (*Archaeology*, 397).

the course of this book, we have seen examples of both types of mistake. We should instead investigate to the best of our ability the text's purpose, how it was written and how it is embedded in culture—the way its author uses various elements of repertoire, including realia before we use it to interpret the archaeological record. Given the composition history and the purpose of various elements in Numbers 21, for example, we should use it with a great deal of caution, if at all, to help us identify the location of sites in Transjordan. But each text must be studied on its own terms. Because of the diversity of genres and literary goals within the Hebrew Bible—even within a single composite text—we should not generalize but deal with the specific goals and techniques of a given text. The conclusions we might draw about the usefulness of Numbers 21 for archaeological interpretation need not be the same conclusions we draw about other texts or about the Bible in general.

The descriptions of the southern boundary of the land in Num 34:3–5, Josh 15:1–4, and Ezek 47:19 and 48:28, although idealized visions, do appear to be related to the landscape we can see archaeologically in the southern Negev of the early Iron II, the same archaeological context in which the Israelite state initially arose farther to the north. Did the authors of these visions select a memory (accessed through sources, as Kallai and others have argued, or otherwise) of the landscape of a golden age as an element of repertoire with which to envision their future restoration? Archaeology cannot answer this question, but it can contribute stratigraphic and chronological information that can resolve the problem of whether this settlement pattern dates to the period that would make it a potentially relevant element of repertoire.[129]

How these texts can in turn be helpful to archaeologists in their search for the people who built these settlements and why is a different matter. The boundary lists could indeed, as Kallai argues, describe the southern limit of a landscape that was built by the earliest Israelite kings. But they are not statements of planning, and they may also describe the landscape at the time with which the Israelites associated themselves, *irrespective of who built it*. When I call a building "*my* house," I am not necessarily making a statement that I planned and built it—although I may have—because I may own or rent it, or I may be referring to a building in which I lived as a child but that is now occupied by others. We face the same type of ambiguity with the town lists and boundary descriptions, and we cannot necessarily take their statements as evidence that these boundaries were planned and executed by Israelite kings. Unfortunately, we cannot ask their authors to clarify.

---

129. On relevance, see D. Sperber and D. Wilson, *Relevance: Communication and Cognition* (Language and Thought Series; Cambridge: Harvard University Press, 1986).

Death on a Mountain

Although the place where Moses dies is identified in the current form of
the Torah as Mount Nebo, it was not originally meant to be specified. Num
27:12 and Deut 34:9 are often mistranslated, with the result that readers in English miss the fact that Numbers 27 identifies the site of Moses' death without
actually naming it. As an example, the new Jewish Publication Society translation has 'ascend *these heights* of Abarim' for עֲלֵה אֶל־הַר הָעֲבָרִים הַזֶּה in Num
27:12 and 'ascend *these heights* of Abarim to Mount Nebo' for עֲלֵה אֶל־הַר הָעֲבָרִים
הַזֶּה הַר־נְבוֹ in Deut 32:49.[130] But הַר is not plural in either verse. The translator
seems to understand הַזֶּה to modify הָעֲבָרִים. Because it is singular, however,
הַזֶּה must refer to the first noun in the construct chain, or הַר. The mistake may
be generated by the fact that הַר and הַזֶּה do not both have definite articles,
because modfiers should match in definiteness. But הַר is definite by virtue of
being in construct with a proper noun (הָעֲבָרִים). In Num 27:12, Moses ascends
הַר הָעֲבָרִים הַזֶּה 'this [*particular unspecified*] *mountain* of the Abarim' in order to
the view the land before he dies. The mountain range is named in Numbers 27,
but the particular mountain is not. The omission is probably a deliberate effort
to obscure the specific site of Moses' death, perhaps to mitigate the chances of
veneration.[131]

The incorporation of Deuteronomy required a shift of setting for the end
of the wilderness narrative from the Negev (Tetrateuch) to Moab (Pentateuch
with Deuteronomy). This shift involved not only moving the Israelites along to
Moab using the itinerary notices in Num 21:12–13a but also truncating Moses'
final scene in Numbers 27 and shifting his death to the end of Deuteronomy,
also with a setting in Moab, as A. Graeme Auld has argued.[132] Nebo provides
an appropriate Moabite setting as one of the major towns in Moab. The Israelites had a quite detailed mental map of Moab, evident in the oracles against
Moab in Isaiah 15 and Jeremiah 48, where the town of Nebo holds a prominent
place. Our knowledge of where ancient Nebo was depends on the relative location provided by Eusebius in his Onomasticon, which is most likely located

130. *Tanakh: A New Translation of the Holy Scriptures according to the Traditional
Hebrew Text* (Philadelphia: Jewish Publication Society, 1985); emphasis mine.

131. E. Cortese and A. Niccacci, "Nebo in Biblical Tradition," in *Mount Nebo: New
Archaeological Excavations, 1967–1997* (ed. M. Piccirillo and E. Alliata; Studium Biblicum Franciscanum Collectio Maior 27; Jerusalem: Franciscan Printing Press, 1998)
62–63.

132. Auld, *Joshua, Moses and the Land*, 72, 98–100.

at Khirbet el-Mukhayyat, "the only site in the area with significant Iron Age remains."[133]

The scribe who wrote Deut 32:49 used the ambiguity about the the the site of Moses' death in Num 27:12 as an opportunity to change the setting. He repeated Num 27:12 with a few updates to deuteronomic style and added הַר־נְבוֹ אֲשֶׁר בְּאֶרֶץ מוֹאָב אֲשֶׁר עַל־פְּנֵי יְרֵחוֹ 'Mount Nebo, which is in the land of Moab facing Jericho' in order to establish the appropriate setting:

עֲלֵה אֶל־הַר הָעֲבָרִים הַזֶּה וּרְאֵה אֶת־הָאָרֶץ אֲשֶׁר נָתַתִּי לִבְנֵי יִשְׂרָאֵל:

Ascend this mountain of the Abarim and look at the land which I give to the Israelites. (Num 27:12)

עֲלֵה אֶל־הַר הָעֲבָרִים הַזֶּה הַר־נְבוֹ אֲשֶׁר בְּאֶרֶץ מוֹאָב אֲשֶׁר עַל־פְּנֵי יְרֵחוֹ וּרְאֵה אֶת־
אֶרֶץ כְּנַעַן אֲשֶׁר אֲנִי נֹתֵן לִבְנֵי יִשְׂרָאֵל לַאֲחֻזָּה:

Ascend this mountain of the Abarim—Mount Nebo, which is in the land of Moab facing Jericho—and look at the land of Canaan, which I am giving to the Israelites as their holding. (Deut 32:49)

In the process, he compromised the purpose of the ambiguous expression הַר הָעֲבָרִים הַזֶּה, which was to obscure the site of Moses' death.

Because the scribe added Mount Nebo to the text of Num 27:12, especially with the modifer explicitly stating that Mount Nebo is in Moab, it now appears as though the *Abarim Range* is also in Moab. Deut 34:1 identifies Mount Nebo as the summit of the Pisgah Range, and many commentators assume that Pisgah and Abarim are two names for the same mountain range in Moab.[134] But Abarim and Pisgah are never combined or otherwise associated elsewhere in biblical literature, which should lead us to wonder whether they were the same in the ancient Israelites' mental map. The oracle concerning Jehoiakim's exile in

---

133. F. Benedettucci, "The Iron Age," in *Mount Nebo: New Archaeological Excavations, 1967–1997* (ed. M. Piccirillo and E. Alliata; Studium Biblicum Franciscanum Collectio Maior 27; Jerusalem: Franciscan Printing Press, 1998) 110–27.

134. So most commentators; e.g., J. Sturdy, *Numbers* (CBC; Cambridge: Cambridge University Press, 1976) 196; Aharoni, *Land of the Bible*, 51, 187; P. J. Budd, *Numbers* (WBC 5; Waco, TX: Word, 1984) 306; D. Baly, *Basic Biblical Geography* (Philadelphia: Fortress, 1986) 62; B. A. Levine, *Numbers 21–36: A New Translation with Introduction and Commentary* (AB 4B; New York: Doubleday, 2000) 348–49. The relationship between Pisgah and Nebo is debated; for a good review of the problem, see M. Dijkstra, "The Geography of the Story of Balaam: Synchronic Reading as a Help to Date a Biblical Text," in *Synchronic or Diachronic: A Debate on Method in Old Testament Exegesis* (ed. J. de Moor; OtSt 34; Leiden: Brill, 1995) 76–78.

Jer 22:18–30 suggests instead that the Abarim Range may be located in southern Canaan. The author here refers to the Abarim as he depicts an outcry of lament from Lebanon, Bashan, and Abarim. Lebanon is a mountain range north of the land of Israel, while Bashan is to the east. If the author is using his knowledge of geography to create an image of lament for the loss of land from the mountains on every side of it, emphasizing the total scope of this loss, that would put Abarim in southern Canaan.

If Abarim was actually somewhere in the Negev rather than in Moab, its apparent location in Deut 32:49—the result of an effort to rewrite Moses' death scene—must have grated against the geographical sensibilities of its original audience, perhaps the same way that a Yam Suf located in the northern part of the Egyptian Delta did. But in this case we do not have the internal conflict that made a Yam Suf in the Egyptian Delta problematic in the context of the wilderness narrative. As many commentators have noted, Abarim (הָעֲבָרִים) resonates with the common reference to Transjordan as the land בְּעֵבֶר הַיַּרְדֵּן 'beyond the Jordan'. This is often invoked as an explanation for the naming of the mountain range in Moab as Abarim.[135] If the ancient Israelite audience heard a similar resonance, it may have made the (mis-)use of Abarim palatable in this new literary context.

Aaron also dies on a mountain. The site of Aaron's death is likewise obscured, but in this case a place-name is *invented* for it that enables it to be a particular mountain and a stop on the wilderness itinerary without identifying a specific known site. Yoel Elitzur has suggested that the name Mount Hor was created in imitation of a typical construct pattern for toponyms in which the first element refers to a specific site, while the second refers to a general region, such as הַר הָעֵמֶק in Josh 13:19. On the basis of this pattern, Elitzur suggests that Mount Hor is really made up of the same common noun repeated, הר ההר, simply indicating a specific unnamed mountain peak in a more general mountainous area. The Qutl pattern (הֹר) was used instead of הַר in order to distinguish the two.[136]

Because it is not a physically locatable site, this Particular Mountain can be read plausibly against any geographical background as long as it is set in a mountainous region. In the Priestly version of the wilderness narrative, Mount

---

135. G. B. Gray, *A Critical and Exegetical Commentary on Numbers* (ICC; New York: Scribner's, 1906) 281; L. E. Binns, *The Book of Numbers* (London: Methuen, 1927) 189; J. Milgrom, *Numbers* (JPS Torah Commentary; Philadelphia: Jewish Publication Society, 1990) 175.

136. Y. Elitzur, *Ancient Place Names in the Holy Land: Preservation and History* (Jerusalem: Magnes, 2004) 281 n. 40, 380.

Hor would be read as though it were located along a route *north* from Kadesh into Canaan, since Num 21:2–3 has the Israelites headed north toward Arad. Yet Num 21:4 situates Mount Hor along the way of Yam Suf, *south* of Kadesh. One might expect this literary "relocation" to be just as confusing and problematic as the mislocations of Yam Suf or the Abarim Range. But, while Yam Suf and the Abarim Range come from the repertoire of places that the author and ancient reader (and modern readers today to a certain degree) knew and could physically visit, no conflict is created when a place-name is invented. Mount Hor takes its place in the Israelites' mental map not as an element of experienced landscape or even as a part of the landscape of memory but, rather, as a part of the landscape of Israelite lore.

Numbers 33

The scribe who wrote Num 33:1–49 needed to contend with a composite wilderness narrative containing remnants of multiple divergent and incompatible routes such as the battle at Hormah near Arad versus the route south from Kadesh toward Yam Suf and the route through Moab versus the route around it to the east. We saw in chap. 6 that he used various compositional techniques to create a coherent, unified itinerary out of what gives only the *impression* of unity in the wilderness narrative. There we saw that he used a single form of the itinerary genre throughout and created explicit connections between itinerary notices where there are fractures in the chain of notices in the wilderness narrative. He also strove to correct various geographical problems in the composite wilderness narrative and create a single, coherent geographical route, shown in fig. 13 (p. 276). We have already seen one example: he omitted the itinerary notice from Exod 15:22, which locates the sea crossing at Yam Suf (a hybrid of *pȝ ṭwf*[*y*] and יָם), and restored Yam Suf to its typical referent (the Red Sea) three stops later in the itinerary.

He also strove to neutralize the divergent routes created by revisions to the wilderness narrative associated with the departure from Egypt, Kadesh, and Transjordan. First, the scribe retained the turn in the Israelites' route (Num 33:7) toward the sea as they departed from Egypt, framing it as part of an itinerary notice rather than as a command (see Exod 14:2). Despite the composite nature of this route in Exodus 12–15, it does also read coherently as a whole. Second, he provided an alternative route through Kadesh. The wilderness narrative has the Israelites go either north from Kadesh into Canaan (Num 21:1–3) or south away from Kadesh toward Yam Suf (Num 14:25; 21:4) depending on whether one reads with the Priestly version of the wilderness narrative or the

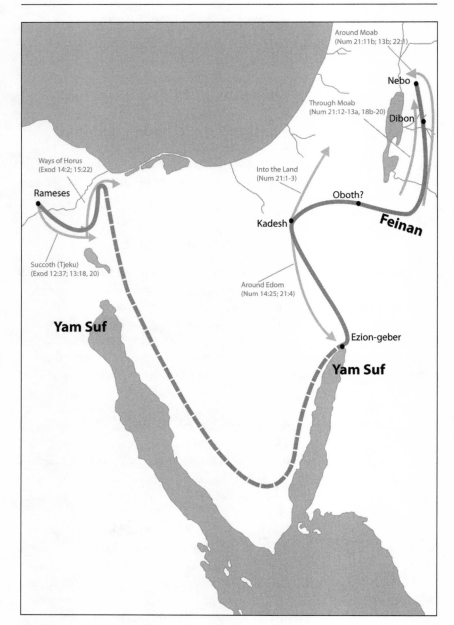

Fig. 13. The "Route" of the Wilderness Sojourn in Numbers 33.

revision to it that takes them around Edom in preparation for wholesale entry into the land from the east in the book of Joshua. The scribe who wrote Num 33:1–49 smoothed out this discrepancy in the route created by the revision to Numbers 21 by offering a clear alternative. Here, the Israelites do not go north from Kadesh toward Arad as Num 21:1–3 suggests, nor do they go south from Kadesh toward Yam Suf (the Gulf of Eilat/Aqaba) as suggested by Num 14:25 and 21:4. Instead, according to Num 33:36, they leave Ezion-geber, on the coast of Yam Suf, and head north from there toward Kadesh, as shown in fig. 13. The scribe has thus abandoned the confusion between the northerly route and the southerly route from Kadesh by offering a different direction of travel altogether, the *opposite* direction from the direction suggested in Num 14:25 and 21:4.

Once the Israelites have arrived at Kadesh from Ezion-geber, the scribe could pull events together as they appear in the wilderness narrative, beginning in Num 20:1, but not without adjustment.

Numbers 20–21	*Numbers 33:37–47*
Kadesh	Kadesh
Mount Hor	Mount Hor
Hormah (toward Arad)	**Zalmonah**
way of Yam Suf	**Punon**
Oboth	Oboth
Iye-abarim	Iye-abarim/Iyyim (in Moab)
Wadi Zered, Arnon, Beer, Midbar, Mattanah, Nahaliel, Bamoth, Pisgah, Jeshimon	**Dibon-gad, Almon-diblathaim, Abarim/Nebo**

The scribe then put Zalmonah and Punon in the slots occupied by Hormah in Num 21:1–3 and the way of Yam Suf in Num 21:4 in order to specify a route from Kadesh around the south end of the Dead Sea. We are unable to identify Zalmonah, but Punon is a reference to the Faynan copper mining region, shown in fig. 13, and takes the Israelites across Wadi Aravah into Transjordan.[137] Beyond being geographically appropriate on a route into Transjordan, Punon's character as a copper mining and smithing region is a good choice to stand in

---

137. For discussion of the two main proposals for where Zalmonah might be, see B. MacDonald, *"East of the Jordan": Territories and Sites of the Hebrew Scriptures* (ASOR Book 6; Boston: American Schools of Oriental Research, 2000).

for a spot in the wilderness narrative that otherwise has a story about a Moses manufacturing a bronze serpent.[138]

The order of names in the resulting itinerary may be a problem. The best identification for Oboth is generally considered to be Ain el-Weibeh, an oasis west of Wadi Aravah across from Faynan and at a crossroads for traveling west toward Gaza, south toward Eilat/Aqaba, and east into Transjordan.[139] If one is coming from the Negev into Transjordan around the south end of the Dead Sea, one would encounter Oboth first and *then* Punon, as shown in fig. 13.[140] Assuming that this identification of Oboth is correct, the author of Numbers 33 has the order backward. If it is indeed backward—and we cannot be sure because the identification of Oboth is not certain; the topographical and linguistic evidence for the Oboth/Ain el-Weibeh identification is good, but there is no archaeological evidence for it—it may be due to a desire to disturb the correspondence of the Numbers 33 itinerary with the composite text of Numbers 20–21 as little as possible.

The conflict between routes around and through Moab in Numbers 21 created by various revisions to this chapter presented yet another geographical problem for the scribe who wrote Num 33:1–49. He first clarified in Num 33:44 that Iye-abarim/Iyyim is בִּגְבוּל מוֹאָב 'in the territory of Moab', correcting the idea that one might receive from reading Num 21:11b that Iye-abarim is in the wilderness *east* of Moab rather than in or on the border of it. This may be another case of reference repair, although we cannot be fully certain where Iye-abarim is, so we do not have the shared context to know what the proper reference is. The scribe further depicts the Israelites as going through Moab by supplying an entirely different set of place-names from the names we find in Numbers 21. This includes not only Nebo—which was pulled from Deut 32:49 because it appears here with Abarim—but also Dibon.

Finally, the middle of the wilderness narrative, especially between the Israelites' departure from Sinai in Num 10:11–12 and 33 and their arrival at Kadesh in Num 20:1, is very problematic with respect to geography. We find few itinerary notices here: only those in Num 11:35 and 12:16, where the Israelites go from Hazeroth to Kibroth-hattaavah to the wilderness of Paran. The main problem, however, is that we find *two* double arrivals. The Israelites arrive in the wilder-

---

138. For the link between this episode and Punon, see J. R. Bartlett, "The Wadi Arabah in the Hebrew Scriptures," in *Crossing the Rift: Resources, routes, settlement patterns and interaction in the Wadi Arabah* (ed. P. Bienkowski and K. Galor; Levant Supplementary Series 3; Oxford: Oxbow, 2006) 152.

139. MacDonald, "*East of the Jordan*," 71.

140. Bartlett, "Wadi Arabah," 155; G. I. Davies, *Way of the Wilderness*, 90.

ness of Paran twice, once in Num 10:12 and again in Num 12:16. They also arrive at Kadesh twice, once implied by Num 13:26 when they return there after the spies' mission (returning there assumes that they had arrived, even though their arrival is never narrated) and again in Num 20:1. The scribe who composed the Numbers 33 itinerary avoided these problems altogether by leaving out the wilderness of Paran, using Kadesh only once in Num 33:36 (where it corresponds to the itinerary notice in Num 20:1), and adding names such as Dophkah and Alush in Num 33:12–14 and the long string of place-names in Num 33:18–35 in order to clarify the Israelites' route.

When we lack access to the ancient Israelite mental map (through texts or other representations) or access to the potential for shared context (through archaeological survey and excavation), we may have difficulty fully understanding the author's use of repertoire and even his literary goals. Dophkah, Alush, and the long string of place-names in Num 33:18–35 illustrate the limitations on our ability to fully understand an author's goals when we lack the potential to develop shared context. We today are unable to securely identify most of these sites, and none except Libnah occurs in another biblical text. Consequently, we are left in a position similar to that of the person whose conversation partner says, over the telephone, "Hey, will you look at THAT!"[141] He does not know what "THAT" refers to and cannot satisfy the referent without asking for an explanation. Without more archaeological data and more texts to tell us where these places were and what associations they had in the ancient Israelites' mental map, we are at something of a loss to interpret the text. Libnah (Laban) appears in Deut 1:1b–2a as part of a list of names that appears to run from a Horeb (Sinai) located in the southern part of the Sinai Peninsula along the eastern coast and into the Aravah.[142] It *seems* likely that both Deut 1:1b–2a and Num 33:1–49 envision the Israelites as being headed north along the coast, although it really is not clear, so I have represented this part of the route as a dotted line on the map (fig. 13). Whether the author meant to convey any other meaning with these place-names beyond simply clarifying a route is even more unclear.

---

141. See discussion on pp. 46–47.

142. Some commentators understand the place-names in Deut 1:1b to identify the sites of Moses' speech and consequently look for them in Moab rather than along a route up the coast of the Sinai Peninsula. The interpretive problem here is whether v. 1b goes with v. 1a, which introduces Moses' speech, or v. 2, which stipulates how long a journey from Horeb to Kadesh takes. A number of commentators mix both views but seem to lean toward the latter; see A. D. H. Mayes, *Deuteronomy* (NCB; Grand Rapids, MI: Eerdmans, 1991) 114; and D. L. Christensen, *Deuteronomy 1–11* (WBC 6A; Dallas: Word, 1991).

These names might have had a rich set of associations in the ancient Israelites' mental map. If so, we currently have no means of accessing what they were.

It is a challenge for us to study the way ancient texts relate to the ancient world partly because some scholars are skilled at literary or linguistic analysis while others are talented excavators. Each subdiscipline makes important contributions, but each has limits. Archaeology cannot tell us what the genre of a text is or what an author's literary goals are. Only study of literary history, intertextuality, and the techniques used to construct a text can do this. Texts cannot clarify the stratigraphy and chronology of an archaeological site. Only ceramics and radiocarbon dating of appropriate items from sealed archaeological contexts can do this.[143] As the closest thing to informants from antiquity we have, texts may be able to tell us something about who built a site or how an artifact was used or valued, but the literary goals of a text and its use of genre and other elements of cultural repertoire must be understood before a text can be used well. Thomas E. Levy and Thomas Higham associate literary criticism with the "minimalist" school and constrast it with the "historicist" (or "maximalist") school, which values "command of the ancient languages, history, and archaeology" and with which they prefer to be associated.[144] This book shows that literary criticism need not and even *should* not be divorced from historical concerns. Command of how literature works—the business of literary criticism—needs to be included alongside the others in their list of valued skills for interpreting the ancient culture in which the Bible was produced, especially if the goal is to *integrate* text and archaeology in a holistic approach to understanding the ancient world.[145] Literary critics likewise must not ignore the potential for shared context that archaeology offers, because it may help us understand the referents of words in a text and therefore help us understand how those elements of realia serve the author's literary goals, whatever they may be. Indeed, we can find ourselves at something of a loss without archaeological information. At the very least, our interpretations of texts are fuller and richer when we understand the social customs, historical events, objects, and places to which they often refer.

---

143. Levy et al., "Lowland Edom," 131.

144. T. E. Levy and T. Higham, "Introduction: Radiocarbon Dating and the Iron Age of the Southern Levant," in *The Bible and Radiocarbon Dating: Archaeology, Text and Science* (ed. T. E. Levy and T. Higham. London: Equinox, 2005) 6.

145. For discussion of this sort of approach, see E. van Wolde, *Reframing Biblical Studies: When Language and Text Meet Culture, Cognition, and Context* (Winona Lake, IN: Eisenbrauns, 2009) 14.

The source of our discontent with relating text and material culture lies, perhaps, in failure to reckon adequately with the fact that, as van der Steen puts it, "the texts as well as the archaeological remains are different sides of one coin, different aspects of one society" or culture.[146] The Torah—indeed, any ancient text—is deeply embedded in ancient culture because the scribes who wrote it represented various elements of that culture in it, often in complex ways. If we understand a text simply to *mirror* the world and look for the way pieces of the ancient environment that we can recover through archaeology *correspond* to it, we go wrong in terms of the insights that recent philosophy, literary theory, and cognitive science have offered us. More importantly, we leave out the scribes. We can access them only implicitly through the texts they wrote. But they are our link between the text and the ancient world, because they made the choices about the shape of the text and the way pieces of their cultural matrix were represented in it. If we look for a direct correspondence between the text and the world, we miss the artistry with which the ancient scribes represented pieces of this world in the text. We may also miss the reasons that they chose an element of repertoire from their contemporary landscape or the landscape of memory, or even contributed a new element of cultural repertoire to the landscape of tradition. Thus, we may misunderstand the meaning and significance of the text as well as the character of its historicity.

---

146. Van der Steen, *Tribes and Territories in Transition*, 296.

Epilogue

Marc Zvi Brettler in *The Creation of History in Ancient Israel* defines history as "a narrative that presents a past."[1] The Torah is a story of Israel's past and can be understood, if only in this very *broad* sense, as history. By the end of his study, Brettler had run up against the same poverty of language that Yosef Haim Yerushalmi spoke of in *Zakhor*, and he came to the conclusion that "the term 'history' or 'historical/historiographical narrative' should be dropped from the form-critical lexicon, since the form of a text has little bearing on its historicity."[2] Biblical narrative is at times quite history-like, yet it often resists this genre classification. We may not be able to give the Torah a genre label, but we can read to understand how ancient Israelite scribes used genre and other elements of cultural repertoire to shape this generative document.

The history-like character of the wilderness narrative derives from the decision of a scribe at one important stage of its development to emplot it using a historiographical genre: the annal. The fact that it *looks like* history in some ways, however, does not mean that it *is*, at least in terms of what we mean by history today or even what typically constituted history in the ancient Near East. The scribe who emplotted the wilderness narrative as an annal used this genre not for its typical purpose of narrating military campaigns but to shape a vision for Israel's return to Zion after the exile. He gave authority to this vision not by putting it in the mouth of a prophet but by giving it historiographical form. Mikhail Bakhtin speaks of the epic past as prophetic but as *finished* prophecy. Instead of looking ahead, it presents the future as rooted in the distant, valorized past.[3]

This future involves both preservation and creation. Yerushalmi notes that reformation involves delving into the past to recover and preserve pieces of

---

1. M. Z. Brettler, *The Creation of History in Ancient Israel* (London: Routledge, 1995) 12.

2. Ibid., 138.

3. M. Bakhtin, "Epic and Novel: Toward a Methodology for the Study of the Novel," in *The Dialogic Imagination: Four Essays* (ed. M. Holquist; trans. C. Emerson and M. Holquist; University of Texas Press Slavic Series 1; Austin: University of Texas Press, 1981) 3–40.

it—pieces that might otherwise be forgotten or that perhaps already have been forgotten—that are deemed significant as a group envisions its future. But this activity is also creative: "every such anamnesis [or, act of remembering] also transforms the recovered past into something new." [4] The wilderness narrative, a vision for the Israelites' return to Zion, became the repository for the pieces of their past that would give their lives new shape. The destruction of the Temple had made enthronement theology problematic in its preexilic form. Using the annals as a mode of emplotment helped the Priestly scribe recover the royal imagery for Yahweh and renew its significance, this time for life in a kingless society. Israel's major festivals appear to have been revisioned in the framework of a 364-day ideal solar calendar, even as divergent forms of the calendar were preserved in the context of the narrative. Old settlement patterns may have been remembered and used to envision an ideal future territoriality. Divergent literatures were incorporated into a single narrative anthology. The scribes also invented, when there was a need to do so. And they borrowed cultural repertoire, making profoundly creative use of it to shape a coherent and memorable narrative so that these pieces of the past might not be forgotten but continue to shape Israelite life under new circumstances.

We do not find such a profound blend of cultural repertoire in administrative documents or military narratives because it does not suit the purposes of these texts. The reports and letters we studied in chap. 3 all serve pragmatic goals. They report on the route of a journey to a supervisor or for deposit in an archive. They instruct about alternate routes to be taken in extreme circumstances or tell where to drop off shipments. The content of these texts is as straightforward as their purposes. They are not creative in their use of either genre or geography, and it is precisely this lack of creativity that enables them to do what they were designed to do. The Egyptian and Assyrian military narratives we studied in chap. 4 use genre creatively in order to meet the needs of a new rhetorical situation. The scribes who wrote them blended chronicles, tribute lists, *jw.tw* reports, and itineraries in order to create narratives that would not only relate the king's military deeds but also convey royal ideology that sustained his image and support for his imperial activities. The itineraries were often sources pulled from an archive and used for information as well as to shape the narrative; although they took on ideological significance in their new literary contexts, they had been simply administrative documents in a former textual life. The scribes who wrote these narratives aimed to report as well

---

4. Y. H. Yerushalmi, *Zakhor: Jewish History and Jewish Memory* (Seattle: University of Washington Press, 1996) 113.

as emplot. While their use of genre was often quite innovative, the content of their narratives was still, at core, the journey. The wilderness narrative is *related* to these neighboring genres, but it can be reduced to them only at the risk of misunderstanding. It is not enough to classify the genre of a text. Indeed, some texts defy classification. Instead, our goal should be to understand how one or more genres *shape* a text and recognize that sometimes this will happen in ways that stretch or break our expectations.

Yerushalmi emphasizes that failing to transmit what becomes part of collective memory is tantamount to forgetting. Thus, "if the achievement is not to be ephemeral, it must itself become a tradition."[5] Whatever its previous shape, the author of the Priestly version achieved a meaningful framework for the wilderness narrative that would last. Subsequent scribes both transmitted and reshaped this literature by incorporating more material into it. Use of the itinerary genre allowed them to integrate their revisions into the narrative—incorporate the *traditio* into the *traditum*—so that it would read more or less as a unity. Like the author of the Priestly version, these scribes sought to reshape the tradition, sometimes in ways that profoundly altered how the whole might be read. Nevertheless, they tended to retain even material that was problematic either *ideologically*, as in the rock/water episode in Exod 17:1b–7 and the appointment of judges in Exodus 18 or the trip through Transjordan into foreign Moabite territory, or in terms of the *shape of the composition*, as in the conquest of Hormah from the south in Num 21:1–3. Rather than excising this material, they recontextualized it, striving to neutralize its prominence in the narrative.[6] However, it is still there to be had. These are not passive efforts at redaction but active efforts to reshape the tradition, preserving it in the process.

Pentateuchal studies is currently in a state of flux. The Graf-Wellhausen version of the Documentary Hypothesis is no longer considered a tenable model for the composition history of the Torah, and scholars working within this subfield are actively seeking a replacement. One commonly adopted alternative is a supplementary hypothesis, a model that makes sense in terms of the material processes of writing. Karel van der Toorn suggests that the need to

---

5. Ibid.

6. For an excellent discussion of reasons that polemics, or alternative viewpoints, were allowed to stand in biblical literature, see Y. Amit, *Hidden Polemics in Biblical Narrative* (trans. J. Chipman; Biblical Interpretation Series 25; Leiden: Brill, 2000) 32–33. Amit addresses this question by asking why *editors* allowed contradictory material to stand. As I showed in chaps. 5–6, however, new material was at least in some cases introduced by revisions to the narrative, and contradictory material was allowed to stand but was marginalized.

replace an old scroll provided the opportunity for making revisions to the text, which could easily have been added as the scribe copied old material.[7] Different scholars advocate different versions of the supplementary model: John Van Seters pushes for a version in which a Yahwistic text is supplemented in spots by a Priestly scribe. Others, such as William Johnstone, speak of a Deuteronomistic version substantively rewritten to create a Priestly version. Some, such as Thomas Dozeman, resist the term *Deuteronomistic* to describe the non-Priestly material, simply referring to it as *non-Priestly* or *pre-Priestly*.[8] What all of these supplementary approaches have in common is the assumption that a compositional effort spans the entire scope of the Torah. Frank Crüsemann warns, however, that the Torah may have a "many-faceted growth."[9] I have shown in this study that there were multiple, smaller-scale, targeted revisions to the Torah even *after* the Priestly version. Attempting to fit everything into only two, Torah-wide recensions flattens what is, as Crüsemann suggests, a multidimensional process of transmitting and reshaping tradition.

Understanding how this literature came to have the shape it now does is a key focus of pentateuchal studies. An old crux is the debate between Martin Noth and Gerhard von Rad about whether the core literary unit is a Tetrateuch (Genesis–Numbers) or a Hextateuch (Genesis–Joshua).[10] Noth understood the literary character of Deuteronomy, along with Joshua–Kings, to be quite different from the character of Genesis–Numbers and posited that the Deuteronomistic History was attached to a once-freestanding Tetrateuch. Von Rad, on the other hand, noted the importance of conquest in various recitals of Israel's early history and argued that the story could not have ended without entry into the land. I suggest that it is a matter not of one or the other but of one *becoming* the other as the tradition grew. The Priestly version of the wilderness

---

7. K. van der Toorn, *Scribal Culture and the Making of the Hebrew Bible* (Cambridge: Harvard University Press, 2007) 146–48.

8. J. Van Seters, *Prologue to History: The Yahwist as Historian in Genesis* (Louisville: Westminster John Knox, 1992); idem, *The Life of Moses: The Yahwist as Historian in Exodus–Numbers* (Louisville: Westminster John Knox, 1994); W. Johnstone, *Chronicles and Exodus: An Analogy and Its Application* (JSOTSup 275; Sheffield: Sheffield Academic Press, 1998); T. B. Dozeman, *Commentary on Exodus* (Eerdmans Critical Commentary; Grand Rapids, MI: Eerdmans, 2009) 39–41.

9. F. Crüsemann, *The Torah: Theology and Social History of Old Testament Law* (trans. A. W. Mahnke; Edinburgh: T. & T. Clark, 1989) 47.

10. G. von Rad, "The Form-Critical Problem of the Hexateuch," *The Problem of the Hexateuch and Other Essays* (London: SCM, 1966) 1–78; and M. Noth, *The Deuteronomistic History* (JSOTSup 15; Sheffield: JSOT Press, 1981); idem, *The Chronicler's History* (trans. H. G. M. Williamson; JSOTSup 50; Sheffield: JSOT Press, 1987) 121–47.

narrative that was emplotted as an annal does seem to have ended in Numbers, but it had an entry into the land, in the now-marginalized little battle episode in Num 21:1–3. The addition of Deuteronomy and Joshua to ultimately form a Hextateuch might best be understood using Thomas Römer's idea of a "rolling corpus" that developed through various additions to the tradition. Römer thinks in terms of the individual books, suggesting that Deuteronomy was attached to Leviticus, and Numbers was set in between.[11] In the Priestly version of the wilderness narrative, however, Numbers and Exodus should be thought of as one piece of literature, emplotted as an annal. But Römer's idea is extremely helpful if we think more organically in terms of smaller, targeted revisions. I have discussed here the likelihood that Deuteronomy was incorporated into the anthology in part by extension of the itinerary in Numbers 21. Materials in Joshua were incorporated in part by diverting the Israelites away from entry into the land at the end of the Tetrateuch, creating a new entry from the east. The itinerary notices are only *small threads* connecting these literatures together; the development of this anthology was obviously far more complex than what I have been able to discuss here. The itinerary notices give us a window into the techniques used to shape it and show us how the ancient scribes simultaneously created and preserved a tradition, whether by adding a new ending or changing an idea.

Although emplotted with a historiographical form and set in the distant past, the wilderness narrative is *not* a work of historiography in either an ancient or a modern sense. *If* we can call it a work of historiography, it is one without parallel. Like Brettler, we should not sit comfortably with this genre label, even if our poverty of language leaves us without a better label. We might even avoid a label, as Brettler suggests, especially as it can mislead us about the character of what we are reading.[12] Hans Frei in *The Eclipse of Biblical Narrative: A Study in Eighteenth and Nineteenth Century Hermeneutics* defines the problem we face as follows:

> [I]n effect, the realistic or history-like quality of biblical narratives, acknowledged by all, instead of being examined for the bearing it had in its own right on meaning and interpretation was immediately transposed

---

11. T. C. Römer, "Israel's Sojourn in the Wilderness and the Construction of the Book of Numbers," in *Reflection and Refraction: Studies in Biblical Historiography in Honour of A. Graeme Auld* (ed. R. Rezetko, T. H. Lim, and W. B. Aucker; Leiden: Brill, 2007) 419–46.

12. For a very helpful understanding of this problem, see the discussion of modal rift in K. L. Sparks, *Ancient Texts for the Study of the Hebrew Bible: A Guide to the Background Literature* (Peabody, MA: Hendrickson, 2005) 18.

into the quite different issue of whether or not the realistic narrative was historical.[13]

The present study was undertaken with the intent to understand where these history-like elements in the wilderness narrative came from, why they were put there, and how they are significant for reading the text. Some may find it frustrating that they turn out to have been used in this case for purposes *other* than writing history. Frei, by giving us a long-term perspective, reminds us that the problem "Is it history or is it fiction?" is a problem of our own intellectual making—and ultimately the wrong way to frame the question.

The fact that the wilderness narrative is not a history does not mean it has no *historicity*. In his argument for a literary approach to biblical narrative that is not divorced from historical-critical concerns, David Damrosch applauds poststructuralist thought that has "sought out a renewed connection to the historical contexts so often obliquely inscribed within the texts themselves."[14] His emphasis on *contexts* in the plural is important, as is his emphasis on the obliqueness with which elements of these contexts appear. We have seen that the scribes who wrote the wilderness narrative drew cultural repertoire from *multiple* background contexts in order to give both shape and place to the narrative. We do not see an account of a single event that took place at one defined point in history when we read the wilderness narrative. What we *do* see is a picture of Israelite history and culture, refracted as though we are looking at it through a kaleidoscope. Wolfgang Iser's approach to the composition of literature, especially the idea of cultural repertoire, holds potential for getting at the complexity of its embeddedness in historical context, helping us within biblical scholarship move toward a *new* historicism.[15]

We must bear in mind the complexity of a text's embeddedness in culture as we consider the context of its composition. Our oldest manuscripts of the Torah are significantly later than the time in which most hold it to have been written, so we are left to make educated guesses about its date. Because there are no external objective criteria we can use, we strive to find objective criteria within the text itself. Geography is frequently held to provide this sort of a criterion, but this is based on the assumption that the realia represented in a text are from the time it was written. We have seen that this assumption is faulty.

13. H. Frei, *The Eclipse of Biblical Narrative: A Study in Eighteenth and Nineteenth Century Hermeneutics* (New Haven, CT: Yale University Press, 1974) 16.

14. D. Damrosch, *The Narrative Covenant: Transformations of Genre in the Growth of Biblical Literature* (San Francisco: Harper & Row, 1987) 31.

15. On New Historicism as an approach to the text/context relationship, see G. Hens-Piazza, *The New Historicism* (GBS; Minneapolis: Fortress, 2002).

Both "maximalist" and "minimalist" efforts to date the exodus and wilderness narratives on the basis of geography run aground on the complexity of repertoire used in the text. A thirteenth–twelfth century B.C.E. date may account for Ramses, but it does not account for a Kadesh outside the land or an Edom in the central Negev. A sixth-century B.C.E. date can account for both, but failure to reckon with the antiquity of Ramses leaves us with an important gap in our understanding of the way geography functions in this narrative.

Language is another criterion frequently held to provide evidence for the date of a text. William Schniedewind, for example, points to features of Classical rather than Late Hebrew as "objective criteria" for a preexilic date for the Torah.[16] There is great value in understanding the historical development of Hebrew language, but it is not *necessarily* an objective dating criterion any more than the geography in the text is. Choice of linguistic dialect or register may be just as much an element of cultural repertoire as geography or genre. It can be used in a typical manner as a scribe writes a text in the dialect he happens to speak or a register that happens to be current for the production of literature, just as a scribe using the itinerary genre to write an administrative document simply includes the places that happen to be on the route. But language *can* also be used creatively to serve a scribe's literary goals. Especially in a literary environment where we are already seeing the creative use of repertoire, we should resist the urge to jump to conclusions about the date of a text solely on the grounds of its linguistic features and instead ask whether and how those features might be serving some literary goal.

Instead of looking for a single objective criterion on which we can pin a date, we should consider *all* of the elements of cultural repertoire used in a text along with the literary goals of the author(s) in order to understand how a text is embedded in context. David H. Aaron has emphasized how important it is for us to be aware that there is a "cultural matrix of signs and information that allows for anything we say or write to be possible."[17] In what cultural matrix (or matrices) would it have been possible to produce a text such as the Priestly version of the wilderness narrative and its subsequent revisions? The geography of the Israelites' departure from Egypt comes from a mental map of the Delta as it was in the thirteenth–twelfth centuries B.C.E. But a scribe in the thirteenth–twelfth centuries B.C.E. could not have known the annals genre because Assyrian scribes were still writing commemorative building inscriptions at that time,

---

16. W. M. Schniedewind, *How the Bible Became a Book: The Textualization of Ancient Israel* (Cambridge: Cambridge University Press, 2004) 82.

17. D. H. Aaron, *Etched in Stone: The Emergence of the Decalogue* (New York: T. & T. Clark, 2006) 38.

and the annals genre had not yet developed. We cannot date the text to all of these contexts but must choose one context in which knowledge of all of these elements of cultural repertoire would have been possible and which could have given rise to the literary goals they were made to serve.

Lacking an external objective criterion for dating a text, we must determine the cultural matrix to the best of our ability based on what best explains the text in front of us. There will always be gaps in our understanding, and any proposal (including my own) must remain subject to revision as new information and better ways of understanding the text arise. The particular form of the annals genre used to emplot the Priestly wilderness narrative presents us with such a gap since it was, as far as we know from extant examples, no longer in use after the eighth century B.C.E. Why not posit an eighth-century date for composition of the wilderness narrative? Because there was no reason in the eighth century B.C.E. to write a narrative about marching home with the vessels of Yahweh that envisions how Israelite culture might be reconstituted in the land. Moreover, if there is indeed direct intertextuality with Isaiah 52, this text had not yet been written. This leaves us with the question of how an Israelite scribe knew this form of the annals genre in the sixth century B.C.E., when the purpose for which he used it would have been feasible. Unfortunately, while we know that literature such as Ezekiel and Deutero-Isaiah was produced in exile, we know little about the social context in which it was produced and what access Israelite scribes had at this time to Mesopotamian literature, especially something like annals, which were not part of the Mesopotamian tradition of scribal education.[18] The best we can do is explain *as many details of the text as possible*, and it is my present judgment that use of this form of the annals genre explains enough features of the wilderness narrative to posit that it was known and purposefully used, despite our inability to trace *how* the scribes knew it.

The revisions to the Priestly version of the wilderness narrative quite likely extend into the Persian period, although just how long they took is not clear. There is disagreement over the precise circumstances that prompted this literary activity. Peter Frei has argued that the Torah took shape under the

---

18. For discussion of literature produced in exile, see Schniedewind, *How the Bible Became a Book*, 152–58. Schniedewind's emphasis on royal patronage should not, however, be pushed too hard, since our picture of Judahite life in Babylon is sketchy and currently in the process of being illuminated by study of texts from al-Yahudu and other enclaves in Babylon; see a critique of Schniedewind in J. Van Seters, "The Origins of the Hebrew Bible: Some New Answers to Old Questions," *JANER* 7 (2007) 105–6; and L. E. Pearce, "New Evidence for Judeans in Babylonia," in *Judah and the Judeans in the Persian Period* (ed. O. Lipschits and M. Oeming; Winona Lake, IN: Eisenbrauns, 2006) 399–412.

influence of Persian authorities, who advocated the codification of local law and traditions. This imperial authorization theory is controversial and depends on a variety of highly debatable factors such as the extent and nature of Persian influence on local government and the historicity of Ezra–Nehemiah. Alternatively, J. P. Weinberg has argued that the formation of a community centered on the Temple prompted the creation of this body of literature.[19] It is not my intent to adopt either theory here but simply to note that ethnic definition is widely held to have been a key concern in this period whether the impetus came from within the group, outside pressures, or (as is more likely) some of both.

These revisions were also most likely the work of a small number of people. We typically assign materials to Priestly or Deuteronomistic schools, but it must be borne in mind that these terms refer to literatures that deal with different concerns, are informed by different traditions, and express different ideologies. They do not necessarily refer to definable social groups. And not all of the revisions to the Priestly wilderness narrative serve discernibly Priestly or Deuteronomistic ideological goals. The efforts to create an anthology by incorporating Deuteronomy, the Balaam narrative, and Joshua into a single narrative may be more compositional than ideological in character. The debate about whether territory in Transjordan should be considered part of Israel's inheritance could have been engaged by a scribe of either ideological persuasion. Karel van der Toorn notes that Chronicles depicts the Levites as being in charge of liturgy, the collection of tithes, and various construction and security activities relating to the Temple. But they were also the custodians of *torah*, responsible for explanation, interpretation, and instruction. He argues that scribal activity during the Persian period was associated with the Temple and suggests that the Levites were largely responsible for it. They were subordinate to the priests, whose duties focused on cultic matters, but they gained ascendancy as Judaism shifted from a focus on holiness and cult to a focus on *text*.[20] One can imagine that matters such as the character of the covenant, the shape of cultic practice, and the extent of Israel's territory may have been topics of debate among scribes and intellectuals in this context.[21] While we *can*

---

19. For an excellent overview of the imperial authorization theory and the issues in the debate about it, see the essays in J. W. Watts, ed., *Persia and Torah: The Theory of Imperial Authorization of the Pentateuch* (SBLSymS 17; Atlanta: Society of Biblical Literature, 2001).

20. Van der Toorn, *Scribal Culture*, 89–96, 104–8.

21. Tension over this matter is reflected in the end of Numbers, evident from a comparison of Numbers 21, which incorporates the Transjordanian plateau into Israelite territory, and Numbers 33–34, which excludes it. Joshua 22 also addresses the status of

often distinguish Priestly from Deuteronomistic ideological concerns, there is value in recognizing that these concerns may reflect differences of opinion held within a relatively circumscribed social group, to which fell the task of reshaping a culture out of the pieces of its past.

The craftsmanship of these scribes is our link between the text and the world represented in it. In his recent work, *The Nature of Biblical Criticism*, John Barton is acutely aware of the gap between us as readers and the scribes who produced the texts we read. He acknowledges that we are involved in our readings of text but pushes for a text-centered hermeneutic: "To try to discover what the biblical text actually means, rather than to impose on it our own theological categories, is to honor the text as part of the givenness of a world that we did not make."[22] Bridging the gap involves negotiation between sometimes vastly different historical, social, and cultural contexts. To negotiate well, I have discovered, means being as conscious of my own role as an interpreter, as curious about the worlds inscribed in (and lurking in the background of) the text, and as attentive to the details and shape of the text as I can be. I can only hope that I have done justice to the text I have studied here. We honor loved ones in conversation by striving to understand their often complex perspectives on the world and resisting the temptation to pigeonhole them in categories into which they do not fit. Reading the Torah is in one sense just such a conversation across time and culture. It is a conversation about ideas that matter as much to those who continue to be shaped by the Torah as they must have mattered to the audience for whom it was initially intended to be a new lease on life.

---

this territory; see D. A. Knight, "Joshua 22 and the Ideology of Space," in *'Imagining' Biblical Worlds: Studies in Spatial and Historical Constructs in Honor of James W. Flanagan* (ed. D. M. Gunn and P. McNutt; JSOTSup 359; Sheffield: Sheffield Academic Press, 2002) 51–63.

22. J. Barton, *The Nature of Biblical Criticism* (Louisville: Westminster John Knox, 2007) 182.

Index of Authors

293

Index of Scripture

Old Testament

Pseudepigrapha

Index of Geographical Names

Index of Other Ancient Sources